BOAT LIFE

IN EGYPT AND NUBIA.

BY

WILLIAM C. PRIME,

AUTHOR OF "TENT LIFE IN THE HOLY LAND," "THE OLD HOUSE BY THE RIVER," "LATER YEARS," ETC.

NEW YORK:
HARPER & BROTHERS,
FRANKLIN SQUARE.

1857.

To the Memory of

Charles Edward Trumbull,

Our Beloved Brother,

Who on the evening of the seventeenth day of March,

in the Year eighteen hundred and fifty-six,

while we lay sleeping in the Valley on this side of

the Jordan, passed over the River into

the City of our God,

I Dedicate this Volume.

Preface.

"HAVE you not a house, O Braheem Effendi?" said my friend Suleiman, on whose shop-front I was accustomed to sit in the bazaars of Cairo. Braheem was the nearest approach to the sound of my name, that an Arab could effect.

"Yea, verily, O Suleiman."

"Have you not a father and a mother?"

"Thy lips drop fragrant truth, O most magnificent of merchants."

"Then why in the name of Allah came you here to Musr?"

"To see men and things. To gather knowledge by travel. To know the world."

"Is it not written, 'Men are a hidden disease?' and elsewhere, 'Communion with men profiteth nothing, unless for idle talk?' Thou mightest better have remained at home, Braheem Effendi;" and the smoke from his chibouk curled in the still air up to the roof over the bazaar, and out into the sunlight, and vanished.

I sometimes wonder whether, after all, the old man was not right.

In the summer of 1855 I left America for Egypt. The immediate object which I had in view was the prosecution of a favorite study. The kindness of my respected and distinguished friend, Joseph Henry, LL.D., of the Smithsonian Institute, and other gentlemen occupying positions in the service of the Government at Washington, provided me with such introductions as enabled me to prosecute my explorations in Egypt with satisfactory success, while the accomplished scholarship of my companion, J. Hammond Trumbull, Esq., of Hartford, not only contributed to this success, but added more than I can tell to the pleasure of the voyage.

The results of my studies are but hinted at in these pages, which are devoted almost exclusively to incidents of travel along the Nile.

The dreams of childhood realized, the hopes of early manhood fully accomplished, I returned home with stories of travel for ears which, alas the day! were closed to my voice by the solemn seal of death.

Whether, that I have seen the sunrise flush the brow of Remeses at Abou Simbal, and touch with passionate, yet gentle and trembling caress—as a lover would touch the lips of his maiden love, dead in her glorious beauty—the cold lips of Memnon at old Thebes; that I have wandered through the stately halls of Karnak, and looked up the stream of time from the summit of Cheops; that I have knelt at the Sepulchre, and felt the night wind on my forehead in Gethsemane—whether all this is sufficient to repay me for the loss of the last gaze out of the eyes of a young, noble, and beloved brother, and, yet more, of the last words of lips whose utterances were the guide of my young years, whose teachings made me love the countries of which old Homer sang, of which old historians wrote, old philosophers discoursed eloquently, whose morning and evening prayers had made dear to me every inch of land that was hallowed by the footprints of the Lord—judge ye, who have heard the blessing of a dying father, or ye who, like myself, have been far wanderers when the God of Peace entered the dear home circle!

W. C. P.

NEW YORK, March 27, 1857.

Contents.

1. Fra Giovanni.

Page

Arles—Malta—Cathedral of St. John, ... 15

2. The Classic Sea.

The Nubia—The Pentapolis—A Sun-worshiper—Sleep and Dreams—Laughter of the Waves—Cape Arabat—Alexandria, ... 20

3. The Dead of Alexandria.

Donkeys—Pompey's Pillar—An Arab Girl—Buckshеesh—Custom-House—A Firman—Needles of Cleopatra—Catacombs—Opening Tombs—Vases—A Painted Tomb—A Large Tomb, ... 32

4. Iskandereyeh.

Rhacotis—An Ancient Lamp—Saint or Martyr—Street Costumes—Female Modesty—Mycerinus—Meshalks—Railway—The Nile—Moslems Praying—Spectres and Angels, ... 50

5. Cairo the Victorious.

Dr. Abbott—Suleiman Effendi—Oriental Method of Reasoning—Streets—Lattices—Dark Eyes—Mosk of Sultan Hassan—Citadel—Mosk of Mohammed Ali—Suleiman Aga and the Coffee—Family Tomb of Mohammed Ali—Murad Bey—Bazaars of Cairo—Buying a Dress, . 60

6. The Footprints of the Patriarchs.

Hajji Ismael, a Dragoman—Founding of Cairo—Topography—Memphis—Heliopolis—Old Cairo—Rhoda—Matareeyeh—Fig-tree of Joseph and Mary—Heliopolis—Gateway of time of Moses—Obelisk—Agriculture—Canals, and Methods of Irrigation—Shooting along the Desert—Tombs of the Memlook Sultans, ... 71

7. Prayers and Coffee.

Page

A Derweesh and an Argument—I Convert him—Punch and Judy—A Donkey Derweesh—Mosk of Amer—The Nilometer, and Island of Rhoda—Howling and Whirling Derweeshes—Description of their Services—The American Mission. 80

8. La Illah Il Allah.

Mosk of Tooloon—Shapes and Shadows—The Destiny of Mohammedanism—English Egypt—Mark the Prophecy, ... 90

9. Sheik Houssein Ibn-Egid.

An Arab Mare—The Old Sheik—Mohammed Abd-el-Atti—How Sheik Houssein came to Cairo—Prisoners—Sheik Houssein is Arrested—I accompany him to the Transit Office—Scene there—A Furious Crowd—A Bail Bond—A Photograph of the Sheik, ... 97

10. Law and Liberty.

A Street Row—Treaties with Turkey—Their Injustice—A Murderer—The Blood Revenge—Procession of the Makhmil—The Bab Zouaileh and the Kutb—Parting with Sheik Houssein—Hearing of him again, 109

11. The Phantom.

Buying Provisions and Furniture—Abd-el-Atti—Contract for the Nile Voyage—The Phantom, my Boat—Description of the Boat—Servants—Ferrajj—Hassan—Hajji Mohammed, the Cook—Money-changer—The Departure—All Aboard—First Night on the Nile, 120

12. Southward Ho!

Sound of the Muezzin Call—An Obliging Government—Nile Mud—First Impressions of the Nile—Benisoef—Abd-el-Atti thrashes a Native—Wild Pigs—Abou-Girg—Going for Milk—Moonlight Scene in a Mud Village—Remains of Ancient Habitations, ... 130

13. Braheem Effendi El Khadi.

Kalouseneh—A Coffee Shop—Boosa—Dancing-Girls—A Disgusting Dish—A Law Question—I turn Khadi and Decide it—A Costly Head-dress—Palm-trees and Moonlight—Mohammed Hassan—A Boy nearly Drowned, and a Row—Convent of the Pulley—Swimming Monks—Medical Advice, ... 143

14. Manfaloot and Es Siout.

Page

CROCODILES—BENI HASSAN—A NEW PASSENGER—ABOU MESHALK—REIS HASSANEIN AND HIS WIFE—MANFALOOT—ES SIOUT—LATIF PASHA—A RECEPTION—BEDOUIN THROATS—TOMBS NEAR ES SIOUT—A VISIT TO THEM, 156

15. Thanksgiving Day.

SUGAR-CANE AND COTTON—PRODUCTS OF THE NILE VALLEY—CHIBOUKS AND LATAKEA—AMERICANS—AN AMERICAN BABY—BRICK-MAKING—ANCIENT BRICKS—A VERY INTERESTING PICTURE IN A TOMB—LATIF PASHA LEAVES ES SIOUT—SALUTES—THANKSGIVING MEMORIES—A NEW POSTAL ARRANGEMENT—A DROMEDARY EXPRESS, ... 167

16. Life Along the River.

BAKING BREAD—SHEIK HERREDDEE—PELICANS—CROCODILES—BENEFITS OF A FIRMAN—MENSHEEH—PIPES OF TOBACCO—HAJJI-MOHAMMED—HASSABO'S FRIGHT—FISHING IN THE NILE—A LONG PULL—A DEVIL, . . . 178

17. Abd-el-Kader Bey.

THE REIS BEATS THE CREW—GHENEH—ABD-EL-KADER—HIS RECEPTION ROOM—THE SOUND OF CHURCH BELLS, ... 190

18. To Love a Star.

THE STORY OF SHEIK HOUSSEIN AND THE CHRISTIAN LADY WHOM HE LOVED—A DEAD MAN—AND BURIED, ... 197

19. The City of a Hundred Gates.

THEBES—RUINS—THEBAN TOMBS—TURF ON GRAVES—THE SULKY GOVERNOR—THE GREAT TEMPLE AT LUXOR—OBELISKS—MUSTAPHA AGA THE AMERICAN AGENT—A CHRISTIAN CHAPEL—COUNTERFEIT ANTIQUES—SUNRISE ON MEMNON—PILGRIM FOOTPRINTS—EXCAVATIONS, ... 206

20. The Ancient Dead at Esne.

THEBES TO ESNE—TEMPLE AT ESNE—MUMMIES LYING IN THE TEMPLE—I EXAMINE THEM—PRIESTESS AND PRIEST—SUMMARY JUSTICE ON A NATIVE—MEDICINE AND SURGERY—DONKEY TRADE. 220

21. Buying Antiques.

SUNDAY ON THE RIVER—EL KAB, THE ANCIENT EILEITHYAS—ANTIQUES, TRUE OR FALSE—COST OF ANTIQUES—BUYING THEM—AN ARAB HORSE—RAIN IN EGYPT—RUINS OF EILEITHYAS—LIZARDS, ... 227

22. Edfou.

Page

A Desert Mare—Edfou—The Temple—Suleiman, the Governor—Funeral of a Boy who Died of a Devil—Buying more Antiques—Another Governor—A Court of Justice—Government of Egypt—Eastern Tobacco—Latakea—A Strong Pull, thanks to Mohammed Roumali, 236

23. The Tower of Syene.

A Row on Shore—Hagar Silsilis—Temple at Koum Ombos—Hassabo Arrives at Home—Arrival at Es Souan—Elephantine—The Cemetery at Es Souan—The American Agent—The Reises of the Cataract—The Contract for Going up—The Start, ... 247

24. The First Cataract.

The Rapids—Ascent of the Cataract—Incidents of the Ascent—Bag Boug and the Brandy—Philæ—Moonlight on Philæ—The Pass of the Cataract, ... 262

25. Moonlight.

Jackals and a Wolf—Hassan Shellalee and his Mother—Old Women in Egypt—Moonlight on the Ruins—Nubia—Miserable Life—Nubian Villages—An Eventful History, ... 273

26. The Nubians.

Medical Advice—A Horrible Case—A Devoted Wife—Korusko—Derr—Abdul Rahman and his Physician—Hassan Kasheef and his Hundred Wives—Fruit and Wine—Chameleons—Abou Simbal—Tombs of the Sons of Israel—A Fight on Deck—The Second Cataract—Christmas Eve. 283

27. The Second Cataract.

Wady Halfeh—A Dromedary Ride across the Desert—Gazelles—A Chase—Alone on the Desert—Abou Seir—The Second Cataract of the Nile—Names Cut in the Rock—Christmas Dinner—Preparations for the Return Voyage. 295

28. Abou Simbal.

Rock Temple at Ferayg—I Fall into a Tomb—Abou Simbal—Illumination of the Temple—Brilliant Effect—Nubian Fellaheen—The Colossi—The Temples of Abou Simbal. 302

29. Northward in Nubia.

Page

Derr Again and Abdul Rahman—Temple at Derr—Ostriches, and a Monkey—Temple at Amada—Letters from Home!—I tell my Crew about Dr. Kane—Saboa—A Heavy Sea—A Nubian Girl—Left Behind —Old People—Dakkeh, ... 310

30. Northward in Egypt.

Gerf Hossayn—Turbulent Natives—Justice Administered—Kalabshee —New Year's Day at Philæ—Descent of the Cataract—New Year's Calls at Es Souan—Travelers' Boats—Jessamine—Hagar Silsilis—The Quarries and Grottoes, ... 318

31. Arrakee and Antiques.

Edfou—The Temple and its Dark Chambers—An Arrakee Distillery—Wild Fowl—Roman Ruins at Eileithyas—Ancient Homes—Tombs at El Kab—Four American Boats—Tobacco, ... 326

32. Achmet the Resurrectionist.

Esne—The Mummies Again—Strolls Along Shore—A Dumb Beauty —Luxor by Night—A Light Among the Tombs—An Ancient Prince—A Theban History, ... 337

33. Thebes the Magnificent.

The Tent on Shore—Medeenet Habou—Evening in the Tent—Tombs of the Assaseef—The Remeseion—Theban Tombs—Achmet Again—Mummies—Private Tombs—Number 35, ... 346

34. The Palaces of the Dead.

An Unexpected Meeting—Mr. Righter—An Antique Shop—Discovery of Mummy Shawls—Mummies in Wrong Boxes—Tombs of the Kings—Belzoni's Tomb—Bruce's Tomb—My Friend Whitely, ... 362

35. He Sleeps Well.

Cabin of the Phantom—Mustapha Aga's House—A Dying Artist—Karnak—Digging a Grave—The Last Look—The Funeral and Burial, ... 372

36. The Glory of Karnak.

Extent of Karnak—Egyptian Ideas of Immortality—Approach to Karnak, Shishak and Rehoboam—Champollion and his Discoveries—Melek Aiudah—Moonlight on Karnak—That Lonely Grave, . . 386

37. Memnon and his Daughter.

Page

A Jereed Performance—Ghawazee Girls—Finding a Ladder—Memnon—Climbing into his Lap—Houssein Kasheef the Governor—Old and Lonely—The Last Evening at Luxor—The Surly Nazir—Leaving Thebes—Taking a Mummy on Board, ... 397

38. A Turkish Nobleman.

Gheneh—Abd-el-Kader Bey—Ducks and Foxes—Houssein Kasheef made Happy—Dendera—A Present from Abd-el-Kader, . . . 411

39. The Crocodile Pits.

Maabdeh—A Party for the Crocodile Pits—Mr. Legh's Account—Road to the Pits—Entrance—First Chamber—Perilous Advance—Narrow Place—The Crocodile Mummies—Coming Out—Attack from the Natives—Manfaloot—The Governor's Administration of Justice—The Coptic Bishop, ... 417

40. Desolate Places.

Beni Hassan—Tomb of Joseph—Latif Pasha at Minieh—Sakkara—A Row on Shore—Memphis—Sesostris Fallen—Tomb of Apis—A Brief Battle—Seizing Soldiers—The Pyramids of Ghizeh—We Leave the Phantom, ... 429

41. Vision and Realities.

Bucksheesh—Tobacco and Kief—Suleiman Effendi's Shop—Story of Selim Pasha's Love—A Rich Soil—The Dust of Benjamin and Judah—The Wife of Manasseh—Joseph and Benjamin—The Departure for Holy Land, ... 444

Appendix.

A.—Sketch of the History, Religion, and Written Language of Ancient Egypt, ... 471

B.—Advice to Travelers Visiting Egypt, ... 493

I.

Fra Giovanni.

Fra Giovanni was a Franciscan. His face was one that you loved to look at. A calm and beautiful face. Sometimes, when the long black lashes fell over his cheek and his mind went wandering over the hills about San Germano in the fair land of Italy, I used to think I was looking at the face of him of Patmos, the beloved disciple, who, much as he loved the ascended Christ, yet remained longest of all the twelve away from him; and when my friend prayed, as I have seen him pray, with tears, and yet very bright hope, in his eyes, I used to remember the same John, and think I could see his eyes, when he uttered the last fervent prayer that his Lord would come quickly, from whom he had been so long separated.

We met in the theatre at Arles, that old town of the south of France which boasts a rival to the Roman Coliseum. I was sitting in the twilight, with no one but

Miriam and the guardian near me, and I was dreaming, as I suppose any enthusiastic American may be permitted to dream the first time he finds his feet on the boards—on the rocks, I should say—of an ancient theatre. The fading light was not unfavorable to such an occupation. Ghosts came at my call and filled the otherwise vacant seats.

I saw fair women, brave men, magistrates, soldiers, senators, and an emperor, yea verily, an emperor, in the seat between the marble columns. There were wrestlers, just come from the games near by in the amphitheatre, standing by the stage, and dancers, and jesters, and masked figures flitting to and fro. All was silent. But the silence grew intolerable, and at length I interrupted it myself.

You need not laugh at me for talking Greek. Those Roman ghosts could understand Greek as well as English, or, for that matter, as well as Latin, and if they knew any thing they should have known Æschylus. So I acted prompter and gave them

> "Χθονος μὲν εἱς τηλουρὸν ἥκομεν πέδον
> Σκύθην ἐς οἶμον ἄβροτον εἱς ἐρημίαν,"

whereupon the ghosts vanished. In a flash, in the twinkling of a star, the scene was one of cold bare rocks in the gray twilight, a ruined hall, fallen columns over which countless snails were crawling, and Kaiser and actor were dust of a verity under my feet.

But a voice answered my voice. For in a nook among the confused stones near the stage had been sitting, all this time, a person that I had not seen, whose clear soft voice came pleasantly to me as he hailed congenial company in this place of ruins.

"Who is there, that would renew old and familiar echoes in these walls?"

"Why? Do you think they ever heard that before?"

"The Prometheus? Yes—why not? There were scholarly days when the fashionable Romans delighted in Greek plays."

We walked out, all together, and down to the miserable forum and the hotel, where, in the evening, over a bottle of St. Peray that I had brought from Valence with my own baggage, we talked down the hours. Thus I became acquainted with Fra Giovanni—and our acquaintance fast ripened. He was an Italian, young, wealthy, of good family, and a priest. He had not been long an ecclesiastic. There were moments when the former life flashed out through the fine eyes under his cowl. The memory of other times alternately lit and darkened his face. There was some deep grief there of which he never told me, and which I never sought to know. He was a good, gentle, faithful friend. That was enough.

Some time after that, we were standing in the crypt of the cathedral of St John's at Malta. That day we were to separate. I to go eastward, and he to travel he scarcely knew whither, on the work of his sacred calling. Before us, in marble silence, lay the stout Villiers de l'Isle Adam, and a little way off the brave Valetta, sleeping after his last great battle with the Turks, who surrounded this, his rocky fortress.

He who goes to the East should always go by way of Malta. It is a proper stepping-stone between Europe and the Orient, where the last wave of the crusades rolled back from the walls of Jerusalem, and sank in foam.

"You will find yourself always looking back to this little crypt in the middle of the sea, wherever your footsteps turn," said Fra Giovanni. "No place in the Mediterranean is so intimately connected with the history of the East as this island of Malta, and there is scarcely any part of the Orient in which you will not be reminded of it. This fact alone, that it is the place of the death and burial of that mighty order who for so great a period swayed the sceptre of power in Europe, is enough to connect it with Egypt and Holy Land, indeed with all the possessions of the Turks. Here, when Valetta was Grand Master, the arms of the Moslem had their first great check, and the followers of the false prophet learned that their boasted invincibility was a fable. Here, too, but yesterday, when the great leader of the French had garrisoned the island, your stout cousins of England, who followed his swift feet as the hounds follow after the deer, drove out his soldiery. You will think of that when you see the boastful inscription of Desaix at the cataract of the Nile. There have been valiant deeds done on this rock. If the sea could have a voice, it would tell of men of might, and deeds of might done here, that are themes for bards who love to celebrate the great acts of men. But the sea is the only living thing that knows them. For there are no trees, nor ancient vines, nor any thing here but the great rock, and the living, moving, throbbing sea around it."

I don't know but my friend would have talked on all day, had not a gun from the harbor announced that the steamer was heaving up her anchor.

We left the crypt and walked over the splendid floor of the cathedral, which is inlaid with a thousand tombstones of knights of the Cross. I glanced once more at the picture of the Beheading of John, which Caravaggio painted that he might be admitted to the order, and painted in fading colors (water some say) that the evidence of his debasement of the art, and their debasement of the order, might disappear; and then, rushing out into the Strada Reale, and plunging down the steep narrow streets to the landing-place, overturning a half-dozen commissionaires, each of whom swore he was the man that said good-morning the day previous, and became thereby entitled to his five francs (for no one need imagine that he will land at Malta without paying, at least, three commissionaires and five porters, if he carry no baggage on shore, or twice as many, if he have one portmanteau), I parted from Fra Giovanni, with a warm pressure of the hand, a low "God bless you," and a long, earnest look out of those eyes of John the Saint.

When the *Nubia* swung up on the port-chain, with her head to the opening of the harbor, and ran out to sea, she passed close under the Lower Barracka, so close that I could recognize faces on it. In the corner, by the monument of Sir Alexander Ball, I saw my friend. As he recognized me, he waved his hand toward me, and even in that motion I caught his intent; for he, good Catholic that he was, could not let me, his heretic friend, go to sea, and especially to the East, without that last sign of the redemption by way of benediction. I thanked him for it, for he meant it lovingly, and so I was away for the Orient. We met again at the Holy Sepulchre.

Such was my step from the modern world to the ancient. From good old Presbyterian habits and friends to the companionship and affection of a Franciscan brother among the relics of the mediæval world, and then to the heart of Orient, Cairo the Magnificent, el Kahira the Victorious.

2.

The Classic Sea.

There is a comfort, when traveling eastward, in meeting Englishmen. You are very certain, in coming in contact with the English pleasure-traveler, to meet a gentleman. Exceptions are very rare. It is also worthy of remark, that the English gentleman, so soon as he learns that you are American, regards you as a fit companion, which is a degree of confidence that he is very far from reposing in one of his own nationality. Englishmen meeting Englishmen, look on one another as so many pickpockets might, each of whom was certain that each of his neighbors meant to rob him on the first available opportunity.

This perhaps arises from the danger that foreign acquaintances may entail unpleasant and impracticable recognitions at home. There is no apprehension of this in meeting Americans, and this may serve to explain a willingness to find society for the time which will not prove troublesome in the future.

But I am disposed to give our cousins over the water more credit for kindred affection. I have always found them cordial, warm-hearted, frank and hearty companions and friends. I was, perhaps, fortunate in those whom I met, but they were many, lords, spiritual and temporal, soldiers, sailors, and shop-keepers; and I found the name of American a pass to their hearts. Some had friends in our new country, and perhaps I had seen and known them—and once or twice I had—all had an idea that we were a race of brave and active men, given to boasting, but good-natured at that, nearly related to them in blood, and allies of England as champions of freedom against the despotisms of the world.

This last idea was one of new and startling force to me, as I looked back from Europe and the East to England and America. The line between freedom and tyranny runs up the British Channel. It is not the broad Atlantic. Our Constitution is of English origin, based on English law, and the boast which we inherit from our revolutionary patriots was, that Britons would never be slaves.

The sea was still. From Marseilles to Malta, in the little mail steamer *Valetta*, we had experienced a constant gale, sailing almost all the way under water. Ladies had nearly died from the exhaustion of sea-sickness. The day that we passed the straits of Bonifacio was the worst in my memory of bad days at sea. All day long the sea went over us, fore and aft. To live below deck was impossible, the foul air of the little steamer close shut and battened down being poisonous. The ladies who were sea-sick were brought on deck and laid on island cushions around which the water washed back and forth. Here day and night for seventy hours they moaned and shrieked. One of them we thought hourly would die. Miriam and Amy, our American ladies, were brave and good sailors, but the scene was almost too much for them. The gale saw us into the port of Malta, and then flattened down to a calm, and never was there such a beautiful sea as we sailed over to Alexandria. No wind disturbed the profound beauty of that water whose azure I had never before dreamed of. It was a never-ending source of pleasure to lean over the side and gaze into the deep blue, that surpassed the sky in richness, on which the bubbles from the swift prow went dancing gayly before us, white flashing and vanishing, to be followed by others and others, all day and all night long.

The poop cabin had been by some odd chance left vacant, and I had secured it for Miriam and Amy. In a season when the through India passengers crowded the line of the Peninsular and Oriental Company, this was a most fortunate and unexpected occurrence. The cabin was much the pleasantest on shipboard, and they slept in it enough to make up their losses on the *Valetta*.

I passed the night on deck, and could wake at any hour and recognize the stars over me, that had so often seen me sleeping in western wanderings. The old Englishman who had the wheel on the starboard watch on the first night out from Malta, when he saw me rolling a blanket around me and lying down on a bench, grunted a disapproval of it to himself, and even ventured to his mate at the wheel a remark to the detriment of my eyes, expressing also his belief that I would go below before morning. How he came to be on the watch in the morning I don't know, but he expressed unmitigated delight at my visual organs being unaffected by his remarks, when he saw me start up before the break of dawn in the east, and throw off my blanket and sleep together, while I walked over to the rail and watched to see the coming day.

Let him who would see the magnificence of dawn behold it in the Levant, off the coast of the Pentapolis. It is no matter for wonder that the ancients had such glorious ideas of Aurora and her train. The first rays over the blue horizon were splendid. I gazed to see if Jerusalem itself were not the visible origin of that splendor. Then swift in the track of his rays, came the gorgeous sun, springing out of the sea like a god of triumph, and he went up into the heavens with a majestic pomp that the sun has nowhere but just here. There was on board the ship a Pharsee, with his servants. I did not wonder at that longing gaze with which I saw him looking at his rising god. I, too, had I been taught as he, would die a worshiper of that god of light.

The second-class passengers were a motley crowd. Italian, Maltese, French, Greek, Arab, and Lascar, they lay in heaps along the deck until the pumps sent the water flooding over them when the decks were washed, and then climbed into the rigging and sunned themselves dry. I held a general levee among them every forenoon, examining their various developments, and ended it with a handful of cigars on deck, which transformed the crowd into a mass of legs and arms, their heads being absolutely invisible in the mêlée. The first day there grew four separate fights out of this generosity of mine, and the second day three. I omitted it the third, but there were six combats on that morning, and I would have resumed the practice on the fourth morning but that we were in the harbor of Alexandria.

Among the passengers were two major-generals in the East India Company's service, one of whom was capital company. I usually had possession of the port side of the after skylight deck, which being lifted up at each end to allow air in the cabin below, made a very comfortable lounge. As it was close to the poop cabin, I furnished it easily with cushions and pillows, and we were accustomed to make this our reception-room of an afternoon. The general enjoyed a talk about America, by way of introduction to a story, and stories, by himself about India and the Indians, which he much delighted to relate, and to which, I confess, I was not unwilling to listen.

The scene on the deck of the steamer at such times was the gayest imaginable; unlike any other great line of travel, either by sea or land, in that the ladies on board seemed to vie with each other in the elegance of their afternoon dresses. Here lay on a pile of cushions a lady of rare and delicate beauty, dressed in white from head to foot, her dress the finest lawns and laces of exquisite texture; while, by way of contrast or foil to her beauty, an Indian servant, black as an African, and dressed in crimson, with a long piece of yellow cloth wound around his head and shoulders, stood fanning his mistress. There stood a group of young ladies, all in black, but all richly dressed and every neck gleaming with jewels; while a half-dozen young men, officers and civilians intermingled, were making the neighborhood intolerable by their incessant flow of nonsense. Two English generals, with their families, were on deck, and a Portuguese governor-general, with his suite, outward-bound to the possessions of Portugal in the Indies. Children were playing everywhere, and officers hastening hither or thither found themselves constantly entangled in the games of the young ones, or lost in circles of laughing girls, or actually made fast by the endless questions of some elderly mother of a family.

And when the sun went down in the sea, our fellow-passenger, the Pharsee, might be seen on the distant forecastle, standing calmly with folded arms and steadfast eyes fixed on his descending god, and following his course with fixed countenance long after he had disappeared, as if he could penetrate the very earth itself with that adoring gaze. And it did not seem strange here that he should worship that orb. I, too, began to feel that there was something grand, majestic—almost like a god—in the everlasting circuit of the sun above these seas. Day by day—day by day—for thousands of years, the eye of his glory had seen the waves of the Great Sea. The Phœnician sailors, Cadmus, Jason—all the bold navigators that are known in song and story—he had watched and guided to port or destruction.

Is it the same great sun that looks down on American forests? Is it the same sun that has shone on me when I slept at noonday on the rocky shores of the Delaware, or whose red departure I have watched from the hills of Minnesota? The same sun that beheld the glory of Nineveh, the fall of Persepolis, the crumbling ruins of the Acropolis? In such lands, on such seas as this, he is a poor man, poor in imagination and the power of enjoyment, who does not have new ideas of the grandeur of the sun that has shone on the birth, magnificence, burial, and forgotten graves of so many nations. Well as men have marked them, tall as they have builded their monuments, broad and deep as they have laid their foundations, none know them now save the sun and stars, that have marked them day by day with unforgetful visitation. And when the day was gone, and the night, with its deep blue filled with ten thousand more stars than I had ever seen before, was above us, I wrapped my plaid around me, and disdaining any other cover than that glorious canopy, I slept on deck and dreamed of home.

I say I slept and dreamed. It was pleasant though fitful sleep, and I woke at dawn. It could not be otherwise. From my childhood, the one longing desire to visit Egypt and the Holy Land grew on me with my growth. It entered into all my plans of life—all my prospects for the future. I talked of it often, thought of it oftener, dreamed of it nightly for years. One and another obstacle was removed, and I began to see before me the immediate realization of my hopes. It would be idle to say my heart did not beat somewhat faster when I saw the blue line of the American horizon go down behind the sea. It would still be more idle to say, that I did not weep sometimes—tears that were not childish—when I remembered the silent parting from those dear lips that had taught me for thirty years to love the land that God's footsteps had hallowed, and whose eyes looked so longingly after me as I hastened away. (God granted me never again those dear embraces.) It would be idle to deny that in my restless sleep on the Atlantic in the narrow cabin, my gentle Miriam, who slept less heavily, heard me sometimes speak strange words that might have puzzled others, but which she, as the companion of my studies, recognized as the familiar names of holy places.

But notwithstanding all this, I did not, in my calm, waking hours, feel that I was approaching eastern climes and classic or sacred soil until I had left Malta, and felt the soft north wind coming down from Greece. That first night on the *Nubia* was full of it. I could not sleep more than half an hour at a time, and then I would start up wide awake, with the idea that some one had spoken to me; and once, I could not doubt it, I heard as plainly as if it were real, my father's voice—as I have heard it often and often—reading from the old prince and father of song.

Just before daybreak I crossed the deck and bared my forehead to a soft, faint breeze that stole over the sea. The moon lay in the west. The night was clear, and I could read as if it were day. I leaned on the rail, and looked up to windward, where, here and there, I could see the white caps of the thousand waves, silvered in the light of the purest moon I ever saw, and thinking of my friend, Fra Giovanni, and of my first meeting with him, and yielding to the temptation of a quotation, where no one was near to hear me and to call it pedantic, I began to recite that other splendid passage from the Prometheus, which was born in the poet's brain on this identical water which now rolled around me :

'Ω δῖος αἰθὴρ καὶ ταχύπτεροι πνοιαὶ
Ποταμῶν τε πηγαὶ, ποντίων τε κυμάτων
'Ανήριθμον γέλασμα, παμμῆτόρ τε γῆ
Καὶ τὸν πανόπτην κύκλον ἡλίου, καλῶ.

"And what's the use of calling on them?" said a clear, pleasant voice behind me, as I started around to recognize one of the English generals whom I have mentioned as with us on the ship.

"I say, what's the use of calling on them when they won't come? Times are changed. There are no gods in Greece now, and, by Jupiter, no men either, and the river nymphs are all gone; and the smiles of the waves, look at them—they come when they will, and go where they will; but the good old days of poetry are gone, gone, gone! Even as the glory of yonder cities is gone!" And he pointed to the southern horizon, where I now saw the low line of the coast of Africa for the first time. We were just seventeen hours from Malta when we came up with it. It was Cape Arabat, and here were the cities of the Pentapolis. Here was Berenice the beautiful; Ptolemais was here and Cyrene. That long line of sand, deserted and desolate, was all that I was to see of their grandeur; but I was not sorry that my first view of Africa should be connected with such associations.

In the forenoon we lost sight of land again, and were then left to our own resources in the ship. The sea was in a generous humor. From the hour we left Malta there was almost a flat calm. We did not suffer a moment's discomfort, and I think there was not a case of sea-sickness on board.

Around our cabin doors, on the after deck, we assembled a gay group daily. The ship's band made pleasant music for us in the afternoons and evenings, once delighting us with "Hail Columbia" and "Yankee Doodle," which sounded the more home-like for the unexpectedness of those familiar sounds on an English ship along the coast of Africa.

Night after night came over us with never-diminishing wealth of beauty, and each successive dawn and sunrise woke me from deep slumber on the deck of the vessel. Thursday evening came. At midnight the deck was deserted, and I was alone. In that soft air and exquisite climate I preferred the deck to my cabin, and had made my bed every night on the planks under the sky. This night I could not sleep. The restlessness of which I have spoken had increased as we approached the shore of Egypt, and I walked the deck steadily for an hour, and then threw myself into one of the dozen large chairs which, in the day-time, were the private property of as many English ladies. At one o'clock I heard the officer of the deck discussing the power of his eyesight, and springing to the rail, I saw clearly, on the starboard bow, the light of the Pharos at Alexandria.

You may be curious to know what were my emotions at the visible presence of Egypt before my eyes, and the evidence that I should tread its soil to-morrow. I did not pause to think of the magnificence of the old Pharos which this one replaces, or of the grandeur that made it one of the seven wonders of the world. The great mirror that exhibited vessels a hundred miles at sea; the lofty tower that shone in the nights of those old centuries, almost on the rocky shores of Crete; the palaces that lined the shore and stretched far out into the blue Mediterranean; none of these were in my mind.

Enough to say that, before I thought of this as the burial-place of the mighty son of Philip; before I thought of it as the residence of the most beautiful of queens; the abode of luxury and magnificence surpassing all that the world had seen or will see; before the remembrance of the fabled Proteus, or even the great Julius came to my mind, I was seated in my chair, my head bowed down on my breast, and before my vision swept a train of old men of lordly mien, each man kingly in his presence and bearing, yet each man in his life poor, lowly, if not despised. I saw the old Academician, his white locks flowing on the wind, and the Stagyrite, the mighty man of all old or modern philosophy, and a host of the great men of learning, whose names are lost now. And last in that visionary procession—calmer, more stately than the rest, with clear bright eye fixed on the heaven where last of all he saw the flashing footsteps of the angels that bore away his Lord, with that bright light around his white forehead that crowned him a prince and king on earth and in heaven—I saw *Mark*, the Apostle of Him whom Plato longed to see and Aristotle died ignorant of.

With daybreak came the outlines of the shore and the modern city of *Iskandereyeh*, conspicuous above all being the Pillar of Diocletian, known to modern fame as Pompey's Pillar. We lay outside all night waiting for a pilot. The only benefit to be derived from the modern lighthouse at Alexandria is its warning not to approach the harbor, which is entered by a winding channel among innumerable reefs and rocks. We threw rockets, burned blue-lights, and fired cannon; but an Egyptian pilot is not to be aroused before sunrise, and it was, therefore, two hours after daylight before he came off to us, and we entered the port on the west side of the city.

The instant that the anchor was dropped, a swarm, like the locusts of Egypt, of all manner of specimens of the human animal, poured up the sides of the ship and covered the deck from stem to stern. It would be vain to attempt to describe them. Moors, Egyptians, Bedouins, Turks, Nubians, Maltese, nondescripts—white, black, yellow, copper-colored, and colorless—to the number of two or three hundred, dressed in as many costumes, convinced us that we were in a new country for us. There were many who wore elegant and costly dresses, but the large majority were of the poorest sort, and poverty here seems to make what we call poverty at home positive wealth.

Of a hundred or more of this crowd, the dress of each man consisted of one solitary article of clothing—a shirt of coarse cotton cloth, reaching not quite to the knees, and this so thin as to reveal the entire outline of the body, while it was usually so ragged as to leave nothing to be complained of in the way of extra clothing. They went to work like horses, and I never saw men exhibit such feats of strength. The cargo of the ship was to be got out as rapidly as possible. Five dollars a day is ample pay for a hundred of these men. A piastre and a half (about eight cents) is the highest rate of wages in Egypt.

With the crowd who came on board were the usual number of anxious and officious dragomans.

The word dragoman, derived from turgoman, and meaning simply an interpreter, has gotten to signify a sort of courier, valet, servant, adviser, and traveling companion, all combined, on whom the Oriental traveler must expect to be dependent for his very subsistence from day to day, from and after the moment he becomes attached to him.

A friend of mine, speaking of the servants, was accustomed to call them "the young ladies who boarded with his mother." The dragoman may be defined as the gentleman who travels with you. He becomes a part of yourself, goes where you go, sleeps where you sleep, you talk through him, buy through him (and pay him and through him at the same time), and, in point of fact, you become his servant. All this, if you choose. But, if you choose otherwise, you may make him what he should be, a very good servant, and nothing more. He who can not manage his own servants should stay at home and not travel. The man whose servant can cheat him, should not keep servants, or should submit to his own stupidity.

I may as well pause here, to advise the Egyptian traveler under no circumstances to take a dragoman until he reaches Cairo. He will find English, French, and Italian, spoken everywhere in Alexandria, and on the railway to Cairo, so that he will need no assistance until he begins to make his arrangements to go up the Nile; which *he should not make* in Alexandria.

One of the importunate, who came on board the Nubia, may serve as an example of the rest.

He was a Nubian, black and shining; dressed in the Nizam costume, embroidered jacket, silk vest, and flowing trowsers, all of dark green. He offered a handful of testimonials, but I rejected these, and asked him a question for the sake of getting rid of him.

"What languages do you speak?"

"All de kinds. I had school went to—sixty, seventy year. I ought know."

"Perhaps you ought, but you won't do for me."

I had observed a respectable-looking Maltese, who was the commissionaire for Cesar Tortilla's Hotel d' Europe. Placing the baggage in his charge, we made our way down into a boat, and a tall, half-naked Arab, standing up to his oars, pulled us slowly in to the crowded landing-place at the custom-house of Alexandria.

Here I entered Egypt; and, at this same spot, on a moony midnight five months later, I departed for the Holy Land.

3.

The Dead of Alexandria.

ALEXANDRIA is a strange medley. The West and the East have met and intermarried in her streets. The great square presents the most singular spectacle that can be imagined in any city of Orient or sunset, from the strange commingling of races, nations, costumes, and animals. The great modern institution of Egypt is the donkey, especially to American eyes.

The Egyptian donkey is the smallest imaginable animal of the species. The average height is from three feet and a half to four feet, though large numbers of them are under three feet. These little fellows carry incredible loads, and apparently with ease. In the square were scores of them. Here an old Turk, fat and shaky, his feet reaching to within six inches of the ground, went trotting across the square; there a dozen half naked boys, each perched between two goat-skins of water. Four or five English sailors, full of wonderment at the novel mode of travel, were plunging along at a fast gallop, and got foul of the old Turk. The boys, one of whom always follows his donkey, however swift the pace, belaboring him with a stick, and ingeniously poking him in the ribs or under the saddle-strap, commenced beating each other. Two ladies and two gentlemen, India passengers, taking their first donkey ride, became entangled in the group. Twenty long-legged, single-shirted *fellaheen* rushed up, some with donkeys and some with long rods. A row of camels stalked slowly by, and looked with quiet eyes at the increasing din; and when the confusion seemed to be inextricable, a splendid carriage dashed up the square, and fifty yards in advance of it ran, at all the speed of a swift horse, an elegantly-dressed runner, waving his silver rod, and shouting to make way for the high and mighty Somebody; and forthwith, in a twinkling, the mass scattered in every direction, and the square was free again. The old Turk ambled along his way, and the sailors surrounded one of their number who had managed to lose his seat in the hubbub, and whose curses were decidedly home-like.

No one could be contented in Alexandria more than fifteen minutes without going to Pompey's Pillar, as fame has it, or the Pillar of Diocletian, as it is now more frequently and properly called.

Leaving the ladies to their baths and a late breakfast, we mounted donkeys at the door, and being joined by a half dozen English officers bound to India, who were detained in Alexandria for the train until evening, we dashed off up the square at a furious gallop; furious in appearance, but the rate of progress was about equal to a slow trot on horseback. Nevertheless, a donkey carrying a heavy American on his back has some momentum when he gallops, as the guard in the gateway found to his cost; for he was dozing, after the prescribed manner of an Egyptian noon-day doze, and he dreamed that he heard the Frenchmen coming again, as they came once in his time; and before he had time to pick up his scattered intellect he had more to do in picking up himself, for we went over him like a thunder-storm, rattling on the draw-bridge, across an open space, through another gateway, across another draw-bridge, and so out into a long, broad street, on each side of which was a row of acacia trees (known as the sont), and so to a hill that overlooks the city and the harbor, on which stands this solitary column, the lonesome relic of unknown grandeur. Of what it formed a part, whether of the great library, or of some gorgeous temple, no one knows.

We sat down in the dust and looked up at its massive proportions, and admired and wondered, as hundreds of thousands have looked and admired in past years, and commented as they had, and dreamed as they had.

Shall I confess it? There was an Arab girl, who came from a mud village close by, and who stood at a little distance gazing at us, whose face attracted more of my attention than this mysterious column, in whose shade I sat. She was tall, slender, graceful as a deer, and her face exceedingly beautiful. She was not more than fourteen. She was dressed in the style of the country; a single blue cotton shirt. As it was a female who wore it, perhaps it deserves another name; but that will answer, since the sex did not vary the pattern. It was open from the neck to the waist, exposing the bust, and it reached but to her knees. She stood erect, with a proud uplifted head, and to my imagination she answered well for a personification of the angel of the degraded country in which I found myself. The ancient glory was here, but, clothed in the garb of poverty, she was reduced to be an outcast among the nations of the earth.

As I sat on the sand and looked at her, I put out my hand to support myself, and it fell on a skull. Bones, whether of ancient or modern Egyptians I knew not then, lay scattered around.

When I would have apostrophised the brown angel, she started in affright, and vanished in a hut built of most unromantic materials, such, indeed, as lay sun-drying all around us. It was gathered in the streets, and dried in cakes, which served the purpose of fuel, and occasionally of house building. Six naked children of eight years old and under remained. No imagination could make them other than the filthy wretches they were. Here we learned the sound of that word which is omnipotent in Turkish lands, and which travelers now too much ridicule, as if its benefits belonged to the beggar.

Before the gate of El Azhar, in Cairo, I whispered it in the ear of the Sheik, and it opened the old college to my profane feet. At the mosque of Machpelah, in Hebron, I said "Bucksheesh" to the venerable guardian of the place, and though five hundred howling Arabs were outside the door shouting for him to bring me out to them, he said: "Come in the night, when these dogs are sleeping, and I will show you the tomb of Ibrahim." I sent it by my dragoman to the Bim-pasha of Jerusalem, and he gave me fifty soldiers, and marched me through every corner of the mosque of Omar, or the Mesjid El Aksa.

It is a magic word, of value to be known: spoken interrogatively, it is offensive; spoken suggestively, it is powerful. If you doubt it, try it, as I have.

I have said that I did not sleep on board the ship the night before. Neither did I sleep on shore the first night in Egypt. But the cause of my wakefulness was different. Dogs abound in the city of the son of Philip. They have no special owners, and are a sort of public property, always respected. But such infernal dog-fights as occurred once an hour under our windows no one elsewhere has known or heard of. I counted fifteen dogs in one mêlée the first evening, each fighting, like an Irishman in a fair, on his own account.

Besides this, the watchmen of the city are a nuisance. There are a large number of them, and some twenty are stationed in and around the grand square. Every quarter of an hour, the chief of a division enters the square and shouts his call, which is a prolonged cry, to the utmost extent of his breath. As he commences, each watchman springs into the square; and by the time he has exhausted his breath they take up the same shout in a body, and reply. He repeats it, and they again reply; and all is then still for fifteen minutes. But as if this were not enough, there was a tall gaunt fellow, who had once been a dragoman, but was a poor and drunken dog now, and, in fact, crazy from bad habits, who slept somewhere in the square every night, and who invariably echoed the watchmen with a yell that rang down the square, in unmistakable English, "all right;" and once I heard him add, in the same tremendous tones, "Damn the rascals!"

And just before the dawn, when the law of Mohammed prescribed it, at that moment that a man could distinguish between a white thread and a black, there was a sound which now came to my ears with a sweetness that I can not find words to express. In a moment of the utmost stillness, when all the earth, and air, and sky was calm and peaceful, a voice fell through the solemn night, clear, rich, prolonged, but in a tone of rare melody that thrilled through my ears, and I needed no one to tell me that it was the muezzin's call to prayer. "There is no God but God!" said the voice, in the words of the Book of the Law given on the mountain of fire, and our hearts answered the call to pray.

My first business in Alexandria was to get on shore, from the steamer, the various articles which we had purchased at Marseilles and Malta for a winter on the Nile. One of these, a cask of Marsala wine—Woodhouse's best—must necessarily pass through the custom-house, and I was not sorry to have an opportunity of witnessing the fashion of collecting the revenue of the Viceroy of Egypt. The cask had been landed from the

Nubia, and, as all the other goods here landed, was in the public stores of the custom-house. Business is transacted in Arabic or Italian, or in the mixed Arabic and Italian which forms the Maltese. We—that is, Trumbull and I, accompanied by a servant and interpreter—went first to look for the wine. Having found it, I was amused at the simple fashion of getting it through the business which, in other countries, is made so needlessly tedious.

A tall Nubian, black as night, looked at the barrel, weighed it with his eye (it was over two hundred weight), twisted a cord around it, and wound the cord around his head, taking the strain on his forehead, and then, with a swing of his giant body, he had it on his back, and followed us to the inspector. This gentleman, an old Turk, with a beard not quite as heavy as my own, but much more gray, addressed us very pleasantly in Italian, and passed us along to his clerk, who sat by his side, each with his legs invisible under him. The proper certificate of the contents was here made, and sealed—for a Turk or Copt never writes his name, impressing it on the paper with ink on a seal—and the black carried the wine to the scales to be weighed. This was done in an instant, the weight noted, and another man received the duty, whereupon it was ready to be carried up to the hotel. All this was done in fifteen minutes or less, and the majesty of the viceroy and ourselves were equally well satisfied.

My next business was with the viceroy himself, and its object to procure a firman which should enable me to make excavations among the ruins of Upper Egypt. Mr. De Leon, who so successfully fills the post of American consul in Egypt, was absent on a visit to Greece. This consulate is by far the most important foreign consular appointment of our government, since it amounts to a

Chargéship, the Egyptian government being, in all commercial matters, independent of the Porte, and receiving communications through the consul direct. The power of this functionary is absolutely startling to an American, who suddenly finds himself in a land where he has no protection from the government, no obedience to render to it, where he is not liable to punishment for any offence against its laws, and where, in fact, he may commit wholesale murder with no penalty other than being sent out of the country by the American consul. I shall speak further of this in another place, and I allude to it here only to say that Mr. De Leon is most remarkably successful in his difficult and responsible position, having secured the confidence of the government, and thus enabled himself more effectually to protect travelers, who find themselves in constant need of some strong friend to appeal to the government in their aid.

During his absence the seal of the consulate was in the custody of Mr. Petersen, the vice-consul of Sweden and Norway, and I take this opportunity of expressing my thanks to him for his unremitting kindness and attention to us during our stay in Alexandria.

On my representing to him my wishes, and presenting the papers on which I relied for the furtherance of my application, he went immediately to the viceroy, and within the forenoon of the day sent to me the desired paper, which was a letter directed to Latif Pasha, governor of Upper Egypt and Lower Nubia, resident at Es Siout, requiring him to furnish me with all necessary papers and assistance, letters to inferior governors and officers of whatever grade, and to provide men and beasts as I should demand, at any point on the river.

The cost of this paper was a polite "thank you," which I repeat here, as well to Mr. Petersen as to the Egyptian government. How invaluable it afterward proved to me I shall frequently have occasion to describe. Without reference to its usefulness for the immediate objects of my visit to Egypt, it operated as an introduction to all men of rank in the upper country, and enabled me to become acquainted with some whose friendship is among the pleasantest recollections of my winter on the Nile, as well as the pleasantest anticipations of a return.

Alexandria has been visited by many travelers, and is described in all the books on Egypt, but with the exception of the Pillar of Diocletian (Pompey's Pillar) and Cleopatra's Needles, there are no antiquities which have attracted their attention.

The modern city stands on a neck of land, to the eastward of which is the old and deserted harbor, and on the west the new, and rather inaccessible, but safe anchorage in which vessels of every nation are found. As a port, it is one of the most important on the Mediterranean, especially as the western terminus of the Suez railway, which is soon to be completed across the isthmus; and which renders the proposed canal, across the isthmus, more than ever undesirable. The chief trade of the port is in coals from England, and grain and cotton thither.

But around modern Alexandria, in all directions, lie mounds of yellow dust and sand, destitute of the slightest vegetation, and burning in the hot sun. Under these mounds lie the ruins of the city of the Ptolemies. Excavations are carried on continually, but only to obtain stone for building purposes, to be used in walls or burned for lime. No investigations have been made by antiquarians, as yet, among these hills, where there is, without doubt, a rich store of treasure to be opened. Here, indeed, but little of the very ancient is to be expected. It was in the later days of Egypt, when the

Pharaohs had been succeeded by the Ptolemies, when Memphis was old, and Thebes was crumbling into ruin, that the Alexandrian splendor filled the eastern, though it was then called the western, world.

I had no desire to spend time or money here, further than to take one step backward in time before I found myself treading the halls of Remeses.

The Pillar of Diocletian I have already mentioned. The Needles of Cleopatra, as they have been long called, are in their old sites, one standing erect where the spray of the sea washes over it, in the eastern part of the city, the other lying on the ground, almost under ground indeed, near it. But not being in their original positions, having been brought here in Roman times, they possess but little more interest than that at Paris, scarcely so much as those at Rome.

The Baths of Cleopatra, as they are called, ancient tombs open and partially sunken in the sea, on the west side of the city, are interesting only as deserted tombs, without name or mark. Having visited these, we supposed the antiquities of Alexandria were "done."

But the Maltese *Abrams*, whom I have mentioned, and whom I recommend as a capital servant, told us of certain catacombs that he knew of, three miles east of the city on the sea shore, where the natives were digging lime-stone for building purposes and for burning. Accordingly we rode out one day to look at them.

It proved a fortunate discovery, especially as on my return to Alexandria I found that these catacombs were entirely dug away and all appearance of them had vanished, although there remain doubtless many tombs under the ground never yet reached, for future explorers to open.

We were no novices in donkey-riding by this time; you would have supposed that we were used to riding them all our lives, had you seen the four which we mounted, and the speed at which we dashed down the long street that leads to the Rosetta gate, followed by our four boys, shouting and screaming to the groups of people walking before us. We raised a cloud of dust all the way, and elicited not a few Mohammedan curses from women with vailed faces, whose black eyes flashed contempt on the bare faces of Amy and Miriam. Now working to windward of a long row of camels laden with stone, now to leeward of a gathering of women around a fruit-stall, now passing a funeral procession that went chanting their songs along the middle of the way—we dashed, in a confused heap, donkeys and boys, through the arched gateway, to the terror of the Pasha's soldiers who sat smoking under the shade, and who had heard doubtless of our victory over the guard on the first day, across the draw-bridge with a thunder that you would not have believed the donkey's hoof could have extracted from the plank, through the second arch, and out into the desolate tract of land, without grass, or tree, or living object for miles, where once stood the palaces of the city of Cleopatra.

Winding our way over the mounds of earth that concealed the ruins, catching sight here and there of a projecting cornice, a capital, or a slab of polished stone, we at length descended to the shore at the place where the men were now engaged in digging out stone for lime and buildings in the modern city.

Formerly the shore for a mile or more must have been bordered by a great necropolis, all cut in solid rock. During a thousand years the entire shore has sunk, I have no means of estimating how much, but not less than thirty feet, as I judge from a rough observation; it may have been fifty, or even more. By this many of the rock-hewn tombs have been submerged entirely, and those on shore have been depressed, and many of them thrown out of perpendicular, while the rock has been cracked, and sand has filled the subterranean chambers. Of the period at which these tombs were commenced we have no means now of judging. It is sufficiently manifest, however, that they have served the purposes of successive generations of nations, if I may use the expression; and have in turn held Egyptians, who were removed to make room for Romans, who themselves slept only until the Saracens needed places for their long sleep.

Already great numbers of tombs had been opened and their contents scattered. The fellaheen who were at work proceeded rapidly in their Vandalish business. Some long corridors stood open in the white limestone of the hill, and broken pottery and innumerable bones lay scattered around. An afternoon was consumed in the first mere looking at these catacombs. Returning the next morning, we selected a spot where the workmen had gone deepest, and hired a dozen men to work under our direction. Miriam and Amy sat in a niche of an open tomb, shaded from the sun, and looking out at the sea, which broke with a grand surf at their very feet.

After breaking into three in succession of the unopened niches, we at length struck on one which had evidently escaped Saracen invasion. It was in the lowest tier of three on the side of an arched chamber, protected by a heavy stone slab inlaid in cement. It required gunpowder to start it. The tomb was about two feet six inches wide by the same height, and extended seven feet into the rock. The others on all sides of the room were of the same dimensions. There were in all twenty-four.

Upon opening this and entering it, we found a skeleton lying at full length, in remarkable preservation, evidently that of a man in the prime of life. At his head stood an alabaster vase, plainly but beautifully cut, in perfect preservation, and as pure and white as if carved but yesterday. The height of the vase is seventeen and a half inches, the greatest diameter nine and a half inches.

It consisted of four different pieces—the pedestal, the main part of the vase, the cover, and the small knob or handle on the top; not broken but so cut originally.

This vase Mr. Trumbull subsequently shipped to America, where I am happy to say it arrived safely. (The cut at the end of this chapter exhibits the form of this vase.)

Pursuing our success, we removed the bones of the dead man, reserving only a few to go with the vase, and then searched carefully the floor of the tomb, which was

EARTHEN VASE FOUND AT ALEXANDRIA.

covered with fine dust and sand. Here we at length hit on the top of another vase; and after an hour of careful and diligent work, we took out from a deep sunk hole in the rock, scarcely larger than itself, an Etruscan vase, which on opening we found to contain burned bones and ashes, as fresh in appearance as if but yesterday deposited.

This vase or urn is fifteen inches high, and its largest diameter is eleven inches. It is of fine earthenware ornamented with flowers and devices.

This vase was too fragile to attempt to send to America, and I left it with Mr. De Leon. The reader will observe the peculiar position of this vase, in the bottom of a tomb under the bones of a dead man. There was another similar hole in the same tomb, but no vase in it. In the bottom of another tomb we found another alabaster urn similarly sunken. It was of ungraceful shape, being simply a tub with a cover.

In one of the lowest excavations we found a tomb which was painted in ancient Egyptian style, but it was so filled with damp sand that nothing remained of the paintings except near the roof which was arched and plastered. There was nothing to indicate the period of its occupation, but it is interesting as being the only tomb I have ever heard of as discovered at Alexandria which was of ancient Egyptian character. All the sarcophagi and tombs hitherto found here have been considered of Greek or Roman period. This, however, was unmistakable, the heads and upper parts of the figures being as brilliant and fresh as the tombs at Thebes. Being on a much lower level than any other that we penetrated, it was possibly of ante-Greek times; but it may have been the tomb of an Egyptian who retained ancient customs after Greek dates.

With this we finished our day's labor, then strolled along the shore, and looked at the gorgeous sunset, right over the Pharos, and then mounting our donkeys, and carrying our vases and sundry pieces of broken pottery in our hands, we rode slowly into the city. I wondered whether the old Greek or Roman whose burned bones I was shaking about in the vase on the pommel of my donkey-saddle had any idea of the curious resurrection he was undergoing in modern Iskandereyeh, or whether it disturbed him beyond the Styx when I shook out his ashes on a copy of the London Times spread on the floor of Cæsar Tortilla's Hôtel d'Europe. Cæsar is a good fellow by-the-by, and his hotel admirable for the East.

The next morning we were up and away at an earlier hour, but fearing to fatigue the ladies too much by a second long ride, we took a carriage to drive out as near as possible to the catacombs. It was not the Oriental fashion. We had no right to try it. The driver said he could do it easily, he had done it before, and lied like an Italian about it, so that we trusted him. We had hardly gone out of the Rosetta gate, and turned up the first hill over the ruins of the ancient city, when one of the horses baulked, and the carriage began backing, but instead of backing straight, the forewheels cramped, and the first plunge of the baulky horse forward took him and us over the side of the bank and down a steep descent into an excavation. The pole of the carriage snapped short off, the other horse, dragged into the scrape by his companion, fell down, and the carriage ran directly over him, and rested on his body. The ladies sprang out as it stopped, and we all reached the ground safely; but there was another ruin on the top of the old ruins. It was, in point of fact, what we call in America a total smash, and we sent back for donkeys, while we amused ourselves with wandering over the site of the old city.

This day I determined to go deeper into the vaults of the catacombs, if possible, than before, and I commenced on the side of the sea in the room that was painted in the brilliant colors of the Egyptians. Setting my men at work here by the light of candles, I was not long in penetrating the bottom of the chamber by a hole which opened into the roof of a similar room below. I thrust myself through the hole as rapidly as possible, but found that the earth had filled it to within three feet of the top. Two hours' work cleared it out; but I found nothing, for the dampness of the sea had reached it, and all was destroyed except the solid walls.

A few moments later one of the men came to tell me that they had opened a new gallery of tombs, and I hastened to see it. Though not what I expected from their description, it was sufficiently strange to be worth examining.

Crawling on my hands and knees about twenty feet through an arched passage cut in the stone, and measuring thirty-two inches in width by thirty-six in height at the centre, I found myself in a chamber twenty-one feet long by fifteen broad. The roof was a plain arch. Its height it was impossible to tell, for the earth had sifted into it through huge fissures in the rock, and by the slow accumulation of two thousand years or less, had filled it on one side to within eight feet of the roof. But the earth had come in only on that side, and had run down in a steep slope toward the other side, which was not so full by fifteen feet. Nevertheless there was no floor visible there, but the lowest stones in that wall were huge slabs of granite, and on digging down I could see that the slope of the earth ran under them, into what I have no doubt was a stone staircase, arched with granite, leading down into the catacombs below. The room was plastered plainly with a smooth whitish-gray plaster on three sides. The fourth side, that over the granite stairway, and, as I have explained, the side where the earth was lowest, was solid rock, with two immense shelves of rock, one six feet above the other, left there in the excavation, and evidently intended as places on which to stand funeral urns and vases. But what struck me as most remarkable, was that a rough projecting cornice was left across the chamber, corresponding with the fronts of the shelves, in which were five immense iron nails, or spikes, with heads measuring two inches across. The heads of but two were left, the others

TOMB IN THE CATACOMBS OF ALEXANDRIA.

having rusted off. I could not imagine any object to which these nails were applied, unless to hold planks which may at some time have covered these shelves.

Upon the shelves were lying masses of broken pottery and vases; but nothing perfect or valuable. I then proceeded to strike the plastered walls with my hammer, and at length found a place that sounded hollow. Two fellaheen went to work instantly, and soon opened a niche which had been walled up and plastered over. It was in the usual shape, two feet eight inches wide, by three feet high in the centre, and seven feet deep. In it lay a skeleton and the dust of a dead man, nothing more. I proceeded, and in an hour I had opened twelve similar niches, or openings, some larger, and containing as many as three skeletons each. It was a strange sensation that of crawling into these resting-places of the dead of long ago on my hands and knees, feeling the soft and moss-like crush of the bones under me, and digging with my fingers in the dust for memorials of its life and activity. My clothes, my eyes, my throat, were covered and filled with the fine dust of the dead, and I came out at length more of an ancient than modern in external appearance.

During the process of my investigations the passage-way by which we had entered was darkened, and I soon saw Miriam on her hands and knees, guided by an Egyptian boy, creeping into the cavern to see what was going on. Having opened all of three tiers of graves that were above ground, I found between the tops of the niches smaller niches, plastered over like the others, and containing broken urns and the remains of burned bones. I found nothing in all this gloomy series of graves but a few lamps of earthenware, blackened about the hole for the wick, sad emblems of departed light and life.

We came out from the vaults and walked down to the beach, where the cool wind revived us. Four hundred feet from the shore was a curious rocky island. Trumbull and myself went out to it. It was full of open tombs, a part of the great necropolis sunken in the sea, and all the way from the shore we found traces of the same great burial-place.

We left the catacombs again at sunset, and rode home slowly over the hills. As we entered the gate of the city we met a marriage procession, the bride surrounded by her female friends on the way to her husband's house. She carried on her head a huge box, or chest, containing all her dower, and her friends shouted and sang as they passed us. We quickened our speed as we approached the great square, and dashed up to the door of the hotel at a furious gallop. There the scene in the evening was always the same. A crowd of donkey boys quarreling with their employers for extra fees, shouts, curses in countless languages, a perfect Babel of tongues, from which it was a pleasure to escape to the cheerful dining-room and the capital dinners that we always found there.

ALABASTER VASE FOUND AT ALEXANDRIA.

4.

Iskandereyeh.

Alexandria, or Iskandereyeh, will amply repay the traveler who visits it and goes no further. To find himself in the land of bananas and palms, of prickly pears, and almonds, and oranges, is enough alone to make the trip across the Mediterranean worth while, and to this is added the immediate association with the East, and the intermixture of the oriental with the western, which is sufficiently amusing to repay one for a week of sea-sickness. Beside all this he is in the old world here—the older world than Greece and Rome—for it is undeniable that, long before this city of Alexandria was adopted by the Greeks, there was a powerful and opulent city of the Egyptians on this ground; and, underneath the mounds around it, lie the remains of men and their achievements, not alone of the centuries immediately prior to the Christian era, but of the far remote ages of which we can only hope to know the faintest outlines of history.

Perhaps, hereafter, some excavator, more fortunate than I, may find in Alexandrian catacombs the history of *Rhacotis*, the city which preceded Alexandria.

My time here was limited by engagements at Cairo. To the traveler who wishes to see only the external appearance of things, or to look only at the ground which overlies old cities, or on which they once stood, one or two days will suffice, as well as a month or a year, to see the city of the Ptolemies. But we caught ourselves often standing for an hour before a modern Egyptian house, in the wall of which was worked a piece of old marble, whose exquisite carving and polish proved it to be a part of the old city; possibly from the pediment of a temple; possibly from the boudoir of a lady; possibly from the throne-chamber of a king. To me Alexandria was deeply interesting. Conjecture—or, if you prefer the phrase, imagination—was never idle as I passed along the streets of the modern city, or over the mounds that cover the ancient. It was most active in the tombs, where we found the ashes of the men of Alexandria of all periods in its eventful history, and the memorials of their lives and deaths.

There was one small earthen lamp, one of a dozen which we found in the catacombs, all alike in general form, and every one blackened about the opening for the wick, with the smoke of the last flame that went out in the closed tomb.

Over that lamp I wasted, if you choose to call it waste, many hours in the evening and night, sitting at the open window of my room on the grand square, and listening to the cry of the watchmen and the call of the muezzin at the late hours of prayer. There was nothing peculiar about it except a monogram on the top. It was of the simplest form of ancient lamps, with a hole for the oil and a smaller one for the wick; but there was on the surface a cross, on one arm of which was a semicircle rudely forming the Greek character *Rho*, the cross and the letter together signifying the Χρ, the familiar abbreviation of the name of our Lord. I know not how many centuries that peaceful slumberer in His promises had remained undisturbed; but when I saw that we had broken the rest of one who slept in hope of the resurrection, that we had rudely scattered on the winds of the sea the ashes of one over whom, in the long gone years, had been read the sublime words, "I am the resurrection and the life," perhaps by Cyril the great bishop, perhaps by Mark himself—when I saw those crumbling bones under my feet, and thought in what strong faith that right arm had been lifted to heaven in the hour of extremity, I felt that it was sacrilege to have opened his tomb and disturbed his rest.

True, the Arabs would have reached him next year; but I would rather it had been the Arabs than I. True, he who promised can find the dust, though it be scattered on the deserts of Africa. But I have a more than Roman veneration for the repose of the dead; and, though I felt no compunctions of conscience in scattering the dust of the Arabs, who had themselves robbed the tombs of their predecessors to make room for themselves, yet I did not like the opening of that quiet place in which a Christian of the early days was buried.

Who was he? Again imagination was on the wing. He was one of those who had heard the voices of the apostles; he was one of those who had seen the fierce faith of the martyrs in their agony; he was one who had himself suffered unto death for the love of his Lord and Master. Or possibly that were too wild a fancy, for such a man would hardly have a tomb like this. If so it were, they must have buried him by night, with no torch, no pomp, no light save the dim flickering light of this funereal lamp guiding their footsteps down the corridors of this vast city of the dead; and this they left beside him—sad emblem of his painful life—the light of faith, pure though faint, in the darkness that was all around him.

Men were sublime in faith in those days. It was but as yesterday, to them, that the footsteps of their Lord were on the mountain of Ascension—it was but as yesterday that the voice of Paul was heard across the sea. Perhaps those dusty fingers had grasped the hand that had often been taken lovingly in that hand which the nail pierced. Perhaps—perhaps—I bowed my head reverently as the thought flashed across me—for I do reverence to the bones of the great dead, and though I would not worship, yet I would enshrine in gold and diamonds a relic of a saint—perhaps, in some far wandering from his home, this man had entered Jerusalem, and stood within the porch of the temple when HE went by in all the majesty of his lowliness.

You smile at the wild fancy. Why call it wild? Turn but your head from before the doorway of the sepulchre, and you see that column, at the foot of which Mark taught the words of his Lord; and turn again to yonder obelisk, and read that the king, who knew not Joseph, but whom Moses and Aaron knew, carved it in honor of his reign. Why, then, may not this tomb, which I have opened, a hundred feet below the surface of the hill, contain the dust of one who has traveled as far as the land of Judea, only eighteen hundred years ago; who had seen the visible presence of him whom prophets and kings desired to see; and who, won by the kingly countenance, the holy sweetness of that face, went homeward, bearing with him enough of memory of that face and voice to rejoice at the coming of "John, whose surname was Mark," and to listen to the teaching of the gospel of the Messiah?

It startles those unused to Egyptian antiquities to hear the far past spoken of as thus present with us. But the facts are powerful and undeniable.

One grows terribly old in visiting Egypt.

It is a fact little thought of, scarcely known at all out of scientific circles, that Colonel Howard Vyse, the eminent Englishman whose excavations in the pyramids at

Ghizeh and Sakkarah have contributed to science nearly all that we know concerning those stupendous remains, found in the third pyramid at Ghizeh, the broken coffin of its builder, and the remains of a mummy, bones and flesh, and clothes, that we have every reason to believe are those of Mycerinus.

Any Englishman strolling down Regent street of a winter morning, may turn aside a few blocks and look in a glass case, in the British Museum, on those bones and sinews, and believe with reason that the world knew no greater monarch, in the twenty-first century before Christ, than he whose dust and bones lie there! By their side, is the coffin found bearing his name, and we know from Herodotus, that his period was long before the date of any dynasty that we can connect with known history.

If, then, the bones of the almost immediate successor of Cheops are in a museum in England, why may I not imagine that some of these bones in Alexandria were living even a few brief centuries ago?

The inhabitants of modern Alexandria are of all nations and kinds. Many of the Europeans are wealthy, and live in considerable style, driving handsome equipages, with elegantly-dressed footmen running before and crying, "Clear the way," in the day-time, or at night carrying huge torches made by burning light-wood in an iron frame on the end of a pole, and technically known as *Meshalks*. Much business is done here, and many men are employed in various ways, earning the low wages of the Egyptian fellaheen, which never exceed a piastre and a half, or about eight cents per day. The large standing army of Said Pasha, of which a considerable detachment is always here, is necessarily attended by the wives and children of the soldiers, who lounge about the streets, especially in the sunny and dusty suburbs, in all stages of nakedness.

It is difficult to say what constitutes poverty in Egypt. We should say, were they in America, or in Europe, that the large mass of inhabitants were in squalid, abject, hopeless poverty. But on examination they seem fat, and certainly far happier, than the lower classes of any other nation I have seen, and this when (I speak literally now) the poverty of the most degraded, begging outcast in New York, would be positive wealth to them here. One solitary ragged shirt is the sole property, the entire furniture, estate, and expectancy, of ninety-nine out of a hundred of the inhabitants of Egypt in the cities of Alexandria and Cairo. A man and his wife, or his two or more wives, will possess a shirt to each, and a straw mat, old, worn, and muddy, and have no other possession on earth except naked children without a rag of clothing.

Nakedness is no shame here. Children up to ten and twelve years of age, go about the streets with either one ragged, filthy cloth wound around them, or, as frequently, entirely naked. Groups of ten or a dozen play in the sunshine here and there, without a rag of covering from head to foot. The older people are scarcely more clad. A single long blue shirt suffices for a woman of any ordinary class. It is open in front to the waist, and reaches below the knees. A piece of the same cloth, by way of vail around the head, is the substitute for the elegant head, coverings of the wealthy classes. The upper part of the body is, of course, entirely exposed, and no one seems to think of covering the breast from sun, wind, or eyes. The face is usually hidden by the cloth held in the hand, while the entire body is exposed without the slightest attention to decency. Not unfrequently, when the woman has not the extra covering for her head, she will seize and lift her solitary garment to hide her features, thereby leaving her person uncovered, it being in her view a shame only to exhibit her face.

The women of Egypt are by nature magnificently formed, and the habit of carrying burdens on their heads gives them an erect shape and high cast of the head which continues to extreme old age. I never saw a bent old woman. I remember seeing one woman carrying a small piece of bread on her head from which she occasionally bit a piece, replacing it immediately on its shelf, and Mr. Williams of the Indian Hotel, in Cairo, told me that he had seen a hawk take a piece of meat from the head of a servant as she was carrying it home, an incident that reminded me forcibly of the story of Saad and Saadi in the Arabian Nights, and the loss of the turban.

The men wear whatever they possess in the way of cloth. Doubtless one garment lasts a lifetime, and is ignorant of water oftener than once a year. Their costume is various. Some wear the single shirt; others, a mass of dirty cloth wound round the body, neck, and head; others, a coarse blanket made of camel's-hair, which they throw rather gracefully over their shoulders, leaving a corner to come over the head. The costumes vary so much that I think I counted over thirty entirely different and distinct styles of dress, in the square, in Alexandria, before my windows, at one time.

These remarks, of course, are understood as applying to the middle and lower classes. The wealthy Orientals wear gorgeous dresses. The men usually adopt the Nizam dress, and the ladies revel in silks and jewels that would craze a New York belle.

I obtained admission into one hareem, of which, and the splendor of the dresses, as well as the beauty of a Greek girl that I saw there, I shall speak when writing of the Holy Land.

The railway was completed only to Kafr-el-Aish, on the Nile, and thence we went to Cairo by steamboat. Constructed by English engineers, and under the superintendence of a Scotch gentleman, I think I am safe in saying that there is no railway in America so complete, well constructed, and safe as this of Egypt. It is the private property of the viceroy, and with this fact in view, and the additional fact that it is already nearly complete to Suez, capitalists may judge how probable it is that Said Pasha is sincere in forwarding the canal project, which would cut off all freight-travel to either Cairo or Alexandria. I am convinced that his opinions have been misrepresented to induce capitalists to embark in the scheme of the Suez ship-canal, and that the true interests of the Egyptian government are most decidedly against it.

It was somewhat strange, as may well be imagined, to see a train of cars, surrounded by a hundred guards in turbans and tarbouches, starting out of a city of mud houses, through groves of palms and bananas, winding it way around the Pillar of Diocletian and off into the dismal waste that separates Lake Mareotis from the sea. The speed was at first but slow, even slower than the usual starting rate with us at home; but on reaching the open country we made some thirty miles an hour steadily until we came to Kafr-el-Aish, which was then the terminus of the road on the Rosetta branch of the Nile, eighty miles below Cairo. Here we were transferred to the steamer in waiting for us, the first and second class passengers going on the steamer, and the third class taking an ordinary river boat, which was to be towed three hundred feet astern.

It was impossible to get up any enthusiasm about the Nile. This was indeed one of the branches of the great river, but only one of them, and it was hardly more the Nile than was the Mahmoud Canal in Alexandria, whose waters are the same. The stream was muddy, flowing high between its banks, and sometimes overflowing them, and it was out of the question to admire such a mass of mud. The hot sun shone fiercely on it, and the banks, uninteresting in all respects, seemed to be broiling out a patient existence, while here and there a collection of mud huts, bee-hive like, gave the sole evidence of the life of man in the Delta.

As the sun went down, the deck of the boat began to present a strange spectacle. One by one the Mussulmans went out on the little guard behind the wheel-house and performed their ablutions in the prescribed style, and then ascended the wheel-houses, kitchens, state-room decks, and every other elevated place, and went through the postures and prayers. It was certainly curious to see a row of ten or fifteen men on each side of the deck bowing in the strange but graceful forms of the Mohammedan worship. We lay and looked at them till the evening had passed into night, and then wrapping our shawls around us, slept on the deck till roused by the passage of the *barrage*.

This, it is not necessary to explain, is the magnificent stone bridge intended to operate as a dam, which Mohammed Ali projected, and his successors have continued to its present state, across the Nile, at the point of the Delta where it separates into different mouths, the object being to raise the water somewhat higher and increase the annual inundation. The wild appearance of the stone piers, between which we passed, lit by immense torches of blazing wood, and swarming with half-naked Arabs, whose swarthy countenances glared on us in the flickering light like the faces of so many fiends, roused us from slumber; but we relapsed instantly into deeper sleep, which remained unbroken until we arrived at Boulak, the port of the modern city, and thence we drove swiftly, by the light of a torch in the hands of a swift runner, up the long avenue and into the gate of the Ezbekieh, and were at last in the city of the Mamelukes, Cairo the Victorious, Cairo the Magnificent, Cairo the Beautiful, and the Blessed.

Shall I confess it? There were two trains of thought struggling for precedence in my mind during the first half hour after my arrival, nor did the one gain entire ascendancy until I was in bed and nearly asleep, as the day was breaking over the red hills. The one was full of all the wonderful creations of the Arabian Nights. The heroes and all the natural and supernatural personages of those exquisite imaginations were around me in troops the moment I was within the city of Salah-e'deen. With these spectres angels strove. I could call it nothing else. Sublime and solemn memories, that forever linger in this spot, of all the mighty men of that ancient religion, of which our own is but the new form, of patriarchs and holy men of old, of prophets and priests in later days, who came down with the scattered remnant of the line of Abraham; and last of all, of the mother of our Lord, and his own infant footsteps; all these came to drive away the genii that were around me, and before I slept the seal of Solomon was over them again.

5.

Cairo the Victorious.

AFTER four weeks in Cairo I began to feel at home. With a reasonable amount of curiosity and perseverance, one may accomplish a good deal in the way of studying geography in that time.

What I did, and how I did it, it would be difficult, nay, impossible even, in many instances, to describe. There were morning rides along interminable narrow lanes, where I would often lift my stick, just three feet long, and holding it horizontally show Miriam, whose donkey kept close behind mine everywhere, that that was the exact width of the passage, called here a street, while the overlapping lattices of the opposite houses shut out the sunshine from above us. There were afternoon sittings in the bazaars, on the shop front of Suleiman Effendi or old Khamil the silk and embroidery merchant. One day I was in the unknown depths of the well of Yusef in the citadel, and another I was discussing history with Sheikh Hassan in the Mosk el Azhar, and almost every morning I smoked a sheeshee with Dr. Abbott, and talked of ancient Egypt.

The modern Orient and the ancient East were thus daily before me, and picking up a little Arabic for common uses from day to day, I had soon but little need of a dragoman, except as a guide to spots I desired to visit.

Some months later than this I saw Damascus. I was disappointed in my hopes of reaching Bagdad, but I have little doubt of the universal truth of my remark, that Cairo is the most *oriental* city of the East. I use the word in a sense in which most persons will understand me without explanation. Damascus was more European in external appearance; Cairo is the heart of the Orient.

During our first week in Cairo we had tried various donkeys, and at length selected four which were much the best, and these remained in our service for a month.

I commend Mohammed Olan to all travelers as a donkey-boy, if he be not already grown out of that position: for he seemed in a fair way to emerge into a dragoman's servant, that being first step toward being dragoman. Donkey-boys pick up a little English and French, and thus become fit for servants to travelers.

Every morning, therefore, our donkeys stood before the door of the Indian Hotel, under the large lebbek trees, on the side of the Ezbekieh, and a general shout of good morning welcomed our first appearance. The ladies' saddles were English. All visitors to Egypt will do well to provide themselves with these at Malta. In Egypt, they will find them scarce, poor, and high-priced.

We took a regular morning gallop up the Mouski, which is the chief Frank street, and leads directly to the Turkish bazaars. In the latter our faces were well known.

If you visit them, O traveler, remember Suleiman Effendi, for my sake. He is the oldest man, with the longest and whitest beard, and he smokes the most delicious Latakea of all the merchants in the bazaars within the chains, which chains forbid the entrance of camels or donkeys among the jewels and amber and rare silks and broideries that there abound. Many summery noons I lost in clouds of forgetfulness, seated in dreamy langour, with

Suleiman the Magnificent on his little shop front, discoursing in words that were less frequent than the volleys of smoke, subjects of profound interest: such as the reason why the smoke went upward, and why the fire seemed brighter in the shade than the sunshine, and why the sunshine was pleasant, and why we liked what was pleasant more than what was not pleasant, and many other marvelous and inexplicable things, in regard to all which we arrived at much the same conclusions, and always with complete satisfaction.

Ah, my friend, you may not know the luxury of such discussions—you who waste golden hours in idle words, raising what you call theories, and disputing and annihilating them, and sharpening and hurting one another's intellects with useless and sounding words.

Not so we who have learned the mystery of things in the cool shades of the Cairene bazaars, from whose lips, blue smoke issues in place of theories; and is not the smoke of equal value? For this was the style of our discussion:

"O Suleiman Effendi, wherefore is it that the sunshine falls into the bazaar, and why does it not pause up yonder above the roof of the wakalla?"

And Suleiman heard me, but he was not the man to bother himself about a matter which he could explain in one word, and so he sent a cloud of blue smoke up into the sunshine, and, after a pause of some minutes, uttered the word,

"Inshallah."

"But, O Effendi, wherefore is it that you Mohammedans do not look into these things? One would suppose you did not care how soon the old roof over the bazaars up yonder fell and crushed you. Will it not fall? —look at it?"

The old man poured out a long sunbeam of smoke, for

the window in the crazy roof let the rays fall just before him, and again ejaculated a guttural "Inshallah."

"O Suleiman the honorable, listen to me. I, Braheem Effendi, owe you a thousand piastres for the amber mouth-piece I bought of you yesterday. I am American, and there is no law in Musr to make me pay you. I shall go without paying you."

"Inshallah."

"I am going now."

"Inshallah."

I dismounted from the shop front, shuffled on my red slippers, and, as I bade him good-morning, the old man uttered for once a somewhat disturbed "Bismillah," as if he were astonished that I was in earnest; and then as I vanished in the crowd beyond the chains, he relapsed into his ancient kief and left it all to God.

There is something comfortable about all this to a man who has lived in fast America, and who has always had a lazy inclination to leave matters to take care of themselves.

Sometimes we rode hour after hour around the streets of Cairo, looking at old lattices, quaintly and elaborately carved, catching once in a while the vision of a beautiful face through some small opening, and carrying away with us the blessings of smiles from dark eyes. Ah me, how many smiles I have had from unknown beauties that I shall never see again; and yet, if one meets a fair woman in the street, or on the steamer, or even but sees her on the other side of a Cairene lattice, and exchanges a smile with her, it is a thing of beauty to be remembered forever; for who knows that we shall not meet again somewhere. I wonder if I shall ever meet again that black-eyed girl that looked at me in the street just inside the Bab el Nasr. She was riding on a high-saddled donkey, between two slaves, following three other women, who looked all alike, and all like her. For a woman of Cairo, who belongs to a wealthy hareem, is, when abroad, but a huge bundle of black silk, with a thick white vail, through which two eyes flash like stars.

I was last of our party—she last of hers—and, as she went by me, suddenly her white hand threw back the vail, and all the lustre of her magnificent countenance shone on me. It was like those visions that we have in dreams that remain forever impressed on the memory. I can never forget that face—nor would I, if I could. She was not so exquisitely beautiful as the Greek girl I afterward saw in a hareem in Syria, of whom I shall have somewhat to say there, but her calm white face, her regular features moulded in the most perfect manner, her red lips ripe, full, and overflowing with fun, and, above all, her eyes of deep, splendid beauty were enough to remember for a day or a lifetime.

In one of our rambles about town, going up one street and down another, without heeding whither they led us, we found ourselves one day at the great entrance of the mosk of the Sultan Hassan, and dismounted to enter it. Outside the door were venders of trifles of various sorts; a kind of old junk dealers, second-hand clothiers, and sellers of paste and imitation jewelry. Among them were venders of Meccan curiosities—sandal-wood beads, and the wood, dipped in the holy well of Hagar, which they use to clean their teeth with. All, or nearly all, the Moslems have good teeth, kept white with this wood, a small stick of which, chewed at one end, forms a soft brush, which they use till the whole is worn away.

The mosk is a grand structure, chiefly interesting from being built of the stone which was the casing of the great Pyramid of Ghizeh. It is the most imposing structure in all the Mohammedan countries I have visited, and probably the most so in the Moslem world. The lofty walls surround a rectangular court, one side of which opens by a grand arch into an immense alcove, in the rear of which is the inclosed chamber around the tomb of the Sultan Hassan, who was murdered and buried here. The guide shows the traveler the blood stains on the pavement here, and says something unintelligible about its being the blood of Mamelukes murdered by the sultan; but I am inclined to think the fact is that the Mameluke blood is of the times of Mohammed Ali.

On the tomb lies, as is the custom, a copy of the Koran in a strong box, and sundry old coverings of silk, that were once heavy and gorgeous. The days are past when any one lived to cover the Sultan Hassan with cashmere.

Immediately above the mosk, on the end of a projecting spur of the Mokattam hills, stands the citadel of Cairo, a small city in itself. The vast extent of the walls must inclose ten or fifteen acres of ground, in which are mosks, palaces, and government-houses.

High over all towers the white mosk of Mohammed Ali, built of unpolished alabaster, from the quarries at Tel el Amarna. Within the gorgeous building, which can not be even approached except by first putting off the shoes, the old viceroy lies quiet in a corner untroubled by visions of Mamelukes. He sleeps on the very spot that he once flooded with red blood, when he annihilated that race which had so long ruled Egypt.

Standing by his tomb, I heard a story of his later years that I have not seen printed. Whosoever has read that story of the slaughter of the Mamelukes by Mohammed Ali, has observed, that in whatever volume it occurs, it invariably closes with the friendship that the viceroy always afterward had for Suleiman Aga, who escaped the massacre in the dress of an old woman. The viceroy professed to doubt the method of his escape. Suleiman tried the disguise on his master again, and successfully begged from him in the same costume.

The alleged affection of the viceroy was not uniform, however. He hated a Mameluke, and not even Suleiman escaped his hatred.

One morning as they sat cozily together as of old, Suleiman saw something that disturbed his quiet of soul, either in the face of his master or in the cup before him.

"Why don't you drink your coffee?" said the old viceroy.

"Do you wish me to drink it?"

"Certainly. Drink it, man—drink."

The Mameluke tucked back the voluminous folds of his dress, and exhibited to the viceroy the gold handles of a half dozen pistols, on one of which he laid his finger, while his eye sparkled silently all that he would have said.

"'It is well to die in good company,' saith the tradition; shall I drink?"

There was no one near to seize him. It was literally a case of life and death. The wily monarch saw that he was caught.

"Tush! nonsense, Suleiman! don't make a fool of yourself. If you don't like your coffee, here, I'll pour it behind the cushion;" and he did so. Then they sent for the Koran, and laid it down between them, and swore good faith each to the other across it. After that Suleiman lived to see his master buried in his great mosk standing on the spot once red with the blood of his slaughtered friends.

Another day's ride brought us to the southernmost gate of the city; and thence we pushed on to the tombs of the family of Mohammed Ali, which are not far southwest of Cairo, in the sandy plain between it and old Cairo or Fostat. Here the great viceroy built a mosk for a burial-place, and before he died saw many of his valiant children laid there; but himself sleeps elsewhere, in the great mosk within the citadel.

Here Abbas and Toossoon, and the great Ibrahim are buried. The tomb of the latter is a most superb sepulchral monument; and probably, with the solitary exception of that of Napoleon, it is the most splendid in the world. It is a monumental structure of marble, over which a rich mazarine blue enamel is laid, covering the entire monument. This is broken by the various inscriptions, which are in relief, sharply cut from the marble, in all the styles of character known to the Arabic, and all gilded. The effect is rich and dazzling.

Here and there, in the mosk, men were praying and reading aloud from the Koran, but none seemed disturbed by our entrance. It was with no common emotion that I found myself standing by the tomb of the man whom history will consider as the rival of Napoleon among the great warriors of the past seventy years. From it I walked a little distance across the hot sand to the grave of Murad Bey, the rival of Le Beau Sabreur himself. His tomb is in a sort of inclosed grave-yard, in the dry sand, covered with a rude stone structure that will not outlast this century. If a voice could be found that had power to open these graves and show these dead, as they lie with their hands under their cheeks, and their faces toward the Prophet's tomb, what a scene would the dead of Egypt present! What mighty califs of the old lines, what fierce soldiers of later days, with closed lips, and sightless eyes, and shrunken features—all with their thin faces toward Mecca!

Every one has read of the beautiful and airy structures east of Cairo, known as the tombs of the Mameluke sultans. Some one has spoken of them as exhalations from the sand. They are in sadly ruinous condition now, chiefly surrounded by mud huts, and their doorways thronged by begging fellaheen and naked children. They were our favorite resorts in the afternoons, when we had nowhere else to ride to, and thither, going out of the Bab el Nasr, the gate of victory, we would ride slowly and watch the changing lights on their graceful minarets as the sun went down behind the pyramids.

Such, from day to day, was our employment in Cairo.

Think of looking up your banker at the bottom of a street four feet wide and four hundred long, or of buying a coat over a chibouk and a cup of coffee!

The bazaars of Cairo have been frequently described. The streets are a little wider where the shops abound, and are usually roofed over, admitting sunshine by windows in the matting or close roof, only at mid-day. Business hours are from about eleven to three. No shop is open longer in the principal bazaars. I have more than once found a merchant closing his shop and have been refused an article I wished to purchase.

"Come to-morrow. I am going home now."

"But I shall not be here to-morrow."

"Inshallah!" and he looked up and departed.

At mid-day the bazaars are crowded, jammed, with passers-by or purchasers, women with vailed faces, and donkeys loaded with water-skins, Turks, Bedouins, camels, dromedaries, and horses, all mingled together, for sidewalk or pavement there is none, and it is therefore at the risk of constant pressure against the filthiest specimens of humanity, and constant collisions with nests of fleas and lice, that one passes through the narrow streets.

I remember well the purchase of a common traveling dress which Miriam effected, and which will serve to illustrate the Cairene and Eastern style of business. We went to the silk-merchants in the wealthiest bazaar of Cairo. One and another showed his small stock of goods, but it was with difficulty that Miriam hit on such as suited her. When this was found, commenced the business of determining the price. The shop of the Turkish merchant is but a small cupboard. The front is invariably about the size of an ordinary shop-window in America, say six feet wide by eight high. The floor of the shop is elevated two feet above the street, and on a carpet in the middle of the floor sits the merchant. His shop is so small that every shelf is within reach of his hands. Of these shops there are thousands in Cairo, and whatever the business, the shop is of the same description.

Miriam sat on the right hand of the merchant, with her feet in the street over the front of the shop; I on his left. The silk goods lay piled on the carpet between us, the pieces she had selected being uppermost. The first step toward price was a cup of coffee and a pipe. She took coffee; I smoked quietly a few minutes, and the Turk smoked as calmly and coolly as if there was no silk on earth, and he was dreaming of heaven. For some minutes the silence was unbroken, while he looked at the opposite side of the street, and we blew a tremendous cloud of smoke. At length I broke the silence.

"How much?"

He smoked calmly awhile, sent the cloud slowly up, and the words came from his lips as gently as the smoke itself.

"Three hundred and seventy-five piastres."

"I will give you one hundred and fifty."

"It cost me more money than twice that."

"It is not worth any more."

"It is very beautiful. I sold one like it yesterday for three hundred and eighty."

"I will not give it."

Five minutes of smoke and silence. Miriam most decidedly impatient, and yet full of fun at this novel mode of buying a dress. A fresh pipe and a fresh start. I asked him the least he would take. It was three hundred. I laid down the pipe, sighed heavily, and walked away down the bazaar toward the donkey-boys. He followed us out and down the street, calmly and quietly assuring us that he was honorable in his statements, and offering a reduction of ten piastres more. I offered him two hundred. He exclaimed in despair and retired.

Having made one or two other purchases, we returned to the charge. He had spread his praying carpet, and was kneeling in his shop engaged in his devotions. A dozen other Mussulmans were in sight, doing as he. It was the hour when the voice of the muezzin called to prayer, and though in the din and bustle of the crowded bazaar I had not heard it, yet on the ears of these sincere worshipers it had fallen from the minaret of Kalaoon, and they obeyed the summons.

We waited till he had finished, and then resumed our seats and negotiations, which were finally terminated by our coming together on an intermediate point, and the sale being closed, we mounted our donkeys and rode homeward. This was but the first of a dozen similar negotiations, and is a fair specimen of the Cairene manner of doing business.

But let no one therefore imagine that my friend Suleiman Effendi is not as respectable a merchant as any man on 'change in Gotham, or because he smokes a pipe and not a cigar think him either low in his tastes or susceptible of ignoble influences. Suleiman is a merchant-prince, and his Latakea is of irreproachable fragrance.

6.

The Footprints of the Patriarchs.

We had not yet decided on a dragoman for the Nile. Abrams, our Maltese servant, had accepted an offer from some gentlemen, and was preparing to go up the river with them. Meantime we had for a daily attendant and guide a stately-looking Arab, Hajji Ismael, by name, whose chief virtue consisted in his splendid outfit. Every morning he made his appearance in a new suit from head to foot, now flashing in silk and now dignified in broadcloth. The fellow must have worn some hundred pounds' worth of clothing, but failing thereby to impress us with a sense of his desirableness as a permanent dragoman, he gave up in despair, having at last been reduced to appear twice in the same shoes, although in all other respects his change was as complete as usual.

Marshalled by Hajji Ismael, Hajji (pilgrim) by virtue of having visited the Prophet's tomb at Medina and the holy Kaaba at Mecca, we penetrated all manner of places and saw all manner of sights.

Cairo in itself possesses no interest by reason of any great antiquity. It does not stand on ground that is hallowed by any ancient name, story, or ruins. The founding of Cairo, known formerly as Musr-el-Kahira, was in the year 969, but the city received its greatest embellishments, and became most powerful and wealthy, under the reign of Yusef Salah-e'deen, known to all readers of the crusades.

Ancient Memphis stood on the west side of the Nile, and some four to eight miles higher up than Boulak. Cairo stands on the desert edge, its eastern gates opening on the sand, and its western on the rich fields of sugar-cane and groves of palms and acacia, which, in a belt two miles wide, separate the city from the river. On the river edge, stretching a mile and a half north and south, is Boulak, from which two broad avenues run up to the city. At the southern part of Boulak commences a row of palaces on the bank of the river, which is here divided on two sides of the island of Rhoda, and these continue in unbroken succession two miles southward, to the head of Rhoda, where, on the mainland, is *Old Cairo*, or *Fostat.* This occupies the site of the Roman station *Babylon*, and in its neighborhood are certain ancient Christian churches, of which I shall speak hereafter. Prior to Roman times the cities in this part of Egypt were Memphis, on the west bank, and Heliopolis, on the east, the latter lying six miles north of the site of Cairo, on the desert edge.

Once for all, let me say to those few who do not already know it, that Egypt south of the Delta (which commences about twenty miles north of Cairo) is on an average four miles wide. The hills on the two sides of the river are about that distance apart, sometimes approaching on one side to the very river's edge, and sometimes on the other. Between the bases of these hills the land is for the most part a dead water level, annually covered by the rising Nile. The villages are usually built at the foot of the mountains. Where otherwise, they are on artificial mounds in the plain, or on the ruins of ancient temples. These hills are rocky cliffs, utterly destitute of vegetation. Yellow sand pours down over them from the Arabian and the Libyan deserts, and sometimes encroaches on the cultivated land. The hills on the eastern side of the Nile, after following the course of the river as far as to Cairo, send a single low spur into the city, on the point of which is the citadel, and then sweep off to the eastward and disappear. From Cairo eastward, the desert reaches in general on a level to Suez, and north of this Egypt grows broader, the Nile separating into many streams, and rain not being so unfrequent.

The Nile being now high, for it was yet early in October, the country was still overflowed, and it was impossible to arrange for a visit to the pyramids without taking tents and remaining there over night. The ladies were not yet accustomed to hardship, and we were unwilling to break into nomadic life thus suddenly.

Heliopolis was almost as difficult of access, except by a route along the desert edge, which was some miles longer than the direct route by Matareeyeh. Nevertheless, we tried it one pleasant morning with success.

Hajji Ismael was out in a new dress. It was his eighth morning, I think, and his eighth dress. The donkey-boys were rejoicing in the prospect of a good day, for a long expedition always made necessary a luncheon, which they were very certain of sharing. I can not too highly commend Mr. Williams's Indian Hotel to travelers; though small, it is by far the best and most comfortable in Egypt, and the stranger will find himself there most perfectly at home. They always provided us with a capital luncheon when we went away for a day's ride, and so to-day.

We rattled along the Ezbekieh and through innumerable narrow streets, and at last out of a gate on the north side of the city, and across the country toward the ancient city of On.

Our route lay just within the edge of cultivated land;

we should have done better to keep out on the sand of the desert, for we found ourselves at length in a field from which there was no dry outlet but on the back track. The appearance of the water was not very deep, and we ventured in. But we had not calculated for the mud underneath. Nearly a fourth of a mile we advanced through the water, and then the mud deepened. Miriam's donkey slipped, and but for the boys who caught her, she would have been worse than drowned. They carried her on their shoulders across the rest of the flood, and we then continued our way, through all kinds of paths, wet and dry, mud and sand, sunny and shady, till we arrived at Matareeyeh and the fig-tree of Joseph and Mary.

The tradition that the Saviour rested under this tree is very ancient, but of how early a date it is impossible to say. The Copts and Armenians, I believe, both adopt it. It stands in a fenced garden, and the well of water near it is said to be a fountain that burst out to satisfy the Virgin's thirst.

Passing this, we saw at some distance from us, rising over the dense mass of trees and shrubs that surrounded it, the solitary obelisk of Heliopolis. Just before reaching it we passed three great pieces of stone, evidently parts of a gateway, on which we found the cartouche of Thothmes III. the Pharaoh of the Exodus.

It was the first of the great antiquities of Egypt that I had seen, and I paused here with perhaps somewhat more of respect than I should give those stones now after five months among the mighty ruins of this oldest of countries. But there is nevertheless a something about those stones which give them an interest that scarcely any others have.

If, as we believe, Thothmes III. was the Pharaoh of the days of Moses, then this may well have been part of the gateway to his palace temple through which the great lawgiver passed and repassed, in the days of the captivity and deliverance of the children of Jacob. It was no idle fancy, strangely as it may strike the ear of one unaccustomed to the antiquity of Egypt. A few paces more brought us to the obelisk, the solitary memorial of the grandeur of the great city of the times of Joseph.

This monument bears the name of Osirtasen, and the date of this monarch is probably not far from the time of Abraham. As I shall elsewhere speak of the chronology of Egypt, I shall not pause here to speak of the chronological differences among Egyptian scholars. For our present purposes it is enough to believe that this magnificent column stood here when Jacob blessed his children and departed, and when Joseph charged them to carry his bones into the Land of Promise. Around it then gathered the most splendid palaces of Egypt; and here, perhaps, was held the court to which the old wanderer of Canaan came. But of that old glory nothing remains. The obelisk stands ten feet below the surface of the surrounding earth, in an excavation made to exhibit its base, and under the mounds that lie here and there about it are the buried ruins of the City of the Sun. We sat in the shadow of the obelisk and spread before us our lunch. It was of bread, figs, dates, pomegranates, and oranges, and each of these fruits was growing in profusion within twenty yards of us, as well as olives, custard apples, bamia, and melons of every kind. The obelisk stands in the centre of a garden of perhaps twenty acres of good land, and around this the desert rolls barren and hot. It would seem that the peculiar interest attached to this spot as the City of Joseph, as well as the chief seat of learning in later years, where Plato and the other great philosophers studied and taught, has been specially provided for in the luxuriance of the fruits and products of its soil; so that, instead of the shining sand that covers Memphis and lies around the pyramids, we have the grove of the Academy to rest in while we listen to the voice of its great teacher.

In the neighborhood of Heliopolis I had opportunity to see the method of cultivation adopted by the modern Egyptians.

No land is under cultivation which is not reached by the Nile overflow, or by simple machines for raising water and pouring it on the soil. Rain being no dependence, irrigation is continued throughout the growing season. So soon as the Nile retires the surface of the ground bakes hard. This is broken up by the rude plow of ancient and modern times, unchanged since the days of Sesostris, and the soil then planted and steadily watered till the fruit is ripe.

Canals, large and small, intersect the country everywhere. Let it be remembered that the arable land of Egypt is almost a perfect level, so that when the Nile rises to a certain height it flows over all the land in every direction, and canals continue the supply as the river falls. Some lands, rescued from the desert, are on a level a few feet higher, and others are not so low as to be covered by the Nile in a year like this, when it does not reach its full height. Every field, high or low, is intersected by little canals, made by heaping the dirt up and hollowing a trench in it, so that the field is divided, like a chess-board, into a number of small squares. These trenches are supplied with water by two processes. The larger trenches, which run several miles, are supplied by wheels at the Nile or in the canals, which are turned by cattle, and which raise an endless chain of earthen pots of water. A pump is unknown in Egypt. The smaller canals are supplied by a *shadoof*, which is arranged precisely like an old-fashioned well-pole in America, except that the swing is so short that the man holds the bucket almost constantly in his hand, and dips and empties, dips and empties, all day long. Up the river the *shadoof* is used on the side of the Nile instead of the water-wheel; and everywhere for the purpose of lifting water from one trench to another that will water a few acres of land that is higher in grade.

A very simple contrivance for the same purpose is often found in the fields. It is a basket, made of palm-leaves or some other stout substance, swung on four ropes, two in the hands of one man and two of another. The men sit on opposite sides of the stream or pool of water supplied from a canal or trench, and drop the basket into the water. Then they raise it rapidly, swinging it at the same time over the top of the higher trench into which they wish to lift the water, and at the same instant slacken two of the ropes so as to allow the water to fall out. The rapidity and ease with which they continue this labor from morning till night is no less a source of surprise than the quantity of water they raise, keeping a steady stream running from their place of work.

Oftentimes a piece of land is rescued from the desert and made into a beautiful garden. Almost as often the desert covers over a garden and reclaims it for part of its empire of desolation. Thus at Heliopolis it would appear that the basin, which may be formed by the ruined wall of an ancient temple, over which the sand has heaped itself up, suggested to some one the idea of bringing the Nile into it and watering the sand. With the Nile came alluvial deposit, and with the deposit fruitfulness—such fruitfulness as we seldom see even on our western prairies. In this small farm, around the old stone, grows every variety of eastern fruit. Oranges swing in clusters against its very sides, and pomegranates, and figs, and olives, are all found in the grounds, while vines and vegetables abound. A mud village stands on the edge of the desert, two or three hundred yards from the obelisk, and is the modern successor of the great ON. Alas! for the difference. A crowd of women and children followed us through the narrow winding street, shouting for money, until we were fairly out of their district, and they regarded us as within the "right of begging" of the next village.

On the way home, I found good shooting along the edge of the desert. I had my gun with me, and having missed a shot at a flock of ibis, I loaded my barrels more carefully, and had afterward better success. It is a curious fact, that the air of Egypt is so very light and clear that the same quantity of gunpowder carries shot and ball much further than elsewhere, and the load of a gun is to be reduced nearly one-third for correct shooting. This I found instantly by the peculiar ring of the barrels on firing, and I learned afterward that such is the case in Egypt.

Desert partridges, so called, abound in this neighborhood. They have but one characteristic which should entitle them to be called partridges. That is the feathered legs. In other respects they are more like a large pigeon in shape, and their color is of a nondescript, desert-sand sort of a color, not marked regularly in any specimens that I have seen. I had two or three shots at them, and had some half dozen to bring home for dinner. Add to these a large hawk, and an eagle, as the boys called it, but in fact a vulture, measuring about four feet from tip to tip, and you have the contents of my game-bag, which, by-the-by, was the loose bosom of the shirt of one of the boys, which was our constant receptacle for articles to be carried.

Returning homeward, we diverged somewhat from the direct path, and crossed the hills to look again at the tombs of the Mameluke sultans. Sadly ruinous, and as sadly beautiful, they seemed in the sunset light like representatives of the religion of Mohammed, sprung gloriously from the desert, and fast falling again into the wastes of sand. The most beautiful of these, that of the sultan, Ghait Bey, who died in 1496, is worthy of preservation, as the most exquisite specimen of eastern architecture which the East can produce. Within the mosk which is attached to the tomb, and under the dome, stands a block of black stone, bearing the impress of a human foot, said to be the foot of the Prophet. Another stone in the same mosk bears the perfect impression of two feet, also attributed to the same great origin, but I think the two footprints rather stagger the faith of the Mussulmans. They were very earnest in pressing their kisses on the single footprint, but they only glanced at the other stone, although its casing of silver was as rich, and its impressions were quite as deep.

We entered the city by the Bab el Nasr, the gate of victory.

7.

Prayers and Coffee.

I HAVE met all sorts of derweeshes (I am particular in spelling this word as it is pronounced) in the East, and have been alternately blessed and cursed by an infinite number. There was one fellow in Cairo who cursed me regularly. If there is any virtue in his anathemas my case is hopeless. I met him daily, he was daily impertinent in his demands, thrust his wooden plate, smelling vilely, under my nose, utterly heedless of my refined sensibility of nerve in that region, and stopped my donkey with new impudence every successive day. As soon as I picked up enough Arabic for the purpose I cursed him back, and, after that, almost any pleasant day, you might have seen a funny group at the corner of the Mouski, by the police office. He cursed by Mohammed, and I by St. Simeon Stylites; he invoked Allah, and I hurled at him the anger of Juggernaut. He never dreamed of half the gods and prophets that I showered on his unlucky head, and, at last, I converted him. That is to say he ceased cursing and began to question, and then I had him.

We sat down together on a mat, under the shade of one of the great lebbek trees, on the east side of the Ezbekieh (which, be it known, is a vast open square, once a lake, now filled up, and luxuriant with all manner of trees and herbs). A curious crowd gathered around us, while I informed him of some of the deities I had invoked, their history and powers, and thereby endeavored to enlighten him in the general subject of natural religion as a groundwork to true revelation.

I think I got more out of him than he from me, for I learned somewhat about derweeshes.

A derweesh is a man who has vowed to lead a religious life. This may be esteemed a general definition. There are many classes of them. A sort of freemasonry exists among each of these, but no man because a derweesh is therefore obliged to renounce his business. I know of nothing to prevent the sultan himself becoming one, and retaining his throne. Many classes of them profess to perform miracles, thrusting swords through their bodies, pins through their cheeks, spikes into their eyes, and all this without leaving wounds. The most squalid wretches in the streets of an eastern city are derweeshes, naked, with the exception of a piece of sheepskin around the loins, who go about begging, or lie in stupid inanity in the crowded markets.

My new acquaintance invited me to visit the college to which he belonged, but this was out of my power then. We parted pleasantly, and after that, he looked calmly at me, as a man whose prodigious learning he was bound to respect, and I paid him liberally for his silent flattery.

As we separated, I observed a Punch and Judy tent near by, and, paying five paras (one cent), went in. The scene was undeniably the most ludicrous I ever saw at a theatrical performance, Neapolitan or of a higher grade. Twenty Egyptians, old and young, sat on the ground, with large open eyes fixed on the puppets. Punch beat Judy, and shouted bad Arabic, and Judy screamed in the most horrible of dialects. But it was all Hebrew to

4*

these poor devils. They enjoyed it. It was a sort of miracle of wonderment; but as to fun—that never entered their heads: and when it was over, they retired as solemnly as if they had heard preaching in a mosk.

Voluntary religious meetings, gotten up by the derweeshes, are of hourly occurrence in the streets and coffee shops. A few of them will erect a pole, with flaunting silk flags on it, and begin to surround it with a monotonous dance or motion of the body. Volunteers enter, and join the increasing circle, until it not infrequently numbers from fifty to a hundred persons.

As we were returning one afternoon from the citadel, and entered the Ezbekieh square, near the Oriental Hotel, I caught sight of one of these assemblies surrounding a pole, and commencing their devotional service of dancing and singing. We paused to see them, and sat on our donkeys outside of the ring, in which some fifty men, dressed in various costumes, were swinging their heads and bodies from side to side, and giving utterance, at each jerk, to a hoarse guttural exclamation. This movement became very rapid. Not infrequently one of them would cry out "Allah!" in a voice of thunder. They then formed two rings, those in the inner facing those in the outer, and swinging toward each other, they shouted the same strange sound at each swing. Their faces became convulsed; they foamed at the mouth, they screamed, tossed their hair, embraced each other, and called on God with the same hoarse cry.

We were deeply impressed with the scene. We had gone as closely up to the outside of the ring as we could ride, and the crowd of spectators had made way for us, so that we were directly behind the outer ring, and our donkeys' heads were close to the performers, when suddenly—imagine our horror!—Miriam's donkey, being evidently taken with the scene and affected by it, elevated his head and nose between the heads of two of the derweeshes—one an old man with flowing gray hair and beard, the other a young man with long dark locks—and gave utterance to such a cry as none but an Egyptian donkey can imitate. It was like the blast of a hundred cracked trumpets or fish-horns. Never were men so frightened as were the two derweeshes. They nearly fell into the ring with terror, Mohammed, the boy, in an agony of despair, sprang to his donkey's head and seized his jaws with both hands. Vain endeavor! He but interrupted the terrific sound, and made it tenfold worse as it escaped from second to second, and at length he gave it up and fell to the ground. It was too much for Mussulman gravity. They looked at us furiously at first, but the next instant a universal scream of laughter broke from the surrounding crowd, and we rode off in the midst of it. Even Mohammed Olan, superstitious Arab that he was (for he told me that very day that he had seen an Efrite the night before) enjoyed the fun of the thing, and muttered to his mistress as he ran by her side, "He good Mussulman donkey."

Our Friday is the Moslem seventh day of rest, or of special devotion. We selected one Friday to visit the chief college of the derweeshes on the Nile, where we could see the whirling, and hear the howling. Leaving the hotel at an early hour in the morning, provided with luncheon in case of necessity, we went first to Old Cairo, and visited the Mosk of Amer, which is the most ancient of the buildings of the modern Egyptians. It was erected about A.D. 860, and there is a tradition connected with it, and firmly relied on by the Moslems, that when it falls the crescent will wane. If it be true, the fall of the Moslems can not be far distant. Already the great walls have fallen in, and lie in crumbling heaps within the sacred inclosure; and splendid columns and gorgeous capitals are here and there in the sand and dust, miserable emblems of the fading glory of the power that has so long controlled the East. Near the entrance are two marble columns of somewhat amusing history. They stand close together on the same pedestal; and, in former times, when the mosk was in its glory, these two pillars were the shibboleth of the faith. If a man could pass between them he might hope to pass the gates of Paradise. If he were too great in body—if the good things of the world had so increased his rotundity that he might not squeeze his mortal parts through the narrow passage—then it was very certain that his immortal soul could never hope to see the houries. Alas! for the decay of the mosk and the trembling of the old faith. There was no one of us that could not readily pass between the pillars, though they stand firmly as ever, and do not seem worn by the myriads who have tried themselves here. I did stick at first. I confess that the flesh-pots of Egypt have added to my usually respectable size so much that my vest buttons caught on the inner post, and for a moment I thought my anti-Mohammedanism settled. But doubtless these later years of Frank innovations have tended to relax the strictness of the faith, for I went through without difficulty after one vigorous attempt, and the others followed me.

The service, if I may so call it—the *Zikr*—at the derweesh mosk was to commence at one o'clock. We had an hour before us, and so we took a boat at the ferry from Old Cairo to Ghizeh, and went over to the island of Rhoda to see the Nilometer.

It is on the upper end of the island, adjoining the palace of Hassan Pacha, and consists of a graduated stone pillar in the centre of an open well. Its age has been a subject of much discussion; but no one, I believe, thinks of placing it before Mohammedan times.

We saw but little of it, for the Nile was up to within three inches of the top. But here, on the upper end of Rhoda, for the first time, we saw the Nile, the great river, and our enthusiasm was now at the fullest. We stood on the marble portico of the palace facing up the stream, which is divided here, and saw the lordly river come down in all its majesty, and roll its waves to either side of us, and away to the great sea. Here it was the Nile. No dream, no half river, no small stream of dashing water, but that great river of which we had read, thought, and dreamed; the river on which princes in long-forgotten years had floated palaces and temples from far up, down to their present abode; the river which Abraham saw, and over which Moses stretched out his arm in vengeance; where the golden barge of Cleopatra swept with perfumed breezes, and when, but a few years later, she was dead and her magnificence gone, the feeble footsteps of the Son of God, in infancy on earth, hallowed the banks that the idolatry of thousands of years had cursed; the river of which Homer sang, and Isaiah prophesied, and in whose dark waters fell the tears of the weeping Jeremiah; the river of which all poets wrote, all philosophers taught, all learning, all science, all art spoke for centuries. The waters at our feet, murmuring, dashing, brawling against the foundation of the palace, come by the stately front of Abou Simbal, had loitered before the ruins of Philæ, had dashed over the cataracts and danced in the starlight by Luxor and Karnak. From what remote glens of Africa, from what Ethiopian plains they rose, we did not now pause to think, but having looked long and earnestly up the broad reach of the river, we turned into the palace, and after pipes and coffee, the universal gift of hospitality here, we returned to our boat.

We drifted slowly down the river by the spot where

tradition says that Moses was hid in the rushes, to the village of the derweeshes, that stands on the bank, among the palaces that stretch from Boulak to Old Cairo.

They received us with the utmost politeness. There was no bigoted hatred of Christians visible. On the contrary, they gave us seats in the cool court-yard, under the trees, and brought us coffee, and talked as pleasantly as heart could desire. Fifty wild looking men stood around us, gazing indeed somewhat curiously at our costume, but not in the least offended at our visit; and when the hour for commencing worship arrived, they brought us coffee again, and then conducted us into their mosk, where we took our seats on the matting at the western side. About eighty men stood in a semicircle, with their faces to the south-east, the centre of the circle being the arched niche which is always left in a mosk on the side toward Mecca, by way of guiding the prayers of the faithful in that direction. Musical instruments hung on the wall, and some of the worshipers used them, taking down one and putting up another from time to time. The service consisted in swinging backward and forward in time with the leader, a noble-looking man, who walked around the inner side of the circle, and uttering at each swing a violent groan, or rather a deep, strong sob. For half an hour this motion was steady; then it became more rapid. They swung the body forward, leaning down until their hair swept the floor in front, and threw themselves backward with a sudden, swift bend until it again touched the floor behind them. The velocity of this motion may be guessed at from the fact, that for the space of more than an hour the hair never rested or fell on the head, but continually described a larger circle than the head in this motion.

In the mean time a man dressed in a long white hooped dress, tight at the waist, and some twenty feet in circumference at the bottom of the skirt, slid into the centre of the half circle, and commenced a slow revolution, apparently as gentle and easy as if he stood on a wheel turned by machinery. After a minute, during which he swung out his skirts and started fairly, his speed increased. His hands were at first on his breast, then one on each side of his head; and when the full speed was attained, they were stretched out horizontally, the right hand on his right side, with the palm turned up, and the left hand on its side, with the palm down. For twenty-four minutes, without pause, rest, or change of speed, he continued to whirl around like a top. The velocity was exactly fifty-five revolutions to the minute. I timed it frequently, and was astonished at the regularity. This was not a long performance. It is oftentimes an hour, and even two or three hours, in duration. After this man retired, another took his place, and all the time the excitement in the outer circle was increasing. Some shouted, some howled out the name of God. "Allah! Allah!" rang in the dome of the mosk from eighty voices; and now all the musical instruments, including a dozen large and small drums, added to the terrible noise.

Suddenly the noble-looking man, the leader of the revel, turned and faced the city of the prophet, and instantly all was silent. Some fell on the pavement in convulsions, others stood trembling from head to foot, evidently past all self-control, while others pounded their heads on the stones and gnashed their teeth. Those who were in fits—for it was nothing else—of epilepsy, were taken care of by attendants, who also advanced to those who were still standing, and, placing their arms around them, bent them gently down to their knees, and left them so. It was a scene not a little touching, after the terrible confusion, to see those silent frames bowed down before their God in the dim mosk. We came away and left them there.

All this seems to the reader a story of incredible fanaticism. We think so of such stories when the scene is laid in remote countries; but I can not forbear remarking, that the whole scene was startlingly like to many, very many, that I have seen in America, in religious assemblies, even to the minutest particulars. The excitement, the throwing of the head backward and forward, foaming at the mouth; the loud shouts—"O Lord!" "God!" "God help us!" and the like; the faintings; the epilepsy; every thing was familiar to us, and will be so to many who read this. It is certainly a remarkable fact, and it is a fact, that in a zikr of the howling derweeshes of Cairo I saw a scene more like familiar scenes in America than any other that I saw in Egypt.

I can not close this chapter without contrasting this with another worship that we joined in frequently in the city of Salah-e'deen.

The American mission, by what societies sustained I do not know, is doing its work silently, but successfully, in the city. In the cholera season, when all others, including the English missionary, fled in dismay, these young men, and their young wives, remained at their posts, buried the dead, and consoled, as well as they were able, the living, winning a position that they will never lose. The English residents presented them with a handsome testimonial of their gratitude; and I could wish some more enduring record of their bravery than these pages.

Sometimes a half dozen, sometimes ten persons, always more or less, assembled on Sunday afternoon in the rooms of Rev. Mr. Martin; and here we worshiped God in the old home fashion, with the Psalms of David to sing; and hence I am afraid that I must confess my thoughts oftener than heavenward went wandering back to the old meeting-house in the up-country, and the beloved voices that sang the Psalms there in the long-gone years, and that sing them now with David in the upper country.

8.

La Illah Il Allah.

Days, weeks, and months, go dreamily along in this old land, and the evenings and nights have holier starlight and profounder depths of beauty than in any other country that my feet have wandered through.

For the day-time, whether in the street among the dark-browed, liquid-eyed sons of Ishmael, or wandering over the hills around the city, and surveying the proud sites of old glories, life was like a long dream.

Shall I ever forget that first evening after our arrival, when Miriam and I, far wanderers together through life, and to be yet farther wanderers together on hills of Holy Land, stood on a mound to the northward of the city, one of those inexplicable mounds of broken pottery, fifty, a hundred feet high, and broken earthenware all of it, which surround Cairo on the north and east, and looked at the setting sun beyond the desert? A cool north wind was blowing freshly. The donkeys stood facing it, their sharp ears erect. The boys lay on the sand chattering in Arabic to each other. The dragoman, in full and flowing dress, a short distance in the rear, stood in that attitude of grace that no one but an Oriental can hope to attain to. We four, the only Americans in all the land of Egypt who do not call this their home, stood close together, watching the sun go down the western sky. It was high noon at home. New York was bustling, shouting, noisy New York; and in our homes—how much we would have given to know of them at that instant—who can tell us of the beloved ones there? The moon came out from the sky, silver as never moon was silver to our eyes before. The muezzin calls had ceased, and the faithful had ceased to pray. As the night deepened, object after object disappeared, and only Cairo the Blessed was before us, shining in the soft light; but away on the horizon, standing on the Libyan desert edge, calm, silent, solemn, and awful, we still saw the majesty of the pyramids.

I was off, one morning, among the mosks of Cairo. We directed our way first to the Mosk of Tooloon, which is the oldest in the modern city.

This is said to be the precise copy in miniature of the great mosk at Mecca, and it is certainly the most imposing of the Mohammedan structures of Cairo. Its very age makes it the more stately, though it is now desecrated into a poor-house. It surrounds a square, each side of which is perhaps four or six hundred feet long, and is built with pointed arches, being the earliest known specimen of the style. Its date is about A. D. 880, and its huge columns stand as firmly as they stood a thousand years ago. The minaret, on the western side of the court, is constructed somewhat singularly, having a winding stairway outside the tower. Whereof the tradition is, that the founder, being reproached by his Grand Vizier for wasting his time in twisting a piece of paper, replied that he was planning a minaret to his new mosk up which he might ride on horseback; and so it was made. But it is not very similar, for the staircase makes but one turn around the tower.

Nevertheless, it is profoundly interesting to stand in a spot where, daily, for a thousand years, the prayers of men have been offered up; where the stones are worn with the knees of sincere if mistaken believers; where there has never been a day, since the ninth century, when the voice of the muezzin was not heard across the court and through the shadowy arches, uttering that simple and sublime passage that has been so often uttered above this city, and all the East, that one might think the air would sound it with its own morning winds forever after: "God is great. There is no deity but God. Mohammed is God's apostle. Come to prayer, come to prayer; prayer is better than sleep; come to prayer. God is most great. There is no god but God."

At noonday and at sunsetting the same chant has filled these arches with solemn melody. One can not stand and hear it now without feeling that the voice is the same voice that uttered it ten centuries ago, though the men through whose thin lips it escaped on the air are the dead dust of those centuries. Age is sublime. A creed, though false, is nevertheless magnificent if it be old; and I can not look on these tottering walls, these upheaving pavements, these crumbling towers, without a melancholy regret stealing in along with other feelings, that this worship, this creed, is approaching its end, and that the day is fast coming when Islam and the creed of the Prophet will be to men like the memories of Isis and Apis—shadows flitting around the ruins of old Egypt. In broad daylight, when eyes and intellects are wide awake, the shadows are as clouds dark with memories of crime and wrong; shapes of hideous deeds, blackening the very name of humanity.

But in night time and the moonlight, when we do not see these, there will be shapes like halos around the fallen minarets of Tooloon and Amer as around the obelisk of Heliopolis and the unchanging pyramids; memories of simple but grand faith in the hearts of old men that worshiped God, and died in every year and month of all the thousands that have shone upon these stones; shadows that will forever haunt the places that are sanctified by man's holiest emotions—sincere and prayerful trust in God, though it were in a false god; shadows that are changeful, but always there; long shapes and forms cast on the walls by the altar-flames, that remain and appear, and flit here and there on pavement and wall, though altar-fires be long extinguished, and the wall lie in dust on the broken pavements of the temple.

But is this so, and is the end approaching?

I asked myself the question in the city of Victory, seated at my open window in the night-time, the moon shining gloriously—a dazzling moon—my table drawn to the window, and the flame of my candle rising steadily, and without a flicker, in the profoundly silent air. Two hundred thousand people were lying around me, and I asked who and what they were, and what part they formed in the grand sum of human valuation? Literally nothing. They are not worth the counting among the races of men. They are the curse of one of the fairest lands on this earth's surface.

I had been conversing that same day with intelligent Mussulmans, who not only expressed their belief, but added their anxious hope, that the advance of English power in the East would soon make Egypt an English possession. I heard this everywhere among them.

If they knew any thing about it—and Turks ought to know more of it than Americans—they would see that it is their manifest destiny. England begins to see it, as before she has only wished it.

I answered my question, Yes, the end is not far distant. The mosk of Amer, traditional metre of the duration of the faith, is falling. I saw with my own eyes a huge piece of its wall go crashing down into the dusty court, where the still sunshine fell on it as if it had been waiting for it; and no one will ever disturb its ruin.

Just before break of day, from the mosk of Mohammed Ali at the citadel the morning call to prayer sounds over the city. The Sultan Hassan, old Tooloon, and another and another take it up, and three hundred voices are filling the air with a rich, soft chant, that reaches the ear of the Mussulman in his profoundest slumber, and calls him up to pray. Does he obey? There was a time when, at that call, the city of Salah-e'deen had no closed eye, no unbent knee in all its walls. But the Mussulman is changed now. He heard the call in his half drunken sleep, stupefied with *hashish*, and he damned the muezzin, and turned over to deeper slumber. He heard it in his profound repose, after counting over the gains he had made by cheating his neighbors, and he did not feel like praying. He heard it on the perfumed couch of his slave, and he forgot the prophet's in the present heaven. He heard it—yes, there were a few old men, who remember the glory of the Mamelukes; who heard their fierce shouts when the Christian invaders met them at the pyramids; and who, wearied with long life, look now for youth and rest in heaven, and they, when they heard the call, obeyed it, and theirs were the only prayers wasted on the dawning light in all of Cairo, and when they cease there will be none to pray.

This is no fancy picture. Mark the prophecy. Our days may be few, but there are men living now who will see the crescent disappear from the valley of the Nile, and who will build their houses from the sacred stones of the mightiest mosks in Grand Cairo. The beginning of this end is visible already, but who can foresee what is to follow?

SHEIK HOUSSEIN IBN-EGID.

9.

Sheik Houssein Ibn-egid.

Who that has read eastern travel books for the last half century has not heard the fame of the great Sheik of the Alaween? I remember when I was a boy that I sympathized deeply with some one, of whose robbery by the redoubted sheik I read a sorrowful history, and after that, in book after book, as I heard of this and that traveler driven away from Petra by this old man, or robbed by his extortions, I used to think it would be a pleasant morning's walk to meet him and rid the desert of such an enemy of safe journeying. What a capital shot it would be at the robber sheik, with a cut rifle and a well-greased ball! These boyish notions never left me, and I frequently caught myself wondering whether I should ever meet the sheik and fight him or fly him.

I met him when I least expected it.

As we were riding up the Mouski, Miriam and myself, on our way to the bazaars one afternoon, we were startled and arrested by an apparition that was not to be allowed to pass unnoticed.

Seated on a splendid sorrel mare, whose quick roving eye was ill at ease in the street of the city, was an old man, whose face was the face of a king. His dress was rich and elegant, but such as we had not yet seen in Cairo. He wore no shoes, stockings, nor trowsers. The dust of the desert was on his bare feet and ankles. Over a shirt of the richest brocade was worn a cloak of crimson cloth worked with gold, and over this a cloak of black, concealing all that was under it, except when it was exposed by accident. A cashmere sash was wound around his waist, binding the shirt only, in the folds of which gleamed pistols and knives more than I could count. His head was covered with a shawl of brown silk, the heaviest work of the looms of Damascus, and it was held in its place by a woolen cord, heavy enough to hang a man, wound around the crown of his head above the forehead and ears.

But the dress, strange and elegant as it was, was a matter of subsequent observation to us. It was the face of the man that struck us, and riveted our attention. He was an old man. I did not then know how old. But his eye was brighter than the eye of a young eagle. The suns of the desert for a hundred years had not served to dim one ray of its brilliance. I never saw such an eye. It pierced me through and through. His features were chiseled with the sharpest regularity, and his eye lit them up so that he seemed every inch a prince. And yet he was of diminutive form, small, slender, and his naked foot, that rested in the shovel stirrup, was thin and bony to the extreme.

We had with us Mohammed Abd-el-Atti, a young Egyptian dragoman, with whom we were about closing an arrangement for our voyage southward. As we approached the Bedouin sheik, Abd-el-Atti sprang from his donkey and rushed up to him, seizing his hand and kissing it, and the two exchanged the long series of Oriental blessings, with alternate touches of the breast and forehead, which invariably signalize a meeting between friends long parted.

Meantime we stood looking curiously at the scene, and

in a few moments the old sheik turned his horse toward us, and Abd-el-Atti informed me that he was my old enemy the Sheik Houssein Ibn-egid, the most powerful of the Bedouin chiefs from Cairo to Mecca.

The old man touched my hand, and as we each lifted our fingers to our lips after the grasp, we exchanged a long, steadfast gaze, which seemed to satisfy him, for he laughed quietly to himself, and he asked me if I were going to Wâdy Mousa. Probably he thought me worth robbing, as he saw a lady in my company, and such parties are usually best stocked with plunderable articles.

Sheik Houssein is an old man. Here men say that he is over a hundred years of age, and that his descendants of the fourth generation are full grown men, stout and strong on the desert. Be this as it may, he is a man well known in the world, and his fame has gone from Europe to America in the letters of travelers who have met him on the desert among his five thousand followers. There he is a chieftain to be dreaded. He has but to lift a handful of dust and blow it into the air with his thin old lips, and three thousand Bedouins are in the saddle at his call. He is the guardian of Petra, with whom all who desire to see the Rock City must make peace and friendship.

But how came the Sheik Houssein within the walls of a city, and how came his mare to be treading the filthy streets of Cairo, through the narrow passages shut out from the sky—for where we met them there was no sky visible, the street itself being roofed over with reeds to keep out the sun? The story is somewhat long, but I will make it as brief as possible.

Some time ago the caravan from Suez to Cairo was robbed of a camel loaded with indigo. The Sheik Ibn-sh-deed, who rules the desert from Cairo to the Red Sea, is responsible to the government of Egypt for the safety of the caravan. He has hostages in the city to secure that responsibility. It was immediately evident that none of his tribe had committed the theft, and it was soon as evident that it was the act of two men belonging to a tribe nearer to Akaba, and bordering on the tribes that owe allegiance to the Sheik Houssein. Indeed, some evidence was given that they were actually men under that old Sheik's power.

Among the Arabs still prevails that patriarchal form of government which makes the sheik the father of his entire tribe. If one of them is in trouble—it matters nothing whether it be his son or the poorest wretch of his retainers—he will sacrifice his life for him, and every man of the entire tribe is bound to do the same. The veneration for the sheik, and his care over them, is in every respect like that of a father for his sons, and children for their parent. Accordingly, when one is known to have committed a crime, no trouble is taken to catch him. Any one of the same tribe is quite the same thing. Arrest him if you can, bring him to Cairo, and send word to his sheik that he will remain in prison till the thief is produced at the prison-door, and all the tribe are at work instantly to secure the right man, taking care at first to exhaust all means of effecting the escape of the one who has been taken.

Ramadan Effendi, one of the officers of government in high standing, the third officer in the Transit Department —who is the cousin and the brother-in-law of Abd-el-Atti —went on an expedition to catch one of the tribe at whose door lay the charge of this robbery. How adroitly he managed his business; how he inveigled two of them into an ambuscade, and then sprang on them and bound them; how the whole tribe dogged his returning way with his captives; how he took them in one of the passenger vans to cross from Suez among the English passengers, and thus escaped the vigilance of the Bedouins; and how he deposited them in chains, under bolt and bar, in Cairo, had been the subject of town talk for a month past among those who had known the circumstances. Still there remained a doubt as to whether the robbers were of this tribe, and it was desirable to catch a man from the tribes that acknowledge the supremacy of the Sheik Houssein, and thus make the matter certain.

I went to the prison to see these caged eagles—call them rather vultures—but they were splendid fellows. One of them was the son of the sheik of his tribe, and is celebrated as the man who dared to brave Mohammed Ali. Not many years ago, when that bold man had imprisoned the Sherreef of Mecca in the citadel of Cairo, this Bedouin came under the wall of the citadel on the desert side—where it is fifty feet high—and, with ropes and his own sharp wit to aid him, entered the citadel, liberated the sherreef, lowered him to the desert sand, placed him on his own dromedary, and, with a shout of triumph, dashed away into the desert. Eighty horses, of the swiftest that the viceroy possessed, in vain followed the escaped captive.

He sat and smoked his pipe calmly as I stood and looked at him. It was strongly suspected that he was one of the robbers himself. It was very certain that he would hang at the Bab Zouaileh if some one else were not speedily taken.

But the caravan of the pilgrims from Mecca was coming over the desert. This is the annual event of Cairo. The departure and the return of the Hadg are the two great festivals of the year, and the caravan had just arrived on the desert outside the city on the day of which I speak—and was waiting the order of the pasha to enter the gates and march in procession to the citadel. Three thousand camels were scattered here and there over the sand-hills, and the scene was one of the finest and most picturesque pageants that we have ever witnessed.

A glance at the map will show any reader that the pilgrims, in crossing from Mecca to Cairo, pass immense deserts, and, of course, through the dominions of various Bedouin tribes. To each of these tribes the Hadg pays a certain sum for protection and safe passage. By special instructions sent to them this year, the officers in charge of the caravan made a dispute with Sheik Houssein, on passing through his country, as to the kind of dollar to be paid to him—the rate having been fixed in piastres. The Hadg offered the sheik French dollars at current rates, and he demanded, as no doubt he was entitled, to receive them at government rates, which would give him about three piastres more on every twenty. The result was that they refused to pay him any thing until they should arrive at Cairo, and settle the dispute there. To this he agreed, and accompanied the caravan to Cairo; and he was just entering the city when we met him in the Mouski.

A fate that he little anticipated awaited him. While we talked in the street, some fifty soldiers had gathered around us, and the old man found himself arrested.

But he was not the man to exhibit emotion. No one would have supposed that the occurrence was other than what he had come for, as he quietly asked me to go with him to the diwan of Mustapha Capitan.

It was impossible to desert him under such circumstances. Indeed I had no objection to seizing an opportunity of befriending this universal enemy of travelers. Accordingly we rode with him, two hundred yards, to the Transit office.

We were shown into an upper room, where sat Mustapha Capitan, the chief officer of the Transit Department at Cairo, and Ramadan Effendi, who is the next in rank.

Mustapha occupied the corner of the diwan, and room was immediately made for Miriam and myself on his right, where we sat while coffee was served. Ramadan sat on our left, Abd-el-Atti being at hand to interpret in case of necessity. The room was crowded to suffocation with men in every variety of eastern costume, not less than fifty of them being Bedouins of every tribe between Jerusalem, Mecca, Akaba, and Cairo; the Sheik Ibrahim, whose tribe is between Gaza and Heliopolis, with a dozen of his followers—dark, swarthy fellows, in blankets and shawls; Ibn-sh-deed, whom I have before mentioned, with as many of his retainers; Suleiman, from Akaba, a noble-looking man, with a fine, intelligent face, clothed in a brown robe, over a brown silk shirt, with a shawl of the same color on his head, the ends of which hung to his feet, and with him three darker and more devilish-looking Bedouins than I have elsewhere seen. If one met them on the desert, one would commence turning his pockets wrong side out before they had opened their lips.

The diwan extended across the upper end of the room. In front of it was a small open space, in the centre of which the old sheik stood, and behind him those that I have named, in a semicircle, and then the dense mass in the lower part of the room.

It was not necessary to explain to Sheik Houssein why he was detained. He heard them speaking of the lost camel, and he knew the story well, for every Bedouin in Arabia knew it a month ago. But he strode forward into the semicircle, and while he gathered his cloak around him with his left hand, raised his thin right hand over his head, and stood in an attitude of grace that I have never but once seen equaled. The resemblance to the North American Indian was startling. Every gesture was similar; and the eloquence was the same natural flow of fierce, biting, furious words, yet full of imagery and beauty. I understood but little Arabic as yet, but I could follow him through nearly all that he said—asking Abd-el-Atti occasionally for a word or an idea—so perfect was his gesture, and in such perfect keeping with his subject.

Occasionally Mustapha interrupted him with a question, and he replied. The substance of what he said was that he knew of the robbery, knew who did it, knew where the man, camel, and indigo all were, but that they were all out of his jurisdiction; they were in the adjoining tribe, and he would not undertake to catch the thief, simply because it was none of his business. If he should do it, his own life would not be worth an hour's purchase; and there was no reason why he should throw it away for Said Pasha, a man to whom he owed nothing, and whom he did not love, respect, or fear. If the government of Egypt wanted the man enough to send an officer for him who would take the responsibility of catching him, then he would aid him; but he would not risk his life to do that in which he had no interest.

Some severe expressions were used by Mustapha Capitan, which roused the old sheik's anger, and he shook his fore finger, while the room rang with his deep, guttural voice. "I am an old man; I knew Said Pasha's father; and long before Mohammed Ali sat on the diwan in Cairo I was sheik in Wâdy Mousa. Said Pasha may think himself somewhat of a man, because he is in the seat of his father. My son, you are a boy. You have caught me in Cairo; but if I meet you outside the gates of your city—if I meet you on the desert sand—I will show you who is Sheik Houssein! Kill me here now, if you dare; and I have five sons, old men all, who will seek my blood on the stones of Cairo. No, no, Mustapha Capitan; no no, Hassan Pasha; Sheik Houssein is not to be treated like a boy! What will become of your caravan next year, and the year after that? Send ten thousand men with it to guard it by the mountains of Sheik Houssein, and from every rock and hiding-place, will he rain death on them, and the ten thousand men will lie on the sands. You dare not harm this old head! I am not afraid of you, though I stand here in your strong house, in the heart of your great city. The man does not live who dares to harm me. Woe be to you, Mustapha Capitan, woe be to Said Pasha, if I go not out free from Cairo and unharmed!"

The room was silent for a moment, as the old man took breath after this burst of defiance, and then every voice rang at once in a storm of dissension, dispute, demand, refusal, defiance, anger, and fury. This subsided as Sheik Houssein again raised his voice, and hurled his anathemas on Said Pasha and the Egyptian government. Meantime Mustapha Capitan sat calmly in the corner of the diwan, and Miriam and myself sat as calmly by his side. I confess that I thought once or twice that if this storm of words should result as it would have been likely to result in any other part of the world, our chance would have been poor to reach the door through a hundred Arabs, every one of them fully armed.

But the audience was over. Mustapha had had enough of the sheik, and he broke up the sitting by a nod. We went out with the crowd; and as the room opened out on the large roof of the lower building, the Bedouins sat down on the stones of the roof, and we sat down in a circle composed of the four sheiks that I have mentioned and ourselves, attended by Abd-el-Atti. Here we remained an hour longer, listening to the wily attempts of the others to persuade the old man into a promise to produce the thief. It was in vain; he was not to be caught. Accordingly I proposed to Abd-el-Atti to take the old man with us and visit the other prisoners. I was anxious to see their meeting. He went with us.

As he entered the prison-door they advanced to meet him; and the first one, the son of a sheik, met him with outstretched arms, kissing him on each cheek, and receiving his kiss in return, then pressing his forehead against the old man's forehead, both standing silent and motionless for thirty seconds in that graceful and strange position, their eyes fixed on the ground. The other prisoner received a similar salute, but not so impressive. The first prisoner was dressed in the plainest and most common gray blanket of the Bedouins. It was wound around his body, and the corner was thrown over his head; and yet his slave, who had come to him from his far-off home across the desert, was as richly dressed as any man in the assembly, in silk and cashmere, and I might also have remarked, was one of the loudest talkers in the audience-room; for here slaves talk freely before their masters, and dispute with them fearlessly.

Mustapha Capitan ordered the Sheik Houssein to be detained in the prison all night. Woe to Mustapha if he sets his foot on the desert sand east of Suez after this.

I asked Abd-el-Atti if there was not such a process as giving bail known to Moslem law. There was, but it was only honor. If a man of reputation would promise on his religion to produce the prisoner, he might be given into his custody.

So we arranged it. I never knew exactly how much my word had to do with it, or whether it was Abd-el-Atti's religion or mine that Mustapha Capitan depended on. Abd-el-Atti arranged it with Mustapha Capitan, guarantying his appearance when the government should call for him. The sheik was handed over to him and he brought him down to me at the hotel.

After this he remained for two weeks our constant attendant, passing the nights with Abd-el-Atti at his house and reporting himself every morning to the authorities. He was all this time like a caged tiger, quiet, but with a furious eye. His gratitude to Abd-el-Atti, for saving him from that worst affliction known to an Arab, a night under bolt and bar, knew no bounds. He prayed God that he might see him at Wâdy Mousa, and as he was old he promised the gratitude of his sons and descendants to remote generations.

"What will you do to Abd-el-Atti, when he comes to your tent?" I asked.

He turned his eye up to Abd-el-Atti with a good-natured laugh, and drew his finger across his throat.

I laughed at his jesting threat, and asked him what he would do to Mustapha Capitan if he ever came to Wâdy Mousa. His face sobered in an instant; he looked with his flashing eyes at me, and was silent for a moment. Then he growled rather than spoke,

"You know very well what I will do to Mustapha Capitan or to Said Pasha, if either of them comes within my reach."

"How old are you?" I asked him, as we sat smoking our chibouks in affectionate proximity one morning at the front door of Williams's hotel under the shade of the lebbek trees.

"My children's grand-children ride on horses," was the reply.

While he remained with us, I had his photograph taken by an artist who was passing through Cairo on his way to India. The old man sat like a statue. The first impression taken proved a failure, and, after an interval of ten minutes, the artist proposed to seat him again. It was unnecessary. He was in the chair, and he had not moved hand or foot—I don't think he had winked—since the first sitting.

This picture is an accurate likeness of a Bedouin sheik in full costume, precisely as we were accompanied by him from day to day; the reader may rely on the accuracy of the camera, and not suppose that fancy has added a line.

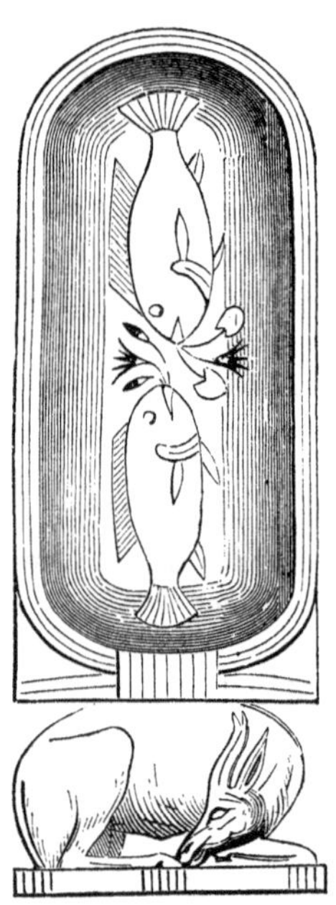

10.

Law and Liberty.

The administration of justice in Egypt is a curious affair. As I was riding homeward that day, after leaving the old man of the desert, I met a camel carrying a large box which contained a huge tiger. The animal was growling furiously, as every swing of the camel sent him now to one end of the cage and now to the other. I was comparing him to the old chief. Never were two more alike. While I was looking at him, two tall stout men, Europeans, dismounted from donkeys which they had hired, and refused to pay the owner for them. On his insisting, one of them struck him. Whereat he became more earnest in his demands for his money, but, was still perfectly respectful, though he held the Frank firmly by the folds of his dress. The latter, enraged at the pertinacity of the Arab, struck him with his cane, and then gave him a terrible beating. I never saw a man so thoroughly thrashed. He struck him over his head and back, his legs and his bare arms, bringing blood at every blow. He beat him across the street and actually into the open court of the police office, where sat fifteen or twenty police officers, smoking sedately and calmly. No one of them moved from his seat, or spoke. Twenty other donkey men rushed in to the rescue, and the Frank broke his cane over the head of his victim, and then took to European swearing. The next instant he rushed out into the street, around the corner of the building, to an old man who sells bamboo and rattans, bought a stout bamboo for a piastre, and returned to the charge. Again the poor Arab took it, and when he was thoroughly tired the Frank left the crowd and walked along the street as coolly as if he had but been whipping a dog.

This is an every day occurrence in the streets of the city, and I mention it in connection with the arrest of the Sheik Houssein as showing what experience I had in one afternoon of the manner of administering justice in Cairo the Blessed.

The explanation of this strange scene in the police office is this.

By our treaty with Turkey, and by the treaties of all civilized nations, it is provided that no American, Englishman, or in general no citizen or subject of either of the powers so protected by treaty, shall be tried for any offense by Turkish law, but every offender shall be tried by the law of his own land. The substance of this is, that he shall be handed over to the consul of his government, and he sends him home for trial without witnesses—of course without possibility of conviction.

Hence foreigners may commit crime with absolute impunity, except for the blood revenge, which authorizes and requires relatives to avenge the death of their connections.

As a result of this, every consul in Egypt has, what are called *protegés*, the list varying from hundreds up to thousands. I beg especial attention to this enormity of fraud, in which our government is an innocent participator, a fraud on the Egyptian and Turkish governments which all civilized nations are combined in perpetrating.

Our present consul, Mr. De Leon, is, I believe, totally free from any blame in the matter. He found a list of

American subjects, entitled to protection, left him by his predecessors, and he has done what he could to diminish the extent of the injury to the nation which this system brings about. But what is he alone among the crowd of foreign consuls, each one a petty sovereign by virtue of this system. Its ramifications extend everywhere in Turkish dominions. I found it at Jaffa, at Jerusalem, at Smyrna, and at Constantinople.

Out of this system wholly arose the Kosta difficulty, and though this has given us a terrible reputation in the East, and one which secures profound respect for Americans, because the Mediterranean nations have gotten the idea that we are a filibustering nation, ready to come and seize on their ports, palaces, and thrones, yet this whole thing was wrong from beginning to ending.

No one in America understood precisely how the thing could occur, or how the commodore and consul dared to act as they did. But this system explains it. If Kosta had been a full-blooded Turk, and never out of Turkey in his life, had his name been found on the consul's lists of *protegés*, the same course would have been taken in carrying out the system. *There are hundreds of such names on our consuls' lists!* Men who never breathed any freer air than that of Mohammedan countries—whose forefathers, to the days of Esau, were Asian, and whom their own government dare not lay finger on, because of this claim of protection on the part of the American government. Observe how it works. A Jew, doubtless direct in his line of descent from the Jews of the time of Jeremiah in Egypt, whose father, and grandfather, and great grandfather, were money-changers in the Jews' quarter of Cairo, killed a man in the street, and was arrested and imprisoned. An Englishman who saw him kill the man, and who caused his arrest, is my informant.

His conviction was certain; his guilt clear as daylight.

But, two days after his arrest, he sent for the French consul, had a long interview with him, and the next day the consul showed his name in his list of *protegés*, and demanded his delivery to him. The government, of course, yielded to the demand.

As a necessary consequence of this system travelers have no protection against each other, and, on the river, every man looks to his arms as his only guard.

The time has arrived when this system should be changed. It is iniquitous, from first to last, and it is only in the fact that our present consul, Mr. De Leon, is an able, upright, and trustworthy man, that Americans can have any confidence for safety while in Egypt.

In connection with this subject, I may here speak of the general administration of justice in Egypt.

The days of Mohammed Defterdar are passed, and better times are come; still the wheels of justice move much on golden axles, and there is room for great reforms in justice and in practice.

The viceroy is an autocrat. He says kill, and they kill.

While I was in Cairo, he gave Mohammed Bey, chief of the police in Cairo, seven days in which to detect a murderer, and on the eighth morning, the murderer being still at large, his friends had permission to bury Mohammed Bey's headless trunk.

The religion is the only law of the country. By it the Khadee rules and judges as he did in the days of Haroun el Rasheed.

I heard one day that a murder had been committed in the broad street of the city, and I went over to the police office to see the process of justice in such a case.

It was a curious scene. On the floor of the room sat the prisoner, literally loaded with chains. He had a chain on each wrist, and one as heavy as a small ship's-cable going around his body and over his shoulders. It was a ridiculous formality, too; for it was very manifest that he had but to shake himself and they would drop off, even to the last link.

Opposite to him sat four women, facing him. They were heavily vailed, but they watched him with flashing eyes. They were the relations of the dead man, attending here to see that he was avenged. The law of blood for blood is omnipotent.

I inquired into the process of the law with such a man.

"When will he be tried?"

"In a month or two."

"Do you make up any calendar of cases for trial?"

"Oh, no."

"How do you remember that such a case is to be tried?"

"They (the women) will see that we don't forget him."

"Is there no other way of remembering it?"

"None; the blood revenge will keep them active. We shall need no other reminder."

"Where will he remain meanwhile?"

"In prison."

"At whose expense?"

"His own."

"Do you feed prisoners?"

"Not a mouthful."

"Who does feed them?"

"Their friends."

"If they have none?"

"What?"

"If they have no friends?"

"Never heard of such a case."

"But if it did occur?"

"I suppose he must starve."

Such is the simple routine of justice. Primitive, and certainly effective. I have no doubt that justice is as evenly administered in this same Cairo, as in Christian New York or London. Look ye to it, who would make Christian lands better than Moslem!

Shortly after my first interview with Sheik Houssein, the procession of the Makhmil took place, which is the final breaking-up of the annual pilgrimage, by depositing the Makḥmil in the mosk of Mohammed Ali at the citadel.

This procession is ordinarily one of the grandest events of the Cairene year. The departure of the pilgrims is the time for more display, but the scene is not more interesting, perhaps not as interesting.

The caravan had been waiting on the desert, outside the city walls, for the pasha's order that it should enter, and this at length was issued at a late hour on the evening before. No one knew of it, and we should not have heard of it but for the faithfulness of our servant, who was up at his prayers before daylight, as every good Mussulman should be, and saw the soldiers passing on their way out of the city to meet the caravan; so he came and roused me, and called a carriage instanter. It had been decided beforehand that we should have a carriage instead of going on donkeys, because, in the first place, we should be better able to see in a crowd, and in the second place, should be less liable to insult from the crowd. For on the day of this procession, from time immemorial, Mussulmans have been permitted to insult Christians with impunity, and the boys are accustomed to do so.

The Makhmil is a somewhat curious affair. Few Mohammedans can tell you what it is, though they venerate it, and look forward and back to its arrival as the great event of the religious year.

Long years ago—let us not be particular about dates—

a certain royal lady, a queen, made the pilgrimage to Mecca, and for her use had a gorgeous car or camel litter made, in which she rode all the way. The next year she did not go on the pilgrimage, but she sent her camel and her litter, and it was carried by the pilgrims each successive year, until they forgot the origin of the custom and made it a religious rite. Each year a most gorgeous canopy is made—a new one every year—at the expense of the government, and this goes and returns empty. On its return, it is held most sacred. The people rush to touch it with their fingers. They press their foreheads and lips to the fringe, and rejoice at the blessing their eyes have in looking at it.

We were effectually insured against insult when we met Sheik Houssein and took him into the carriage. The old man did not exactly like to sit in such an affair. He said he preferred to be on his horse, and when Miriam explained to him that we much preferred carriages in our cities, he promised that when she came to Wâdy Mousa, he would give her such a horse as would make her forswear all wheeled vehicles thenceforth. He looked anxiously around him as we went along through the crowd that was pouring to the part of the city where the procession was to pass. We drove on rapidly, a runner preceding us and clearing the way. I wished to reach the *Bab el Nasr*, the gate of victory, before the entrance of the procession, but I was too late for it. We met them in the narrowest part of the way, and the officers who preceded the procession turned our horses' heads, so that we were obliged to head the procession and drive back till we came to a convenient turn out, where we could stop and let them pass. This place we found and there saw them.

The procession was headed by the camels which had accompanied the Hadj to Mecca and back. Then followed the escort of cavalry and foot sent out to meet them. Behind these came the sacred camel, bearing the makhmil. It was indeed a gorgeous affair, blazing with the purest gold. No tinsel work about this. Its value was incalculable. The camel was almost hidden by the fringe of precious metal, and the balls and crescents shone like suns and moons. The whole crowd shouted and did reverence to it as it passed.

The Mohammedan sign of reverence is made by placing the palm of the open hand on the forehead, and drawing it down to the chin; every man, woman, and child did this, and then shouted. The air rang with the peculiar cry of joy which the women utter on all festive occasions, a long gurgling sound that no one can imitate who is not born in the East. Behind the makhmil, on a camel, sat a derweesh, naked to the waist, who is a somewhat celebrated character, and an important part of the procession. His head rolls as if it were not attached to his shoulders, but only lay there, and every motion of the camel sent it around. This motion is never known to stop from the time the makhmil leaves the citadel of Cairo on its way to Mecca until its return. Possibly in the night time, when no one is near, he may rest and sleep, but this is denied, and it is asserted and believed that he never rests an instant or ceases this strange motion.

Following him are the camels of the pilgrims, with their canopies and their families in them. The camel litter is composed of two boxes, swung on opposite sides of the camel, covered with one tent-like canopy. In each box are some of the riders, or possibly they balance the person on one side by the baggage on the other, if the family is not large enough to fill both.

These are the desert ships of old fame. Five thousand of them were in the caravan when they left Suez, but more than two thousand hastened on, and had been scattered to their various homes a week or more before the arrival of the main body. Hence the procession was not as full as usual.

After the camels came the guard of the caravan, a regiment of wild-looking rascals of every nation under the eastern sun, dressed in more costumes than there are countries in Asia and Africa, and these closed the procession, which was altogether the strangest that we have ever been witnesses of. They passed us and went on through the Bab Zouaileh, which is one of the most stately edifices in the city, and so on up to the citadel. The Bab Zouaileh is, as its name imports, a gate. Before the days of Salah-e'deen it was the most southern gate of Cairo, but when that prince extended the city, and built the citadel, this gate was left in the midst of the houses, and stands to this day a monument of the greatness of that celebrated warrior.

It is withal one of the most sacred places in Cairo, and while superstition even among Mussulmans shrinks from public gaze, here it is displayed to the utmost.

The *Kutb* is the most holy of the Mohammedan saints. No man can tell who, what, or where he is. His residence is always in the flesh, always in some Mussulman. That man knows it, and only he. When he dies, it passes to another. This Kutb, or Wellee, has the gift of ubiquity, or rather the power of instantaneous change of place. One gate of the Bab Zouaileh is never closed, but has stood for hundreds of years shut back against the wall of the archway. Behind this is *the place of the Kutb*, where oftentimes the passing Mohammedan casts a sudden look, hoping to see him.

Upon this gate every Mohammedan who has had a tooth-ache, hangs the extracted tooth, thinking thereby to be insured against a recurrence of the malady. Hence the gate presents, as may well be imagined, a curious appearance. Some hundreds of grinders of every size and sort are placed in the cracks, or attached by strings to various parts of the massive portal; and a dentist might make his fortune by selecting from them. Some of them are inclosed in small bags, but the large majority are in their native purity, or impurity.

Over the gate did hang until it fell away in the winds, the rope by which Toman Bey, the last sultan of the Baharite dynasty, was hung in 1517, and until very recently the ghastly heads of the slaughtered Mamelukes grinned on the turrets above it. Without the gate is the spot still used for the execution of certain criminals, although it is now a crowded bazaar.

The procession over, I drove back to the hotel, dropping the sheik on the way. His release at length came. The government paid him off, and allowed him to depart. He came down to bid me good-by, and urged me to visit him in Wâdy Mousa.

We parted excellent friends. He promised me all manner of attentions in Wâdy Mousa, if I would come, and I have no doubt he would have treated me nobly. But I never saw him again, and the old man will be dead when I go to Wâdy Mousa. I heard of him in the following spring. As I was groping my way by torchlight through the grand caverns that underlie the north-east corner of Jerusalem, a gentleman who was with me on that curious exploration, and who was one of an English party just arrived across the desert from Cairo, happened to mention Petra.

"Did you go to Petra?"

"No."

"Why not?"

"Why, the old Sheikh of the Alaween—"

"Sheikh Houssein Ibn-egid?"

"Yes—do you know him?"

"I think I do;" and I laughed loud and long, without waiting for his story, for I knew that my old friend was at his work again. He had scared them away from Wâdy Mousa. But I had faith to believe that he would be glad to see me there.

II.

The Phantom.

How I wandered about the streets of Cairo; how I visited the citadel, and again and again explored that deep rock-hewn well of Yusef Salah-e'deen, known as the well of Joseph; how I stood, hour by hour, on the front of the unfinished palace of Mohammed Ali, and looked off at the Nile and the pyramids; how, day by day, we rode down to the boat, and watched her progress in fitting up, and bargained here and there for provisions and powder, flags and frying-pans, hams and hammers; how, in one of my hasty gallops up the Mouski, my donkey slipped and plunged me into the open arms of an old Turk, whom I was compelled to console by buying of him a half dozen of brandy, which brandy, O friend, bear in mind when I come to tell of the ascent of the cataract; how Trumbull and myself consulted all night about the comforts for the ladies, and worked all day on little nothings which seemed of huge importance then; how we smoked pounds of Latakea over our volumes of Champollion, and the maps of Jacotin which Trumbull, with infinite skill, had copied in America, and brought with him; how we rode out to the superb Shoubra gardens of Halim Pasha, the viceroy's brother, and sunned ourselves in the corridor that ran around the great fountain wherein foolish and false tradition saith

Mohammed Ali was accustomed to keep pet crocodiles, and overturn boat-loads of his wives; how we did not see the fair odalisques in these bowers, as one fanciful author describes his own good luck, for the reason that they are never open when the ladies are abroad in them, but then rigorously shut even to men slaves of the pasha; how we dreamed away a month of luxurious life in El Kahira the Victorious: are not all these things for our own memories, and too much and too many to be recited here?

Abd-el-Atti was a young, well-built, active Egyptian, with a face much like a North American Indian's. His complexion was copper-colored, his eyes black and rather unsteady. After the Nile voyage I took him with me to Syria; and, having had him for a servant during nearly eight months of constant travel, I think I know the man perfectly.

His temper was violent, but I had no difficulty with it. Like all dragomans, he was anxious to make money, and could see but one view of a money question. I had no trouble with him on that score either. If I yielded to him in one instance, I made him yield in the next. If the traveler will look out for his temperament, and treat him kindly, as a good servant should be treated, I have no hesitation in recommending him as the most accomplished dragoman in Egypt or the East.

He had lived some years in England and France, spoke the language of those countries, Italian, Turkish, and his own, the Arabic—read and wrote Arabic well, which was a great desideratum for our purposes, and had seen travel and adventure enough to be able to tell and manufacture large stories for our amusement, when there was nothing better to do. I give here our contract with him *verbatim*.

Contract.

We, the undersigned, J. Hammond Trumbull, and W. C. Prime, with Mrs. Trumbull and Mrs. Prime, have this day agreed with Mohammed Abd-el-Atti for a trip up the Nile, on the following conditions:

1. Mohammed Abd-el-Atti engages to provide a comfortable boat, with awning and jolly boat; to furnish said boat with beds, bedding, tables, china, glass, water filters, and all and every requisite necessary for the convenience and comfort of first-class passengers.

2. Mohammed Abd-el-Atti agrees to provide all stores, provisions, candles, lights, etc., as shall be necessary for the entire voyage. Also to provide as many courses for breakfast, dinner, etc., as shall be required by the above parties.

3. Mohammed Abd-el-Atti agrees to provide and pay for one cook, one servant, and one assistant, to wash clothes, etc., during the entire voyage.

4. Under the above conditions Mohammed Abd-el-Atti agrees to take Messrs Prime and Trumbull, and party, to Es Souan, and back again to Cairo, for the sum of two hundred and twenty-five pounds in gold, giving them fifteen days' stoppage on the voyage, at any place or places they may wish to stop or remain at, and providing donkeys and guides for visiting any such places.

5. For the first fifteen days of stoppage, exceeding the above period, that they may wish to remain below the first cataract, they will pay to Mohammed Abd-el-Atti the sum of three pounds fifteen shillings per diem.

6. For any period they may wish to remain below the first cataract, after the expiration of the above provided period, they shall pay Mohammed Abd-el-Atti the sum of three pounds per day for each day.

7. Should the above parties, after their arrival at the first cataract, wish to proceed to the second cataract, Mohammed Abd-el-Atti agrees to take them on in the same boat, and same style, and they shall then pay him the sum of sixty-seven pounds ten shillings for the trip between the two cataracts and back, and they shall have three days for stoppage, for visiting such places as they may desire. And if they shall desire to stop more than

three days above the first cataract, then, for every day of stoppage above three, they shall pay him at the rate of three pounds per day.

8. It is, moreover, fully understood that Mohammed Abd-el-Atti is to pay all presents on the voyage; to pay all donkey hire, guides, guards, etc.; to pay the expenses of taking the boat up and down the cataracts, and all and every present to crew, sailors, reis, pilot, or persons on shore, during, and at the end of the voyage.

9. It is understood that, if the party should go to the second cataract, then the provision for days of stoppage over fifteen days below the first cataract is altered, and they shall pay Mohammed Abd-el-Atti, in that case, only three pounds per day over the first fifteen days provided for, for every day more than such fifteen that they may wish to stop.

Dated, at Cairo, this 27th day of October, 1855.

N. B. The boat is to be procured and equipped, and the trip to commence as soon as possible.

Signed by the Americans.
Sealed by Mohammed Abd-el-Atti.

Under this contract he selected a boat, which we examined and approved, and he proceeded to fit and furnish her. When this was done we hoisted the American flag, and, for a signal, a white flag with one large blue star in the centre, and named her from the name of a boat not unknown to fame in our home circles, THE PHANTOM.

There was something pleasant in the idea of calling our Nile boat, that spread her lofty wings on the air, white and very ghost-like in the light of a November moon in Egypt, by the name of that gallant boat which has weathered so many Atlantic gales along the coast of America, and with which many recollections of pleasant days, and pleasant life, and beloved friends, are connected.

But she was a very different craft. Seventy feet long by thirteen broad, she carried a mast stepped away forward, about thirty feet high. On the top of this, swinging by a rough rope tackle, was the long yard, tapering from one heavy end below to a point sixty or seventy feet above the deck, and this carried the large triangular sail. Another smaller mast, stepped at the extreme stern, on the after-rail, carried a small sail of the same shape, which was managed by ropes rigged out on a pole projecting ten feet behind the boat.

The cabins occupied all the after part of the boat, and rose five feet above the deck, the floor being sunk two feet below it. Thus we had ample height of ceiling, and with a dining-room, one large and two small sleeping-rooms, closets, and wash-room, we had a small house in which four persons could live very comfortably. The furniture of the boat was oriental, of course; but two American rocking-chairs, part of a Yankee importation into Alexandria two years ago, made things look somewhat natural within the cabin, and no one could suggest an improvement on our arrangements.

Darkest of Nubians externally, and brightest in intellect, was Ferraj, our first cabin servant. Never was there a blacker or a better fellow. Ten years ago Abd-el-Atti found a crowd of slaves at Wâdy Halfeh, in the slave-pen on the bank of the river. He took a bag of dates in his hand, went among them, and sprinkled them on the ground. The black crowd sprang after them, and gathered them up gladly. He saw one small boy of seven or eight that was unable to get any, and he was struck with his appearance. Eight pounds bought him. He named him Ferraj (Trusty), and took him to Cairo. From that time they have been inseparable, and their affection for each other is an excellent illustration of that ordinarily subsisting between master and slave in oriental countries. He taught him to read—an accomplishment in this country which but one in a thousand can boast of—and having brought him up with the utmost care, made him a good Mussulman and a first-rate servant. He gave him fifty pounds and his freedom two years ago. But they are as inseparable as ever, and the Nubian always accompanies his master on his expeditions with travelers. He is not more than eighteen, but would pass for twenty-two, and stands six feet in his stockings.

Ferraj remained with us as long as Abd-el-Atti, and it would be almost impossible to say how much we became attached to him. Seek him out, O traveler to Egypt, and thank me for telling you of a treasure to a wandering Howajji.

Hassan, the boy, was about fifteen, with a face of perfect beauty, even for a woman's. It was a luxury to look at his dark olive complexion, and into his deep thoughtful eyes. He, too, spoke a little English, but not so much as Ferraj. The latter could think English, if he could not speak it always.

"What's that?" I asked him one morning, as he brought in a dish and placed it on the table at breakfast.

"I not know what you call it. It's what—is—in my head," and he laid his hand on his wool, thereby to signify that it was a dish of brains!

One morning, as we sat smoking at the door of the hotel, Abd-el-Atti brought up a little shut eyed, laughing Egyptian, dressed in flowing trowsers and embroidered vest and jacket, with a turban of voluminous folds on his head, and red slippers, with sharp up-turned toes, on his feet.

"This is Hajji Mohammed Mustapha, the cook."

I looked at him and at Trumbull. Trumbull looked at him and at me.

I was faithless, but submissive. How gloriously I was converted. What royal dishes, what inventions of genius worthy of Ude, what gastronomic powers that wily little Egyptian possessed. I took him to Syria, too. I would have brought him here if I could. His resources were inexhaustible, and he needed thrashing only once in all my dealings with him; that was when an English gentleman, who had dined with me at Nazareth, made him a laughing offer, and he actually deserted me then and there, and left me to starve on a frying-pan and an Arab boy. I reformed him back in a twinkling after I caught him, and I think there was a tear in his eye when I parted from him at Beyrout.

But I linger too long in Cairo. My last piece of work was to sit three mortal hours by a Jew money-changer, who did ten pounds of gold into copper money for me, which we carried, or a man for us, to the hotel, to furnish small change on the upper river. This, and about four times as much more, belonging to Abd-el-Atti, stood on our boat in open baskets during our whole voyage—accessible to any fingers, but always safe.

At four in the afternoon the last cart, car, van, break, or whatever may be the proper name of the Egyptian vehicle drawn by a single bullock, was at the door of the Indian Hotel, where we had now been for six weeks. A half dozen loads had previously gone down to Boulak to the boat, and on this we piled our trunks and small articles, and then surveyed our empty rooms with no regret. We were glad to be away, although every hour had been pleasantly employed, and a year would not suffice to show the stranger all the graceful minarets, strange, quaint lattices, exquisite arches, and lofty mosks of the city of Salah-e'deen. But the Nile was forever flowing by, laden with stories of Karnak, of Philæ, and of Abou Simbal, and we grew anxious to be away on its waters.

The *Phantom* lay at the bank of the river in the rear of the house of its owner. Passing through the house by an arched passage and climbing down a filthy bank, the rubbish-heap of the family, we reached the deck and took possession of the vessel.

The "monarch of all I survey" idea was the prominent one at first; but there was too much work on hand to allow of its being enjoyed. Trunks, boxes, crates of turkeys, coops of chickens, carpets, mats, oranges, fruits of all kinds, guns, pistols, coats, shawls, and the hundred *et ceteras* of a winter outfit lay in indescribable confusion everywhere. Out of this chaos we proceeded to extract order, and having at length accomplished our design in a measure, we discharged our donkey-boys with the customary bucksheesh, and wrapping around us our cloaks and shawls, for the air was chilly as we came out of the cabin, we went up on the cabin deck and ordered all clear for the start.

I could for a moment fancy myself on the deck of the old *Phantom* in western waters, but only for a moment.

"Are you all ready there?" That's the English of my question, which in Arabic was a single interrogative word, "*Hadah?*"

The answer was tolerably good English, if it was pure Arabic—"*Aiowah*," not unlike an American sailor's "Aye, aye." "Cast off then—go ahead Reis Hassanein."

This last command, profane as it sounds, had no reference to the Reis's visual organs. The order in Arabic is "*Godam Ya Reis Hassanein*," literally, "Forward, Captain Hassanein." We fired thirteen guns, and the *Phantom* fell off on the current from the shadow of the houses into the glorious moonlight on the Nile.

Never was such an hour for departure on the voyage. The sky was fathomless in its deep blue beauty. The Nile was yellow gold under us. Minaret and dome stood up in the silent air, and shed a softer light than the moon's own rays, while far away, solemn and majestic, the solemnity that of immortality, the majesty that of centuries, stood the pyramids of Ghizeh, gray and solemn in the light of their old companion. How contemptuously the moon and the pyramids looked down on us sexagenarians of the nineteenth century after the coming of our Lord! How swiftly the river rushed by us, on to the sea that had received it for so many ages, heedless of the passing travelers whose lives would be as brief as the shadow of the sail passing between the moon and the wave!

It was an hour for dreams, if dreaming were possible where all that was real was dreamy—where the trees were lofty palms, waving their crowns to and fro on the starry sky—where the shores were the dust of dead Pharaohs and the children of Jacob and Joseph—where the buildings were domes and minarets, and over all the ancient pyramids—where the stars, calm and steadfast, have looked down on a hundred dynasties of kings, on the graves of a score of nations—where Moses taught and Plato learned, and where the infant eyes of the Son of God looked up to His and our home.

I wrapped my Syrian cloak closely around me, for it was cold at first, and sitting on the cabin deck watched the curious operations of my new crew, and endeavored for an hour to learn the philosophy of their ways of doing things. But I was puzzled beyond endurance. When they wished to turn the boat's head, they pulled precisely the oar I should have let alone; and when they wished to take the wind, they flattened the sail to it with as sharp an edge as they could possibly manage. This was the fashion with every thing, and so continued throughout the voyage. The boat, in fact, managd itself, sailed and steered itself, and did every thing but make itself fast and cast off. Indeed it did cast off once in a while, and I woke to find her drifting quietly to a sand-bank or a rock, while every man on the boat was sound asleep.

An hour passed, and the wind had failed us. We lay under the Ghizeh shore of the river, with lofty palms over our heads, a boat with an English party on board lying a hundred yards from us, and profound silence resting on the river and shore. Even the soft ripple of the river seemed but to make the silence audible, and no one could imagine a city with two hundred thousand inhabitants on the bank of the stream by our side.

This is a strange characteristic of Cairo in the night. With the sunset every one goes home. Here and there a lantern is visible in the evening, as some belated pedestrian hurries along; but there are no street-lamps, no windows to the houses shining out on the passers-by, no sparkling shop-lamps, no shoppers, theatre-goers, diners-out, or other late walkers along the highway; the city is in profound darkness, and the river flows by as silent a shore as where the desert comes down to it on east and west in Nubia. The oldest Egyptian that lay in stone sarcophagus, or painted mummy-box at Sakkara, slept not more profoundly than I that first night on the river.

12.

Southward Ho!

Like the music of a dream, like the sounds one hears in waking hours that are given to visions, sweeter than the voices of birds, far sweeter than sound of organ in cathedral or choir, be it ever so triumphant, came over the river, at the break of day, the muezzin's call to prayer. From the mosk of Mohammed Ali, at the citadel, high up above all Cairo, it came first. The Sultan Hassan took it up, and old Tooloon, and far-off Ghalaoon and El-Azhar, and I even heard, or thought I heard, the old man's voice who sings to the sands of the desert that roll around the tomb of Ghait Bey. It came swelling like the sound of a harp-string, until the four hundred mosks of the City of Saladin took it up, and it filled the charmed air with sweet and holy melody. "Prayer is better than sleep—awake and pray."

It was not yet light, but the footsteps of the day were in the east; and he came on, now with a faint gray light over the Mokattam hills, now with a flush of crimson on the white and gossamer-like minarets of the mosk of Mohammed Ali, and now with the full burst of sunlight on the valley of Memphis and On.

A light breeze now stole up the river, and we made sail. Running slowly along on the west side of the island of Rhoda, and passing the palace of Hassan Pasha and the busy scene at the ferry of Old Cairo, we lost the city, and were on the most lordly of rivers. We were stopped by a hail from the shore, and on approaching found a messenger from the government-office which had sent us the carriage the day previous. It is worth relating, as an illustration of the constant anxiety of this government and its officials to please foreigners. We had left in the carriage a small pasteboard almanac, value three cents on the 1st of January, and much less now that it was the middle of November. When the carriage was cleaned in the morning it was found, and a cawass was instantly dispatched after us with two horses and a government drag.

He went to Boulak, and learned that we had sailed in the evening. Then he went to Old Cairo, and crossed the ferry to Ghizeh, where he learned that we had passed early in the morning. Returning to the east bank, he drove four miles up the river and overtook us as I have related. We sent the small boat on shore for it, and then squared away—if the word is allowable, with a lateen sail—and the wind having now freshened, the boat seemed verily as if she had wings, and flew on, the water parting with a rush and ripple on each side of her bow.

In the afternoon, we passed a boat lying at the shore, and carrying an American flag. It was the boat of Rev. Mr. Martin, one of the American missionaries at Cairo, just starting on a voyage of inspection to determine whether it was desirable to locate a mission at any point up the river. We met them frequently, and had great pleasure in their pleasant companionship.

The pyramids of Ghizeh, of Saccara, and of Dashour,

appeared in succession as we approached them, and watched our departure with changeless aspect; nor was it till late in the afternoon that we lost sight of the lofty citadel of Cairo and the white mosk that shines from it.

It was not to be supposed that we should find ourselves entirely at home on our boat within the first twenty-four hours, and yet I fancy that any one who saw us that day, stretched on diwans, smoking our chibouks, and reading or talking, would have imagined us old voyagers on the return from a long journey; so perfect was every provision for comfort and luxury. The hotel in Cairo was nothing to it, though that was excellent.

The Nile itself, at first, sadly disappointed me. I confess to ideas of a clear and glorious river, like the swift Ohio, flowing over golden sand and shining stones. I had never paused to ask myself whence came its fertilizing powers, or whence the vast deposits of soft mud that enrich the lower part of Egypt; and when I saw the strong stream in the hot sunshine, looking more like flowing mud than water, I was unwilling to call this the Nile. Utility was not what I wanted to see in the river. Beauty, majesty, power, all these I had looked for, and there was nothing of them until the sun went down, and the moon gilded—not silvered—the stream. Then it was the river of my imagination—a strong, a mighty flood, glorious in its deep, strong flow, and the unsightly banks, which, in the day, are abrupt walls of black mud, in layers, looking like huge unbaked brick, become picturesque and fairly beautiful with waving groves of sont and palms, and glistening fields of doura.

We were all awake before the sun rose next morning, and saw him come up after the short morning twilight, which is beautiful beyond words. The sharp outlines of the hills, in morning and evening twilight, surpass belief.

Before the sun was above the mountains, Trumbull and

myself were off on the plain, shooting partridges, for the wind was gone and the boat was lying at the bank. In half an hour Ferraj came off to us with cups of hot coffee, exquisitely made, for therein Hajji Mohammed did excel, and having taken these, gun in hand, we strolled up the river, and the *Phantom* followed us before a light northern breeze. As this increased she picked us up, and we ran on with the lofty sail swinging in the strong, full breeze, and pulling her by the nose through the rushing current of the river.

We reached Benisoef at noon on the third day, and while strolling through the narrow bazaars, with their cupboard shops, I was not a little amused at the dragoman's method of treating his countrymen. Travelers should take a native dragoman in preference to a Maltese on this account, that the inhabitants have no fear of a Maltese before their eyes, and insult travelers without hesitation and without being punished, when they are attended by a foreigner.

But the presence of a native dragoman does not always protect from insulting language.

I did not, but Abd-el-Atti did, overhear a remark made by one of three men seated in a shop front, somewhat derogatory to the character of Christians in general, with particular reference to me. He wheeled in an instant, but the Arab was too quick for him, and vanished around a corner, leaving his shoes on the ground in front of the shop, and his two companions sitting within it. With one of the shoes Abd-el-Atti beat one of the scoundrels, and with the other shoe he thrashed the other, finishing each castigation by throwing the shoe into the face of the victim, adding a little advice to keep better company. Abd-el-Atti was by no means satisfied with the escape of the chief offender, and ten minutes afterward, as we returned that way, proposed to surround him. It was probable he had by this time returned to talk over the affair with his friends. Abd-el-Atti walked on unobserved, and having passed the shop, gave me a signal. We closed up, and he sprang like a cat on his prey.

Never was man more astounded. Abd-el-Atti had snatched a stick from a by-stander, and showered blows on the back and head of the offender, until he made a sudden bolt to escape, and, in his intense haste, stumbled over a boy, and went six feet into the dirt, taking a piece of skin off from his nose—quite large enough to keep him employed in better business for some days, than insulting travelers. Fifty turbaned shop-keepers looked on all this with motionless countenances, neither approving nor disapproving, by word or gesture, though I thought I could detect a smile of satisfaction in some of their dark eyes as he bit the dust.

We left Benisoef with a rattling breeze, but it failed us toward evening, and a dead calm followed. In the morning I went ashore, on the eastern side, to look for game, and found myself on a large island several miles in extent. A native, at work in the fields, assured me that I should find wild hogs in the thickets back of the doura fields, and signaling the boat for two sailors to help me, I went into it with the determination to have them out if they were there.

It was a warm day, but the air was clear and rich, like wine to the lungs, and I scarcely felt any fatigue after a five-mile walk at a fast rate.

Here, I found a thicket that had all the appearance of being a fit place for the game I was after. I had no knowledge whatever of the animal's habits; had never shot one in my life, but I guessed at his taste from his cousins in America, and plunged into the mud swamp with full expectation of seeing my game before me.

Nor was I disappointed. I had not advanced ten rods, when one-eyed Mustapha shouted furiously, and a small, dark pig dashed through the thicket, close to Abdallah's feet. I shot. Abdallah threw himself on him, they rolled and floundered together in the mud ten seconds, and then—presto—the pig was gone, and Abdallah nearly gone. Never was poor devil so muddy. He was a mass of mud. His hair was mortar. His nose was stopped. His mouth was full of his native earth, and his clothes—he had but one shirt, and that could not be harmed or dirtied.

I saw no more pigs or hogs, or tracks of any sort. I shot four rabbits, four partridges, a dozen and a half pigeons, and shot at a curlew that I didn't hit; and have always been sorry since that I missed, as he was different from any other that I have ever seen. I returned to the river four miles above where I left it. The boat was slowly approaching, and I sat down to rest while the men tracked her up. From this time till we reached Es Souan, nearly thirty days afterward, we continued most of the time to track.

The Nile has along each bank a tow-path as well beaten as that of a canal in America. At times, when there are sand-banks near one shore, the boat is rowed across, and the men resume their tracking on the opposite bank. The speed made depends of course on the velocity of the current against which they are pulling, and varies from eight to twelve miles a day with a boat as large as ours.

On the next evening we were at the little village of Abou-Girg, on the west bank; and as Abd-el-Atti was going into the village for milk, I accompanied him. The low water would not allow the boat to reach the bank, and we had directed her to anchor in the middle of the river, as well for the sake of avoiding thieves as for convenience. Nor could the small boat reach the shore; and having pulled up in the mud, I mounted the shoulders of an Arab sailor, who carried me safely to dry land.

The mud village was as quiet as a grave-yard in the moonlight until we approached, and then fifty dogs made the night hideous with cowardly barking. Milk is not as easily procured as might be imagined in a country where cattle, goats, and camels are plenty. Butter brings them so much better prices, that few are willing to sell milk; and hence the propriety of applying to a man in authority to compel the production of the article we wished. I had been furnished with all the necessary authority for this purpose, having with my firman a sort of roving letter of credit from the government, directed to all sheiks of villages, and officials, great and small, requiring them, at all times, to give me whatever I wished, in the way of provisions, at government prices.

It was a mud village, and the streets were but narrow alleys between the walls of the low, windowless houses, whose roofs were corn-stalks or palm-branches. The moon shone very quietly down in those streets. I had never seen it more so. There was an aspect of repose about it that I could account for only in one way, and that was by supposing that the rays of light, having fallen into this vile and dirty spot, had lain down there in the repose of absolute despair.

"Where is the sheik?" we demanded of a naked boy who made himself visible in the moonlight an instant. But he vanished with a howl of terror, and made no reply. We met a woman face to face, as she came around a corner, carrying a calabash on her head. She stopped, drew her dress around her face, set down her calabash on the ground, never removing the gaze of her eyes from my face, and then wheeled, and darted away.

At length we caught a man, and he took us up a street to a point where it made a short angle to the left for thirty feet, and then continued its course. The moon shone up it, but this angle was in the shade; and on a diwan made of dried mud, the customary bench in all the Egyptian villages, sat the sheik and a half dozen of his friends in the shade, with their backs to the moon, looking up the street, where it shone clearly again. Our errand was soon stated, and the pail, which one of the sailors had brought, was placed on the broad bench in front of the sheik, while I sat on one side of it, Abd-el-Atti stood on the other, and a dozen men, women, and boys sat down in the dusty street, just within the line of shadow.

The old sheik puffed his pipe in silence a moment, then handed it to me. One soon forgets prejudices. It would be some time before I could be induced at home to take a pipe from the lips of a white or black man; but I had not been in Egypt a month before I had learned that my Nubian servant always brought me my pipe between his own large lips, and I had accepted the hospitality and wet mouth-pieces of a dozen Turks and Arabs. I did manage at first to get a sly wipe over the mouth-piece with my thumb as I took it; but I gave up this notion at length, and therefore I took the sheik's chibouk unhesitatingly, and puffed as contentedly as his vile Beledi tobacco would permit, while he summoned up his followers. "Hassan! Hassan! Hassan!" The village rang with the voice. No house was there that did not hear it. But Hassan did not appear. Hassan was wide awake. All the village knew that we wanted milk, and Hassan, for the first time in his worthless life, was away from home.

"Some one bring Hassan!" growled the sheik; and while some one was about it, he shouted for "Mohammed." Mohammed was on hand. He had no milk, and was safe in appearing, while they endeavored to convince him that he had a gallon of it. Hassan was brought into the ring, and the sheik ordered him to bring the desired article. Hassan swore he had no milk. He did not know what milk was. If you would believe him, he never drew milk from his mother's breast; and, in fact, on looking at the intense darkness of his countenance, it seemed probable that he was right. He was innocent of the article.

But the sheik knew Hassan. A storm of words commenced that resounded through the village, and Hassan departed growling. The moonlight fell quietly in the narrow street, and the group, which had steadily increased in number, sat in the edge of the light, striving in vain to pierce the darkness that enveloped my corner, and catch a sight of my countenance. The sheik was silent, and I followed his example, puffing industriously at his vile chibouk, which I twice handed back to him with my hand on my forehead, and which he as often returned to me wet from his lips, with his hand most impressively plunged into his loose robe, in the region where ordinary humanity carries its heart, but where an Egyptian carries either a stone or nothing.

It was not so much the mouth-piece as the tobacco to which I objected; but I resigned myself to it after fruitless efforts to get rid of it, and kept at it with commendable perseverance, until I discovered a sleepy-looking Arab on the other side of the sheik, who looked as if he would be glad of a chance at it, and I passed it to him. He seized it and made fast to it, while I yielded myself to a profound sense of satisfaction, and, leaning back, looked up toward the stars. I say toward the stars, but not at them, for not less than twenty heads intercepted my vision. The roofs of the houses were crowded with women, who were looking over into the open space below to see the stranger. I stared at them unobserved, and, though they were villagers living in mud huts and clothed in blue cotton, still they had as beautiful faces among them as I have seen in splendid halls, and eyes that outshone the stars themselves. Ah, those lustrous eyes of the Arab women! one can not imagine the possibility of all the extravagances of the Arabian Nights until he has seen their depths of beauty, and then he understands it all. The dark lines of *kohl*, drawn around the edges of the lids, make them appear like diamonds set in ebony, and their laughing expression is the soul of fun and delight.

I asked the sheik what fruit grew on the house-tops in Abou-Girg? Every head was raised instantly, and the eyes disappeared in a twinkling, while a hearty laugh ran around the circle. At this moment Hassan made his appearance with a bowl containing less than a pint of milk, which he poured into the pail in front of the sheik. Then came a tempest. The sheik groaned, and Abd-el-Atti waxed eloquent. Hassan was overpowered with the storm of words that ensued, and departed to squeeze his calabash or his cows for a little more. Meantime Mohammed had been dispatched to raise some milk under penalty of a thrashing if he failed; and when he was gone, the sheik shouted for female assistance: "Serreeyeh! Serreeyeh!"

She came, wearing the invariable blue cloth wound around her body, head, and face, the eyes alone being visible, and was dispatched on the same errand, while the sheik asked news from the war, and we launched into the sea of politics. The scene was enlivened by the arrival of an Arab mounted on a white horse, and a half dozen tall fellows in red tarbouches, who had been sent for to sit on shore all night and watch our boat. Every village is responsible for the safety of a boat lying over night at or near its banks, and, if robbery occurs, must make good all losses.

At length Hassan returned with another pint of milk,

and poured it into the pail with an air of satisfaction that seemed to claim the approval of his neighbors. The sheik looked in, took up the pail, shook it, looked at Hassan, and set it down with a groan of disgust that was irresistible. I think Hassan's chances for a well pair of feet were poorer at that moment than they had been in some weeks. But Mohammed arrived in the nick of time with a good supply, and filled the pail. As for Serreeyeh, Serreeyeh is doubtless looking for it yet, for we saw no more of her. I took my leave of the sheik and went back to the Phantom, followed by the guard, who spread their mats on the bank while I pulled off to the boat, which was anchored fifty yards from the shore. For an hour the men on board exchanged hails every ten minutes with the guard on shore; after that our hails were unanswered, and from the appearance of the three mats and six dark spots on them, I was convinced that they were keeping watch after the most approved Turkish fashion.

The next day we tracked again all day. But there was nothing tedious in this way of progressing, for it gave us an opportunity of going on shore and walking, shooting, gathering shells, agates, and cornelians, or meeting the natives and talking with or looking at them.

We strolled along a sandy beach, the ladies looking for specimens of the Nile shells, and J—— and myself carrying our guns and shooting an occasional plover or pigeon. We came to a point on the east bank not far below the village of Sheik Hassan, where the desert came down to the edge of the river, and from the Nile to the Red Sea the sand rolled everywhere. There was a rocky point projecting into the river, and on its top the remains of a foundation hewn in it. Nothing but these lines was there. No fallen wall, no blocks of stone, no column, only the trench in the solid rock that marked the outline of the building which had once stood there. There was nothing strange in this, for almost every rock from Cairo to Wâdy Halfeh has interesting memorials about it; but no American, accustomed as we are to the modern, can look on the foundation-wall of a building of three thousand years ago without pausing to analyze the new thoughts and emotions that crowd into his brain. Possibly our monuments are older. Perhaps the mounds that I opened on the banks of the Ohio may be the graves of a race that had grown old when Egypt was young—of a people whose monarchs were mighty men of renown long centuries before the valley of the Nile rang to the sounds of war under the Shepherd Kings. I have looked on those mounds with reverence, but reverence more for the mysterious and unknown than for the ancient and great. I have slept in solemn nights, when the wind was wailing through the forest, wrapped in my blanket, in the turf inclosure that contained one of those strange heaps, and every night ghostly visitors surrounded me, giant men, like trees walking, and with voices like the wind. But I never felt in those dark communions with the unknown past any of that profound awe with which I stand among the relics of a nation whose history I know, and whose age is recorded on granite.

It was but a line on the stone, but it told of the days of princes and kings. We sat down on the rock, Miriam and I, and the sun shone pleasantly down on us, and the river passed on at our feet as we read the story. It was of kingly footsteps on the floor, of the light tread of the fairy feet of princesses, of the tramp of men-at-arms, the sound of music, and laughter, and song, and dance, and revel. Soft passages were not wanting, that told of pure and gentle love; and those we paused to read, for human love hallows the earth more than any other incident in all the life of man. I care not where it is

—though in the hut of an Egyptian Fellah or the hovel of a miserable Berber, if the sanctifying influence of love have been there, it has made it a sacred place. And the thought that arms had been twined around each other here, that lips had wooed each other's kisses here, that hearts had beaten against hearts, and strong embraces held young beauties, and voices whispered low soft words of human fondness, and eyes looked love here—this thought hallowed the rock, though arms, lips, and young beauties were all dead dust a thousand years ago—dead dust carried away on the river to the sea, and by the sea scattered to the islands and continents of an unknown world. If all the dust of all the earth could but start into life and clear perception for an instant where it now lies, what strange, wild countenances of affright and horror would men see staring on them from the earth beneath their feet in every land!

13.

Braheem Effendi El Khadi.

We reached Kalouseneh that day. When within four miles of it, I left the boat, and crossed the country on foot, gun in hand, shooting along the way.

At the village I found it market-day. There are about a hundred acres of palm-grove here—it might almost be called a forest—and in the shade sat literally hundreds of men, women, and children, with their various wares and merchandise. All the fruits, grains, and products of the country abounded, and there were long rows of temporary shops, consisting only of shawls spread on the ground, covered with beads and other trinkets, to tempt the Bedouin or Egyptian women. I sat down under a palm, tired out, and endeavored to cool and rest myself; but a gaping crowd, scores and scores of the people, surrounded me, stifling the air, and nearly suffocating me. I left the market and entered the village. It was the usual mud structure of Egypt, and but for the beauty of its palm-grove, would have been as detestable as any other. I found a coffee-house on the bank of the river, where I sat down to wait the coming of my boat. It was already occupied, but they vacated the coolest diwan on my arrival, and I took it.

Do not imagine a coffee-house on the European or American plan. Far from it. A mud wall in the rear, seven feet high, and two posts at the front corners, supported a roof of reeds or of corn-stalks. This is the Egyptian coffee-shop, found in every village of any size, and furnishing coffee at ten paras the cup, araka at a little more, and boosa at five paras for enough to get sick upon. Forever be the memory of Egyptian boosa detested! It was here that I first encountered it, and, unsuspicious man that I was, invested my paras—five of them constituting almost the smallest coin known in Egypt—in ordering a cup of beer—Arabic, *boosa*. It came, and I looked at it, and elevated my gaze to the faces of the group around me. They did not understand my horror, except only a ghawazee, a dancing-girl, whose intense black eyes flashed her fun as she saw me posed by the earthen dish full of a vile abomination that—on my faith it did—smelled as if it had already served the purposes of two Arabs, and refused to stay on their stomachs. I tasted it. I taste every thing, clean or unclean, that Arabs taste. No, I am wrong: there is a dish that Abdul Rahman Effendi, the governor of Nubia from Es Souan to Wâdy Halfeh, called my attention to, and which I did not taste. It was the entrails of a sheep, chopped fine, with the gall broken and sprinkled on them, which a half dozen Berbers were eating raw, with a gusto that might have tempted a less fastidious man; as I said, I did not taste that. But I did taste the boosa, and I handed back the dish, cup, bowl, whatever its name was—it held a quart—and I begged the proprietor of the shop, as a special favor to me, to pour it all back into his reservoir, and shut the cover down. I shudder as I remember it now!

I sat for two hours in the coffee-shop, and I am sorry to say that my company was none of the most reputable. There were three filthy-looking Arabs, half-civilized Bedouins, belonging to a tribe that Mohammed Ali persuaded to occupy arable land and raise camels for his uses, and whom Said Pasha has converted into enemies by attempting to tax. There was a great rascal, in the shape of an owner of a boat, who was endeavoring to extract a sum of money out of a poor reis by a summary process, not unlike some attempts that I have seen in other countries, in which attempt there were some ten or twelve villagers deeply interested, while two ghawazee—dancing girls—dressed in the voluptuous, half-naked style of their profession, swindled the various parties out of successive cups of coffee, or the money to buy them, by the same arts that women of their character practice all the world over.

The dispute about the boat, between the owner and the reis, grew furious. All shouted at once, and now I learned that the sheik of the reises was present endeavoring to settle the difficulty.

This is a feature of Egyptian government. Every trade or business has its sheik. In Cairo you will hear constantly of the sheik of the donkey-owners, and, on any dispute arising among your boys as to the division of the day's pay, you had nothing to do but to throw down your money, and let them go to their sheik and settle it.

Achmet, the boat owner, had contracted with Reis Barikat to let him his boat for a year at a fixed rate per month, and he had had it a year and a half, and paid regularly. Just at this time freights were very high, and the boat was loaded with grain, and ready to go down the river, when the rascally Achmet demanded the boat, on the ground that his contract was for a year and no longer, and although it ran on six months longer, that was no reason why it should six months more.

The dispute waxed furious, and came at last to the true western style.

"You lie."

"You lie yourself."

And then they went at each other. Loud shouts arose on all sides, and the ghawazee danced in uproarious fun at the idea of a fight, and ran up to me with the most decided indications of their intent to embrace me as they had embraced every body else.

I was sitting on a bench of mud a little elevated from the mud floor of the coffee-shop. I drew my feet up under me, and felt for the handle of a friend in my shawl-belt as the roaring, screaming mass came over toward me, and just then Abd-el-Atti made his appearance with koorbash in hand. A koorbash is Arabic for cowhide, the cow being a rhinoceros. It is the most cruel whip known to fame. Heavy as lead, and flexible as India rubber, usually about forty inches long and tapering gradually from an inch in diameter to a point, it administers a blow which leaves its mark for time.

I had not been on the Nile a week before I learned that the koorbash was the only weapon of defense necessary to carry, and we soon gave up knives and pistols and took to the whip, of which all the people had a salutary horror.

Abd-el-Atti made the crowd fly as he swung his weapon among them, and silence ensued with astonishing suddenness.

"How dare you make such a row in the presence of Braheem Effendi?"

"Who is Braheem Effendi?" asked the reis of the boatmen, for up to this moment he had not observed that the stranger in the coffee-shop was a Howajji. This was owing not to my oriental appearance so much as to the extremely shabby costume that I happened to have on that morning.

"Yonder he is."

The reis advanced immediately to pay his respects

and apologise for the row. I had to be frank and tell him it needed an apology. Then he stated the difficulty, and Achmet interrupted him, and Reis Barikat sat silent on the ground just outside the shade of the coffee-shop, sullen as if he expected, as a matter of course, that, now that his affair was referred to a rich man and his turgoman, the decision would be against him, a poor devil without friends, right or wrong.

Abd-el-Atti interpreted rapidly and fluently, much to my admiration, and when I expressed surprise that any doubt could arise on so clear a case as this, and asked if they had no law to punish the man who had sat, day after day, on the bank and seen his boat loaded while he waited for the opportunity to attempt extortion like this, old Reis Barikat looked over his shoulder at me in astonishment gradually changing into delight, and then I proceeded to deliver a lecture on the doctrine of bailments, contracts, executory and executed, and all the law that could be applied remotely or nearly to this case, or any case like it. The crowd around the coffee-house increased to not less than a hundred persons, all profoundly silent, while I amused myself by watching their dark faces, among which the bright countenance of one of the ghawazee girls, white as a Circassian's, and rosy as a Georgian's, shone conspicuous with delight, for she had all along favored the old reis, who had, doubtless, given her a free sail down to Cairo once in a while.

The scene was worth remembering. I sat on the bench, over which a straw mat, crowded with fleas, had been spread. Abd-el-Atti stood before me. The sheik of the boatmen sat on the ground in front, Achmet by his side, and the villagers stood crowded behind them. By the time I had finished my address the *Phantom* was in sight, and rising from the seat of justice, I gathered my robes about me with as much dignity as might be, and quietly walked down to the boat, leaving the reis and Achmet to the tender mercies of the sheik enlightened by American law.

Abd-el-Atti remained behind, and informed me that the sheik's decision was based on the profound views that I had suggested, although, to say truth, he did n't remember the precise order of them or what they were about. But he gave Reis Barikat the boat on the same terms for the voyage as before, and administered justice to the feet of the extortionate owner.

While we were lying here, I saw a woman sitting on the bank tearing sugar-cane to pieces with her teeth, and feeding it to her child. The mother's beauty of teeth attracted my attention, and I approached her to look at them. Her head-dress was of the shape common in her country, consisting, as I supposed, of round pieces of brass attached to each other. Her form was not ungraceful, and most liberally exposed by the single blue shirt, open to the waist, which alone covered it. Abd-el-Atti asked her something about her head-dress, and told her he would give her five paras apiece for the ornaments. I looked at him in surprise, and told him he was making her a large offer.

"Do you think so? Look at them," said he—and I walked up and took hold of them. They were gold pieces, Constantinople money, worth twenty odd piastres each, and the woman had on her head actually more than a hundred dollars' worth of gold coin. This style of head-dress is everywhere common. Women wear all they possess on their heads, and nearly every coin in circulation in Egypt has a hole in it, showing that it has been used for this purpose. The young children of the poorer classes wear the base metal coins of the value of a half piastre and upward, and it is an evidence of the general honesty of the people, that young children of five and ten years old are seen everywhere with head-dresses covered with these coins.

It was not yet evening, but there was no other village for some distance above, and we thought it best to pass the night here. Accordingly we laid the boat up at the bank, and spread our carpets under the palm-trees. Here we sat till the sun went down, and the moonlight came gloriously over us. Never was there such a moon, never such skies, never such stars as these. And when the night comes, and I sit in the holy light that sanctifies even this apparently God-forgotten land, I think there can be no life in all the world like this. Palm-trees, moonlight, and the Nile! What more? Sometimes—sometimes, I say—not often—on such nights as these, I remember a distant land of cold storms and biting frosts. Often—how often! how earnestly, how fondly, I remember a land of gleaming firesides and beloved faces; and I see the sad countenances of two who look for my coming, and then I long to be away. God keep us all to meet in a land that I love better than Jerusalem itself, for all my darling memories of childhood and of you!

At break of day we glided away from the shadow of the palm-trees, and pursued our course slowly up the river—I, as usual, taking my gun and one of the men with me, and walking on shore, in advance of the crew who were at the tracking-rope. The current was strong, and we had not advanced far when we met a boat in which were a man, his wife, and two boys coming down on the stream. It was heavily loaded and near the shore, and the man was unable to row off and give our boat the track, as was our right. It was manifest that unless he stopped her we should be afoul, and that with force enough to sink one or the other, or both. The usual Arab shouting commenced, and the eldest boy plunged into the stream with a rope for the shore. He reached it, but the current swept him by the steep bank. I gave him the end of my gun, and my man caught the rope, and between us we swung the boat in to the shore. At the moment that her bow struck, the other boy jumped for the shore, and missing his footing, fell into the stream just in time for the boat to close over him and absolutely extinguish him. I thought he was done for. But Mohammed sprang to the rescue, pushed off the boat, and seized him literally *in extremis.*

All Arabs, men and boys, have their heads shaved, leaving only a scalp-lock, said by some to be left in imitation of the Prophet, who wore his own thus; and by others said to be for the convenience of the angel who will pull them out of their graves when the day of rising shall come. The tuft of hair served the boy's purposes at an earlier date than had been anticipated. Mohammed lifted him bodily by it, his feet and hands spread out like a frog. I thought his scalp must be pulled off; but no. He picked himself up from the mud into which Mohammed threw him, and stood, without a whimper, an unconcerned spectator of the scene which followed. His father was indignant at Mohammed for saving the boy's life so rudely. He should have been more polite about it. The old man struck a good blow, but got a better one in return. By this time the crew had come up with the tracking-rope, and some natives had run down to the shore. The *mêlée* became general. I was the only one not in it, and I amused myself with seeing their harmless blows, which were showered furiously on each other, while the shouts were hideous. Blows and shouts at length became milder, and the difficulty was ended. The crew resumed their tracking-rope, turning occasionally to hurl a general volley—a sort of company-fire of words—in the rear, until Reis Hassanein, who had been foremost in the fray, resumed his walk by the side of his men, and gave the time for the invariable towing chorus—

"Ya Allah! ya M'hammed!"

which they continued right cheerily until afternoon, when we were under the Jebel e' Tayr, or "Mountain of Birds," which, saith tradition, the birds annually visit for the purpose of leaving one of their number imprisoned until their next return. The why and the wherefore who knoweth?

But the mountain is better known as the site of the "Convent of the Pulley," or of "Sitteh Mariam el Adra" (our Lady Mary the Virgin), and, more briefly, "Dayr el Adra." It is a long range of cliffs, singularly broken, and full of rifts and chasms, rising perpendicularly from the east side of the river for four miles. The convent, which is in fact but a Coptic village within mud-brick walls, occupies the highest part of it, and access to it is had by a well-hole, a natural break in the rock, up which men may climb from the river's edge. Otherwise one must go some miles around to reach it.

Coptic convents are not such places as we are accustomed to imagine convents. Marriage not being forbidden to the priests, their wives and families necessarily form part of the inhabitants of a convent, which thus becomes a village, often of no small dimensions. A church, surrounded by mud huts, and all inclosed in a wall to protect them from the incursions of Bedouins, who have no fear of the church before their eyes, composes the residence of the monks. They live as they best can—by begging, cultivating land, and possibly in less honest ways. I have not much admiration for the Copts. A Mussulman is worth a dozen of them, and a much safer companion. The Dayr el Adra boasts a church built by the Empress Helena, but it is nearly in ruins, and there is nothing interesting outside of it.

Long before we were up with it, two black heads were visible on the surface of the water under the hill, and two of the monks came off to the boat, swimming more than two miles to meet us. Their robes were not according to any monastic order that I have before heard of, nor could any opinion be formed from them of the rank of the individuals. In point of fact, the only opinion one could form was of their physical developments, and these were magnificent. They were naked, and two more stout, brawny, heavily-built specimens of humanity were never seen in or out of a monastery. They made the air ring and the cliffs echo their shouts from the time they took to the water until they reached us, "Howajji, Christiano; Christiano, Howajji," and would doubtless have added the demand for bucksheesh in the approved Egyptian style if I had not anticipated them. I was on the upper deck sketching the hill, and when they were within two hundred yards of us, rapidly approaching, throwing their long arms out of the water and drawing themselves along, I called to them to give me bucksheesh. I begged more vociferously than an Arab—I shouted, I howled it out: "Edine Bucksheesh, Edine Bucksheesh, Khamsa, Ashera, Bucksheesh, Bucksheesh!"

They were taken aback. It was not what they came for. I had mistaken them. It was they who wanted money. They had not come on a benevolent mission to the travelers' boat; so they dropped astern very quietly and swam ashore on the west bank, along which we were tracking, where they held a small council and took each other's advice according to priestly rule. It appeared to be a new question in their experience. For something like a thousand years the monks of the monastery of the Sitteh Mariam had been accustomed to ask gifts from passing travelers, but never before had one demanded aid from the convent; and yet it looked proper; even their thick skulls felt the penetrating power of the idea.

Five minutes closed the council, and they advanced along the sand to the side of the boat.

"Howajji," commenced the leader. I have an idea that he was the father abbot; he was six feet in—no—*not* in his stockings. His tone was subdued. It was by way of introducing a conversation that he called our attention. I was busy over my sketch with my head bent down, though I watched him steadily.

"Howajji."

"Howajji mafish," replied Trumbull. "There's no Howajji here. What do you mean by calling me a shopkeeper?"

Again he paused to consider. There was a point in the remark. The term Howajji, or Howaggi, as it is pronounced in Egypt, is applied indiscriminately to all travelers, originally as an expression of contempt, though it has become the common phrase for a foreigner who travels for pleasure. The Turks consider all other nations mere shopkeepers, but the Christian monk had no excuse for using the word. At length he began again.

"Sidi" (gentleman), and proceeded to state his case. It was a somewhat unecclesiastical affair altogether, but I think he did not appreciate that. When he had explained his wishes, which resolved themselves into the usual demand for charity, only it was somewhat novel to hear it asked in the name of the Saviour, we invited the monks alongside. They swam off to the boat and held on to the rail, with their mouths open and heads thrown back, and we administered the silver in due form, laying it on their tongues. But the ceremony was incomplete, and the next instant they shouted for "wine, wine," with mouths yet wider open. This exhausted our respect for the church, and I swung a whip over their heads so suddenly that they disappeared like divers, and swam ashore again. They walked by our side three miles or so up the river, and then took to the water again, and swam across to the convent, where, I trust, for the benefit of future travelers, they referred the question I had suggested to a chapter of the worthy brethren of the Dayr el Adra—a forlorn hope verily.

In the afternoon, while I was away shooting geese, one of the men cut his hand badly, and I found on my return that Miriam had bound it up skillfully, and it was doing well. But he insisted on my examining it, and I did so. Every man on the boat thereupon presented himself with a wound, bruise, or sore of some sort to be attended to, excepting one only, who, after diligent search over his body, could find nothing but an ancient wart on his finger that he begged to have removed.

Medical advice and medicine are the most frequent demands, next to the invariable bucksheesh, which we have to reply to, not alone from our men, but from men along shore. Women bring their children with sore eyes and bruised bodies, and beg medicine, advice, and bucksheesh.

In the evening the deck of the boat presented a scene that I much wished to have before me for preservation on canvas. Reis Hassanein had an old uncle who came with us from Cairo, by permission, as far as Manfaloot, where he resides. He was an ancient reis himself, having navigated the Nile for fifty years, and was fifty times the man that his nephew was. All the evening he was sitting on one side of a lantern, while Abd-el-Atti read aloud to him from a ponderous volume of the Arabian Nights, and the old man's face would light up with a glow that was positively fine, as some passages of special beauty or spirit struck his ear. Abd-el-Atti read well, and his volume of the Arabian Nights proved a valuable addition to our library. Thereby hangs a story, too, which is worth the telling, as illustrating the manner in which things are sometimes done in the East.

Mohammed Ali, among his other good deeds, published a large number of books at the government press in Boulak, and among other books he printed an edition of the Arabian Nights, and another of geometry, both large books, the former in two volumes. But who in Egypt could be found to purchase books? The edition lay unused, unsold, and unread, till the government issued an order requiring every person in their employ to take five or more copies of each. A capital way of disseminating information this. Some hundreds of men who could not read a letter were thus supplied with several copies of valuable books. The result was that they were glad to sell them for whatever they could get, and for a while books were cheap in Cairo.

14.

Manfaloot and Es Siout.

"Braheem Effendi," said Reis Hassanein, as we left Minieh, after examining the sugar factories there and tasting Said Pasha's rum which he distills "in spite of Mohammed's law." The effendi was in his usual place with his chibouk, on the larboard side of the cabin deck, and acknowledged the low voice of the reis by a look.

"The wely yonder, under the fig-trees, is death to crocodiles."

It was a Moslem tomb standing on the river bank in the village of Minieh.

"Why so?"

"Inshallah! They never pass it. If they do they turn wrong side up and float down dead."

Such is the story. Certain it is that the first crocodile I shot at going up was a little way above here and the last one coming down was near the same place.

The river now began to grow more interesting. The hills on either side were more or less pierced with tombs, and early the next morning we were abreast of *Beni Hassan*, one of the most interesting points on the Nile. But a breeze from the north is never to be thrown away, and we did not stop now even to see the reputed tomb of Joseph.

At evening, under the foot of a lofty bluff, we passed a

small Moslem wely, or saint's tomb, with a white dome over it, known as that of Sheik Said. A superstition of the river leads all sailors passing this to throw into the water some bread for the birds, of which there are hundreds here. They are a common white gull, called by the sailors *Abou Nouris*, and are said to inhabit the tomb. No boat refusing the gift of bread can hope for a safe passage. The birds swooped down in clouds to pick up the floating pieces, and we saw the ceremony repeated by four boats in succession descending the river as we went up.

Reis Hassanein had a new passenger on deck that morning. It appeared that while we were lying up in the night a downward going boat had stopped near us and proved to be in command of Hassanein's father, and to have his own little daughter on board, going down to see her father in Cairo. He took her out and was now conveying her back to Manfaloot, her and his home; that is to say as much his home as any place, for these Nile reises are roving people and have wives and families, sailor fashion, in every port. The fact was that his Manfaloot wife became uneasy at his absence of more than a year, and had packed off this child to hunt him up.

Hassanein applied for permission to remain in Manfaloot over one night. I warned him that I didn't like this sort of thing, a wife sending a child to look after her father's habits and haunts, and that he must look out for squalls at Manfaloot. But the misguided wretch insisted on his desires, and after due consultation Trumbull and myself agreed to leave him to his fate, and promised to stop at Manfaloot for a night.

Next day we passed the cliffs of Aboufayda, celebrated for wild and furious tempests, but we found them calm, and went ingloriously by at the end of a tow rope.

Trumbull and myself went ashore in the afternoon, and

walked some miles along the foot of the cliffs, examining empty tombs with which the hills were honey-combed. Bones and mummy cloths abounded. The dead had been here, but were gone on the winds. I climbed one hill two or three hundred feet, and looked into innumerable tombs on terraces, but found nothing. I found one narrow cavernous entrance which penetrated far into the hill. I had not then adopted a plan I learned soon, never to be without a candle in my pocket. I went in two hundred feet by the light of successive pieces of paper, and then my supply was exhausted, and I was obliged to retire. I have little doubt that an exploration of this cavern would repay well. It is not mentioned in any of the books. It was about three feet wide by an average of six high, and seemed to have been worked in the rock. A little way above this we passed a great collection of modern Christian graves in a ravine that came down to the river, and which I suppose to be near the village *Ebras.*

Descending from a hillside where I had been in tomb after tomb, I found myself almost literally on the top of the wely of Sheik Abou Meshalk (Father of the Torch), wherein for nearly or quite a hundred years one man lived and grew old and fat on the bucksheesh of passing boatman. He always left a light burning in the dome or wely, and however fierce were the winds around Aboufayda, the sailor was secure who caught sight of the steady gleam of Abou Meshalk.

The old man died about six years ago, and his grandson, a brawny Arab, has succeeded him. As I leaped to the ground at the very door of the tomb he demanded bucksheesh, and I gave him some coppers, whereat he retired, and I marked him as the first and last man in Egypt I have seen satisfied with a gift.

Reis Hassanein left the boat to cut across lots and reach Manfaloot early in the day. We arrived at evening, and he was already satisfied. He stood on the bank waiting our arrival, and he did not venture to raise his eyes to mine.

"Was all right, Reis Hassanein?" I shouted.

"You are always right, O Braheem Effendi," was his melancholy reply.

He had found not only a squall but a tempest in his house.

"She said she knew I had another wife in Cairo," said he the next evening as we sat on deck together, smoking quietly, as he told me his wrongs and afflictions; "and when I denied it, she beat me, and she called in her father and her mother and her brothers and all her family, and they put me in a corner and kept me there till the boat came. And when I went back in the evening, they cornered me again, and one or another talked to me all night and abused me, and called me all manner of names; and if you please, O Howajji, I will not stop at Manfaloot when we go down the river."

We could not oblige the reis in this request, for one of my most interesting adventures in Egypt occurred in the crocodile pits at Maabdeh on the opposite shore, and at Manfaloot, when we were descending the Nile. I believe that the reis made it right with the family on the second visit by virtue of cash and presents of dates from Nubia.

We awoke early in the morning on our approach to Es Siout, the chief city of Upper Egypt.

The city lies back from the river, but the palace of Latif Pasha, the resident governor, is directly on the bank. A row of stone steps, designed especially for the use of the viceroy, descends from the palace gate to the water, and at the foot of these Abd-el-Atti laid up the *Phantom*, assuming that the American Howajjis were sufficiently noble to walk up such steps, especially as they carried the firman of the viceroy himself.

We fired some guns on approaching the land, and a few moments after touching the stakes two officers in uniform came down by the side of the steps—to ask the names and character of the new arrivals. Abd-el-Atti received them on deck while we were at breakfast, and we had scarcely finished when another officer in full Nizam costume, attended by two aids, came on board and announced that the governor himself would visit us.

We could not consent to this, and hastened up to the court of the palace, where we met him just coming out, and he returned with us to the boat.

The reception of guests in the East has been so frequently described that I may run the risk of a repetition. Yet I think I may venture, once for all, on a minute account of this visit as an illustration of eastern manners.

Latif Pasha is one of the finest-looking men I have ever seen. His complexion is white and clear, eyes black and roving, an exquisitely-cut lip over which was a moustache, closely trimmed, and his beard, in Turkish style, also cut short; for a well-dressed Turkish gentleman never wears a long beard. He was dressed in the Nizam costume, all his clothing being of black cloth, his shawl a heavy Damascus silk, wound around his waist, and a red tarbouche on his head, with white takea showing under it.

As he entered, two officers took their position at the door of the cabin, one on each side, and his pipe-bearer advanced with his pipe ready-filled and lighted.

He seated himself on the starboard diwan, and Abd-el-Atti stood in the centre, while we sat opposite, and then commenced the usual salutations, repeated in various forms. Latif Pasha understood French and English, but he would not converse except in Arabic or Turkish, through Abd-el-Atti as interpreter.

Coffee was served instantly on his taking his seat.

Oriental coffee is a dense, dark decoction, sweetened

and served in tiny cups, each cup fitting in a silver or gold cup a little larger. The receiver touches his hand to his breast and forehead as he takes it, and the host at the same moment goes through the same form. The coffee is sipped with a loud noise of the lips, and the empty cup returned to a servant, who receives it on the palm of one hand and covers it with the other. A wealthy Turkish gentleman carries his own pipe with him, having his pipe-bearer as a constant attendant. We were abundantly-well provided with chibouks, and not unfrequently filled ten or twelve at a time in the cabin.

The conversation, which began in the usual formal style, gradually ran into general politics, and then into general matters, and his excellency, finding our tobacco and coffee and conversation all agreeable, sat the morning out.

I am under very great obligations to Latif Pasha for a pleasant winter in Egypt, and I passed a morning with him afterward at Minieh, where I had opportunity to thank him for his kindness. He furnished me with full letters of credit on all Upper Egypt, by virtue of which I was able to command all the assistance I desired at any time, and was enabled to make my journeyings rapid, pleasant, and successful.

He smoked splendidly, lipping his jeweled amber mouth-piece as if he knew what a superb lip he had, and sending clouds of smoke through his moustache and around his fine face.

He apologized for not returning our salute in the morning, as he had no gun loaded. He made up for it in the evening.

When he left us we accompanied him up to the top of the steps, the distance the host goes with his guest being the measure of his respect.

A few minutes afterward ten donkeys, of the most rare

and elegant breeds, made their appearance, being placed at our service, and several officers having orders to accompany us and see that we wanted nothing. We mounted for a ride to the city and the mountain beyond.

As we were riding up the long avenue, an officer, splendidly mounted, rode up to us, and with profound respect handed me a package of letters to various officials on the upper Nile, which had been instantly prepared by the governor's directions, and at the same time informed us that Latif Pasha was fearful he should not see us again, as he had received despatches calling him down the river.

We knew what this meant, and not long afterward heard the result of his mission. I have already mentioned the Bedouins, whom Mohammed Ali reduced to civilization and Said Pasha has driven into revolt.

Latif was the man for them, and was sent to look after them. Our gentlemanly friend has the reputation of a devil among the Arabs. Some time after this I met a Bedouin near Abydos, and heard of the manner in which he suppressed this revolt. The Bedouin cursed him with all the curses of his race.

"What did he do?"

The fellow's wild eye flashed at me, as he drew the back of his hand across his throat for answer.

"How many?"

"One hundred and fifty!"

I could not think it possible, but I learned that it was probably true. The law requires him to report a sentence of death to Said Pasha. He obeys the law, but only after executing the sentence.

As I before remarked, the city lies more than a mile from the river, near the foot of the mountain; but it is separated from the latter by a branch of the river, which makes the site of the city in fact an island. Over this branch stands an arched stone bridge, and below it the picturesque ruins of an older one similar to it; while immediately after crossing the bridge commences the abrupt ascent of the mountain, which is filled with tombs and grottoes. From the river to the city the road is raised some feet above the level of the plain, which is overflowed at high Nile. The approach by this curving route is very picturesque, and the appearance of the city is, in all respects, more beautiful than any thing I have seen in Egypt. Fifteen or twenty mosks lift their graceful minarets among groves of palms; and the private houses of the city, which are built in much better style than in Cairo, present an appearance that is refreshing to the eye so long accustomed to mud and crude brick.

Es Siout occupies the site of the ancient Lycopolis, "the City of Wolves," so called from the worship, by the ancient Egyptians, of the god to whom the wolf was sacred, and a consequent respect to the animal, evinced by the immense number of them found mummied in the catacombs among the hills. Of the ancient city little or nothing now remains, and of its ancient inhabitants no memorial, except their empty tombs, which darken the mountain-side like melancholy eyes looking over the plain that once gleamed with art, and arms, and wealth, and magnificence. Sometimes, indeed, an industrious Arab, mindful of the value which is set on the bones of his dead predecessors, excavates a new tomb, and dislodges the occupant who has slept so many thousand years in its gloomy silence. But this is not often, and most travelers who have visited the catacombs of Es Siout record the sight of wolves prowling among them, and Mohammedan funerals in the cemetery below, as the only things worthy of record that they saw from the hill.

We saw the funerals, but no wolves. Perhaps those who have been before us have seen foxes, which we did see, and mistook them for wolves; or possibly they did see wolves, which are not so very uncommon on the Nile. We rode rapidly through the city. The bazaars were very busy, and the people were apparently less accustomed to the sight of a Christian than those in other cities of Egypt, for they crowded around us as children around a menagerie, so that at times the cawass had difficulty in clearing our passage. On the hill we paused awhile to survey the magnificent view over the plain, and then entered the Stabl Antar, the great tomb of some unknown grandee of the old time, whose dust was long ago scattered on the Nile.

It is an immense chamber, cut in the rock, having a lofty doorway opening out on the side of the mountain. The vaulted roof of the room is nearly or quite fifty feet in height, and from this chamber arched passages lead in various directions, now nearly filled with sand and the crumbling stone of their roofs.

Into one of these passages I crawled on my hands and knees for two hundred feet, where it spread out into an immense chamber, but I could not stand upright anywhere in it. Under one side of it there was a lower chamber, into the roof of which some rude hands had broken an opening in former years, and around it lay dead men's bones and the relics of ancient humanity. My feet crushed them at every step. I held my candle down in the chasm, and could see indistinctly the bottom ten feet below. I let myself down, and dropped, safely indeed, but with a fearful rattle of bones around my feet.

The spoiler had been here long ago, nor was there any evidence who, or how many, had slept out the centuries here in darkness, nor when their slumber was disturbed. There was evidence, indeed, of nothing, save only that, somewhere in God's great universe, there are souls, spirits of light or gloom, who once wielded these bones for earthly uses, and who now know nothing and care nothing for their fate: Perhaps this is not so. In fact it does violate one of our dearest fancies—call it belief, for I believe it—that the dead do linger with somewhat of affection around the clay homes they once inhabited, and best love the flowers that spring from the dust which was once their own. If so, what ghostly companies are in this valley of the Nile! for here there is little trouble in finding their bodies. In other lands they pass into grass, and trees, and all the mutations that are the course of nature; but here, in black hideousness, they lie in rocky sepulchres, millions on millions, the dead of two thousand years of glory such as no nation before or since has equaled; and could we but speak into visible existence their haunting spirits, what room above this narrow valley would there be to let the moonlight through their crowded ranks? What maidens would sit on white rocks over the burial-vaults of lovers! what mothers, in white-robed sorrow, would bow their heads over the forms of beloved children! what angel-watchers would be seen at head and foot of countless fathers and friends!

We ate our lunch in the large room, spreading our carpets in the centre, where we could look out across the valley and feast our eyes with the glorious view. In the foreground was the city; beyond, its groves of palms, and then the lordly river, on which the only visible flag was our own—the only memorial before us of home. While we ate, the cawass and ten or a dozen attendants, men and boys, sat outside the doorway, and one of them chanted to the others a chapter from the Koran. It rang in the vault of the room, and, closing our eyes, we could imagine ourselves in a cathedral of Europe, so priest-like was the sound.

Lunch over, I left the ladies and climbed to the top of the hill, looking into a hundred tombs on the sides of the rocky terraces, and finally crossing the summit, where I descended into a wild ravine, the habitation of desolation itself. Here, musing as I walked, I started a fox from his hole in some recess of a tomb, and as he dashed down the side of the hill I sent a ball after him. It did not stop him, though it killed him, for he went a hundred feet down and fell into the ravine, while the sound rang through the rocky chasms with a hundred echoes that might well have startled the sleepers under those gray hills. Descending to secure my game, I returned to the party by a path around the hill, and came upon a crude brick ruin, which may be Christian or possibly Roman. It was remarkable only for the abundance of scorpions which were in the walls, and I killed a dozen within a minute, perforating two of them with a thorn for exhibition to the ladies, who had heard much of them, as common in Egypt, but who had never yet seen any.

I found them still sitting in the doorway of the Stabl Antar, looking out on the valley view, and on a mournful procession that carried a dead man to the burial-place in the sand near the foot of the hill. The loud cries of the mourners, mingled with the chant of the bearers, came up to us with peculiar effect. We sat silent in the broken entrance of an ancient prince's tomb, to watch the burial of the poor fellah, and wonder how many days the wolves and jackals would let him repose.

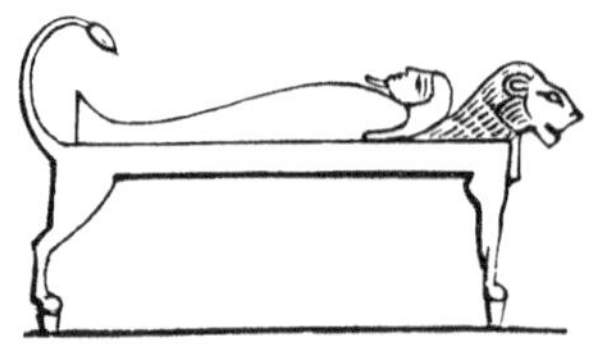

15.

Thanksgiving Day.

From the hill above Es Siout we obtained one of the finest views of agricultural Egypt, that the country offers. I have already spoken of the simple method of cultivation. Here we began to learn the nature of the crops of Egypt.

Sugar-cane began to abound, and above here cotton was plenty. At Es Siout as indeed throughout Egypt the great crop is corn, doura and wheat being most plenty. Doura is of two kinds, and but two. The millet, growing one large ear on the top of the corn-stalk, and the *Doura Shamee*, or Syrian doura, as it is called, which is our ordinary Indian corn. The latter is of poor quality as to the yield, but is sweet, and makes excellent meal. The antiquity of the millet, or native doura, is great, as is evident from the monuments, where we find it often represented in farming scenes. It is not, however, to be supposed that these are the only products of Egyptian soil. Beans grow in great quantities, lupins and lentils abound, and immense fields of *bamia*, the edible hybiscus, (sometimes called ocre), are found near all the large towns. Onions abound, and a large bulbous root, known as the *ghoulghas*, or *oulas*, is used as a substitute for the potato, which does not flourish here.

There is but one form of tool for hand use by one man

that I have seen in Egypt. It is a species of hoe, but more like a broad pick, very heavy and unwieldy, known as the gedoom. It is in fact a carpenter's adze, and is used as ax, hammer, hoe, rake, spade, and shovel. Another form of hoe or scraper, used for making the small squares which I have described, is a flat piece of board, with a handle held by one man, and two ropes held by two others, who draw it while the one guides it over the ground. Thus three men do less work than one would do with a good tool.

Threshing is done, as of old, by the oxen treading out the grain, and it is winnowed in the wind. Some instruments are in use to assist in this work; but they are simple and rude, and but little advantage is derived from them, most of the natives preferring the simpler process. I wish a thousand Yankee farmers could be in Egypt for ten years, and I believe it would be the garden of the world.

We took a shorter path down the hill than that which we had ascended, and made some heavy plunges over steep places, where two Arabs to a lady and a third to the donkey were hardly sufficient to keep them safe from accident. But the foot of the hill was safely reached at length, and we trotted rapidly across the bridge and into the city again.

Before returning to the boat we paused in the bazaars to make some purchases, and especially to replenish our stock of pipe bowls, which had become low.

Forever to be remembered are the chibouks of Egypt, and the tobacco called Latakea, from the city that was the ancient Laodicea, not the Laodicea once celebrated for the Christian Church, but its namesake in Syria. The chibouk, O my friend! is not very different from the pipe that you and I used to smoke in college days, when we had reeds bored, some six feet long, and rested the bowl on the other side of the room. It is but a long stick with a clay bowl for the tobacco, and the wealth of the owner determines the elegance of the ornaments. The amber mouth-piece is a necessity on an eastern chibouk, and on this are set jewels of every description. The stick itself is common dog-wood, or cherry, or jessamine; and as the pipe-maker is always at hand, and will bore a stick in two minutes at any time, it is not uncommon for a host to have branches of roses or other plants loaded with fragrant blossoms bored for pipe-sticks, and handed to his guests fresh from the garden. Es Siout is celebrated for its manufacture of pipe-bowls, whence come the best in Egypt; and besides these, the workers in clay make many small affairs—match-boxes, cups, and plates, vases, and like articles, which are curious and even beautiful in appearance, and with which we loaded ourselves as we returned to the boat.

On our way back we met a party of Franks whom, on approaching, we with pleasure recognized as our missionary friends whose boat we had passed on the first day out from Cairo.

It was a keen pleasure to meet American faces in such a spot, and the sight of an American baby, born in Cairo indeed, but no less American for that, in the streets of Es Siout, is a sight that Upper Egypt does not often furnish to the eyes of a traveler tired of gazing on the miserable, squalid, and filthy *scarabœi*, that are called children in Egypt. The missionary boat continued in company with us as far as Es Souan, and I shall hereafter describe our parting with them in the moonlit gorges of the cataract.

Near the landing was a brick yard, which attracted our attention, as had numerous others in Egypt.

The manufacture of brick in the land of bondage will

always be an interesting subject of investigation to travelers.

It was not common among the ancients to burn brick. It is no more common now. It is almost incredible, to one who has not visited this country, that immense ruins remain of buildings and walls, composed entirely of these unburned brick—mere Nile mud sun-dried—which date quite as far back as the time of the children of Israel. Large structures remain, of which every brick bears the name of THOTHMES III., the supposed Pharaoh of the Exodus, and he who is incredulous of the genuineness of these may convince himself by visiting Egypt, where he may turn hundreds of them over with the toe of his boot, and read the ancient legend.

The making of brick, in those days, was much more of a business than now, for the great population of the country doubtless required a constant supply of building material, and the mud was probably then, as now, the chief article in use for this purpose. But aside from this, kings built pyramids of brick, which yet stand, and inclosures of temples, and residences for priests, and city fortifications, and all the other massive structures for which other countries use wood and stone. There was, therefore, employment enough for the miserable sons of Israel.

Doubtless the modern process of brick-making is similar to that then in use, and a brief explanation of the method, which we saw here and often elsewhere along the river, will serve to make the history of the Israelites mere intelligible to many readers. The mud of the Nile is the sole article now in use for Egyptian house-building, and this is either roughly plastered up in mud walls, or shaped in the form of brick, and dried in the sun.

I passed by some men who were building a tomb. It

FOREIGN CAPTIVES EMPLOYED IN MAKING BRICK AT THEBES. FROM TOMB NO. 35, AT THEBES.

Figs. 4, 5, 1. Carrying brick and returning.
Figs. 7, 9, 12, 13. Digging the clay or mud.
Figs. 14, 15. Fetching water from the tank.
Figs. 3, 6. Taskmasters.
Figs. 8, 16. Making bricks with a mould.
Figs. 2, 10, 11. Collecting and carrying mud.

was made of crude brick, and they paused in their work to make their bricks, which was done by preparing a bed to hold water, into which they threw mud, and, over all, large quantities of cut straw. This they trod into the mud with their feet; and when the whole was thoroughly mixed, they took out large lumps with their hands, which they dexterously shaped into bricks, and laid down to dry. At another place I saw two men at the same work, with only this difference, that they held in their hands a rude mould, into which they thrust the mud, and from which they almost instantly shook out the brick, and left it to dry in the sun. The tenacity of the Nile mud almost passes description; and until one has his foot in it, he can not fully understand it. That a similar process was used by the ancient Egyptians, and probably by the Israelities, we are not left to doubt. We are fortunate in an illustration of the ancient manufacture, copied by Wilkinson from a tomb at Thebes, which is known there as number 35, and of which I shall speak fully when describing Thebes. On the wall of that tomb we find all the process of brick-making, from the gathering of the mud to the drying and counting of the tale.

Of course great interest has been felt in this tomb and representation, very many persons supposing the captives here laboring under the lash to be Israelites. This, however, is not the case, as appears from various reasons, of which the style and character of the faces, the color of the hair, and eyes, and beard, and the name of the captive people given on the tomb, are sufficient.

As I sat at my table writing at midnight that night I was startled by the flashing of brilliant lights on the bank, and looking out saw Latif Pasha coming from his palace, on the way to his dahabeeh, which lay a few rods astern of ours. Twenty or thirty glaring meshalks, each one a furnace of flame, on a long pole, glared on the white wall of the palace, and on the boats at the shore, as he came out, attended by a guard of not less than two hundred soldiers. He rode a white horse; and catching sight of me at the cabin window, waved a graceful bow as he passed on.

A steamer was waiting to tow his boat. He had been detained until this late hour. As the steamer turned her wheels, he commenced firing a salute, and as I had some thirty odd barrels loaded, I began a reply. Every one else on the *Phantom* was sound asleep, except Abd-el-Atti, and he re-loaded as fast as I fired. So we kept it up till the pasha was far down the river; and I could hear the faint sound of his guns from miles away in the still air of the Nile.

The next morning was Thursday, November 29th. We knew very well that it must be Thanksgiving day in some of the States at home, and we had tolerable certainty that it was so in New York and Connecticut. As we were to leave at noon, our American friends accepted an invitation to breakfast with us, and we made our Thanksgiving feast at about the time that you were sleeping your hardest in America.

And with the day came thronging all the memories that hallow that day. Who has not pleasant, who is so happy as not to have sad memories of the annual feast? What table is full, without one empty chair?

In my Nile boat I sat down alone at sunrise to watch the coming of the day on this strange land; and with his coming I seemed to have new light poured on the dim and distant past, by which I read the story of my first affliction over and over.

How often have I thought of him here, my boy-companion, my guide, my brother, counselor, friend! It was always the saddest thought I had in connection with this visit to the East, that he had died without seeing it. I could not bring my mind to the idea that he has seen a city whose foundations, in adamant and gold, surpass the splendor of the Jerusalem toward which I travel. But since I have come here—since I have looked up into these skies, whose deep blue beauty and unfathomable glory seem to bear the memory of the days when they received our ascending Lord into their radiant depths—since I have breathed the east wind from Bethlehem, and begin to see clearly my pathway to the cross and the tomb of our Master and Saviour, I say now I realize that he whom I so loved in boyhood, whom I have so mourned in secret in all my years of wandering life; whose lips have whispered to me a thousand times in the solemn nights—that he has seen, with clearer eyes than mine, the grandeur of Egypt, and the olives of the hills of Jerusalem.

Did I not tell you once, my friend, that I thought the sky must be lower down over the Holy Land than elsewhere, from the crowding thitherward of the footsteps of the angels, and that heaven must be nearer there than our cold western clime? It is so, I think; and already I am where the arch is lower, for I never felt so near him as here. He sleeps—not where we laid him then, but where we laid him last, on the forest hill, near our great city, in the congregation of the dead. He does not hear aught of the long, loud roar of the city, the tramp of the thousands, the sounds of warring, wrangling life there. He hears not that, but he did hear me, as the morning sun rose up above the Arabian desert and poured his flood of light on this slavish land—he did hear me praying for a blessing on the 'old folks at home' on that Thanksgiving morning, and I heard his voice, too, from the deep sky. It was not till the sun was far up, and the sounds of Arab life were heard on all sides of me, that I lost the influence of that morning reverie.

The coolness of these Arabs is amusing. It was not enough that we should occupy the viceroy's steps with our boat, but our men erected their poles on lines at the top of them in front of the palace gates, and all manner of clothing, unmentionable articles of ladies' and gentlemen's apparel, were floating in the wind before the door of the governor of Upper Egypt, doubtless much to the edification of the ladies of his hareem, who had an opportunity of studying Christian styles of dress and American costumes. Nor was this all. One-eyed Mustapha, the cook's servant, killed a sheep on the steps themselves, and when I went out to see what was going on, I found the Arab hound actually skinning the animal before he was dead. I was strongly inclined to have him flogged till he understood the meaning of flaying alive.

The mails of Egypt go by a curious sort of post. All Egypt is on the Nile, as every one knows, and one line of mail service up and down the river goes through every city and village from Cairo to Es Souan. This line is cut into sections, and on each section is a foot runner, who goes over his course three or four times a day, back and forward, meeting the next runner at each end of his section, and passing along from one to the other any letter he may receive. Thus no mail-bag is made up, but letters are passed singly. I sent my letters to the local governor at Es Siout, to be posted in this way; but he had orders to take special care of me and my wishes, and forthwith despatched an express with them. This is the method with all government letters. They go by dromedary, crossing the desert and avoiding the long bends of the river. It was somewhat strange to follow with my imagination those letters on their wanderings, and I sat that evening thinking of the dromedary carrying an Arab charged with those precious words of affection, crossing the desert back of the lofty hills of Aboufayda, guided by the stars as he hastened northward. In what wild and dark pass of the mountains he might lie down to sleep, who could tell? What howling wolves or fierce hyenas would follow his steps, who might know? On what sandy plain, in what Arab tent or hut of fellah, might they rest! What moonlights would look down on their swift course across the desert—what hot suns would weary the carrier before they reached the city of Victory! It was something to have a dromedary express despatched with one's letters, hoping only that the envelopes would be kept at home in some safe place, that I might look on them and endeavor thereby to learn something of their eventful travel.

16.

Life along the River.

The bread was ready. Have I or have I not mentioned that the object of a stay of two days at Es Siout was to give the crew of the boat an opportunity to bake bread, which is their sole article of food, and which is always renewed at this point, and again at Esne?

The Nile boatman is *sui generis*. There is no other race of men in the world like this. They live a miserable life of hard labor without enough pay to be able to save a farthing, and yet they seem to be always happy. Their songs make the night musical, and all day long, at oars or the tow-rope, they go chanting and singing as cheerfully as if they received thirty instead of three dollars a month, and were well fed and clothed, instead of having to feed and to clothe themselves out of this miserable pay. Their food is but the poorest sort of bread, baked and broken into pieces and dried on deck in the sun. A heap of several bushels of it always lies on the cabin deck, and this is boiled in Nile water, making a sort of mush or soft mass, which the men surround three times a day, and eat with their hands, dipping out of the one wooden bowl, which is their sole possession in the shape of plate or dish.

At Es Siout they stopped, as I said, to renew their supply. This would seem to be an easy matter. But it is not so easy. They arrived at eight in the morning, and went instantly to purchase wheat. This they took to a mill to have ground. When ground, they took the flour to the baker's, where they mixed the bread themselves, and then handed it over to the baker, who is in fact only a baker, and not a maker, of bread. At twelve at noon on the next day the bread had arrived on board, and we sailed from Es Siout, and were now fairly on the upper Nile.

The dôm palm-tree now appearing on the shore, changes the hitherto uniform aspect of the palm groves, and the shadoof poles seem to grow more abundant. The irrigation of the land is kept up by steadfast, hard labor, and it is remarkable that no pumps or other improved hydraulic machines are used in Egypt. No improvement has been made on this in three thousand years. I have no doubt that the banks of the Nile present now in many places the exact aspect which they presented so many centuries ago.

At evening of the next day we were under the cliffs of Sheik Herreddee, whereof the tradition saith that a serpent resides there, gifted with miraculous powers to heal all manner of diseases. It would cure a blind man, could he but have a momentary glimpse of the splendor of the hill in the light of a setting Egyptian sun. This was the last night of the autumn, and the winter came on us next morning right gloriously with a flush of gold in the east, and the full-orbed splendor of the sun, and an air balmy as June, and a sky that tempted one heavenward. Pelicans began to be plenty. That morning we shot two, and in the course of the day half a dozen geese and as many ducks. We made no count of the pigeons that we shot; they were innumerable. There was one day, when we were at Negaddeh, that we shot three hundred and six, which we distributed to our neighbors in other boats, giving our men as many as they could eat for three days.

All along the river game began to abound, and crocodiles were frequently seen on the sand-banks. I shot at several, as all travelers must do; but I killed none, as all travelers must say. There was one which I came very near to killing. Had he waited for me, I should have hit him. He was sunning himself on a bank, and I crawled quietly toward him; but when I got there, he was not there. The *trochilus*, the bird celebrated as the watching friend of the crocodile, who is said to warn him of the approach of enemies, flew before me with a loud cry, and perhaps alarmed him. I can not say that I verified the story of this bird's habits and friendship for the huge water monster, but I have no doubt that in this case he did act as ancient and modern writers say he is in the habit of doing. But he also acted precisely as he and a thousand like him have done every day that I have been on the Nile, and I am quite certain that if there had been no crocodile there, he would have gone along before me in the same way, with the same sharp, shrill cry.

As we approached Mensheeh, I had walked along the shore ahead of the boat, and on reaching the village met Suleiman Aga, the local governor, taking a walk with his old uncle on the bank. He was apparently delighted at seeing the face of a stranger, for he said he led a life of imprisonment in his village, and was glad of any relief to its monotony. He walked up the bank with me, and when the boat came to the land near the upper end of the village, he came on board and spent an hour with us. While we were lying here, our friends, the American missionaries, who were lying near us, had a difficulty with their servant, who was an impertinent scoundrel, and whom it became necessary for them to discharge. The governor begged hard to be allowed to thrash him into respectability, but to this, of course, our friends would not consent. I have seldom seen a more disappointed man than was Suleiman, after sitting for an hour and hearing the fellow complain of his master, when he was not permitted to put on the bastinado. It is a luxury to some of these governors to thrash a man; and it is even related of the Defterdar, Mohammed Ali's son-in-law, that he often whipped men to death for his amusement. But this is not all. It is also a luxury to the men oftentimes to be whipped, if one may judge from the headlong manner in which they rush into the necessity of being punished. "You may give me a hundred if these eggs are not fresh," says the fellah, and the clerk of the market breaks three spoiled eggs in succession, and down goes the fellah and gets his hundred, with fifty to boot.

A roving letter of credit on the Nile is a marvelous assistant to one's traveling comforts, and at the same time affords much amusement in the way of incident. I was not a little amused that same evening at Mensheeh by overhearing a conversation on deck between Abd-el-Atti and the sheik of the village. When we left Cairo, among other articles of boat furniture we were particular in ordering a good cat; but we were sent away with two worthless kittens, both of which found their way into the river within the first week after sailing, and we repeated the order to provide another. It seemed that Abd-el-Atti had directed one to be brought down to the boat, and the sheik, who very naturally didn't want to be bothered about it, was protesting that there was no such animal in the town—no, not a kitten, not a piece of the skin or tail of a feline animal.

The war of words grew furious, and at length the dragoman rushed into the cabin for the firman, and infinite was my amusement to see the government seal exhibited, and condign punishment threatened if the cat were not forthcoming. It had the desired effect, and the sheik instantly and silently departed, and an hour later a row and general outcry on deck called me out to see five cats, black, white, and yellow, each led by a string, and all now tangled in an inextricable knot, fighting, spitting, and uttering all manner of Arabic sounds, brought for us to select from.

We took three; and I may as well pause to record their fate. The yellow one took a flying leap from the boat to the bank, about thirty feet, struck heavily, and fell back into the water. I have forgotten what was the immediate impulse which induced this catastrophe, but the cat was worthless. The next, a small black kitten, met with an unhappy fate. We found a dead rat in a closet, and, from the appearance of Miriam's Indian rubber overshoes, we concluded he died of caoutchouc. He lay on deck dead, when the kitten caught sight of him, and made a dash at him, seized him by the neck, and swung him up and over the rail, and, presto! rat and cat fell overboard together, and we swept on, leaving them to their fate. The last one was a furious wretch, with the eye of an arch devil, and one day in Nubia I loosened the rope by which he had been tied, and gave him a chance to run. The last I saw of him he was crossing the desert twenty miles below Abou Simbal.

I have said but little thus far of our manner of life on the river, preferring rather that it should be guessed at from what I might write. But I find that nothing I have yet said will convey any idea of the perfect *dolce far niente* of the Nile boat. The day is one long dream of delight, the night a paradise of beauty. We never weary, yet we do nothing. We have books, but we do not read. We have paper, but not the courage to write. If there be no wind, and the boat was tracking, we walked along the shore, and shot whatever we could find. Game is plenty everywhere, for there is almost no one in Egypt to disturb it. If the wind sprang up, a hail from the boat called us; we jumped on board, and were off, perhaps for only a mile or two, when we again tracked and again walked. We eschewed all manners of dress. It would be impossible to say what style or national costume I wore, unless it was a remote approximation to the French blouse-man: I wore but a thin pair of linen pants and a blue shirt—nothing else, on my word—that is, when the weather was warm. On my head, I always wore the tarbouche. With this dress it was not difficult to follow the example of the Arab sailors and jump overboard at any moment, or wade in deep water after game. Sometimes I followed the men at the tracking-rope, and crossed the branches of the river which came down around islands, wading where it was up to my waist; and, never thinking of changing my clothes, I pushed on through villages and fields, to the manifest astonishment of the natives, who were not accustomed to see a Howajji so nearly on a parallel with themselves in dress. Oftentimes I was far in advance of the boat, and then, if near a village, I usually sat down in front of a coffee-shop—which is very certain to occupy a prominent point on the river-bank—and while the ghawazee sang and danced, and the natives smoked silently and looked on, I took the first pipe offered me, and curled my legs under me as well as I was able (I soon began to have a knack that way), and waited the coming of the boat, while the fumes of the beledi tobacco ascended in the still sunshine. How many pipes of tobacco I have smoked in such spots in Egypt!

At other times, I would push the reis from his place, which is the top of the kitchen on the extreme bow of the boat, and, as this was altogether the best look-out, Ferraj would bring me cushions from the diwan and my chibouk, and, with my gun close at hand, I smoked and watched the river and the shore. From this point I have gotten not a few shots at crocodiles that lay basking in the sunshine; and if I did not hit them, it was worth the shot to see the splendid start the fellows made as they heard the crack of the gun, and how they leaped into the air and the water with a grand flourish of the tail and a tremendous plash. Hajji Mohammed, the cook, was a great hand for a shot at a crocodile, and never sent word to the cabin that he saw one, but on the instant that he got sight of him, whether near or far off, sent a bullet after him, if it were half a mile. He wasted an awful amount of lead and powder, and got nothing. But not seldom I have gotten geese and duck from my seat on the kitchen, and Halifa, a capital swimmer, stood always ready to swim off and bring them to me.

It is vain on the Nile to attempt late sleeping in the morning. I was usually on deck at break of day, and almost always on shore before sunrise. The mornings are delicious beyond expression, and the beauty of the dawn is only equaled by the brief evening twilight. But early as I was out, I was never ahead of my prince of cooks, who sent me a cup of coffee the instant he heard my footstep, and then went to work at breakfast, which he made a meal fit for the most fastidious of tastes or appetites.

The twilight always found us on deck, and there we remained till midnight. There is enough to see in air and sky, whether it be or be not moonlight. There were sofas on the cabin-deck, well-cushioned and perfect, and here we lay, looking up at the stars. We talked little, and when we did speak it was mostly of the dear ones at home, of the pleasure they would have with us there—never of the glorious past, the fallen grandeur of Egypt, the march of history, the trampling feet of time. Of all those we would think—think—think—till thought became soul, and we were bodiless, and the moon and stars looked down on a silent, verily a phantom boat, floating slowly along the river of Egypt, surrounded by the princes and priests of Osirian days.

The blackest and the best-looking man on the boat was Hassabo, the mestahmil or steersman. One evening, I was writing a letter at the table. It was late, all was silent outside, and I supposed every one was sleeping, when I was startled by the abrupt entrance, rather say rush, into the cabin of Hassabo, supported on either side by Ferraj and Hassan, the two cabin servants. Black as he ordinarily is, Hassabo was now blue with fright or pain, I could not tell which. Blood was running from his finger, which Hassan and Ferraj held in their hands, grasping it as if they thought it would get away from them. From something that he muttered about fish, I understood that he had run a fish-hook through his finger, and I proceeded to wash the wound and put on some common plaster. In the midst of this, Hassabo, who was by far the most pious Mussulman on the boat, was constantly muttering, "Allah! Allah!" and trembling and growing weaker, until suddenly he turned from me with a bolt toward the door, which was open, and threw the contents of his stomach on the deck. Unfortunately a deck plank was up, and, as he rushed out, he tripped in the hole thus left and went down on deck with a tremendous fall just as he heaved a second time; and then the poor fellow lay frightened and badly hurt in the scuppers. I soon learned the cause of his fright, for I saw that the wound was a trifle. Hajji Mohammed, the cook, had invited Hassabo to an extra good supper, and the poor fellow, glad as they all are of a chance to get any thing better than sour bread to eat, had accepted the invitation, and overfed himself at the kitchen with sundry relics of fowls and mutton. Now Hassabo was rigid in his observances, and always washed before and after eating, so that when he had finished his supper he stepped into the small boat, which lay alongside, to wash, and, as he dipped his hands in the water, a huge fish seized his finger. *Hinc illæ lachrymæ.* The fright and the overfeeding were too much for him.

I had fishing-tackle for the river ready on deck at all times, but had as yet hooked nothing, having been unable to get any idea from books or persons of the habits of Nile fish. The natives take them in a way peculiar to the river. They have a rope, two hundred feet long, armed with large hooks at every few inches, which is sunk by weights, and dragged up or down the river. By chance they sometimes hook a large fish in this way, and only by chance.

This accident of Hassabo's gave me a clew to the ways of at least one species of fish, and in ten minutes I was diligently trolling for him, and in ten more I had him. He struck my hook as a blue-fish would strike, from below, with a sharp, swift blow, turning on his tail as he took hold, and carrying away my line with him, which I gave him for six fathoms before I struck him. I needed not to wait, as it afterward appeared. He had swallowed the hook instantly. I had him fast, but that was very little indeed toward getting him into the boat. He was a strong swimmer, and tried my tackle severely; but it had held heavier fish than he in American waters, and landed them, too, and I did not give him up when he had fifty fathoms of line out, and was pulling straight down the river. Jumping into the small boat, I cast her loose myself and drifted down stream, helped not a little by his pulling. It was nearly an hour before I killed him, and during that time I had never for an instant thought of where I was or whither I was drifting. And now I found myself alone on the Nile, the night dark, the moon not yet risen, my boat four miles away, a strong current against me, and an uncommonly lively fish raising the devil in the bottom of the boat. I had no time for consideration. Every minute was a loss, and carried me further away. I sat down to the oars. I remembered all the heavy pulling I had done in my life as I leaned to those clumsy sticks which they called oars, any one of which will outweigh two long boat sweeps. I thought especially of two scenes in my past life; one when I rowed against a fierce gale off the north point of Block Island, and the other when, with Miriam wrapped up in oil-clothes and India-rubber, seated in the stern of my boat, I pulled up from the ferry-stairs at Niagara to the foot of the American Fall, and across to the milk-white basin of the Horseshoe. But in neither of these instances, said I to myself, did I hear these hungry jackals that are barking on the shore to-night. Then I sang, and I made the Egyptian darkness ring to Yankee songs, until it occurred to me that I was inviting the Ababdee scoundrels, who are all along that part of the river, and always awake at night, watching for chances to rob passers-by on the water; and so I kept myself quiet, and pulled steadily, and counted stars.

There were never half so many visible to my eye in the heavens. That night, and every clear night since I have been in Egypt, I have seen eleven stars in the constellation of the Pleiades, and one night I saw twelve distinctly. But I did not pause long to count stars. I looked northward and pulled southward with a will. In an hour I saw the red light which we always carried at the end of the high yard, and in half an hour more I was pretty much used up, alongside the boat, where every one was sound asleep. No one knew of my lonesome adventure until they saw the fish lying on deck the next morning.

Administering to the diseases of the crew became an every-day matter. Hajji Hassan, the cook's mate, a tall, bony Arab, had never before been in the upper country, and the sun effectually skinned his face, so that he was as miserable an object in appearance as one will meet in a year, and, I have no doubt, was equally miserable in feeling. His head, bones, back, all parts of him, and a number of other parts, that he imagined he had, ached unendurably, as well they might. I applied cooling lotions (I believe that is the phrase), and the next morning he was much better, only needing a mild dose of medicine to complete the cure. My stock of drugs was small, for we eschew the use of them; a Seidlitz powder would fit the case tolerably well, and I gave him one, explaining before he took it the effervescing character of it. But he did not understand it. And as he held one glass in his hand, while I poured the acid in from the other, telling him to drink quick, he raised it to his lips, but the foam touched his nose, and he was astounded beyond measure. He dropped the glass as if he were shot, cried out, *Efrit! Efrit!*—"A devil! a devil!" and no persuasion could induce him to try another. I substituted the half of one without the acid, which answered all the purpose.

That same evening I shot, for the first time, a bird that the Arabs consider almost sacred. It is much like our curlew, in size, shape, and habit; but its peculiarity is that it utters a note that the Arab understands to be a distinct address to God: *El moulk illak, La shareek illak*—"The universe is thine; thou hast no partner!" This cry is remarkably distinct and musical, and we heard it all the evening, in the twilight, across a waste of halfeh grass, which marked the position of a forgotten city. I know no picture on all the earth's surface more striking than that of this bird, standing erect, in the gloaming, on a mound that covered the palace of a long-forgotten prince, and uttering, on the desert wind, that simple and sublime tribute of praise to Him who alone knew the history of the dead that lay below.

17.

Abd-el-Kader-Bey.

When on shore, two days after passing Girgeh, in the morning I came on the ruins of a village which was evidently Arab, and whose destruction was manifestly violent. Such village scenes are not uncommon in this miserable land. Not infrequently the inhabitants of one of these mud heaps—they can hardly be called any thing else—rebel against the authority of the viceroy. More foolish or mad conduct could not be imagined. Entirely destitute of arms, they have no hope of success, and their fate is inevitable; yet village after village, galled by the enormous loads of taxes imposed on them, resists and is destroyed, and such ruins as this mark their sad history.

I asked an old man, who was at work near the ruin, who destroyed this place, and when? He answered, "Ibrahim Pasha, two years ago." Now Ibrahim Pasha rendered his account to an avenging God some eight or more years ago, and the old man was, of course, mistaken, in his date or the person. Ibrahim Pasha had a way of destroying villages, a sort of passion that way, and I supposed it possible that the people might attribute every thing of the kind to him as a sort of matter of course. There is a town not far from New York where, it is said, on good authority, that the people at the last presidential election supposed they were voting for General Jackson, and I fancied this was much the same way. I learned afterward that it was the date only that was wrong. This was one of the monuments of the terrible Ibrahim, and yet I have no doubt the verdict of impartial history will be that the same Ibrahim was one of the greatest men of this age. But I contrasted this ruined village, these deserted houses, fallen roofs, burned thatches of doura, and silent streets, with the gorgeous tomb in which he lies at Cairo, surpassing in its splendor of marble and gold any work of modern art that I have seen or expect to see; and I felt—who could avoid it?—a shudder at the thought of the meeting beyond the grave of the spoiler and the slain!

As I was walking by the men on the shore, one morning, shortly before reaching Gheneh, an incident occurred which, while it illustrates the brutal character of an Arab who has a little power, serves also to introduce more particularly than heretofore to the reader's notice, Reis Hassanein, as stupid and poor a specimen of a Nile captain as could well be found on the river.

I do not yet know what is the process of promotion on the river, or what stages a man should go through to become captain or commander of a dahabeeh. This much I know, that there are fourteen men on our boat, any one of whom is more competent for the office than the man who fills it, and we have been often tempted to hand him over to a governor, and take another in his place.

Some difficulty occurred at the tow-rope. I do not know the nature of it; the first that I saw of it was when Hassabo, the steersman, by the direction of the reis, turned the boat to the land so as to allow the latter to jump on shore, with a nabote, a large club, in his hand, wherewith to make a rush on the row of men who were hauling on the tow-rope, and strike two of them, bringing one to the ground. Had this one been any other man, I do not know that my sympathies would have been so strongly excited, but it was Mohammed Hassan, who was altogether the best man on the boat, and the regular attendant of the ladies when they walked on the shore.

At first I thought his knee-pan broken, and I had a strong notion of administering summary punishment on the reis, then and there. He was himself much frightened, and on my advancing to the scene he retired, leaving Mohammed to me. I had him removed to the boat, where his wound was attended to, and it fortunately proved to be but a bad bruise. Nevertheless, the reis was left to understand that on our arrival at Gheneh, we should hand him over to the governor, to determine whether it was proper for him to beat the men in that way; and in the mean time he was forbidden to punish them with any similar weapons, under penalty of a broken head himself. This filled to overflowing the cup of Reis Hassanein's afflictions, and thereafter he was a milder and a better man.

We reached Gheneh in the afternoon, and I proceeded immediately to pay my respects to Abd-el-Kader Bey, the Governor of Upper Egypt, and next in rank to Latif Pasha, to whom I had letters.

I have met many men of high rank in Egypt, and have been fortunate in making the acquaintance of several of the most distinguished officers of the viceroy, but I have seen no one with whom I was so well pleased, or whose acquaintance I was so glad to have made. The letters would not have been necessary. I found an accomplished gentleman—a Turk, indeed, but affable, polite, and dignified; a pleasant man in conversation, a good soldier, and a grateful protégé of Mohammed Ali, whose name he almost revered.

I found him in his audience-room, a large chamber, forty feet by forty, with a high ceiling and a stone floor.

Across the upper end of the room was a diwan, covered with rich cushions, and this also extended down one side; while opposite was a row of chairs, of eastern pattern, heavily gilded. He led me to a seat on his left, at the upper end of the room, and gave me a chibouk of magnificent pattern. The stick was carved ebony, and the amber mouth-piece was loaded with diamonds. Four young Nubian slaves, handsome in countenance and elegantly dressed in the Nizam dress, brought coffee and sherbet, and then retired, one standing on each corner of the carpet to await further orders. They were manifestly favorites, and a fifth, who had been absent on some errand, entered while the governor was talking, and walking directly up to him, took his hand, kissed it and pressed it to his forehead, and retired to the corner of the room.

Persian carpets covered about one-fourth of the room, across the upper end, and the next fourth was covered with Nubian mats, the remainder being bare. No one stepped on the mats with slippers on his feet, but every one who approached the governor left his slippers on the stone floor, and advanced over the mats as far as the edge of the carpet, but no further unless the governor gave leave. My visit did not interrupt the usual course of business, but he continued to affix his seal to papers that were presented, and to hear petitions and administer justice as usual. He turned from me with a polite excuse each time, completed his business rapidly, and resumed the conversation, which was chiefly on political subjects, with all of which he was more familiar than any man I have met in Egypt.

One poor wretch who had deserted from the army was brought before him by his soldiers, and he turned to look at him. There was a world in his eye, but he did not give the order then. If the power of life and death had not been taken from the governors by recent changes, I have little doubt that I should then and there have heard —what I have so often, and always with deep emotion, heard in America—the sentence of death passed on him. The man held up a bleeding hand, from which he had lately cut two fingers, hoping thereby to render himself unfit for military service. I believe I have already remarked that this is so much the custom in Egypt, that nearly every man has lost a finger or an eye. But this did not avail him now, and he was remanded to await examination. On my return down the river I passed two days at Gheneh, and of the pleasant friendship which I then established with Abd-el-Kader Bey, and of the favors he did me, I shall have occasion to speak fully at another time. He now forwarded letters to every inferior governor on the river, informing them of my progress, and gave me copies to deliver in case of needing any assistance, and so I left Gheneh and approached Thebes.

That night the wind wailed around us, and December voices came flying on it. The starry sky was like the skies of our home-land, but the air was pure, soft, and delicious to the cheek, though the blast was terrible. Once there came on it, from down the river, a long, wild cry—a shriek of women in agony. It was the death-cry of some poor wretches whose boat went down in the tempest. Our men took the small boat and went to their rescue, but in vain. They found the floating evidences of a lost boat, but nothing more.

And in the night I heard the sounds of a distant land come to me distinctly on the gale. You may laugh at me; you may say I write it because others have said and written the same; you may tell me I dreamed it. I care not what you say, but I know that on that stormy Saturday night I heard the church bells of my old home sounding over the tossing waves of the Nile. Yes, I heard them. I, too, laughed when I read in the books of travels of others that they heard such sounds on the desert, but I did not laugh now, for I have learned the truth of those sounds right well.

I was sitting just here where I now sit, writing a letter home, to be mailed when we should reach Luxor. Profound silence for a moment rested on every thing. There was a lull in the wind. The flow of the river was swift and noiseless. Miriam was sleeping. All the others on the boat were sleeping. It was midnight, I say; but far away, in that pleasant land that I call home, it was just sunset, and the hour of prayer. I leaned my head forward on my hands a moment, and perhaps—I will not say it was so, but perhaps—perhaps there were some tears in my eyes; for on a winter evening like this, in the long-gone years, I saw the light of life fade out of eyes that I loved, and deep gloom take its place forever, and so, perhaps I wept as I remembered it—and then I heard those bells. They sounded sweetly—clearly, and I sprang to the door of the cabin, and out into the starry night, and leaned my head forward to listen to the melody.

Soft, soft and sweet they came over the swift river; clear, rich, and full. There could be no mistaking them. I might have doubted, but the tones were all the same. There was the Presbyterian bell, deep, stern, and solemn in every stroke; the Episcopal church bell, more musical and silvery; the old Scotch church bell, that was forever chanting the Psalm, "They that go down to the sea in ships"—all clear and loud; and then the wind arose, and they went away over the desert, and I heard them far off, and then no longer.

There was an hour when, before I left America, I stood with a friend—the best friend of all my years of life, the companion of boyhood, youth, and mature years—and talked with him of the same subject.

He had been in Egypt, and had once heard that same

sound, and with all the calm thoughtfulness of his nature, he believed that the bells did verily sound in his ears with their own metallic notes. We were speaking then of Eothen, and the same story as related by its author, in his own inimitable style; but I had little faith then in my friend or in Eothen. I have more now. You may tell me it was the wailing over a dead man in a village along the bank, or you may say that it was a creaking sakea, or a palm-tree moaning in the wind, or whatsoever you please to believe it. I am content to know that my ears heard the church bells, and since my feet might not tread the accustomed path, my heart went there with those that trod it, and the old altar had a worshiper there that none knew who surrounded it that evening, but whose worship was sincere and fervent, though the waters of the Nile were under him, and the skies of Egypt, starry and clear, over his head.

18.

To Love a Star.

It was one of those glorious nights of which I have spoken, such as no land knows but Egypt, and no river but the Nile. Strangest of all things, in the economy of nature, is this waste of glory on the degraded race that are unable to enjoy it, or to thank God for it. Night after night, for a thousand years, the undimmed moon and stars have seen themselves reflected in the river, have silvered the hills and mellowed the otherwise haggard face of nature; and no one has thought of its exquisite beauty, its holy splendor, except, perhaps, some lonely traveler who beheld in it the melancholy memorial of ancient grandeur, or a dying Bedouin, who looked longingly up to the deep beyond, and wondered whether he should hold a star in his hand when he should have shaken off his clay bonds.

I was seated on deck alone, for all the rest of the party were sleeping, and I was revolving in my mind all the traditions and legends of the stars that I had heard in former years.

Pleasantest of them was that which I somewhere read or heard long ago, that some of the wandering tribes believe that the stars are torches, held in the hands of the beloved dead, who light with soft rays of love the pathway of the living over the desert hills of life. And thereby hangs a story which in long gone years I heard or read, and which I now believe must have had some foundation in truth, so exactly are all the particulars in accordance with the truth of scene and character.

In a valley among the hills of the Arabian desert, where a spring of water kept living a few palms to relieve the otherwise barren aspect of the visible world, lived a small family or tribe of Bedouins, consisting of a hundred persons or thereabouts, possessing ten or a dozen black tents, and as many horses and camels as men. From this point they made their excursions over the plains, and sometimes returned with strange goods for such a place. Costly silks, rare and splendid jewels, the richest cashmeres, were common articles in their household furniture; and he who saw the outer appearance of the dark camel's hair cloth, which kept the sun off from their heads, would never have dreamed of the magnificence and elegance within those low huts. We will not pause to ask whence these treasures came.

There was in this tribe a young man of higher mental structure than his companions, who was the son of a sheik dead long before, and who had been educated in the City of Victory. Education, by-the-by, in this part of the world has a peculiar meaning. It does not consist in the learning that is hidden in books, in amassing stores from the brains of the dead sages, in drawing curious lines on paper, and proving strange and incredible things to be true by mathematical calculations. It is little more than teaching the boy to read and write the language of the Koran, and then teaching him the Koran so well that he will not need to read it to be able to quote any chapter or verse. And, besides the Koran, there are hosts of unwritten traditions in the Mohammedan religion handed down from lip to lip, which are always part of the finishing accomplishments. In all these the young Sheik Houssein was learned, but he was not satisfied with these. He knew nothing of that hackneyed story—hackneyed by the school-boys and school-girls of ancient Rome, and ever since—of an indescribable longing after "the far-off unattained and dim;" but he felt within him a thirst that no fountain of Arabia could allay—a thirst that many have felt, and none have quenched until their lips were wet with the waters of the river of the throne! His world was a small one, and he had searched it through. From the Nile to the Euphrates, from Akaba to the Bosphorus, in Mecca, and in Jerusalem, he had looked with earnest eyes, had sought with feverish lips, and sought in vain.

Do not expect me to describe what it was that he sought. He did not know; how should I? He but knew that his life was not all that it should be; that he had capabilities beyond the narrow boundary of a Bedouin's wanderings; that there was something more in existence than the fray of the desert, the midnight descent on the unarmed village, the dastardly robbing of the peaceful caravan; something more in death than the sensual paradise of the Prophet, and the traditions of his fathers.

There is a moment, in every man's existence, on which turns his future destiny. There are many such moments; for oftentimes life hangs on a thread, and if the thread is not cut it requires but a touch to change the whole direction of the future. But in every man's life there is at least one, and in his it occurred thus:

It was not often in those days that travelers crossed the great desert. Few Europeans came to Egypt, and fewer still went on to Sinai. But there was a time when Houssein was called to Cairo to meet a noble party of western travelers, a gentleman and two ladies, who were making a pilgrimage to Sinai and the Holy Land, and who wished his protection in crossing the desert. He saw but the gentleman, and readily engaged to perform the desired service.

It was not till the party had left the Birket-el-Haj that he met them, where they were encamped, by moonlight, on the sand that stretches away to Suez. As he sprang from his mare, before the tent-door, he was startled by such a vision as he had never seen before, but thought he had dreamed of in his waking dreams.

She was slight, fair, and, in the moonlight, pale as a creature of dreams. Was this one of the houris of his fabled paradise? No; he rejected the thought if it rose. There was no spot in all the heaven of Mohammed fit for an angel like this. Away, like the sand on the whirlwind, like the clouds before the sun, like the stars at day-break—away swept all his faith in Islam, and, in an instant, the Sheik Houssein was an idolater, worshiping, as a thousand greater than he have done, the beauty of a woman. Perhaps he might have quenched his thirst for the unknown at some other fountain, but this was enough now. He had found that wherewith to fill the void, and he was content.

Love was a new emotion, a sensation he had never before experienced, and it satisfied him. Did she love him? That was a question which never occurred to him. What did he care for that? He was not seeking to be loved. He was looking for employment for his own soul, and he had found it, and that was enough.

The tradition goes to describe his long crossing of the desert. How he lingered among the hills of Sinai; how he led them by Akaba and Petra, and detained them many weeks in the City of Rock; how the fair English girl faded slowly away, for she was dying when she came to Egypt; and how, weary, well-nigh dead, he carried her to the Holy City, and pitched their tents by the mountain of the Ascension. And all this time he watched over her with the zealous care of a father or a brother, and the quick heart of the lady saw it and understood it all. And sometimes he would try, in broken words, to tell her of his old belief and his ideas of immortality, and she would read in his hearing sublime promises and glorious hopes that were in a language he knew nothing of, but which he half understood from her uplifted eye and countenance.

How he worshiped that matchless eye! He worshiped nothing else, on earth or in heaven.

It was noon of night under the walls of Jerusalem, and in a white tent close by the hill on which the last footsteps of the ascending Lord left their hallowing touch, an English girl was waiting his bidding to follow him.

Outside the tent, prone on the ground, with eyes fixed on the everlasting stars, lay a group of Bedouins, and apart from them a little way their chief, silent, motionless—to all that was earthly, dead. A low voice within the tent broke the stillness of the night, but he did not move. A voice was uttering again those words, of which the sound had become familiar to him already, the Christian's prayer.

"Sheik Houssein!"

He sprang to his feet. It was her voice, faint, low, but silvery. The tent-door was thrust aside, and as a hand motioned to him to enter he obeyed.

She lay on the cushions, her head lifted somewhat from the pillow by the arms of her sister; her brother, who spoke the language of the desert well, stood by her as the young sheik approached. His coofea was gathered around his head; only his dark eye, flashing gloriously, was visible. She looked up into it and whispered; he half understood her before the words came through her

9*

brother's lips, as she told him the story of Calvary and Christ, and the cloud that received the King and Saviour returning to his throne.

It were vain to say he understood all this. He only knew that she was telling him of her hope ere long to be above him, above the world, above the sky; and his active but bewildered mind inwrought all this with his ancient traditions, and having long ago rejected the creed that did not teach him that she was immortal, as he fell back on the idea that the immortals had somewhat to do with the stars, and as he lay down on the ground, close by the side of the tent, listening for every sound from within, he fixed his eyes on the zenith and watched the passing of the hosts of the night until she died. There was a rustling of garments, a voice of inexpressible sweetness suddenly silent, a low, soft sigh, the expiration of a saint, and at that instant, far in the depths of the meridian blue, a clear star flashed on his eye, for the first time, its silver radiance, and he believed that she was there.

For three-score years after that, there was on the desert, near that group of palm-trees and lonely spring, a small turret built of stones, brought a long distance, stone by stone, on camels. And in this hut, or on its summit, lived a good, wise man, beloved of all the tribes, and especially followed by his own immediate tribe, who, with him, rejected Mohammed, and worshiped an unknown God, through the medium of the stars, and especially one star, which he had taught them to reverence above all others.

And at length there came a night when the wind was abroad on the desert, and the voice of the tempest was fierce and terrible. But high over all the sand-hills, and over the whirling storms of sand, sedate, calm, majestic, the immutable stars were looking down on the plain, and the old man on his tower beheld them, and went forth on the wind to search their infinite distances.

That night, saith the tradition, another star flashed out of heaven beside the star that the Arabs worshiped, and the Sheik Houssein was young again in the heaven of his beloved.

Let us leave him to the mercy of the tradition, nor seek to know whether he reached that blessed abode.

All this story, that I have perhaps wearied you in relating, passed through my mind that night as I lay on deck on the softly-cushioned sofa, and looked out of the cape of my Syrian cloak at the sky. In the midst of my endeavors to recall such parts as had faded from my memory, I was roused by a deep groan near me.

One of my crew, a man from the upper country, black, but with finely-cut features and straight hair, had been ill from the time of our leaving Cairo, and steadily rejected any Christian remedies. One case of bilious fever I had managed with my small stock of medical knowledge and medicines, and had cured. But Abd-el-Kerim refused medicine, preferring to die a natural death, and I did not much blame him. I was of opinion from the first that his case was hopeless; and as these Arabs lay all cures to their own charms, and not to our medicine, but charge all deaths on the unlucky adviser, and call it poisoning, it is quite as well to let their diseases alone, unless one is tolerably certain of being able to effect a complete cure.

He was dying. Delirium had set in with high fever three days before, and two of the men had been detailed to watch him constantly. It was as much as they could do to keep him quiet until that afternoon, when the fever abated, and he began to sink. I had forgotten him entirely during my reverie, and was startled, and even alarmed, by the groan. He lay on his back, wrapped in cloaks and blankets, which we had provided for our own uses, but yielded readily to his greater necessities. I have seldom seen as fine a countenance. The Nubians are not all like the colored population of America, but many of them have finely-chiseled Grecian faces, with high foreheads, and sharply-cut outlines. He was a man of thirty-five, stout and athletic in body—in fact, Herculean when he was well, but he was weak as a child now.

Religion he had none—positively none. Of the Mussulmans four fifths, or five sixths, are infidels. On my boat, which had nineteen professed Mussulmans on board, there were but three who prayed.

This man had never shown the slightest knowledge of Moslem faith or doctrine; and what were his thoughts at this moment of departure I have no idea. He died like a dog, and his companions treated him as such. It was a strange scene, to say the least of it, that on the deck of the *Phantom*, at midnight. Stretched at full length, his dark face glistening in the moonlight, lay the dying Nubian. Around him sat four of the crew, his companions. The rest were forward, sleeping. These were smoking a goza, a water-pipe, made of a cocoa-nut shell, in which they smoked tombak, breathing enormous quantities of it into their lungs, and ejecting it in clouds. I stood at his feet, looking down on his huge form, and wondering, as usual, as I shall never cease to wonder, as men will wonder till they know more than here and now, that life could leave such splendid machinery mere dead clay. He breathed slowly, and with difficulty. His eyes roved from face to face of his companions with a sort of wistful expression or longing for life, or shrinking from the terrible unknown into which he was plunging, and then he looked up at the sky. But he saw nothing there. To him the stars were but lights, the moon a greater light; and he had no thought of them as I had at that moment, as marks along the way his swift soul would travel to the place of judgment. No hope of immortality was in his eye or heart; no looking beyond the gloom. The swift, dark river that flowed below him was to him no emblem: he saw nothing on the moonlit bank that spoke of heaven or God, but shuddering fearfully, he lifted his stout arms twice into the air, clenched his fists, muttered in a hoarse voice, "Allah!" and was gone.

His companions smoked on in silence, passing the goza from mouth to mouth, and I stood and looked at them, and at him, and the night hastened on apace. I could not sleep below that deck; so wrapping closer the cloak around my face, I lay down on the sofa and slept and dreamed.

I awoke at sunrise. The deck was clear. The dead man was gone. I asked for him, for this hasty resurrection surprised me. He was buried. They had taken him at daybreak to a burial-place near a village, dug his grave a few inches deep, and left him for the wolves and jackals. I little thought to see such a scene on the Nile. How much less one that I saw later, when I felt the quivering pulse fail in the white temple of a fellow-Christian, who had lain down to die in the great temple of Luxor, and with my own hands closed forever his eyes, whose last gaze was on the magnificent columns of the great Amunoph. But of that hereafter.

19.

The City of a Hundred Gates.

It was a quiet Sunday morning when we reached the great city of Egypt, Thebes of a hundred gates. We had tracked from about daylight; and after the sun rose I took my position on the upper deck to watch the appearance of the hills and the banks of the river. It was not difficult to imagine ancient Thebes, still mighty and magnificent, guarded by those lofty mountains. It was more difficult to imagine Thebes gone, dead, departed, buried in caverns and unknown sepulchres of these dark ravines that come down to the water from among the rocky piles. I could more easily expect to find a million men living in the valley that opened luxuriantly before me, than I could believe that unknown millions lay in the earth below, or the rocks around it. Nowhere in all Egypt do such rugged hills embrace so beautiful a plain, and nowhere is there a spot so well suited for the capital of a great nation. The mountains are here, and the river flows between them, and Memnon sits calmly on his throne, and looks over the plain and the river with stony eyes, unused to tears, and nothing appears to lament the dead glory. Not even the sun, not even the moon shines less brilliantly, less joyously, that kings and princes, matrons and virgins, wise and foolish, weak and strong, are all alike dead in the past, dead in the valley, dead in rock-hewn sepulchres; the palaces ruins, the temples ruins, the homes gone, the hearth-fires ashes long ago, the hearts of the men of Thebes dust—insensible, still, silent dust.

I do not know that you understand what I am endeavoring to express. It is, in plain language, this, that before approaching the valley of Thebes you can readily expect to find there a great city, but on seeing it a broad plain, level as subsiding water can level it, and covered with corn and grain, you can not believe that it is the site of a ruined capital, once the wonder of the world for magnificence. There is nothing to indicate it. You expect to find mounds, heaps of rubbish, or some of the usual marks of an ancient town. But there is nothing of the sort, except immediately around Luxor and Karnak. Fields of waving grain, of lupins, lentils, and doura, or Indian corn, cover the flat expanse of the valley, broken nowhere by ruin, rock, or mound, except in these localities, and excepting also the two colossi, who sit in lonesome majesty among the fields of green on the west bank of the river. That temples and palaces have been here, their vast remains indicate; but those on the west side of the river are at the foot of the mountain, and not on the cultivated land; and Karnak stands solitary on the eastern side, a majestic solitude indeed, among heaps of earth that may cover the floors of ancient habitations.

In fact, I am induced to believe that Thebes never was a city of large population. It was, probably, a city of temples, possibly of colleges—an Oxford or a Cambridge, and a place to which men were carried for sepulture in holy ground. But I do not believe that any great crowd of inhabitants were ever found here.

We saw, first of all the ruins of Thebes, the old temple

at Goornou on the west bank, and then the Remeseion, the colossi, and Medeenet Habou, all distant; and at length, on the east, over the high banks along which we were tracking, the obelisks and the lofty towers of the propylon of Karnak looked down on us.

The valley of the Nile widens at this point. I have no means of comparing it with other places on the river, but it is as wide, I should imagine, as at any point above the Delta. On the western side the plain is from two to three miles wide, and on the eastern at least five, perhaps eight or ten.

The mountains on the west are higher than at any other place in Egypt, and their character is so peculiar that no one can form a just idea of the appearance of Thebes until he understands this.

I think I have before remarked that all Egyptian hills and mountains are absolutely destitute of vegetation. No shrub, or tree, or blade of grass takes root on their rocky sides. They are, in fact, only vast piles of rock, the sides being either precipitous or formed of the *débris* of the stone. The hills of Thebes are intersected by numerous ravines, which wind their way through them in almost cavernous gloom. Frequently the hills are nearly a thousand feet high on each side of these ravines, ascending by terraces of several hundred feet each. On the front of the hills overlooking the valley they show the openings of tombs, hundreds and thousands, while hundreds and thousands remain unopened. On these hills the eye of the traveler rests with more intense interest than on the ruins of temples and palaces, for there, during a thousand years of royal prosperity, the Theban princes, priests, and people, buried their dead,

> "And there the bodies lay, age after age,
> Mute, life-like, rounded, fresh, and undecaying,
> Like those asleep in quiet hermitage
> With gentle sleep about their eyelids playing;

And living in their rest, beyond the rage
  Of death or life; while fate was still arraying,
In liveries ever new, the rapid, blind,
And fleeting generations of mankind."

It is always so. Men will turn their eyes from a palace at any time to look at a tomb, and in a landscape will forget the beauty of hill and forest to gaze on the white stones of a grave-yard. I remember well that once in my life I fell upon a grave in a grand old forest. The trees were lofty and majestic, and the sky, seen through their branches, was far away and deep, and winning and glorious. The voice of the mountain wind was musical, and the voice of a stream that wound its joyful way around that solitary grave was even more melodious. But I forgot the sky, and trees, and wind, and sat down among the dead leaves of the last autumn to hold communion with the unknown spirit of him who slept below. I did not know whether he was Indian or white man; nay, I did not know that he was a man, saving only that I did not think any human being would have laid a woman there to sleep alone in the forest through all the days and nights of the dismal years; but I knew by that strange consciousness that every one has felt, but no one can describe, that human dust lay in its kindred dust below, and I paused to look on the turf that hid it.

The turf! It is comforting when the cold is coming over one, when the eye is dimming, the hand failing, the lip trembling, the heart hushing—it is comforting, I say, to think that one will be laid under green sods, whereon violets may grow, and that this vile dust of humanity may have a resurection in roses or myrtle blossoms. There is no such comfort here. No grave in Egypt has turf on it, nor grass, nor flower, nor tree, nor creeping plant. It is but sand, or the decaying dust of ancient houses in which they laid their dead, and the winds sweep over them, and mounds increase to gigantic size or wholly disappear in one night's blasts. I do not think I could sleep here at all. I do not think that my dust would consent to mingle with this soil. Those ancient Thebans doubtless felt all this, for I have less faith than formerly in the idea that they wished to preserve their bodies till they should come to reclaim them. The Nile plain was no place to lay their dead. It was annually flooded by the river, and no man would be laid there. The sandy desert was a wild spot, and hyenas could find their way into deep graves. It was horrible to think of it. Only the rock was left, and the rock they chose, and cut their tombs in it, and wound their bodies in spices and gums, and slept well. Yea well. Blessed is he who can find a grave in Egypt that will last him a century; more blessed far if it last him three thousand years.

We had ordered our letters to be forwarded from Cairo to Luxor, and Abd-el-Atti left us slowly tracking up the river, and hastened on to the village to get them for us. He was disappointed, and unwilling to see our disappointment, sent a messenger back to meet us, with intelligence that we had no letters, and on my word we thought but little of Thebes after that until we found ourselves at the shore by the great temple of Luxor.

We were scarcely at the shore when Mustapha Aga, the American agent, came down, and after him Islamin Bey, the governor or nazir of this section, a bad-looking Turk, ignorant and stupid, whom we received without much attention and left to smoke and drink coffee alone on the upper deck while we strolled up to the temple. Perhaps this inattention on our part was the cause of his subsequent rudeness to us, but as it cost us nothing and him his governorship he had the worst of it, and it is to be hoped he learned better manners for the next time.

The first idea that I received, when a boy, of the magnitude of the ruins of Egyptian temples was from hearing that one of them was so large that a modern Arab village stood on the roof of it. I had not retained the locality, but the moment that I looked up at Luxor I recognized the ruin of which the story was told. Doubtless this was the temple, though afterward I found the same thing true of Edfou, and of one or two others, but they were small temples compared with this.

Luxor, or El Uksorein—" The Palaces," is on the east bank of the Nile, and the ruins of its great temple rise among the crude brick and mud houses of the modern village. Nothing remains here of the ancient except only this temple. Karnak lies two miles from it on the north, but the fields between contain no memorials or relics of the city that once connected them.

The temple, or those portions of it which now remain, are on a line parallel with the main part of the river as it flows by them, but a branch or arm of the Nile, which flows around a large island above Luxor, comes into the main channel again here, and the rear of the temple is on this branch. The total length of the temple is about a thousand feet. The front was originally connected with Karnak; how or when, it concerns not my purpose now to discuss. But the great entrance to the temple is now surrounded by the mud and brick houses of the inhabitants. Nevertheless they have had the decency, unknown in some places, to leave an open space before the great propylon, where the astonished traveler may pause in awe before the vast entrance, or lie down in the dust and look up at the obelisk and the huge towers sculptured all over with the representations of the valiant deeds of kings long dead and forgotten.

But if any one were inclined to lie down there, let him be warned that it is a Coptic neighborhood, and fleas love Coptic blood and Christian blood of all kinds, and fleas are plenty here. He will do well not to lie down, but to stand and rather break his neck with looking up at the obelisk and trying to read its large characters.

The other obelisk is gone to Paris. It stands in the Place de la Concorde, on a pedestal, whereon are graven in gilded letters the deeds of Louis Philippe, King of the French, and the old gray granite looks down scoffingly on the gilded lines and figures below. The remaining obelisk, solitary but stately, is far more grand and imposing in its appearance than its ancient companion, and rumor said that the wandering obelisk of the Place de la Concorde was not to be allowed to remain in its present place. The view of the Arch of Triumph from the Tuileries is obstructed by it, and Louis Napoleon loves a long prospect, especially when he can secure it by removing monuments of the reign of his predecessor. It is sorrowful to think that the stone had remained almost four thousand years on its base at Luxor, and now has begun an existence of changes. The next Louis Somebody will find it obstructing his view in some other direction. Nothing remains stationary in Paris.

The doorway is guarded by colossal statues of granite, of which the heads only are above the earth. But these are highly polished, and enough is visible to show their former grandeur and beauty. Passing between these, you enter the doorway, and find yourself in a narrow, dirty street or alley, of the modern Arab village. The splendid columns which once flanked the court of the temple are yet standing, many of them, but the huts of the village inclose and cover them. Entering these miserable hovels, you find the women and children, with sheep, dogs, and goats, in promiscuous heaps, and all manner of filth and dirt around the sides of these half-buried columns; whose glorious legends of ancient princes stare solemnly on the entering stranger, as if to ask him what hard decree of fate has led him into the same prison in which they are doomed to darkness and oblivion.

This court of the temple was about two hundred feet long by a hundred and seventy wide, and another propylon here opened into the grand hall or colonnade. The hovels are closely packed here, and the alley turns to the right, and again to the left, bringing you to the great pillars beyond.

Up to this second propylon the temple was built by the second Remeses, the great Sesostris of Greek history, and the builder of almost all the most magnificent temples and palaces of Egypt. He added these portions to the older parts, which were built by Amunoph III., whose period was about 1430 B. C., and within the century after the exodus of the Israelites. Remeses II. was within a century later. I am now following Wilkinson's chronology.

Passing through the second propylon, as I have remarked, you would enter the great colonnade; but this you are now compelled to avoid, and re-enter the temple at the great pillars, of which two rows, of six in each row, are standing. The earth covers their pedestals, and the columns themselves, to a height of perhaps twenty feet, and as much more remains uncovered, with the immense stone architrave on each side.

These columns are among the largest known in Egypt, but they are small in comparison with those of the grand hall at Karnak. In the midst of these massive columns, stands the house of Mustapha Aga, the American consular agent, of whom I may be pardoned for pausing here to say something.

Mustapha is getting to be an old man, but a better, or more capable one for his place and position, could not be found. There is no place in the East where a consular agent is more necessary than at Luxor. A large number of American travelers annually visit the place, and every one needs advice, assistance, and protection from the rapacity of dragomans, sailors, or Coptic antique dealers. Mustapha fulfills these duties admirably; and the only regret about it is that he does it gratuitously, receiving no pay whatever, except in the way of presents which travelers may think of giving him, and these are never in money, and therefore generally mere nothings. Ordinarily they are wine, and as Mustapha drinks no wine himself, the stranger who leaves it is only supplying the others who follow him, for Mustapha gives it all away again. Can not this be improved? The old fellow would be made abundantly happy by an allowance of five hundred dollars a year, and it is sincerely to be desired that our government might direct this to be made. I am confident that no American traveler on the Nile has failed to experience his hospitality and kind attentions, and I know that every one would join in a request of this kind to the government. I have paused to speak of him in my description of the temple because he is now a part of it, and from your boat you scarcely ever look up at the grand columns without seeing Mustapha seated on the porch of his house, between two of these massive pillars, under the gigantic architrave, quietly smoking his chibouk, and entertaining some friends, either foreign or native.

His house is the most comfortable private house in Upper Egypt. It is all on one floor, and covers a large space. The halls are roomy and airy, the chambers papered, dark and cool, the furniture plain and comfortable, while the grand front of ancient columns gives it a more royal appearance than the citadel of Cairo.

The remainder of the temple, after passing this colonnade, is inclosed in or covered by the modern houses, and the rear chambers, the adytum, and the holy rooms, are still perfect, while on their roof stands a large part of the village. I shall not attempt any description of these various halls, courts, and chambers, which cover a space of nearly five hundred feet in length. One observation alone will suffice to convey an idea of the splendor of these buildings. Every stone in an Egyptian temple which exposes a surface to the eye, whether within or without the temple, is elaborately sculptured with pictures or hieroglyphics. No wall is without its legends and representations. Outside the temple on the lofty walls are often represented battle scenes elaborately carved, in which the builder shows himself as a victor, usually of gigantic size as compared with those whom he conquers. The same, or similar scenes, cover the inner walls, on which are also found mythological representations which are a puzzle to the student, and are likely to remain so forever. Of the minuteness and beauty of these sculptures no idea can be given by description, nor would those who have not seen them be ready to believe that three thousand years have left them so exquisitely perfect as we now find them.

The rear, or southern part of the Temple of Luxor, is divided into several apartments, each covered with sculptures indicating its peculiar design. The roof of this part is now occupied by the huts of the natives, and filth and vermin abound in the silent rooms below. One of the rooms, now open to the sky, was used in early times by the Christians as a chapel for the worship of Christ, and around it are the remains of their paintings on plaster, which covered and preserved the hieroglyphics on the stone walls. This is the case with many of the temples of Egypt; and while the early Christians defaced and destroyed much which they regarded as idolatrous and profane, they have preserved much else by covering it with plaster and mud, which being now removed, leaves the sculptures as fresh and clear as they were a thousand years ago.

Of the grandeur of the Temple of Luxor, no adequate idea can be formed, even by the visitor who stands among its ruins. From its great propylon, or from some portion of its massive walls, an avenue stretched away to Karnak, ornamented with all the splendor of ancient art, and guarded on each side by colossal rams, the emblems of the deity of Thebes. Of this avenue only the northern end remains, in ruins, but majestic even in ruins, and a lofty gateway, of Ptolemaic times, closes it. Thus Karnak was, in some sort, a continuation of the Temple of Luxor, and, in fact, all the temples of Thebes were connected by avenues, and possibly by bridges, so that it was a city of temples.

I left the *Phantom* and walked around the village, my footsteps dogged by twenty donkey-doys, and as many donkeys, each of the former hoping that I would grow tired and patronize one of them. At every corner and turn a Coptic scoundrel would produce a lot of antiques for sale, and I amused myself by asking prices. At Luxor rates, Dr. Abbott's collection is worth a million.

O! confident Howajji, beware in Luxor of Ibrahim the Copt, and on the western shore of Achmet-el-Kamouri, the Mussulman. Skillful manufacturers of every form of antique are plenty in the neighborhood, and these men have them in their employ, and sell to unwary travelers the productions of the modern Arabs as veritable specimens of the antique. Achmet is the chief manufacturer himself, and has a ready hand at the chisel.

The manufacture of antiques is a large business in Egypt, and very profitable. Scarabæi are moulded from clay or cut from stone, with close imitation of the ancient, and sold readily at prices varying from one to five dollars. At Thebes is the head-quarters of this business. Still, no antiquarian will be deceived; and it requires very little practice to be able in an instant to determine whether an article is ancient or modern. When the Copt finds that you do know the distinction, he becomes communicative, and readily lets you into the secret of his business; and while he is confidentially informing you of the way in which the Arabs do it, and how this is modern and that is not, beware lest you become too trusting, and he sells you in selling a ring, or a vase, or a seal. He is a wily fellow and sharp, and he knows well how to manage a Howajji.

A strong breeze from the northward was not to be lost on our upward voyage, and after one night at Luxor we pressed on.

But I could not go without one view over the plain, and at break of day I went up the hill to the foot of the propylon towers of the temple, and looked up to their summit. There must be a way to climb them, and while I was looking for it, a bright Arab boy made his appearance and offered to show me. I followed him readily, and he led me through the propylon to the narrow alley already spoken of, and around the corner into a low door in the mud wall. This opened into a yard or court, full of sheep and doura, or corn-stalks, and passing through another like it, I climbed a mud wall and walked along this to the corner of the tower, which was somewhat broken. Climbing this some twenty feet and going around the end, I discovered an opening into the body of the tower, where, crawling in, I found a stairway, encumbered with huge masses of fallen stone, and up this I ascended, with no little difficulty, to the top of the tower. Here I sat and watched the coming of the sun. The Libyan hills were first lit, and the golden line of light came slowly down their rugged sides—down, down, until it reached the tombs that open to the east, and the Memnonium and Medeenet Habou, and then it touched the lips of Memnon and his old companion. I saw the red flash on the giant head, and I bent my head forward to hear the sound of the salutation; but there was no sound—Memnon is vocal only in tradition.

A peculiarity of the tower on which I was standing I have never seen noted by any travelers. Every stone on the summit is covered with footprints, cut more or less deep in the surface. By whom these were cut no record remains to tell.

It has been supposed that they are the marks of pilgrim feet, but who were the pilgrims that thus recorded their accomplished vows? Afterward I found similar marks on stones on the river bank in Nubia, but always on elevated bluffs, where perhaps pilgrims standing could catch a view of some far shrine. Sometimes they were simple parallelograms, two side by side, with four short marks at the end of each, to signify the toes of the foot, but oftener they were well-drawn feet, large or small, as if marked out around the foot itself.

They are not the rude scratchings of the modern Arabs, or of those who drew the boats and animals that are found on the rocks of Nubia and elsewhere. That there was a design in their being placed here is evident from the number of them, and from their being only on the summit of the lofty tower, and only on the topmost course of stones. There are none below this. Was there any idea of the footsteps of angels here, or of departing souls, or of departing prayers?

It is not the intention of this book to record any of the results of study in Egypt, and I shall therefore pass entirely over that subject. As we remained at Luxor but one day, reserving a long visit for our return trip, the time that I had was, of course, too brief to make any examinations of places or things; but I had informed myself previously, as well as books and papers and charts could assist me, and after a hasty inspection of a few spots, I directed the commencement of some excavations to be continued during my trip up the river. The governor, on my requisition, furnished me with fifty men for work; but, alas! for Egyptian excavations, they had no tools of any sort or kind save only the fingers God gave them, or as many of them as each man had not cut off. For I have before remarked, that the natives are thus mutilated to save themselves from the conscription. With their hands and palm-leaf baskets these fifty men might do as much in a day as five Irishmen with shovels and wheel-barrows, and their pay was about the same, being a piastre and half to each, or about eight cents American per day, making the whole pay about four dollars for the fifty. Placing them under the direction of Mustapha Aga, the worthy consular agent, and giving him a letter to the governor as my agent, I left Luxor to seek more remote antiquities.

20.

The Ancient Dead at Esne.

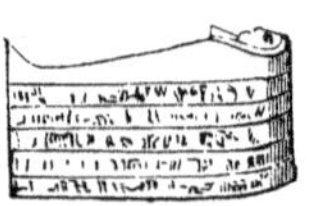

We left Thebes with regret. I believe that almost any one of us would most willingly have paused here and rested, going no further up the river. But there was much to be seen beyond, and it is best, as a general rule, to reserve all stoppages for the return trip, especially if the wind blows.

We had no incidents of voyage between Thebes and Esne worthy of record. To us the most important was the supply of fresh vegetables and fruits, which we had from the garden of Mustapha Pasha, at Erment. We were two days between the two places.

At Esne I awoke in the morning early, and walked up into the town, intending to see the bazaars only, and return to breakfast. To my surprise, I found myself at the door of the temple, which is one of the most beautiful remains in Egypt, and I entered it.

It is not my intention, as I have already said, to describe the various ruins of Egypt as I see them. Books are already full of these descriptions. It will be enough if I succeed in giving a general idea of them, sufficient for the reader's convenience in following my personal adventures.

Esne stands on mounds, the accumulated heaps of an

ancient city. The temple itself is totally buried in these piles of rubbish, and the city is built over them, so that its former extent or appearance is now unknown. Only the portico remains, and this being some feet higher than other parts of the building, remained standing above the earth. A few years ago the visitor could walk into it, just under the roof, and see the capitals of the columns and the splendidly carved ceiling. Mohammed Ali, being one day at Esne, and having nothing better to do, ordered the excavation of this portico, and a thousand fellahs were set to work, with hands and baskets, to carry out the earth which lay between the columns, and find the pavement, which was thirty feet below. It has been insinuated that the pasha wanted a powder magazine, and that this, and not respect for antiquity, induced him to undertake this laudable enterprise. Be this as it may, the result was the exposure of one of the most beautiful buildings, ancient or modern, in the world.

The earth in front remains at the old level, kept by a brick wall from falling into the inclosure. You enter a small yard or inclosure, among the houses, which stand, with their walls, not more than fifteen feet from the front of the temple, and passing along this narrow alley, descend by wooden steps into the excavated area of the portico, finding yourself then in an immense chamber, the lofty stone ceiling supported by rows of massive columns, and the walls and columns alike covered with a profusion of sculpture characteristic of the late period at which this temple was built.

The light which comes in through the narrow space left between the cornice and the ground, greatly diminished by the proximity of the houses, leaves a sepulchral rather than a "dim, religious" gloom within; but to this the eyes at length become accustomed, and then the forms of gods and men start from the walls and salute the stranger with their cold, calm eyes. Strange figures, hideous forms of gods and sacred beasts, unknown even to old Pliny, are found here on the stones, and on the ceiling is a zodiac, with curious representations of the heavenly bodies.

Three doorways, opening formerly into the chambers of the temple, are now closed with stone to keep out or in the earth on which the city stands, and we are left to imagine the secrets which the earth covers. Perhaps some national expedition may hereafter excavate these rooms, and show their treasures of legend and pictures to the world.

The temple portico does not antedate the time of the Cæsars, and is therefore comparatively a recent affair. It is a matter of chronological interest that possibly and probably these columns were carved during the lifetime of Christ on earth, and perhaps while he was in Egypt.

I came out of the temple after a brief visit, and hastened back to the boat to breakfast, after which I returned with the ladies.

There were lying in the alley, or small yard of which I have spoken, five or six mummies, badly broken to pieces. They had been here for ten or fifteen years, being government property, taken from the Arabs who had found them. The government monopolizes all antiques here. It was manifest that these were considered worthless and would soon be scattered, and I felt at liberty to investigate their condition and contents.

But two proved to be of any interest. One was probably a woman, doubtless of the priestly order, and from the same circumstances by which we ordinarily judge the age of a horse, I judged that she was young. One of her teeth, beautifully shaped, white, and perfect, lies now by me as I write, and I am wondering what kisses were pressed on them, what words of love escaped through them.

She lay in a coffin that had been elaborately painted, but the paint was now covered with mud and filth. On raising her body from its position, I found that she was laid on a bed of flowers. The bottom of the case was filled with them, worked in wreaths and garlands. There were more than a peck of them, lying precisely as they were laid when she was placed upon them, and I never felt more profound regret at the disturbance of a repose than that. If I had known the tomb from which she came, I would have been strongly tempted to carry her back, and close it up, and in some way forbid entrance to it thenceforth forever. As it was, I but laid her back on the wreaths of ancient leaves, dry now and dead as her name and memory, and turned to another of her companions.

He was a stalwart man, full six feet high, and the shawls in which he was wrapped were of rare and costly fabrics, decayed now, and worthless. Outside of all his wrappings had been a shawl of beads, not uncommon as an ornament of mummies. The beads were earthen, of various colors, blue predominating; some of them long, such as ladies call *bugles*, and others small. They were arranged in a diamond-shaped figure, the centre of the back being a large *scarabœus*. The scarabæus, let me remark, for the benefit of the unlearned in Egyptian antiquities, is the common black beetle of the country, which was sacred to the sun, and was itself an emblem of that God. It became the most common form of religious ornament, worn, perhaps, as some moderns wear a charm, and always buried with the dead. On the faces of the earthen or stone scarabæi are often found inscriptions—either the name of the king in whose reign it was made, or of the person, or of some religious object. Thus a scarabæus often determines the age of a mummy; and the curious in this subject will be interested in Dr. Abbott's collection, on seeing the small and beautiful mummy of a female which stands there, to learn that from its broken case a scarabæus fell, marked with the name of Thothmes III., the Pharaoh of the Exodus.

I found the beads and the scarabæus in a mass at his feet, but there was no vestige of the threads that had formed the shawl. Gathering nearly a quart of them, I examined the localities of his feet and head and breast for other antiques. Alas! feet and head were gone. Some plunderer like me, less scrupulous than I, had cut them off and carried them away, and the breast—a huge fissure was where his breast had been, and vacancy—nothing more.

Miriam and I sat over him, while an Arab attendant, sent by the governor, sat at a little distance, growling and grumbling at a furious rate. I paid no attention to it, but Mohammed Hassan, one of our sailors, who is our constant attendant when on shore, and who was helping me to overhaul the priest of old time, took careful notes of all the fellow's remarks, which were far from complimentary. I did not think that Mohammed observed it, but on leaving the temple I passed the governor's diwan, which was near the exit. I exchanged a few words with him, and went on, but missing Mohammed, I turned back to find him. Imagine my surprise at seeing the Arab on his back before the governor, his feet upturned to the tenth blow, as I arrived to put a stop to it. Mohammed had pocketed all the insults on my account, and produced them seriatim to the governor after I had gone by, and the governor had proceeded, in the summary manner to which the Turks are accustomed, to administer the ordinary form of punishment. A great nation that!

The scene presented on the shore near our boat was curious and amusing. I believe I have heretofore mentioned the custom of the modern Egyptians of shaving their heads. One might imagine it to have originated in some ideas of cleanliness, were it not for the amount of filth and the number of vermin found elsewhere on their persons. While we were at the temple the men had sent for a barber, and he came down to the boat, bringing his instruments with him, and on our return we found them seated in a row undergoing the shaving process.

In this, as in so many other of the customs of the modern Egyptians, we find the ancient usage still preserved. In one of the tombs at Beni Hassan is a representation of a barber at his work, which has been, not unnaturally, mistaken for a doctor and his patient. Whether the same effect is produced by the same process in modern Egypt as in ancient, I am unable to say. Herodotus tells us that it hardened their skulls, and in this respect contrasts them with the Persians. I have never seen men so susceptible to the influence of a hot sun as were the sailors on our boat. There was scarcely a day in which there was not one or more of them on his back from the effects of it, and the effects of the treatment he received from his fellows by way of medical assistance.

I was astonished one afternoon at finding Yusef, one of the crew, administering a severe pounding to Hassan Hegazi, another; and, on inquiry, learned that it was medical treatment for a stroke of the sun. He pommeled him terribly about the shoulders and breast. Then he pulled his two ears nearly out of his head, laid him down on one side and filled his ear with salt and water, and shook his head to shake it in, pulled his ears again, then seized him by the solitary scalp-lock on his head, and twisting it severely, gathered his hands around the back of his head, and rubbing them forward as if he were scraping the disease off from the surface to the forehead, he suddenly bit off the imaginary lump of illness which he had collected, and pronounced the patient cured. Per-

10*

haps he was, but Yusef had pounded him into a fever, of which I had to cure him. And he did not thank me for it, but did attribute his final recovery to Yusef's nonsense.

Esne was the last point on the passage up the river at which the men might bake bread, and here they laid in a supply to last them to the second cataract and back again.

After two days of delay, we were ready to be away; and now, think of my surprise at finding myself in a new trade. I never imagined that I should be in the donkey line; but Abd-el-Atti was very desirous of procuring a good donkey, and Esne is the best point on the river for those useful animals. Abd-el-Atti might have looked in vain for a donkey to suit him, but the Howajji, with the firman of the viceroy, was another sort of person, and he begged me therefore, on his account, to write to the resident governor at Esne, and direct him to have in readiness on our return a number of first-class donkeys, from which we should select one that might suit us. I consented, and the order was despatched, and his excellency did me the honor to assure me in reply that it should receive his profound consideration and devoted attention, or words to that effect in Arabic diplomacy.

21.

Buying Antiques.

It was late in the afternoon when the bread was brought on board, and the shaving operation being finished, Hassabo resumed his position at the tiller, and the men shook out the sail, and pushed off from the shore. The wind was fresh, and the foam dashed up before us as the crew gathered on deck near the mast, and sang to the music of the *darabooka*, which is but an earthern jar, over the large end of which a skin, or the loose bag of a pelican's bill is stretched. So with a long chorus and a lively repeat, and an occasional shout of "Allah!" (for they are profane dogs, those Mohammedans, though commonly called religious) we were again off on our voyage.

Above Esne the game on the river became more plentiful, and I devoted myself to it with considerable zeal. Pelicans abounded, especially on Sundays, when we did not shoot. Every one knows that an American crow is thoroughly acquainted with the succession of days, and the return of the seventh brings him down with fearless boldness on the cornfield. It would be difficult to suppose that in this worse than heathen land, where the Sabbath is unknown, the birds keep the run of the day; and yet it was a stubborn fact that every Sunday on the river, the game was not only more plentiful than on other days, but approached the boat as fearlessly as if the animals knew that we kept the day of rest. One Sunday evening a flight of quite two hundred pelicans sailed around us, and lit at length on a sand-bank close by our boat, and within a near gun-shot.

But whether or not the animals and the inhabitants know the Sabbath day, I do verily believe that the land knows it, and the winds and the sky. Beautiful as they are on other days, calm and clear as are the skies, they have, nevertheless, on this day a glory and a quiet that I can not describe, except by saying that it is like a Sabbath morning at home in the country, and the air like that still, soft air that a summer Sunday morning brings in at the open windows of the church on the green; and no heart can fail to keep in unison with sun and sky on such a day.

We enter the sand-stone country now, and the appearance of the hills along the river totally changes. They slope away from the banks, leaving their sides and bases covered with immense boulders. The country is narrower, and cultivation is becoming more difficult.

The day after we left Esne I shot a pelican from the boat with a pistol-ball; and the same afternoon, while on shore after pigeons, I found myself close on a flock of wild geese before I knew it, and got one of them with each barrel as they flew away. They proved to be the best we had found on the river. Their color was precisely like our common American tame goose, white and lead-color mingled. That night we slept at *El Kab*, the site of the ancient Eileithyas, and one of the most interesting points on the river.

Waking early in the morning, I sprang ashore and up the bank, to find where we were. The plain stretches away two miles to the mountains, in parts of it much more. Only the edge of the river is cultivated; the rest of the broad level is a sand and gravel barren, extending up and down the river some ten miles. The site of the ancient city was considerably to the north of the point at which we lay, and I saw at the base of the hill the modern village, toward which I immediately determined to direct my way.

My object was simply to purchase antiques, which the fellahs who cultivate this plain find in large quantities.

I have already warned the traveler against the frauds of the antique manufacturers at Thebes or Luxor. It is easy to imagine how important the business of purchasing curiosities has become in Egypt. Hundreds of travelers going up and down the river demand them wherever they stop; and the natives, who formerly thought of them as trifles, have now begun to learn their value. The scarabæus, which is usually more highly valued than any other of the small antiques, on account of its possessing a religious interest, as well as because it usually bears a name on its face, was formerly sold at a few paras, while now it commands from five piastres to a dollar, according to its style and preservation. Other and larger antiques bear proportionate prices, and there is no limit to the demands of an Arab who finds a gold ring or a jewel. There are plenty of foolish Howajjis who will pay him ten times its value for it, and he knows this well enough to wait for a purchaser, who is sure to come in time. But there is really no necessity whatever for paying such prices as these, and the knowing traveler will never be deceived by a modern, or in the price of an antique. I very soon learned at Luxor that the Copt was not to be deluded into parting with any of his stores at their fair price; but that by stealthily asking every Arab, fellah, or boy, and especially every woman that I met, if they had antiques or coins or scarabæi, I frequently found them, and purchased them for mere trifles. Thus at Karnak I bought a scarabæus for a piastre and five paras, for which the

Copt offered me ten piastres the same day, and told Mustapha that he would readily give a dollar, to sell it for two.

I had learned from Abd-el-Atti that El Kab was a favorable place for such purchases, as the village lay four miles from the site of the ancient city, and hence no travelers are apt to visit it. I started at sunrise across the plain, hailing every Arab that I met with the usual question, "Mafish goouran, mafish gedid, anteeka?" (Have you no scarabæus, or coins, or antiques?) Abd-el-Atti accompanied me, and we made the same demand on each side, picking up small affairs here and there, until we reached the village, which was on a rocky mound near an isolated mass of stone that had been left from the ancient quarrying.

Here, seating myself on the ground in an open space among the mud houses, I dispatched every boy and woman I could find to call up their friends and tell them to bring me whatever they had in the way of antiques. In a few minutes I was surrounded by the men, women, and children of El Kab, in all the various degrees of nakedness, and all in one state of filth. The nameless vermin that I found on me after that expedition were intensely disgusting. The animals themselves partook of the filthy appearance, as well as the dark color of the skins they had fed on.

Naked children presented handsfull of pieces of ancient pottery, or coins, or broken images of gods and sacred objects. Women leaned down to show their necklaces, on which were strung beads and scarabæi, and pieces of agate and cornelian, cut into strange shapes known only in old mythology. A small coin satisfied the most anxious of them; and they expressed aloud their regret that they had sold a great many—all that they had—a few weeks before to the Copt from Luxor, who had been up here on a purchasing expedition. They said I gave them twice what he did. They had nothing that was very valuable, for this reason, and what they had were what had been found within a few days. Some scarabæi, two or three small vases for toilet purposes, and one ring of the time of Amunoph III., the Memnon of Thebes—or, rather, him whose statue is called that of Memnon—and a handful of coins, and curious small images and earthen objects were all that I obtained.

One very curious antique which I picked up here, was a die, of ivory, resembling modern dice in all respects but one. The well-known power of the die, which is commonly called seven, from the fact that the sum of the opposite sides is always seven, and out of twenty throws of a pair the average result will be seven to a throw or very near it, was in this instance lost. The ace was not opposite to the six nor the two to the five.

The crowd became thicker and more noisy. One man was loud in his remarks which were not complimentary to the Howajji. I paid no attention to him but, continued my purchases. The press increased, and when at length a half naked woman with a quite naked baby in her arms, tumbled over my feet and almost into my embrace, to the detriment of my personal feelings, and the baby's as well, I rose and decamped leaving the crowd in glorious confusion over a half dozen coppers that I scattered among them.

The sheik, I have forgotten his name, but the chances are that if it was not Achmet it was Mohammed, was waiting for me at the upper end of the village where he knew I must pass in going out, and had two horses ready saddled for me and my servant. He knew that the boat had gone on so far that to attempt to overtake it on foot was out of the question. I accepted his offer with gratitude, and was preparing to mount, when a tremendous row arrested my attention. Some twenty or thirty of the villagers were approaching, vociferating a demand for more bucksheesh, based on the fact that they had failed in getting any of my scattering. Foremost among them was the huge rascal who had been personal in his remarks. He came to a sorrowful fate. Abd-el-Atti seized him by the back of the neck and walked him up to the sheik. He was strong enough to throw the dragoman over the sheik's head, no hard job, indeed, for the sheik was lamentably small, but the big fellow walked up to him with sufficient humility and my astonishment was immense when the little sheik ordered him to be laid down on his face and administered to his back about thirty blows of a tolerably large cane. Up to this moment I had not, in the confusion of tongues, understood what it was about, but now the thrashed man rushed up to me and attempted to seize my hand with a view to defile it with his dirty lips, a ceremony which I always preferred to have honored in the breach.

The sheik renewed his proffer of the horses. One of them was wicked-looking but a magnificent animal, and stood eyeing the crowd with furious countenance, while two Arabs held him by the nose.

I advanced to mount, and set my foot on the shovel stirrup. A shovel stirrup is—a shovel stirrup; nothing else; a flat shovel of iron, sides turned up, and four sharp points turned out, on which the whole foot rests.

The Arabs ride with short stirrup-straps, and knees up to their chins. As I touched the stirrup it touched his side, and—presto—his heels flew into the crowd behind him, and Abd-el-Atti, struck full on the breast, went a rod backward, and howled as if Sathanas himself had struck him. I never saw a horse's heels fly so fast and so many ways at once. I vanished through the open doors of the nearest mud hut, and found myself in the hareem of a worthy of El Kab, among all sorts of women and children, in all sorts of dresses and no dresses. When I looked out the scene was more quiet. Abd-el-Atti was moaning and groaning. The sheik was looking in horror of mind for the vanished Howajji, and wondering if he were really annihilated by the furious animal, whom the two Arabs still held by the nose, around which one of them had twisted a halter.

I glanced at the saddle-girths and the reins. They did not look over strong, but I resolved to risk them. I had boasted from childhood that no horse had ever mastered or thrown me, and I was unwilling to give up the attempt on this wild specimen of the Prophet's own breed.

My precipitate retreat had not given my Arabian friends any exalted ideas of my courage, but they did not appreciate as fully as I that I had not come to Egypt to have my brains kicked out by a horse, and that discretion is sometimes valor. I shouted to them now to clear the way, and with a short run went into the saddle. It had a back-board eight inches high, and a short post or handle four inches high from the pommel. It was no small operation to settle myself between these two in the short space of time allowed. As I struck the saddle the Arabs flung him off, and went rolling heels over head as they scattered out of the way of the first plunge.

It was a magnificent leap; another, and we were out of the village, a third and we were at full speed on the plain which stretched away five miles, a dead, hard level of gravel, without a break or a blade of grass. For twenty rods the pace was tremendous. The peculiarity of an Arab horse is that he is at full speed on the third leap. I became alarmed at the first, and checked him with a sharp rein. He came down in a heap, nearly thrown, and nearly pitching me over his head. After trying this once or twice more, I learned that he would not bear the lightest drawing on the rein. Then I talked to him, and for a wonder he understood my Arabic, and then we began to understand each other, and, at length, went along at an easy gallop over the plain toward the ancient city of Eileithyas. I saw nothing more of Abd-el-Atti till I reached the boat. He was entirely distanced.

The site of the old city is still surrounded by the crude brick wall which incloses the ruined brick houses, and the remains of stone temples and palaces that were once the habitations of men, but are now the homes of wolves and jackals.

The size, height, and thickness of this wall are a source of astonishment to the stranger, and illustrate the remarks I had occasion to make in a former chapter, on the subject of the enduring nature of crude, unburned brick in this country. This is the more astonishing when one is informed, that the common story that it never rains in Egypt is entirely destitute of truth, a remark exemplified by the fact that I have seen on the Nile, sixty miles above Cairo, as hard a rain-shower as one is apt to see in America. It is true that this is not a frequent occurrence, but there is more or less of rain in Upper and Lower Egypt every year, and mountain-torrents are formed that have left their dry rocky beds in every ravine on the side of the Nile. And through these storms, for thousands of years, the brick walls have stood, decaying, indeed, but massive yet, and are likely to outlast the storms of thousands more, if they are not carried away by the Arabs; for the only manure I have seen applied to land in Upper Egypt is the old dust of ancient brick walls. These they dig down, and loading panniers on donkeys with the dust, scatter it on the plains, to add richness to the soil, which is not sufficiently enriched by the overflow of the river.

Leaving the tombs to be visited hereafter, I rode

around the wall, and overtook the boat three miles above. At the instant of approaching it I saw three or four large lizards in the river, much like a crocodile in appearance, but destitute of scales. I shot one, and Abd-el-Atti another. The one measured four feet eight inches in length, the other three feet six. These are the monitor lizard, I suppose, celebrated as the enemy of the crocodile, whom they destroy by crawling into his open mouth and down his throat, whence they eat their way out through the animal and destroy him.

A picture of the scene on shore that evening was worth preserving. We lay at the bank, near a small village called *Kella*, and as usual a guard was sent down to watch the boat, lest robbers should make free with our property, and we should thereupon hold the village responsible.

The guard spread their dark boornooses on the ground and slept profoundly. I glanced out of the window late in the evening, and saw Ferraj and Halifa busy, with earnest countenances flashing in the light of a lantern, over the bodies of the lizards, which they were skinning for preservation.

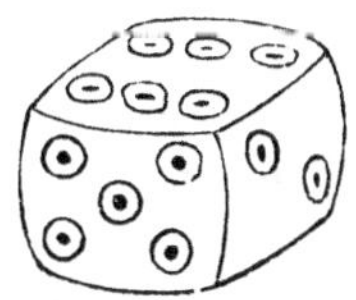

22.

Edfou.

Mohammed Hassan had been sent on from El Kab to Edfou to order sundry provisions that were necessary, and especially charcoal, which we could not obtain above here. In the morning after leaving El Kab when I awoke I saw a group of horses on the bank, keeping along with the boat, which was tracking slowly. It appeared that the governor had sent them down for us to ride up to Edfou in advance of the boat; and accepting them willingly, I mounted one and was off over the fields, attended by Abd-el-Atti and the governor's messenger.

We rode some two miles through the fields of doura, now leaping the trenches, through which the Nile water ran over the fields, and now pushing our way through the standing corn, until at length we struck the dry bed of a canal, full only at very high Nile, and followed this up to the village, high over which we saw the lofty propylon towers of the vast temple.

Speaking of horses; as we rode along, one of the governor's officers told me a story of an old sheik of the Bedouins that I have seen in print in two or three forms, but never precisely in this:

He was old and poor. The latter virtue is common to his race. He owned a tent, a Nubian slave, and a mare; nothing else. The mare was the fleetest animal on the desert. From the Nile to the Euphrates, fame of this animal had gone out, and kings had sought in vain to own her. The love of a Bedouin for his horse is not that fabled affection that we read of in books. This love is the same affection that an American nabob has for his gold, or rather that a poor laborer has for his day's wages. His horse is his life. He can rob, plunder kill, and destroy *ad libitum* if he have a fleet steed. If he have none, he can do nothing, but is the prey of every one who has. Acquisition is a prominent feature of Arab character, but accumulation is not found in the brain of a son of Ishmael. The reason is obvious. If he have wealth he has nowhere to keep it. He would be robbed in a night. He would, indeed, have no desire to keep it; for the Bedouin who murders you for a shawl, or a belt, or some gay trapping, will give it away the next day.

Living this wandering life, the old sheik was rich in this one mare, which was acknowledged to be the fleetest horse in Arabia.

Ibrahim Pasha wished the animal, as his father had wished her before him. He sent various offers to the old sheik, but in vain. At length he sent a deputation, with five hundred purses (a purse is five pounds), and the old man laughed at them.

"Then," said Ibrahim Pasha, "I will take your mare."

"Try it."

He sent a regiment into the desert, and the sheik rode around them, and laughed at them, and the regiment came home.

At last the sheik died from a wound received in a fray with a neighboring tribe. Dying he gave to his Nubian slave all that he had—this priceless mare—and the duties of the blood revenge.

The faithful slave accepted both, and has ever since been the terror of the eastern desert. Yearly he comes down like a hawk on the tents of that devoted tribe, and leaves a ball or a lance in man or woman. No amount of blood satiates his revenge; and the mare and the black rider are as celebrated in Arabia as the wild huntsman in European forests, and much better known.

But one incident interrupted our morning ride. We met two tall men riding on one miserable donkey, and held a temporary court to inquire into the proper punishment that should be administered in the case. It was decided that they should be made to carry the donkey; but the donkey wouldn't be carried, until I made one of them tie his legs together, and take him up, sheep fashion, on his shoulders, with the legs before him. After they had each carried him a hundred yards, we dismissed them with a lecture and rode on to Edfou.

Old Suleiman—that was his name—every body was named Mohammed, or Selim, or Suleiman, or Abdallah, or some derivative of one of these names—old Suleiman, the governor of Edfou, was not at the temple. He had an idea, perhaps, that I would ride to his house and wait on him; but I had a temple in my eye that shut out all governors and governors' houses.

I rode around the rear of the temple, followed by my train, which had now increased to a larger number, and dismounted on the top of the inclosing wall of the grand court, for the earth was banked up to this height on the west side. Entering the stairway of the great tower west of the grand door of the temple, I forbade any human foot to follow me, for I was tired out by the Arabic gabble, and climbed, lonesome, and sole possessor for the time, that grand propylon. At length, coming out on the lofty summit, I threw myself down on the vast stones that crown its top, gazing in silence and profound awe on the court, and corridors, and temple below me.

Where, where are they now? Hackneyed old question, indeed, but I tell you, man, that when you stand on the tower of the temple at Edfou, or in the awful hall of Karnak, you will ask the question with new and overwhelming interest. Gone! gone! and whither? Where are the men, when their works stand here sublime? Where are the maidens, when their voices have not ceased to echo here in choral hymns? Where are the worshipers, when the gods sit yet on their seats, and the altars wait the kindling of the fire and the victims?

It was a golden morning. The sunlight lay like a dream on the Nile valley. Five miles down the river I saw the flag of the *Phantom* slowly tracking up the stream, which approaches within about a mile of the village and temple.

After a little I saw the governor and his suite approaching the temple through a street or lane in the mud village which reached up to the front of the propylon, and after I had finished my inspection of the country I descended to the court where he was waiting me.

Suleiman was a hard-looking old Turk, much the worse for wear and arrakee. When I came back to Edfou I found where he got his arrakee, but of that hereafter. He was attended by a one-eyed scribe, an eight-fingered cawass, and half a dozen minor officials. I was obliged to walk down into town with the old fellow, and to his seat of justice, a bench in an archway on the side of the only mosk at Edfou. I sat on his bench awhile, drank two or three cups of coffee, and smoked a chibouk, and then, very fortunately for my purposes, a funeral procession came up into the open square before the mosk, and the loud wails of the women drowned all conversation and afforded me a chance to escape.

It was the funeral of a child, who was carried on an open bier, and followed by seventy-five or a hundred women. Fresh mourners poured in from every corner and byway and joined them. Each one as she came walked up to the mother of the child, placing one hand tenderly on her head and pressed the forehead gently to the forehead of the old woman, and then looked in her face and uttered a low wail, to which the mother answered.

The latter was a tall, gaunt woman, with one of those faces of Egyptian old women, utter abject woe incarnate. She carried in her hand a stick seven feet long, which she used by way of support as she stalked back and forth in the square, exchanging those mournful salutations and uttering loud laments and praises of her dead boy.

"Is it a boy?" I inquired of the one-eyed scribe of the governor, as the face of the child, calm and unearthly, as are the faces of all dead children, passed my seat after the procession went around the square twice or three times.

"Yes; and he died of a devil."

"Of a devil?"

"Yes; he was well, playing about the house, and he suddenly sprang up and spat on the ground, and fell down dead."

"He choked, did he not?"

"No, it was a devil; a devil entered into him and killed him."

So be it, thought I. It will do you no good to argue the matter. I told the governor I was minded to follow the funeral and see the burial; and as this was out of his line and quite beneath his dignity, he let me go, and I mounted my horse again and joined the procession, which now left the village and wound around the rear of the temple. Here I deserted the funeral, rode back to the sunny side of the temple, and, dismounting, sat down in the dust of old and modern Egypt and called for antiques. In five minutes I was surrounded by a motley crowd, of various colors, and chiefly naked. One girl, a well-shaped child of ten or eleven, improved on the general style of undress by having a single string of beads around her waist. Nothing else on her from head to foot. Her appearance was novel if not picturesque.

I bought the usual quantities of trinkets and coins, and one very beautiful vase, or plate, of clear, translucent stone, much like an agate, but not so hard, with two cupids holding a heart between them. It was as modern as possible in design, but I had sufficient evidence of its antiquity in the place and the price.

The sheik of the field men, that is of the agricultural part of the community, who could always control the discoveries of antiques, promised me to preserve any new treasures that might be dug up until my return, and having exhausted the stock on hand, I remounted and rode through the town again, to go down to the river and rejoin the *Phantom*.

Suleiman was waiting for me. The wily old fellow was not to be baulked of a bottle of brandy, which he made sure he would receive if he hung on, and he fell in behind me on the way to the boat.

I gave him a run of it. His politeness made it necessary for him to keep up with me, and I gave the horse the rein, taking the fields instead of the winding path that led through them to the usual landing-place. The old fellow stuck to his saddle like a cat, and went over trenches where I made sure I should shake him off, as if he had done nothing else but ride steeple-chases all his life, nor did he pull up till I did, at the bank of the river, where the *Phantom* lay along the shore, near a boat which evidently belonged to a man of distinction. Suleiman's face grew some inches longer when he recognized his superior, Mohammed Romali, the nazir of this section. Him I found, seated on a carpet under a sont tree, with Trumbull, and the two were discussing sherbet and chibouks as confidentially as if they had known each other from childhood.

He had arrived a short time before, and had summoned the resident khadi before him to hear a report of the late litigations which he had decided. The khadi had come down, attended by several litigants, and Trumbull, on his arrival, had found the nazir listening to the statements, and affirming or reversing decrees, as the cases were severally laid before him. But he interrupted his court on the arrival of the *Phantom*, and between them they had drank some half-dozen cups of coffee each, and had finished nearly as many pipes of tobacco.

The form of government of Egypt is somewhat of a puzzle to the natives, and to the governors themselves, but Mohammed Roumali, the governor with whom I found Trumbull, informed me of its general nature, and it is somewhat thus:

Every thing here is autocratical. The viceroy is supreme, and makes laws as he pleases, appointing and disappointing, moving and re-moving, as his will inclines. Next to him are the superintendent governors of the three great sections of Egypt. The first section reaches from the sea to a point not far above Cairo. The second section from this point to Semneh, just above the second cataract, and the last from Semneh as far south as the viceroy can collect taxes. Of the second section, which covers all that part of the Nile that travelers ordinarily go over, Latif Pasha is the superintendent governor, exercising supreme power. Although the law requires all sentences of death to be submitted to the viceroy, he does not wait for this, but executes when he pleases. Under him, and as a sort of associate officer, is Abd-el-Kader Bey, who is governor of the same section, under the superintendence of Latif Pasha. Under him again are governors of minor sections, as, for example, Abd-el-Rahman, who is governor from Wâdy Halfeh to the first cataract, and Suleiman Effendi, who is governor from the first cataract to Thebes. Under these governors are traveling governors, who go along the river from place to place, examining the conduct of various villages and cities, hearing appeals from the local magistrates and judges, and attending to similar business. Besides these, each village and city has its local governor, whose power extends only to the next village; every city and village has its sheik, as also has each separate trade or business. Thus the boatmen have their sheik in every large place; the laborers in the field have their sheik; the merchants, the donkey owners, and the water carriers. The office of the sheik is hereditary, descending from father to son.

The interpreter and judge of the law is in the first instance the khadi, who is a sort of clergyman, thoroughly acquainted with the Koran and its provisions. Any man dissatisfied with the decision of a sheik, may go to the khadi, and from him to the nazir. Thus far an appeal is safe. But to carry it further, is risking lands and life, in an autocratical country like this.

The khadi, in this instance, was a sort of chief justice among the khadis hereabouts. He was a plain, elderly man, dressed in the simplest costume—shirt and turban—but a man of dignity, and apparently much respected.

He, too, came on board the boat, and, shortly after, took me aside and begged a prescription for a chronic disease with which he was affected, and which I gave him as cautiously as I could, knowing nothing about the proper treatment. I recommended what I knew would not hurt him, and, as it afterward turned out, I was very fortunate, for on my return to Edfou, three weeks later, he pronounced himself a well man, and, wonderful to relate, attributed it to the medicine.

The charcoal was all in, and still they sat. Old Suleiman had received his congé long ago. The nazir knew what he came for, and found business for him elsewhere; and when he was gone, frankly told us why he sent him away.

I believe it was the first time that Trumbull and myself acknowledged ourselves smoked out. I counted pipes until I was on my eleventh and he must have been on the seventeenth, and there was still no sign of the nazir yielding.

He was a very intelligent man, and talked freely of the state of affairs in Egypt. We picked up much information from him. "Don't be in haste about going," said he, observing certain signs of impatience. "There is no wind, and I will see that you lose nothing by chatting with me an hour or two longer. It's a comfort to meet some one from the lower country. I pass the summer here among these people, and don't see an intelligent man till the travelers begin to come up the river in the winter." And so we filled up our pipes again, and went at it afresh.

I like tobacco moderately and immoderately, nor have I any hesitation in pronouncing myself a judge of tobacco. And, strange as it may seem, although on first tasting it, I condemned Latakea as no tobacco at all, I became at length inordinately fond of it, and smoked it in quantities incredible.

The tobacco of the East is of many varieties. The Turkish, or Stambouli, found in Constantinople bazaars, is strong, somewhat sharp, and not pleasant. It is now imported to America in quantities, and may be bought anywhere in New York. It is of light color, and very finely cut, so as to appear almost like threads. In flavor, to lips that have been pleased with genuine Latakea, the Stambouli is detestable.

Next comes Syrian Jebeli, or mountain tobacco—a

fine-flavored article, but acrid, and although preferable to Stambouli, it is stronger than Latakea, and inferior in delicacy. My American taste led me to mix it with the Latakea, and thus bring the latter up to the strength of good Cuba tobacco; but, as I grew to liking the Latakea, I dropped the Jebeli entirely. Egypt has its *beledi* tobacco, that is the native tobacco of the country, and it is of the lowest grade. The common people use it, and not infrequently it is inflicted on guests by village sheiks and petty officials, as I remember to my cost at Abou Girg.

There are two cities of old times known to history as *Laodicea:* the one Laodicea of Asia Minor, celebrated as the site of one of the seven churches; the other in Syria, on the sea coast, not far from the north-east corner of the Mediterranean. In wandering through that country I found the place, a modern Syrian village, in the heart of which stood two stately ruins of Roman glory, a temple and perhaps a tomb. In this latter city, Latakea, as it is now called, much tobacco is sold. It is carefully prepared in a way not elsewhere known, by hanging the leaves in a smoke-house, and burning under them chips of a fragrant wood. This it is which gives to the tobacco that slight taste of smoke which Burton and other travelers mention without knowing its origin, and which leads them to condemn it. It is mostly sent to Egypt, where the demand is never supplied. Little of the best Latakea travels elsewhere, and I have sent to Cairo for all that I have imported since my return, being certain of getting the best there. Its fragrance is ambrosial, its effects on brain and nerves beyond description calm.

Come and see me some evening, O my friend, and we will close the windows, and drop the curtains, and shut out the sight, if not the sound, of the rattling, driving, furious western world, and you shall wrap my old and travel-stained boomoose around you, crown your head with my tarbouche that has been wet with the spray of the second cataract of the Nile, the sea of Galilee, the frozen dews of Hermon, and the waters of the Pharpar, and you shall sip mocha (veritable akwa of the orient), black and fragrant as the drink of gods, while we make the air blue with the delicious aroma of Latakea, fit for the shapes and shades that haunt my memories of the East, which you shall share.

Mohammed Roumali kept his promise, that we should not suffer by our delay. While he talked, his messengers had collected the people in all directions, and he had at length a hundred fellaheen waiting his orders. At three in the afternoon he went ashore, and they took hold of the tow-rope, and went up the bank with a will. It was child's-play to them, so many on one boat, and they drew us in two hours further than our own men would have been able to track in a day. The current above Edfou is very strong, and the assistance was most timely. Toward evening a light breeze sprang up, and, taking in the tow-rope, we shot ahead of the dusky group, who stood in a body on the shore, and watched us for a long time as we went up the river.

23.

The Tower of Syene.

I WAS roused from a sound sleep by a terrible row on shore. My room was six feet by four, of which four two feet were occupied by my bed. Trumbull's room, of the same size, was opposite to mine, and the entire stern of the boat was in one room, which was occupied by the ladies. I raised myself on my elbow high enough to look out of my window which stood open day and night, and seeing a general skirmish going on between the crew and some natives, I seized my koorbash and sprang from the window to the bank.

The appearance of the Howajji suspended hostilities, and I now learned for the first time that Mohammed Roumali had placed an officer on the boat with orders, whenever the wind failed, to press fellaheen into service on the tow-rope, so that our lost time at Edfou should be fully made up. We could not, without incivility, refuse this aid, and yet it was by no means pleasant, except in the result. Leaving the cawass to exercise his authority, I turned back to the boat and we pushed, or rather they pulled us, on. Ten minutes later there was a loud outcry on the bank; Abd-el-Atti rushed into the cabin for his pistols and I followed him out with mine, under a sort of imagination that not less than a thousand Bedouins must be in the neighborhood waiting to attack us.

The crew, taken mightily with the notion of getting help on the tow-rope, had organized in a sort of roving party, and with the cawass at their head were marching about three hundred yards from the river, where they could cut off all natives who attempted to escape inland and drive them down to the tow-rope. By this means they had now about fifty and were in high spirits, as indeed were those that were caught, who the moment they were at work, entered into the pleasure of catching others. The rascals so much enjoyed entrapping their friends that I lost all pity for them. But the crew had met their match in a group of nearly forty natives who were assembled in an opening among the standing corn, and who had gotten the idea that a government boat was coming to catch and press them for soldiers in the army of Said Pasha. Death has no such horror for Egyptians as this fate of being pressed as a soldier. To avoid it they cut off their fingers, pluck out their eyes, and mutilate themselves in every way.

The little group were assembled with all the determination of rebels in a brave cause, and as the cawass made his appearance through the corn, a lance went by his head within an inch of it, and struck the shoulder of Hassan Hegazi, but being nearly spent wounded him but slightly. A tremendous yell from both sides announced the determination of both to fight out the battle thus commenced, and Abd-el-Atti hearing it rushed to the rescue with the Howajji close behind him. The combatants were still facing each other when we arrived, and Hassan brought me the spear which I preserved as a trophy and have with me now. The arrival of fire-arms put an end to the contest. The poor feellaheen dropped on their knees and begged for mercy.

Abd-el-Atti explained to them what was wanted of them, and their faces lit up with delight, while the scoundrels instantly proposed to inveigle all the men of a neighboring village into the trap. But at this moment a breeze came and we hastened on board, drew in the track-rope, scattered a liberal bucksheesh on shore, and were away. News flies swiftly even in Egypt. For miles up the river the shadoofs were deserted, the corn fields empty, nor could we see man, or woman, or child, so that you would have thought the land deserted of its inhabitants, such was their terror of the government boat.

I regretted the whole circumstance as exceedingly painful, nor have I yet forgiven myself the pain of apprehension that I unwittingly inflicted on these poor wretches already weighed down with the oppression of their miserable life.

Toward evening the breeze freshened and blew a steady gale. In a clear laughing moonlight we entered the narrow pass at Hagar Silsilis, and swept with a full sail and a long swinging roll through this rocky gate of the upper country, catching in dim outline the carved grottos that adorn the western shore, and the high rock from which the gorge derives its name.

Of this more when I come down the river.

As we rushed out of the pass into a broad, moonlit, lake-like sheet of water, we saw a boat lying at the shore, and then with a thump that sent every thing flying over the deck, we struck a sand bar, and were fast aground.

Perhaps this was the twentieth time since we left Cairo, and, as in each former instance, a dozen of the crew were overboard in an instant, heaving under the side of the boat. It was an hour before we got off and dropped down stream again to stand up another channel. We passed a boat that was lying at the shore, little dreaming then, that by the light that flashed out on the Nile were sitting two Americans, although we might have guessed it had we reflected that our friends,

Mr. and Mrs. Martin, had left Es Siout a day before us, and where somewhere hereabout.

Early the next morning we were under the high bluff on which stands the temple of Koum Ombos, and we climbed the hill before breakfast, all four of us, to see the ruins and the view up the river.

The temple was founded in the time of Ptolemy Philometor, B. C. 180, and continued and completed during the reigns of his successors, and is singular in being, as it were, a double temple, having two shrines, in which two contemplar gods were worshiped, the one in each.

There is a gateway of another temple standing, but the stone of the temple itself is fallen down the hill, and lies in irregular masses even to the edge of the water. No one can even trace the former shape of this building. The chief interest in looking at the large temple consists in the fact that its sculptures were never wholly finished, and the marks of the artists, the outline drawings of the figures, and the squares into which the surface of the stone was marked out before drawing the figures, all remain freshly visible, even to the places where the chisel had but touched the rock. There is something melancholy in the unfinished painting of a dead painter, the half-hewn marble of a dead sculptor, the half-written song of a dead poet. How much more oppressive the melancholy, where the painter and sculptor have been dead two thousand years, and the stone remains as it was left, and the lines still stand on the surface!

While we stood looking out alternately to the south and to the north-west, the boat of our American friends came up the river with a fair breeze, and we ran hastily down the sloping side of the hill, plunging our feet into the loose desert sand, and were on board as the first breath of wind reached us. We dashed up the river rapidly, and as the breeze freshened to almost a gale, we flew before it. The golden sands now came down to the edge of the water on both sides of us, often seeming ready to overflow and destroy the groups of palms that stood on the shore. As we approached Es Souan the villages improved in appearance, and every thing seemed to be smiling. Even the desert was beautiful, exceedingly, and the sky was glorious.

Hassabo, the steersman, the best man on the boat, had his family in a small village below Es Souan, and of course must take this opportunity to see them. As we could not ascend the cataract till the next day, we gave him leave of absence to rejoin us above the cataract, and he made ready his baggage and the little presents he had brought from Cairo.

All along the bank of the river, for miles before we reached the village, his acquaintances hailed him, and he exchanged with them the graceful phrases of eastern salutation. The news of his approach ran along the shore faster than we flew, and many voices out of the fields and villages hailed us with shouts of "welcome Hassabo!" At length we came up to a group of dark-faced persons (for Hassabo is a Nubian, and black), and here we let the sheet fly, and the boat's keel scraped the sand. Over flew all his baggage far up the bank, and then Hassabo sprang into his mother's arms. The old woman stood trembling on the shore, looking wistfully for him till he left the boat. Then she threw her arms around him, and clasped him close, and wept over him, and kissed his cheeks, and all the time he stood silent and motionless, only looking at her and the surrounding group. She touched his cheeks and his hands as if, like old Isaac, her eyesight were dim, and she would know him by the softness of his shining skin, and then she laid her withered hand on the top of his head, and leaned forward and threw herself again on his breast. Yea—verily—it was her boy.

O, Philip, my friend, who will read these lines as if you heard my voice speaking them, you will understand how my heart yearned to that mother, though she was black and poor. There was a day, long, long after that, when another wanderer reached his mother's house, and found her alone where he had left her with his father's presence. And when the far-traveled boy pressed her quivering lips, though it was in a sunny American home, among trees and vines, and with fair white faces around them, his heart went back to the cataract and black Hassabo and his glad old mother.

We stood on deck in front of the cabin doors, and looked admiringly on the scene. The crew entered into it with keen delight, and as the sheet was hauled home, and they heaved her bow from the shore, they gave three genuine hurras, as we had taught them how, for Hassabo, and on rushed the *Phantom* to far Syene. It was three in the afternoon when we dashed by the hill on which stands the ruined citadel, and among the rocks which here fill the bed of the river, and fired our salute to the cataract as we came to the land at its foot under the tower of Syene.

Here, again, was a point in my wanderings that was full of interest, as one of the ancient boundaries of the world. Here, in old days, men paused, and hesitated, and turned back. The dwellers beyond Syene were unknown heathen. But here were four travelers from a land beyond the Pillars of Hercules, who had come thus far to look at Syene, and pass its rocky barriers, and go on to a more distant point, whose feet had already traveled six thousand miles from home, and would walk many thousand more before they returned to that threshold again. The world ended here, and the world ends not far from here now;

but men live beyond, and temples and palaces lie in ruins beyond, and the palm-trees flourish, and the Nile flows, and yet, if all that lies beyond Syene were blotted out of existence, swept off from the chart of the world and the page of history, who would miss any thing? Verily the world ends just here.

A crowd were waiting for us at Es Souan. Being the first boat of the season, we were likely to be victimized by all the venders of curiosities, and they manifestly regarded us as legitimate prey. There were sellers of gigantic ebony clubs, the weapon of the Abyssinians, and rhinoceros hide shields, wherewith to ward off the blows of the clubs, and there were naked children with baskets, curiously plaited, and pipes of clay well made and well burned, and koorbashes, and dates, and ostrich eggs, and all sorts of antiques from Elephantine.

The crowd beset the shore, alongside the boat. When I went ashore, hearing my name called out in good English, they turned it into Arabic precisely as all others had done, and shouted, "Braheem Pasha, buy our wares."

After a vain attempt to stroll quietly along the shore, we took refuge in our small boat, and pulled across to the island of Elephantine.

The glory of Elephantine has departed long ago. In ancient days its temples and palaces surpassed in splendor all the fables of antiquity. No wealth could again rear such buildings; no nation of modern times, with all the wealth of modern days, could erect one such temple, much less the hundred that crowded this sacred island. Here magnificence and beauty held their court and swayed the hearts of men. Here alternate love and hate, and all the passions of the human breast, held for their brief times the reins of power. Here men reigned, women loved, kings and priests and princes lived and died, and the change came, and time trod on them and crushed the palaces, and the avenging angel swept his wing over them, and their very dust went away on the wind. Elephantine lay in the Nile, and other nations took the place of Egypt in the roll of time. There is, perhaps, no place in Egypt that, could it have a voice, would utter more strange and splendid histories of men and kings than this island.

It lies in the river, from the foot of the cataract, stretching down in front of Es Souan about a mile, and is nearly half a mile in breadth. It surface is a mass of ruins, shapeless and hideous. Ruin sits triumphant here. Not even the plowshare of ancient history, which has run over so many ruins, could prevail here to penetrate the mass. A small part of the island is cultivated, but a large portion still remains in the condition I have described, and so will remain so long as the world stands. Fragments of statues, a gateway of the time of the mighty son of Philip, an altar whose fire was long ago extinguished in the blood of its worshipers; these and similar relics remain; but nothing to indicate the shape, extent, or date of any of the buildings that formerly covered the island.

On the shore a group of Nubian girls met us with their small worked baskets and mats, and a few antiques, for sale. They were the first specimens of the Nubians we had seen at their homes, and they were as different a race from the Egyptians as we ourselves. Black in color, but with sharply-cut features and beautiful eyes, they are as fine-looking a people as the world can produce. Nor do they hide their beauties. The full costume of the unmarried females is a simple leathern girdle around the waist, with a fringe hanging a few inches below it. There was one girl among those at Elephantine that was exceedingly beautiful. She was tall, slender, and graceful as a deer, and quite as timid.

She would not approach us near enough to offer her mats for sale, but coming within ten feet would start suddenly, and spring into the air like a fawn and dart away, and then coming slowly back approach us as nearly again, only to retreat in the same way. Her face was the soul of fun, and her eyes were brimful of laughter. We watched her for half an hour, offering her money to induce her to come nearer, but we were obliged at length to lay it down and let her take it up when we had gone three or four yards away, and then she stooped with her eyes fixed on us, never removing her gaze. We wandered over the island until sunset and dark, and then, when the moon was bright, we rowed up the river into the gorge between the island and the rocky bluff above Es Souan, and let our boat drift slowly down by the ruined temples and the dark rocks.

I found the cabin of the *Phantom* in possession of a fat and comfortable looking Copt, in a rich dress, who called himself American agent at Es Souan. I knew that Mustapha at Luxor was the only agent on the Nile above Cairo, but the fellow was so sincere about it that I couldn't doubt his own belief that he held some such official appointment.

As he wanted the opportunity to make a little money out of us, and as I wanted nothing at Es Souan so much as three or four handsome koorbashes as ladies' riding-whips (for they carve them very skillfully), I requested him to bring some down early the next morning, as we were going to leave in the forenoon; and so getting rid of him, we had time for dinner, coffee, and profound slumber.

Early in the morning Trumbull and myself walked out alone into the vast cemetery that almost surrounds Es Souan. The tombs extend over miles square of desert, and date from the very earliest periods of Islam. It is the largest and the most desolate burial-place in the world.

No tree sheds its leaves on the mounds, no blade of grass springs up to cheer the mourners with the emblem of resurrection. Not one solitary palm looks heavenward from this dry, sandy waste of death.

Near the village, just at sunrise, we saw a funeral ceremony, but did not pause. We wandered an hour in the hollows and over the hills of this curious Golgotha, and then climbed a hill that overlooks the outlet of the cataract, and lay down on the sandy summit to gaze on Elephantine and the Nile.

"Ya Braheem Effendi—Braheem Effendi."

The shout came as if from the tombs themselves. Deep down in the hollow we saw two Arabs leading horses, and they seeing us, came up the hill to say that the governor of Es Souan was at his diwan, and had sent horses to request us to honor him with a morning visit. We had not yet breakfasted, but promising to see him after breakfast (he had called on us the evening previous, and wasted a half-hour of his and our time in dull formalities of talk), we cantered down to the boat.

The soi-disant American agent was waiting for us outside the cabin with his pile of koorbashes. Ferraj had wisely kept him out lest he should spoil by his presence one of Hajji Mohammed's inimitable breakfasts. He apologized for not coming earlier, as he said his son had died in the night and he was detained in the morning to bury him. He was as cool about it as if he had spoken of a dog, and this sudden change in his family since he had parted from us the evening before—a son sick in bed then, but buried three feet deep now—did not appear to him a matter worth mentioning except by way of apology for his delay. Such hasty burial is the eastern custom. Doubtless this was the burial we had seen.

The expense of taking the boat up the cataract was, as the reader already knows, no concern of ours, but Abd-el-Atti was in a fair way to be swindled unless we would aid him in person, and we consented.

Every one who has read books on Egypt is familiar with the fact, that the first cataract of the Nile has been from time immemorial under the charge of a reis or captain, who monopolized the fees for dragging boats up its rapids. Of late years the increase of travel has been so great that there are four reises in partnership who attend to the business; and it is so profitable withal that they have a great many other persons in the partnership, even to the governor at Es Souan himself, who, for the sake of having his own boat taken up free, as well as for the sake of part of the pay, never interferes with the reises of the cataract in their rapacity.

But we were fortified with a firman from his highness; and if it were of no use here, it was not likely that it would be any where. Besides this, a letter from Latif Pasha to the governor at Es Souan, and another from Abd-el-Kader Bey, instructed him to pay special attention to us. We accordingly sent him word to have the reises of the cataract at his diwan, where we would meet them. As soon as breakfast was over we went up to the residence, where we found the governor already in conclave with the *shellalee*, or men of the cataract.

Old Reis Hassan was conspicuous for his gray beard and broad shoulders. He is celebrated in story, as was his father before him. Bag Boug was a giant, a bony Nubian, gaunt and stout-framed, with an eye like a devil's, and an arm like a Titan's. The other two, Ibrahim and Selim, were younger and more silent; but the four looked abundantly able to lift the boat on their shoulders and carry it over the hills. We had manifestly broken in on a consultation among the worthies, in which the governor's son-in-law, a sharp-looking Greek, had taken a conspicuous part. He was apparently governor of the old man.

We sat down on dingy cushions, and accepted pipes and coffee before the conference began, and at length opened the subject by requesting the governor to inform us what the reis of the cataract proposed to do for us.

The governor hesitated a moment, and his ready son-in-law answered for him, that the reis said our boat was too heavy and large to go up the cataract at all.

We smoked a while in silence, deliberating on this communication, and, in the mean time, I was looking over the faces of the four reises, and studying out their separate capacities and influence with each other.

"Our boat has been up the cataract every year for four years."

This was no answer. That a thing has been done once or four times is no reason that it can be done again in Egypt.

"She will break. The water is very low this year. It was earlier when she went up before."

"It was February last."

This was a point-blank difference, but it produced no effect. We conversed a few moments in English, and then smoked silently a while.

"Very well; we have given up the idea of going up the cataract."

"There are very good boats to be had at Es Souan that will go up the cataract easily."

This meant that the governor or his son and the shellalee had a boat that they would like to force us to hire.

"There isn't a boat within five hundred miles of Es Souan fit for an American to go in. We are going back."

This was a poser.

"Perhaps, if you took out the kitchen, the stores, and all the baggage, she might be light enough."

"Perhaps she would; but if we go up at all we go as

we are. But we have given up going. We will go down the river this afternoon. Perhaps the governor will forward a letter for us to Abd-el-Kader Bey?"

There was a strong hint in this suggestion, and the governor felt it. There was another brief time of smoke and silence, and Bag Boug then growled out his opinion. He did not see any difficulty in taking the boat up if there were men enough to pull her. But it would cost a great deal.

"How much?"

A long silence. Hassan spoke suggestingly, "Fifteen hundred piastres."

I looked at him, at the governor, at his son-in-law, laid down my chibouk, gathered my shawl around me, and walked toward the door.

"Tell the governor I will send a letter for Abd-el-Kader Bey, which I wish him to despatch immediately, and we will sail as soon as possible."

The governor sprang to his feet, and the reises united in making a new proposition. One thousand piastres would cover it all. I came out and left them. Then Abd-el-Atti thundered at them.

"What is the use of the effendi having his highness's letter if this is all he gets by it? When did you ever get a thousand piastres for taking a boat up the cataract? You are all a set of thieves together. I understand you, and Braheem Effendi understands you, and I can tell you that when Abd-el-Kader Bey hears of it he will make you move up here. He will understand it, too, eh? What do you think he will say, eh? when he hears that the gentleman with his highness's letter could not go up the cataract, eh?"

They endeavored to soothe him, and gradually came down in their offers, and at length he got a chance to speak to old Hassan alone, and whispered to him a promise of an extra bucksheesh above the contract price, unknown to the others. This converted Hassan, and he yielded slowly to the offer of four hundred piastres, which the others finally came to most reluctantly, and then it was closed, and I returned to the room.

The next question came to be discussed: this was the when. It was now eleven o'clock, and of course too late to go up to-day.

"Why too late?"

"No one can go up without starting very early in the morning."

"How long does it take?"

"Two days; one day to go up to the foot of the last fall, the next to go up *the gate* (which is the first great fall at the head of the cataract)."

"Two days! In the name of the Prophet what is the use of taking two days? It ought to be done in four hours, and it can and must."

"Impossible!"

"There's no such word in America. The thing must be done. It is now eleven—not yet noon. We must be at Philæ by sunset. We will not spend another night here, or in the cataract. Up the river or down, whichever the reises please," and I left them disputing.

At length they came to it, and then the troop came down to the river, the old governor leading, and the procession following. We had crossed to Elephantine again, but returned when we saw the procession, and instantly made all ready for a start. The governor remained long enough to smoke a pipe, and endeavored to retrieve his character by telling all sorts of stories of the shellalee, laying the blame of the slow contract to them. I suspected him the more for his anxiety to be rid of the imputation, and having bowed him ashore, we were ready to start.

For the benefit of travelers who pay their own way up the Nile, I record the terms of the contract as concluded.

For four hundred piastres they were to take us up and down the cataract, but in addition to this there was a private agreement with old Hassan to give him a hundred and fifty more. Half the money to be paid on the safe delivery of the boat at Philæ, and the other half on her safe return to Es Souan after the completion of our Nubian voyage.

Mr. and Mrs. Martin were going no further than Es Souan, but joined us on board the *Phantom* to go up the cataract with us, and return from Philæ on donkeys.

The reises were in good spirits, and as well satisfied as if their utmost demands had been yielded to. They only begged us to inform every body, as they would, that we had paid a thousand piastres, and help them raise the price this year.

We stowed away all glass and movables, lashed every thing that was likely to be thrown down, and then, with a shout and a salute of ten guns, we dashed away before a grand breeze, and, rounding the bluff of black basalt, which frowns over the upper end of Elephantine, we breasted the last rush of the rapids, which are called the Cataract of the Nile.

24.

The First Cataract.

THE cataract is not a cataract in any sense to Americans. It is but a rapid, broken up by thousands of boulders of granite and black basalt. One might well imagine that here occurred the battle between Jupiter and the Titans, and that the rocks hurled against the throne of the Thunderer fell back here, shattered and broken, but gigantic still. Every where through the cataract these rocks lie, piled on each other, or singly, black and polished, above the foaming river. The cataract is not narrow. The river, in fact, spreads out as wide as in any other part of its length, and the rocks lie across its entire breadth. The length of the cataract is not more than four miles. The principal descent of water is at its head, where the river comes down through a narrow pass called the Gate. Below this it is broken up, and turned, and vexed, and dashed hither and thither, but there is no great fall at any point.

Still the water was black, and dashed furiously against our bows, as if to warn us back from the far-famed barriers of Syene. A moment later we swept around the point, the rocks closed before and behind us, and we were in a lake-like inclosure. But there was nothing lake-like in the waves that dashed around us as never lake was vexed. The wind was now a gale, and howled over our heads, and drove the boat into the current, whose strength increased at each moment. Two miles of this navigation, turning frequently short around rocks, now skirting the edge of a foaming mass, now sliding with a grating jar over a smooth stone that lay hidden under the boiling foam, brought us to a point where the river came down several passages through the rocks into the one broad stream up which we had come.

Selecting the easternmost passage, down which the waters poured in yellow foam, we breasted the current with a full sail and straining spars. The *Phantom* rushed at it as if she knew what was before her, and enjoyed the contest. Just so I have seen her gallant namesake breast the rushing ebb-tide off Watch-hill, in a stiff north-easter, coming up before it, and rolling heavily, but plunging through bravely.

The water flew from the bow, and the short ascent was almost won, when she hesitated, trembled, and then, slowly yielding, she paused.

We were all on deck among the men, the three ladies seated in front of the cabin door, and the gentlemen standing by them. There was just wind enough to hold us where we were; and we stood in the middle of the stream, neither progressing nor receding.

Reis Hassan looked up stream and down stream, now on this and now on that side. Sellm was steadfast at the tiller, Ibrahim was on the look-out forward, and Bag Boug was every where at once.

The old man watched the full and straining sail; and as he saw her slowly yield and give back to the heavy rush of the river, he shouted for a rope, and, seizing the coils of the heavy *liban* (the tow-rope), dropped his turban, two tarbouches, and all his clothes, quick as lightning, and sprang into the furious current. Ten strokes of his powerful arms, and he was on a black rock, around which the water was raging. From this he dived again, up stream, and disappeared. The next instant he came above water, far up stream. No human power could swim that distance in that current. He had, doubtless, helped himself along by rocks on the bottom of the stream; but he had never let go his hold on the heavy rope. A dozen Nubians followed him, made the rope fast around a rock directly ahead of us, and then, throwing themselves into the stream, came flying down to the boat, which they caught as they swept by, and swung themselves in, and all hands commenced hauling with a tremendous chorus of "Hah, Allah!" All this occupied a briefer time than I have taken to describe it, and the boat was still breasting the stream; but now she began to go up, up, with every repeat of the chorus, until, just as she was on the very crest of the rapid, and entering the smooth water, crack! The rope flew high in the air as it parted, and she sagged over to the side of the passage, and thumped heavily on the rocks, where she rested.

The shouts that arose from fifty Arab throats drowned the roar of the waters as this mishap occurred; but in a moment twenty men were in the water, other ropes were carried forward, and then, with a long, steady haul, she was swung off the rocks into the stream, and up into a safe eddy at the top of this part of the cataract, the men swimming to her from all directions, and she flying on before the wind to the next place of trial.

Again, as before, the wind carried us half way up this; and then the black skins flashed through the water, and ropes were sent out to the rocks, and she was drawn into an eddy half way up, where she rested again a moment. Here I was not a little surprised to see her headed into a narrow passage, not ten yards wide, down which the water fell a foot or eighteen inches in a hundred feet.

The broader stream foamed and dashed high up on the rocks, around which it flowed. This passage seemed deeper, and Reis Hassan knew his business. It was evident that sheer lifting alone could get the boat up this fall, and three ropes were got out while we lay in the eddy. Old Hassan sprang to the rocks, and threw a handful of dust into the air. In an instant men started up in every part of the rocky bed of the Nile. The valley that a moment before had seemed to be only the abode of rocks and the great river, where from hill to hill there was only black stone and white foam, now swarmed with life, and three hundred men, women, and children, rushed down to the boat to aid in the hauling, and claim their share of the reward. The children, whose name was Legion, stood on the shore and shouted "Bucksheesh Howajji!" in every tone conceivable, while some threw themselves into the current, and came dancing down the water, and went by us in a twinkling, soon coming up, with their logs or floats on their shoulders, to claim their pay.

We were ready for another attempt. Bag Boug made his appearance at the cabin door, where I was standing. He was wet, and cold, and shivering. He begged hard. Bag Boug is always wet, and cold, and shivering, and always wants brandy. We had a lot on board, reserved for such purposes. Possibly the reader remembers my purchase of it in the Mouski from the ancient gentleman into whose arms my donkey threw me. Old Hassan never drinks, and I did not care how drunk the others were, for he was, after all, the man of the party. I handed Bag Boug the glass—a large tumbler—and a bottle to pour for himself. He filled the tumbler to the brim, and poured it down his throat as if it were water, and while I looked on in astonishment he repeated the dose. On my honor that shellalee drank a full pint of raw brandy without a wink, and there was not in his conduct afterward the slightest indication that he was affected by it. His throat must be copper to stand such stuff as that was.

We were now all ready; and fifty men took hold of the ropes, and as many more stood on the rocks to keep her off and push when they could. Up, up, up! But she paused again. Twenty good steady men to haul would have sent her up; but the Arabs pulled one at a time, and they could not move her. As she went back, we all sprang to the ropes, and three Americans hauling did more than thirty Arabs. She went forward, the water parted over her bow, she shot up the fall and on into the eddy before the gate of the cataract.

Down this gate the Nile pours in one solid stream, parting instantly around a hundred rocks. As we shot forward in the eddy before the strong wind, we struck a rock, and ran high up on it. Fifty men were under her instantly, swimming till they found points of rock on which to rest their feet, and then lifting and pushing, and as she sank off and floated, they swam hither and thither like fish, and we ran on to the foot of the gate.

Here large and strong preparations were necessary for the final pull, and while these were in process we went on shore to see how the boat looked in the current. This was a view not to be lost; and we clambered on the rocks to a high point overlooking the boat and the crowd, which was steadily increasing. I think there were a hundred naked boys and girls around us vociferating for bucksheesh. Whips and clubs were of no use whatever. They thronged us.

The boat certainly looked gallantly, and most gallant of all was Hajji Mohammed, our prince of cooks. I think I have mentioned that the kitchen occupies the extreme bow of the boat, forward of the mast; and as there is no bowsprit or forward rigging, there was nothing to interrupt the view forward from his stand. But he was steadily at work boning a fowl, and attending to his usual duties as quietly as if she were lying at anchor in a calm. A dozen naked Nubians were sitting forward of the kitchen, and clinging to its sides, but he paid no attention to them whatever, nor did he once cease his work in all the passage of the cataract. Enough for him that we had ordered an early dinner, and he was hastening it as fast as possible.

Now they announced the boat ready for her last trial. An immense hawser was made fast literally around the boat, and this was long enough for two hundred men to take hold of. The sail was stowed away; no one could manage it in this place. And now with a long steady song, and as steady a pull as they could make, the *Phantom* entered the gate and mounted the rapid, and emerged from Egypt into Nubia up the last reach of the cataract. Tumbling overboard every body but the reises and their immediate attendants, with the sails shaken out to the breeze, we swept on, now to the left, around a lofty pile of rocks, and now to the right, opening before us the loveliest view in all Egypt, perhaps in all the world, the burial-place of Osiris, the beautiful Philæ.

The island of Philæ, lying at the head of the cataract of the Nile, is in one of the most wild and picturesque spots on the face of the earth. High black rocks, heaped up to the sky, lie all around it; and from any point of view, it is a jewel set in a rough inclosure, to make it the more beautiful by contrast. The entire surface of the island is covered with ruins, the great temple of Isis, which is the most perfect among them, occupying the western side. It is not of a very ancient period. One learns in Egypt to call every thing modern that is not three thousand years old; and the temples of the Ptolemies are of less interest after one begins to learn the history of the Pharaohs of older times, and look on their monuments. It is a strange passion this that men have for the old. What is it in the intellect of man that makes him do such homage to age—to great age? Is it because we always admire the inaccessible, and that we, whose dust holds together but seventy years, therefore admire the dust that has outlived thirty centuries? Not so; because the hills and mountains of our own country are old enough for all that. It is not age alone. It is something in the fact, that human hands wrought on these rocks; that human intellect shaped and planned their order. It is the memorial of dead men's thoughts to which we bow in reverence; and perhaps it is somewhat akin to our own desires after immortality. Perhaps the feverish thirst of the boy for fame—the thirst that long life can never satisfy—is somewhat similar to the profound awe with which he looks on the carved name of an ancient king, or the exquisite sculpture of an ancient artist. And men are but grown-up boys; and the boy's anxiety for fame may have vanished among the more immediate and practical desires of manhood, but the admiration for the fame of others, and the veneration for the mere approximation to immortality which he fancies he sees in the ruins of old temples and palaces, lingers with him; nor does it leave him ever.

But there is something more than all this, which we all feel, but which none of us can well explain, when we look on an ancient ruin, and which makes the difference between old hills and old houses. If one fell on the ruin of an ancient shop, wherein men of old times bought and sold goods and wares, there would not be any very profound admiration excited, nor would he sit down long to reflect on the scenes which had occurred within those walls. Still less did he discover a butcher's stall or a drinking-shop. The ordinary employments of men in former ages interest us, but only momentarily.

We stroll through Pompeii with interest, astonishment, and melancholy delight, if I may use the expression, and we remember its shops and counters as curious places, but we scarcely think of the men that stood in those shops and bought and sold by those weights and measures. But what thrilling imagination does that mould of a young breast arouse! The memorials of the hearts of ancient men and women, of their great emotions, their passions, most challenge our respect and fix our minds. The houses in which they lived remind us of these, in that we recall the home scenes, the thousand affections of home; and man's love always sanctifies a place. But the palaces in which they reigned, where all day long, and all the year long, were heard the sounds of royalty, with which are always mingled the fiercest emotions of humanity, the temples in which their altar fires burned, and their hearts burned as well, these are the places in which the foot of the thoughtful man lingers, from daylight and sunshine till sunset and moonlight hallow them with softer rays, and around which he sees always in sunshine or moonlight the flitting shadows of ancient memories. Altars are crumbled, and altar fires have long been quenched, but the memory of men's worship remains to sanctify, and the impress of their tears is visible in the crumbling pavements.

Philæ was the most sacred spot in Egypt. Hither, from all directions, men came for worship. But none were admitted to set their feet on the sacred island except by special order. Here was the fabled burial-place of Osiris, or near here, for antiquarians dispute much on this point. But in the temple of Isis is now found a remarkable subterranean vault, near the holy of holies, from which a concealed stairway passes through the solid walls of the temple up to the roof, and which gives every indication of having been used by the priests for their secret purposes, possibly to show to strangers as the grave of the great Osiris.

But for the present I have nothing to do with ancient Philæ. It is only the modern; the palm-trees and the ruins; the fallen altars and columns that I have to speak of. They lay in the utmost beauty of desolateness as the moonlight came over them that night, and we wandered about among their wastes.

Again I might write, as I have written before, never was such moonlight—certainly never was such a place for moonlight. It fell on the columns of the ancient temple at the upper end of the island, and the small obelisk seemed to grow larger in the silver light. It lingered in the great court of the temple of Isis, as if it loved the memories that resided there. But purest, holiest of all, it fell in the open temple on the eastern side of the island, where Miriam and I sat silently as the night swept along with its load of glory, while the others wandered up and down the island looking vainly for one spot more beautiful than another.

Our American friends were with us still, and it was now time for their return to Es Souan. Donkeys had been ordered to be ready for them on the opposite side of the river, and, taking them in the small boat, I pulled across to the main land. The boys stood under the palm-trees, but when they were mounted and ready to be away, I could not permit them to go alone and unattended through the wildest and perhaps the most dangerous mountain pass in Egypt; for the men of the cataract—the *shellalee*, as they are called—are not much more merciful or human in disposition than the wolves and hyenas which abound among their hills, and I felt unwilling to trust my friends—one of them a young and delicate lady—to the mercy of either class of brutes. So I accompanied them myself, with a six-barrelled Colt and an endless volcanic repeater. I walked along by their side in pleasant talk across the arm of the desert on which stands the village, under a branching sycamore that grew up from the very sand itself, and then into the wilderness of rocks that lie as the hands of the Almighty cast them, here and there and everywhere, on the east bank of the river. It was a strange group that, for such a scene and such a night. Sometimes the donkeys climbed the sides of rocks on which their feet seemed scarcely able to retain foothold; often they passed through narrow chasms, that seemed impassable till we had tried them. The hills grew higher on the right, the noise of the cataract louder on the left, the scene more wild, the moonlight more beautiful. And so we continued until I had accompanied them beyond the mountain pass and into the more open and safe country which lies along the line of the portage from Es Souan around the cataract, and here I left them to pursue their way downward to their boat, and thence to Cairo, while I turned my back and again resumed my way southward toward the tropic, toward Abou Simbal and the second cataract.

I know no point in my wanderings at which I felt so much the distance from home, or that I was leaving all that bound and connected me to that home as here.

Behind me lay Egypt. Close behind me the only two Americans (except ourselves) within almost a thousand miles, had their faces turned northward, and were leaving us to our lonesome journey. Around me was desolation, its very abode, where the rock and desert held every thing. At my right the roar of the rapid, sounding as when the Greeks heard it, warned me, as it warned the Romans of old, that I had passed "far Syene," and that the world lay behind me and unknown wastes before. Grim, silent, solemn rocks, lifting their dark countenances in the air, looked on me with stern gaze, that sometimes seemed, in the clear moonlight, to change into a smile of contempt, and sometimes into a sneer of derision. What was I, a puny mortal of six feet, in these slow-coming years, what was I, that I should be walking so carelessly and recklessly along that mighty river, by the far-famed cataract, in that light that had guided the footsteps of kings and priests ages ago, among those stately rocks that had been the witness-bearers of forty centuries? What was I, that I should look with unshrinking eyes on all these ancient memorials, and troll a song—a dashing modern song—as I walked among them? For an instant a shudder came over me, and I verily feared lest the old guardians of the barrier should stop me there. But that was a momentary half-defined feeling that vanished on the instant, and I gathered my wits together as well as I was able, and walked on over sand and stone, as I fancied millions had walked, in years when there was a shrine for devout worship on the beautiful island, on moonlight pilgrimages to Philæ.

25.

Moonlight.

I WAS weary. I know not why, but I was weary that night, and I thought, as I trod the wild path among the cliffs, of a fireside in a far off land, by which could I but have warmed my feet, I would have lain down content to sleep such sleep as God giveth his beloved, and wander never again. I wondered whether I really knew what sleep was. Sometimes I thought I had not slept for months, and I had not, save only that dreamy, restless sleep that is filled with visions of dear faces looking on me through impassable bars, or out of unapproachable distances. And that night, as I walked along, the moonlight falling all around me out of that fathomless sky, I felt as if to lie down on the sand would be blessed, and to sleep there glorious, if I could but dream once more of home.

For an instant, lonesome and weary, though I had with me the dearest company in all the world—for an instant I thought of proposing to turn the boat, and go down the cataract, and northward to the sea; but the next instant drove all such thoughts far off.

I have described the pass. The high black rocks,

seamed and riven with ancient convulsions of nature in the childhood of this old world, now towered on my left, and the river ran blackly and with a heavy roar on the right. A low, long, snarling bark or yell startled and stopped me.

It came from the river-side, five hundred yards before me, and was followed by the quick barking of the jackals, of whom I saw three or four dash across the path and disappear in the direction of the sound.

The first bark was not a jackal, nor was it a fox. So far as I can learn there is no distinction now made in Egypt between those two animals, unless in the Delta. I have shot a number of them, and the people call them *taleb* (fox), and *abou l'houssein* (jackal), indiscriminately; nor am I able to learn that there is any other animal known to them as a jackal than this, which is but a small fox.

But that the voice did not proceed from one of these I was very certain, and the more so as their sharp, piercing bark now arose furiously and increased in noise; so that I imagined a council of the little rascals disturbed in a banquet by a wolf or hyena. The prospect of getting a shot at either of these animals was too good to be lost, and I examined my pistols and advanced cautiously in the direction of the angry disputants.

I had proceeded two hundred yards or so when a second loud and now more fierce yell or howl interrupted the sounds, which were then renewed with tenfold earnestness; but one of the foxes was snarling, howling, and yelping in a broken, disconnected way that could not be mistaken. Some strong compression was on his lungs. He was, in fact, in other hands than his own. I judged, as it afterward proved correctly, that the wolf had made a dash among his foes and seized one of them.

I started on now at a fast run, and at length the ascent

of a rock over which the path led brought me in sight of the battle. A large wolf—large here, but what I should call at home a very small one—was standing over the body of a dead donkey on the shore of the river, and half a dozen foxes were fighting him in true Arab style, with terrible voices, but at a safe distance. One poor little villain of a fox was in his jaws, and he would shake him for amusement occasionally. There was no need of it. He was dead, or shamming dead, and I do not think there was any sham about it. There certainly was none when he dropped him, as he did a moment afterward, when a ball from my Colt went down through his shoulder and broke the bone. The howl that he uttered on that night-air rings in my ear this moment. It made the rocks of Biggeh echo. It filled the whole pass with its unearthly sound. It was a long wild cry of intolerable anguish and pain.

He threw up his head as it escaped him, as if he were invoking the gods of Lycopolis to avenge him, and then leaped into the water. A second ball bounded from the stone as he left it, and went glancing over the river in the moonlight, leaving a sparkling track; and a third dashed the water about him, if it did not hit him, as he swam out for the current, which swept him downward, and I lost him.

The silence that followed was as startling as the cry had been. Only the river among the rocks sounded as steadily as it had sounded through the centuries, and the moonlight seemed to be in harmony with the sound.

Ten minutes afterward I came out by the village on the sand above the pass, and we entered it in search of our new pilot, a shellalee, who was to take charge of the boat to the second cataract, and back to Philæ.

Under a tree, the sycamore fig, in the middle of the village, was a curious seat which is not uncommon in Nubia. It was circular, made of mud, on a raised platform of the same material. A seat or diwan ran round this platform, having a high back, so that a dozen or twenty persons could sit here in a circle, all facing the centre. It was occupied by women, who were busy talking over the village gossip, and who answered very pleasantly our inquiries after Hassan. He had gone to the next village, which, like this, consisted of two rows of mud houses, a hundred yards apart, with the moonlight on the yellow sand between them. We walked through them, shouting "Hassan! Hassan!" and at length he emerged from a low doorway, and replied to his name.

He was six feet two at the least, and black as ebony. He did not know that we expected to sail that night or he would have been on board; so, hastening off for his baggage (a pipe, and an empty bag in which to bring home dates from the upper country), he promised to join us at the small boat, and we walked on. We found her where we left her, and Hajji Hassan and Abdallah both asleep in the bottom. What did they care for the moonlight and Philæ? And yet, I dare to say, that nowhere, on the face of the earth, is there a moonlight scene more rich in all that reaches and rouses the heart of man than was that same view. I looked on it as one looks on the faces of a dream when he knows he is dreaming, and fears to move or approach lest they vanish.

At length Hassan Shellalee, made his appearance, accompanied by his mother. She was an old woman, and though it was but a two weeks' parting, she wept bitterly, and embraced him again and again. When we pushed off, she begged me to treat him kindly, and then knelt on the moonlit bank and prayed for him: "God bless him! God keep my son! Allah, Allah, bring him back safe!" and, as we crossed, we could hear her mournful voice sounding over the river.

I know not what comfort there is in all the universe for an old woman among these miserable people, or what hope there is in her heart to keep out the cold. To the young, life is always bright, and the future presents joys in anticipation, as well to the poor as to the rich, which are enough to make them glad. But to the old, with dim eyes gazing on the sand, and feeble footsteps scarce prevailing to pass through it, without love, without God, without heaven, saving only the uncertain belief that it is remotely possible that they may have souls—a belief utterly rejected by half their teachers—and, even when trusting to that belief, entirely forbidden to expect, in any future life, to meet the beloved of this; hopeless of ever renewing the embraces that death has unlocked; hopeless of ever opening their eyes again on son or husband, daughter or mother; to them I know not what spirit there can be to live, what endearment to life, unless it be the horror of death itself.

For if the grave were pleasant, they might long for its repose. To lie down in some pleasant spot under the trees and find rest, even though it were dreamless and eternal; to sleep where the breath of the wind would be laden with odors of roses; to have resurrection in the sweet scent of flowers and shrubs; to have sunlight love to linger over one's place of rest, and moon and starlight fall with delight among myrtle leaves—all this would be delicious hope to them, if this might be. But a grave here! God forbid that I die here! to be laid, coffinless, three feet deep in the dry sand, and to-night disentombed by the jackals, or to-morrow by the wind. Such burial, and no immortality, who would not abhor?

We strolled an hour longer on the island. The moonlight was brighter each moment. Trumbull and Amy sat down in the front of the great Temple of Isis, and I could hear him occasionally discoursing to the ruins and the moon in almost every language with which those hallowed spots were familiar. Miriam and myself sat near them; but we selected the shade, and looked out of it on the wild scenery with indescribable admiration and awe. We could not tear ourselves away. It was midnight; but still we lingered in front of the Temple of Isis; still gazed up the shining river from the corridor near the small obelisk; still sat on the terrace and looked over at Biggeh and its lofty rocks. Yielding at length to the persuasive breeze that freshened every hour, we came down to the boat, and while we slept she sprang away before it, and in the morning was far up among the mountains of Nubia.

We were told by the reises of the cataract, that our boat was the first which had been taken up the cataract in a single day. They solemnly asseverated the truth of this, but I did not believe them. Nevertheless, at noon the next day, just twenty-four hours after leaving Es Souan, we were fifty-two miles from that place, having ascended the cataract and passed the evening at Philæ in the meantime. This, I have no doubt, surpasses any thing ever before done by a traveler's boat. The wind failed us in the afternoon, and I walked a while on shore taking my first view of Nubia.

The difference between Egypt and Nubia is marked and great. Not alone in the color of the inhabitants, but in almost every respect. Egypt may perhaps average five miles in width, exclusive of the river. Nubia averages just about as many rods. This is seriously true. The mountains of rock rise abruptly a few yards, or at most a few hundred feet, from the river's edge, and in large portions of Nubia nothing is cultivated but the actual slope of the bank, one or two rods in width. The inhabitants live on the scanty supply of beans and doura (corn) which their small amount of land yields, but chiefly on dates, for palm-trees abound, and their produce is most excellent. The people are generally industrious. They must work or starve. Their clothing is simple, many of them being nearly naked, and all the unmarried females wearing the fringe around their waists, and in cold weather wrapping a piece of cotton cloth loosely about them.

The women plait their hair in heavy folds, which they soak with castor-oil and with butter. Hideous shining masses cover their heads, which they exhibit with all the pride of a city lady, and they like the intensely disgusting odor quite as well as we like the most delicate geranium.

The people are quarrelsome, notwithstanding their industry, and many Nubian villages have been burned, and many Nubian bodies have swung between trees and ground for this bad trait of character, without producing very great effect.

One of the features of Nubia is the sakea, or water-wheel, for raising water from the river to irrigate the land. It is seen at every hundred rods, and heard all day and all night long, creaking a most melancholy and mournful creak. The small amount of land which each sakea waters, makes the contrast with Egypt more forcible in this respect, and shows the greater amount of labor required of the Nubian to produce the same result.

I know no part of the world in which life is so very small and worthless a matter as here, nor do the inhabitants themselves appear to set any high value on their own existence or that of each other. Life is but existence; nothing more. They rise from the ground on which they sleep, or the heap of doura stalks, or mat which keeps their naked bodies from it, and eating a coarse lump of corn meal, half baked, if they are so fortunate as to have it, but generally eating a dozen dried dates for breakfast, they go out to the bank of the river and work in the scanty soil, or watch the sakea, relieving their companions who have kept it going all night. And when the day is done, and work is done, they sit in groups in the dark or in the moonlight, and talk at intervals, but mostly keep silence, passing around from lip to lip the small pipe of native tobacco, and one by one rolls himself up in his own nakedness, curling his knees up to his head, and sleeps profound and dreamless sleep till morning.

Their huts are miserable substitutes for even the vile huts of the Egyptians. Many travelers mention the contrast between the Egyptian villages and the neat cottages of the Nubians among the trees, speaking of the beauty of the latter, and one traveler even calls them "neat white cottages." He must have been far away from Nubia when he wrote that, and had doubtless forgotten the low piles of Nile mud, never, or scarcely ever, high enough for a man to stand erect in, which constitute a Nubian village; and as to trees, I saw none in Nubia that were near the houses. On the contrary, without exception, so far as my observation went, the Nubian villages were built on land where trees or plants would not grow. Soil is too valuable there to be wasted for building purposes. Hence the houses, which are of the rudest form and smallest possible dimension, are usually built in a honeycomb mass at the foot of the mountain, and it requires a quick eye to detect them, their color being similar to the sand and rock.

One night I went into some of these huts at a late hour. No doors prevented intruders, nor was there any safeguard against robbers. The inhabitants lay on the ground, huddled together in masses, sound asleep like so many hogs, and grunted, as hogs would, when we stirred them up with our feet and voices. Life in such a country has no great amount of variety, as one might well imagine.

There was an old man that I found one day on shore as I walked by the boat, whose history was strange and worth the hearing.

He was a puny, dried-up old fellow, whose weight, I think, might come within seventy pounds. He sat on the end of the pole of the water-wheel, immediately behind the tails of the bullocks, and followed them around the little circle which they walked, his knees up to his chin, which was buried between them, and his blear eyes gazing listlessly on the cattle and the outer wall of the sakea, for it was inclosed in a stone and mud wall. The everlasting creaking of the wheels—that strange sound that no other machinery on earth emits—seemed, and was to him, the familiar music of his life.

I questioned him, and his story was simply this: He was born just there. It was long before the days of Mohammed Ali, when Hassan Kasheef was king, that he was a boy, sitting on the pole of the sakea, and following the bullocks around. He sat there more years than he knew any thing about, and grew to be a man. Life was to him still the same round. His view was bounded by the mountains around him, and he never went beyond them. He rode the sakea, and at every circle he caught through the open doorway a vision of one mighty hill, with a grove of palms at its foot. In the night he saw it still and solemn among the stars, and sometimes he had seen tempests gathered around it. It was the one idea of his life, and it was something to find in such a brain one idea, though it was but a rock. He looked out at it as he told me of it with a sort of affection that I well understood, but which surprised me none the less. But so he had lived. He grew heavier as he grew older, and then he could not ride the pole, but sat down in the doorway and watched his bullocks, looking behind him often at the hill, and so the years slipped along, and age came and he wasted away, and when his second childhood was on him, he mounted the pole again, and was riding to his grave.

He had been a great traveler. I know not how many thousand miles he had been carried around that centre pin. Had he never been away from the valley? Yes, once; he climbed the hill yonder, and from its summit saw the dreary wastes of sand that stretched far away in all directions, and he came back contented. Did nothing occur in his lifetime that he now remembered as marking some one day more than another? Nothing. Yes! one day the wheel broke, and he was startled and frightened; but they came and mended it, and all went on as before.

I left him there to follow his weary round till death overtake him; and if I find life oppressive at any time hereafter, I shall know where to seek a hermitage and undisturbed calm.

26.

The Nubians.

I DID not stop to look at any ruins in Nubia on my upward voyage, until we reached Abou Simbal.

We tracked a little toward noon of the day after leaving Philæ; that was December 19th, and I walked on shore for a while, crossing the tropic on foot.

Medical treatment had been demanded from time to time, along the river, by the natives, who imagine Franks omnipotent in medicine, but now the demands were oppressively frequent.

As I was walking along, gun in hand, looking after game, which was very scarce in Nubia, a dozen applicants presented themselves for the treatment of ophthalmia, sprains, and some bad wounds. I directed them, one after another, to follow up the river with the boat, which was tracking a half mile behind me. Arriving at a convenient spot, I sat down till the party arrived, and stopping the boat for my medicine-chest, proceeded to administer to their wants as I knew how. It was always a dangerous business, for if a man were not cured, his friends would be certain to lay it to the medicine, and if he died, would seek revenge on his supposed murderer.

There was one case presented to me here that was intensely horrible. I beg pardon of my gentler readers for asking them to pass over this page or two, unless they wish to be shocked by an instance of womanly affection that surpassed, in my view, any story of ancient or modern history or romance that I have read.

A tall, slender, and graceful woman, erect as a queen, but naked as a Nubian (great, indeed, was the contrast between her carriage and her costume), led down to the boat a man of thirty or thereabouts, whom she called her husband. He was a splendidly-formed fellow, black as charcoal, but with a frame that looked as if he could carry a world on his shoulders. Its developments were manifest, for he wore nothing but a cloth around his waist, and a bundle of rags on his right hand.

This hand she unbound, and exposed to me a most horrible wound. In a fray with some neighboring village, he, holding one of the heavy Nubian clubs in his hand, had received a blow on the back of it from another, which crushed the small bones to a pulp. This was some weeks before, and the hand had now no semblance of a hand. The fingers were one solid mass of flesh, the whole swollen to enormous size, and in the centre of the back, was a hole, an inch in diameter, from which oozed foul matter that made me sick to look at.

Now pass over what I am about to describe, I beg you, fair lady.

The wound had not been washed. The whole hand was a mass of dirt. Miriam threw me a cake of soap from the window of the boat, and I made the wife wash the hand.

She did it as gently as a mother could handle a dying child. Her fingers could not cause him pain, so lightly did she move them over the wound, and after a few minutes I could see the skin.

It was a hopeless case. Mortification followed within a week, I have no doubt. But I could not tell her so. The lightest touch pressed out foul discharges from the opening. I told her to clean it out. She did so till I could look in it. There were stringy pieces of white substance looking like pieces of the tendons. They were accumulations of ropy discharges, and I told her to get them out. She tried with her fingers, but they were too slippery, and she could not. Then she took up the hand and put her lips down to the wound, and took one of these foul pieces between her teeth and—I suppose she drew them out—I didn't see her.

When she told me it was done, I was leaning against a palm-tree, a little way up the bank, with my tarbouche off, trying to get a little fresh air.

I tell you, my bachelor friend, that woman was worth her weight in diamonds, and she was a widow within a fortnight.

There was a boy, who professed to have some disease, and after thorough examination of him, I gave him the old remedy, a bread pill. He took it, and then followed what he had really come down to the boat for, a demand for bucksheesh.

"What?" said I.

"Bucksheesh."

I seized him by the loose shirt that enveloped his active limbs, and threw him into the river. He swam like a fish, was ashore in a twinkling, and, as he shook himself, demanded, with an air of perfect certainty that he had now a right to it, "Bucksheesh, Ya Howajji."

Toward evening, of the next day, we came up to Korusko.

Korusko figures largely in the geography of Upper Egypt, and I had expected to find there a village of considerable size, if not a flourishing city. But there was nothing of the sort. There was not even an ordinary village. A few scattered huts along the foot of the mountain were the only residences of the natives. Along the shore were tents, and camels, and piles of goods, and bales of various sorts of merchandise, for this is the point at which the caravans leave the Nile to go to Upper Nubia. The river here returns to its course after a great bend to the westward, which bend the caravans avoid, as well as the many cataracts which forbid navigation. We approached it in the evening, just at sunset, and, sending the boat on ahead, we went ashore to walk through the grove of palms which covers the bank. We found groups of traders around their camp-fires, and the effect of moonlight on them became very picturesque. One party of Europeans surprised us not a little. It appeared that they were going to the upper country on a trading expedition, and their camels were ready for the journey.

We lay all night here, and in the morning tracked up to Derr, the chief city of Lower Nubia.

We had sent on word that we were coming, as the course of the river from Derr to Korusko is nearly southeast, and it was necessary to track all the way, no wind blowing against that current, and we wished additional men to take the ropes.

Abdul Rahman Effendi, the governor of this section, who resides at Derr, sent us down a small army of nearly a hundred men, under charge of Mohammed, one of the sons of Hassan Kasheef, the old king of Nubia, and they took us up at a flying rate. About eight miles from Derr, Abdul Rahman himself met us on horseback, and came on board the boat.

He is a young man, who has been a favorite with Latif Pasha, and has been steadily promoted by him until he has reached his present elevation. But he is not exactly contented, for he is in a place of exile to a man of his peculiar tastes. He was accompanied by his physician, who was a keen old fellow, full of fun, and sharp as a razor. In reply to his inquiry whether in America the law made any distinctions in favor of the rich over the poor, I enlightened him by the history of some medical men, of good position and connections, who had recently suffered its penalties, and he seemed greatly astonished. I think he gathered from what I said that medical men in America were not the most safe class in the community, and were somewhat given to killing other people. But I disabused his mind on that score very soon.

Abdul Rahman was sent to Derr some time ago to settle the division of the property of old Hassan Kasheef, the last king of Nubia before its subjugation by Mohammed Ali. Having successfully accomplished his mission he was sent back as governor of Lower Nubia, not precisely to his own liking, for he would have much prefered a place below the cataract.

He told me afterward the history of the old king and his property. Hassan Kasheef was a giant in his day. He was seven feet high, could eat a lamb for his breakfast, and a sheep for his dinner, had over a hundred wives, and left more children than could be counted. He was in the habit of marrying every girl that he fancied, his ceremony being simply to ride up to the door of the hut in which she lived and fire his gun. The people shouted instantly, "the Kasheef is married!" and after remaining a day or two with his wife he went away, and she never heard of him again. Thus he had wives everywhere. The first Turkish governor endeavored to reform his morals; but Hassan could be a Mussulman in all but that. He got rid of all but seven of the women, and when he died, seven years ago, these appeared to claim a share in the property. But there were three more than the Mohammedan law could recognize, it allowing only four wives to one man. It was this knotty subject that Abdul Rahman was sent here to untwist, and he succeeded admirably, by inducing them all to submit to his arrangement and make an equitable division of the property.

His sons, in the regular line, now living, are fifteen. Their names are almost a complete catalogue of the names of all Moslems. Suleiman, Ali, Daoud, Rashwan, Mohammed, Houssein, Ibrahim, Abdul-Rahwan, Khalil, Achmet-Asim, Mohammed-Manfouh, Mohammed-Dahib, Mustapha, Shahin, and Mohammed-Defterdar.

Abdul Rahman and his physician proved jolly companions. They smoked, talked, laughed, and joked, with the ease and freedom of western society. Wine they both declined. Every one knows that the Moslem religion forbids wine.

They ate freely of pomegranates. "Doctor," said Trumbull; "don't you think that a little wine or brandy with his fruit would be proper for the governor to take by way of medicine?"

"No—I don't think wine agrees with Abdul Rahman's constitution," said the doctor; "but I find that I need it myself with fruit, and it is good for me." He filled a tumbler with Marsala, and poured it down with a sly wink of his eye at the laughing governor, and after that the doctor stuck to the decanter till it was empty.

I had heard all along the river that the great temple at Abou Simbal was closed with sand, and had not been open for two years. I accordingly requested Abdul Rahman to send up an order to the nearest sheiks, to have a hundred men there on the day I expected to be there coming down the river, for it was out of the question to leave Nubia without seeing the interior of this, the greatest curiosity in Egypt—perhaps greater than Cheops or Karnak.

Abdul Rahman was most hearty and earnest in his attentions. I regretted the impossibility of staying a day or two with him at Derr, where he promised us all sorts of jollifications. But I had work to do at Thebes, and every day was important. He sent a cawass with us to hasten our progress above Derr, and after making us promise to call on our way down, he suddenly discovered that we had carried him two miles above his house, on the river bank at Derr, and shouted to be put ashore. His train of fifty or more horses and men had kept along the bank by our side, and we now turned up to the shore. Chief among the followers was Suleiman, eldest son of Hassan-Kasheef, a noble man, nearly seven feet high, heir to his father's fallen throne.

We lay a couple of hours at the bank. The boys brought us lots of chameleons which abounded on the bean vines along the shore, and we bought them at a copper each till we had more than we wanted. They were a source of great amusement to us afterward, fighting one another with most furious slowness, biting as an iron rail-shears opens and shuts its jaws, once in half a minute, swelling and changing their colors, now brilliant green, now dull gray, now straw yellow, now, when angry, covered with a hundred shining spots, and then relapsing into their natural brilliant green. They remained on the boat for a month, and then as we came northward died one by one until all had disappeared.

Toward evening we left Derr, tracking slowly. Abdul Rahman and his suite rode along shore three or four miles with us, and then a breeze springing up, we left him and dashed on a mile or two further. Here the breeze died away, and we came to the land under a precipitous mountain, on which all night long the moonlight lay in silent splendor. We sat, all four of us, on the rocks till nearly midnight, and the boat of an English gentleman and lady (residents of Cairo), who had been all the fall on the river, joined us here, and remained with us to the second cataract.

It was on the afternoon of the 23d of December that we came in sight of the grand front of Abou Simbal, the most impressive of the monuments of Egyptian grandeur. I say the most impressive, because here is all that can impress the heart. Here are the remains of ancient wealth, splendor, and taste united. Here the sublime idea of the great Sesostris stands graven on the rock, and the men of the nineteenth century after Christ respond with their hearts to the call which the man of the fourteenth before Christ utters on the face of the mountain. Human power may not hope to accomplish more than this, or to equal again the magnificence and beauty of this temple. It was the thought of a kingly intellect to hew down the face of the mountain, leaving four colossal statues sitting before it, and then to excavate a temple in its very depths, and leave the statues of the gods looking from its inmost chamber out to the bank of the swift Nile. The thought has long outlasted the man—outlasted his dynasty—outlasted his race and nation. The desert sands have in vain sought to hide it and cover it up. It is the grandest remaining monument of old Egypt.

Three colossal statues sit silent and majestic in a niche cut in the face of the mountain. The fourth has fallen into ruin, and only his throne remains. The sand of the desert, yellow as gold, flowing around the end of the mountain and across the front of the temple, has covered the northernmost statue to his neck, the second to his knees, the throne of the third, which is vacant, and the feet of the fourth. The doorway, between the two middle statues, is not now filled with the sand, though it appears to be so. The highest ridge of the sand is thirty feet in front of the doorway, from which it slopes each way, to the river on one side and into the temple on the other.

It had not been our intention to stop at all on the way up the river, but I could not pass those stupendous statues thus.

There are two temples at Abou Simbal, alike hewn in the face of the mountain. The smaller one is two hundred feet from the greater. A ravine of sand comes down between them.

Trumbull and myself looked longingly as we slowly forged by them, with a light breeze blowing, and I saw that he felt as I did.

"What say you?"

"Let us stop."

Hassabo put his helm down, and we ran up to the land between the two temples. To our surprise we found that the great temple was not closed, as we had heard, and access to the interior was not impossible though difficult. We could sit down on the loose sand, and slide, feet foremost, under the top of the doorway, and lying down on our backs, let ourselves down the hill of sand that sloped into the great chamber.

Eight immense pillars of square stone support the roof. In front of each pillar is a statue seventeen feet high, with folded hands and countenance of calm majesty. Beyond this is a second and a third room, opening at last into the holy of holies, where the altar yet stands, before four seated statues of gods, to which the great Sesostris offered his sacrifices three thousand years ago. A screen has formerly crossed this room in front of the altar, but it has gone long ago; doubtless it gleamed with gold and jewels once. Nine other chambers opened in various directions in this strange subterranean temple, whose walls are every where covered with legends and paintings of old triumphs of the great king.

The smaller temple of Abou Simbal is also hewn in the rock like this, and presents a front much smaller but more elaborately executed. Seven large buttresses, sloping backward from the base, have between them six colossal statues standing. The temple itself consists of five rooms, on a smaller scale than the great temple, but possessing quite as much interest historically.

We paused a very short time here on our way up the river. Wâdy Halfeh and the second cataract were close before us, and we were anxious to be there and on our return. So as the breeze freshened toward evening, we again shook out the canvas, and the *Phantom* again sprang forward to the gale. The mountains of Nubia now assumed a new appearance. Solitary hills rose out of the desert plain like sugar-loaves. Others had long levels on their summits, and some were covered with ruined villages. Behind one ruined town, which the men called Diff, we saw strange tombs with domes, like the ordinary skeik's tomb of the Mussulmans; but which they (the Mussulmans) say are not of their faith. I think they are. Some of the men, when we asked about them, said they were tombs of the Beni-Israel (children of Israel).

We passed the ruins of Ibreem, which gives its name to the finest dates in Nubia, much prized in the lower country, and as the evening came down we were in a country whose scenery had totally changed. The desert views were distant and fine. The hills scattered and broken.

In the night the breeze freshened, and as we dashed swiftly up the river, Hassan Shellalee, the pilot, trusting entirely to his good luck and nearness to the end of the journey, went to sleep, and the boat brought up on the rocks with a terrible thump. Then ensued a scene. Such a row as we had on deck! We rushed out and found Abd-el-Atti laying on his whip. Every one who came within his reach took a full share, and the poor pilot got most of all.

An hour afterward we again grounded with a tremendous crash. I thought the *Phantom* was done for. Abd-el-Atti dashed out on deck and cursed the unlucky pilot with all the phrases known to the Orient. He stood it all until he was called a Jew and a hog, and then he struck at the dragoman, and they clinched with a yell and rolled on deck together.

I don't know exactly how we managed it. Trumbull dragged the shellalee out by his bare legs, and I hauled Abd-el-Atti aft by his coat—for he wore a European overcoat. They clung to each other like dogs, and it was like tearing flesh apart to draw them asunder.

We had a midnight session of the court to consider the case, which we adjourned to the next day at Wâdy Halfeh, warning Hassan Shellalee that if the *Phantom* struck again, he might address himself to the Prophet, for nothing short of Mohammed himself could save him.

The day rose clear and glorious on the desert, and we were flying on. The white wings of the *Phantom* were stretched on the fresh air as she swept gracefully up by hill and island and village until at two o'clock after noon we fired a salute of ten guns to ourselves as she folded her wings for the last time at Wâdy Halfeh, the ultima thule of our Nubian travel.

That night was the birth-night. In what countries of the round world were not Christians singing carols as the sun going westward left the holy twilight of Christmas eve with blessings on every land?

Wherever a man may be on Christmas eve it is pardonable in him to give at least one hour to memory. And if there be not the broad fireside and the flashing logs in the chimney, if his far-wandering feet are hot with desert sands, and his forehead is burning with the sunshine of Sahara, he will be excused for remembering with even more distinctness the forms of old times, on which the blaze of the Christmas log shines so gloriously.

A few rods from the boat, on the sand, lying down and looking starward, I was able for awhile to forget Nubia and recall America.

Able!—I couldn't help it—voices called to me out of distances that I did not try to fathom. Eyes looked at me, but I didn't think to ask whether they were this side or beyond the stars. Lips kissed me—and I never dreamed of their being ghostly lips, for they were not cold—and arms enfolded me—warm embraces—and hearts were throbbing loud against mine as one and another of the beloved ones of old times and all times lay on my breast.

27.

The Second Cataract.

Wâdy Halfeh (the valley of *halfeh*, a coarse species of grass) is on the east side of the Nile four miles below the last rapid of the second cataract. It is a small village scattered among the palm-trees which abound here. The west shore of the river is barren, the yellow sand of Sahara pouring down to the water's edge. To see the cataract it is necessary to ride about seven miles on the western shore, either directly along the water's edge, or behind a range of hills that are here much broken and scattered. Small boats can approach very near the foot of the cataract. But the *Phantom* could not. The khadi, who was resident post-master, governor, and whatever other official might be necessary at Wâdy Halfeh, had received from Abdul Rahman Effendi, by express, news of our coming, and was on board with proffers of all manner of attentions so soon as we came to land. But we did not see him ourselves, for, having taken the small boat and crossed to the west bank of the stream we were lying on the golden sand, picking up splendid agates and other beautiful stones, until the sun went down.

Early on Christmas morning, however, he came down, with from thirty to forty dromedaries, horses, and donkeys, offering us choice from among them for our ride to Abou Seir, and such as we selected were immediately sent across the river, to await our time of starting. When we were ready he announced his intention of accompanying us for the day.

We mounted on the west bank near a curious crude brick ruin which stands like a church tower on the very edge of the river. The English gentleman and lady had arrived in the night and joined us this morning, so that we were six Franks and about twenty Arabs, forming no small caravan. I rode a fine white dromedary, and the khadi kept close at my side on a capital horse. Our route lay back of the mountains over the yellow desert, and after traveling slowly a couple of miles we were in the sand hollows as far from any sign of life or vegetation as if we had been a thousand miles distant in the heart of Sahara.

"Will the Howajji try the Haggin?"

Certainly I would try him, if the khadi thought him a good animal (and so I began to get his paces out of him). He was not as good a dromedary by much as I have seen, but he could travel fast enough, and when he proposed a race I beat him easily. Possibly, probably, he let me do it, but the dromedary is a swift animal. We were going fast, I leading the khadi by about a length, both animals warming up to it, and one of the attendants, on another dromedary, close behind, when five gazelles sprang up, three hundred yards ahead of us, and were off like the wind. I shouted to the khadi, never thinking of a gazelle chase on a dromedary, and pulled up.

"I have no gun," said he.

"Here is one," said I, reaching out to him my larger pistol.

What notion the dromedary had I know not. Perhaps I used a word that he misunderstood, for down went his fore legs and off went pistol and Braheem Effendi together, striking some twenty feet or less from the camel's nose.

I was not on the ground any sooner than the khadi who was horrified at the idea of a dead Howajji on his hands to answer for, but as he sprang from his saddle I rebounded, and leaping into his place, shouted and shook the reins, and away we went after the game that was fast vanishing over the sand hills: all this had occupied but an instant. I looked back, however, and beheld the usual winding up of such a scene, the poor camel driver on his back, the khadi pronouncing sentence and the other Arabs around ready to execute it. Miriam interfered to save the poor devil's soles, and I went on after the gazelles. I rode three miles on a full gallop, but the drove of gazelles kept just ahead of me, pausing occasionally, as if in wonderment at what I could be riding so furiously for, and then going on with their long, easy leaps, that put to shame my poor horse in the heavy sand.

Once I had got within two hundred yards of one of them, and sent a pistol-ball after him, but he only leaped into the air, I think quite ten feet high from the sand, and was off like the wind.

Still I followed them, mile after mile; and suddenly I looked around me, and the desert had closed in, and I was alone. There was an excitement in it I had never before felt. On—on! I drove the shovel stirrups into the sides of the horse, and we went like the desert storm over the hills and through the hollows. Sand, sand, sky, and sand—nothing else was visible! It was my first realization of the solitude of the desert, of its desolation and loneliness. I saw at length something white lying among the yellow gold around me, and riding toward it I found an empty basket, a broken water-gourd, the pieces of a jar, and some rags. Was this the spot where some desert wanderer, having exhausted his last drop of water, lay down and died, never dreaming that the Nile, with its glorious flow, was within ten miles of him ? I picked up the basket, remounted, and rode slowly to the south-east, hoping ere long to catch sight of my companions from some hill-top on the desert.

In a few minutes, four of the Arab attendants came over the hills to the eastward, in search of me, and rode up swiftly. As we went on, one of them, thinking that I might be disposed to try another race, challenged one of his companions, and they went ahead at a furious gallop. My horse looked at them awhile, and then pricked up his ears and went off at a bound after them. I was close on them when I saw one of them stagger in his seat. His saddle-girth had broken, and the next moment he and his saddle rolled over on the sand. I went over him at a leap. He swore I had killed him, and made it a plea for a large bucksheesh that evening, which, I am happy to say, restored the erectness of his back, which had been lamentably bent before its bestowal.

Five miles brought me to a hill-top, where I saw the party as many miles distant, moving slowly over the sand, and in an hour more I rejoined them at the hill of Abou Seir, on the second cataract of the Nile.

This cataract is less a cataract than the first. But the river spreads wider among more minute islands, and is broken up into a thousand streams, up which no large boat can be taken. The rapids extend through twelve miles, and the breadth of them may be from three to five, but in this space little of the river is visible. The rocks and islands are covered with a low shrub, or bush, somewhat like the *sont*, or *acacia nilotica*, in appearance, but I think it is not the same, though I did not examine it, and it may be. The green appearance of this makes the view over the cataract exceedingly fresh and beautiful, contrasting forcibly with the desert around. Under the rocky bluff of Abou Seir, the last plunge of the Nile is seen and heard, and it ascends, with solemn roar, around the hill, as it has since the rift was made and the waters let through.

Here we spread our carpets and our luncheon, the wind blowing over our heads. We read the names of travelers carved here and there on the stones. They were numerous, and we found among them many friends. We carved our own here. It was the only place in all my Nile travel that I had been willing to cut my name; but I enjoyed the pleasure of reading those of my friends so keenly, that I could not forego the hope that in some future day some one would come to this spot who would find a momentary pleasure in looking at mine. It is under the edge of an overhanging piece of the rock, and Miriam's is by it. If they last but half as long as some that we found there, they will be read when we are dust, and when the stones that friends shall carve at our heads will long ago have crumbled in our stormy land.

Eliot Warburton's was cut near Belzoni's. Before the former some one has cut, "Alas! poor," and no one could read the name without a passing shadow of sadness at the memory of his fate.

The romance of travel is well-nigh over. We had no discomforts to boast of in Egypt. We spread Persian carpets, rich enough to win the heart of a lady of gorgeous tastes in New York, on the rocky bluff at Abou Seir, and opened a bottle of Chateau Lafitte, of sparkling St. Peray, and of Bass's pale ale. A luncheon-bag from the back of one of the camels furnished metal drinking-cups that improved the ale, if they did spoil the claret, but we lunched on cold turkey and sandwiches, and the only romance about it was, that we threw the foam out of our cups into the air, and it went down two hundred feet into the cataract of the Nile.

Luncheon ended, the moment was somewhat serious.

There was nothing beyond that point that had any attractions for me. It would have been pleasant to loiter month after month along the great river, but there were pleasanter loitering places in the great world we had yet to travel over, and I could not regret that I was to turn my back on the South. One long gaze into the distance above the cataract, that distance so imperfectly explored, though so many have visited it, a half-uttered promise that when the world had nothing else to be seen of more interest, we would return and find our way up to Dongola, and on to Kartum, and on—on—on. And then—

"Miriam—we turn our faces now to Jerusalem."

Standing on the lofty hill at Abou Seir, we sent westward, over the desert that stretched away across Africa to the shores of the sea, westward over desert and sea, our messages to the waiting hearts at home, and then, with willing steps, turned on our way toward Holy Land.

We found the boat dressed by Abd-el-Atti for Christmas. She was covered with green palm branches from stem to stern, and the cabin was a bower fit for a queen. And such a dinner-table as Hajji Mohammed got up that day who shall be able to describe! There was a turkey, made drunk on brandy before he was killed, and consequently as tender as a partridge—so said the cook—and I saw the brandy administered myself, but I can't say it was that which made him tender, though tender he was. There was a roast goose, wild and delicious; four roasted teal, and chickens in three forms. There was a pigeon-pie made of macaroni, and one whole lamb, with folded arms and bent legs, and head and tail complete, every inch of him, stuffed with almonds, raisins, and rice, and done to a turn. There were innumerable dishes of kabobs and small bits of meat and game, and there was a curry of chicken that would have suited an Indian general. Then there were calves'-feet jelly and blanc-mange in moulds, and mish-mish and apple and mince and pumpkin pies, and there was a cake made of sugar and almonds, which you struck with a stick or a knife, and when you broke it, out flew a white pigeon; and this was but half the variety wherewith our indefatigable dragoman had loaded our Christmas table.

That night the weather changed. We had been on deck always before this until nearly midnight, and now we went up to see the boat illuminated. Fifty colored lanterns, crimson and blue, yellow and green, were hung out from all the spars and ropes and awning-posts. Blue-lights sent their glare over the surface of the water, and altogether it was about as strange a scene as Wâdy Halfeh is likely to have in the next half century.

The boat was rigged for the return voyage; the great yard was taken down, and laid fore-and-aft over the cabin, while the small yard from the mast at the stern was placed on the fore-mast, and the deck-planks were taken up, leaving the seats for the men to row. At midnight, when the wind had gone down, the boat was cast off, and with a long shout and a new chorus she swung her head to the current, and the downward voyage had commenced. It was cold and clear, and looking upward one might imagine that the night was a Christmas night at home, when the stars hold their most joyous revel. I sat on deck till long after the voyage commenced, and then slept. So ended Christmas at Wâdy Halfeh.

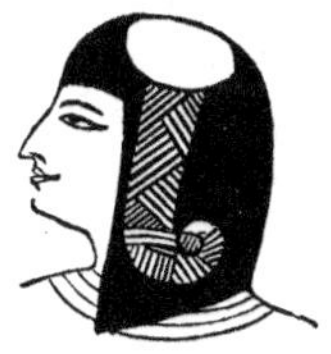

28.

Abou Simbal.

The next afternoon, as the sun was setting, we approached the rock-hewn temple at Ferayg, a few miles above Abou Simbal.

It was nearly sunset, and, to avoid delay, we took the small boat and pulled down the river ahead of the large boat to land and examine it. The entrance is a plain, lofty doorway in the rock-face of the hill, without ornament. The boat grated alongside the rocks, and springing out we climbed the terraces, some thirty feet, to the doorway.

Entering the hall, the roof of which is supported by four square pillars, we were astonished at finding the principal object in view a picture of the Saviour on the ceiling, his head surrounded by a halo. This, like many other of the Egyptian temples, has been used in later years for Christian worship, but not in late years. I have much veneration for these evidences of the faith of the early Christians. Here martyrs worshiped in days when martyrs suffered for the name of their Lord, and in many of these places martyrs died with eyes fixed on the image of their Saviour. There was an inner room, opening from this hall, and I walked into it, tapping the floor in front of me, as was my custom, with a long stick which I carried in my hand when exploring a dark place. I found a solid floor, as I supposed, and advanced, but as I entered the dark doorway I stepped on nothing.

There are moments when one thinks the thoughts of years. I had sounded some of these graves in rock-hewn chambers, and found them thirty and forty feet deep. As I began to descend I thought of those, and gave up all for lost. It was not the fate I had hoped for, to die in a hole like that. I wondered what sort of a paragraph it would make in the newspapers at home under the head of "melancholy occurrence," among steamboat explosions, railway smashes, suicides, and swindles. I wondered whether they would ever get me out, dead or alive, or whether they would not come tumbling after me one on another into the same trap; and then my feet struck bottom and I shouted, "Miriam, stand back—don't come in here," and she, hearing a voice from the tombs, was terribly startled, as well she might be. It was but ten feet deep. It might have been fifty. It had been much deeper than now, but it was filled up with rubbish. I struck on my feet, in the corner, standing upright. I put my hand in my pocket, took out a candle and lit it with a match, caught the end of Mohammed Hassan's turban, which he let down to me, and he and Trumbull lifted me out. Till then I did not suppose that I was hurt, but when this was accomplished my left arm fell powerless, and I was not able to use it for a month.

I stowed myself in the bow of the boat, my shoulder aching intensely. The others took the stern. It was a calm, delicious evening. The sun was just gone, the swift twilight had come down on us, and in a few moments starry darkness followed. The men pulled slowly, and the oars made the only noise that broke the profound stillness of the scene. Silence, the deep silence of ancient countries, that which every one has noticed among ruins, and which was majestic always on the lordly Nile, the stillness of that repose which ages have but deepened, never disturbed, was on land and river.

Resting awhile without rowing we lost count of time, and suddenly began to wonder if by any possibility we had passed the *Phantom*, which had gone on while we were in the temple, and was to wait for us at Abou Simbal. She always carried a crimson light at the peak in the night time, but we could not see it any where. Trumbull fired his pistol three times, and a moment afterward we heard three discharges in reply, and saw the red light going up. Pulling for it, in a few moments we saw her lying at the shore, but our eyes were instantly directed elsewhere. For in the light of the stars, calm, unearthly in their majesty, we saw the forms of the three colossal statues of Remeses, and as we came nearer they grew in size, and looked upon us with that cold and stately smile that has been wasted so many centuries on the fast flowing river—and that seems to signify in those rocky watchers some conception of the destiny of human life and national grandeur, which they behold aptly typified in the everlasting flow of the drops to a distant and unknown sea.

Mindful of the brilliant illumination of the boat the evening previous, at Wâdy Halfeh, it occurred to us that we might realize somewhat of the ancient glory of Abou Simbal by lighting it with our colored lanterns.

Abd-el-Atti entered into the idea with his accustomed alacrity, and although my shoulder was exceedingly painful I went up into the temple to advise and assist in the disposition of candles and lanterns, while the ladies, who did not go into the temple on our passage up, waited on board until the illumination was complete.

The sand hill was almost impassable. It was like climbing a snow bank fifty feet high, the feet going in deep and slipping far back at every step, so that we had to lie down and breathe several times before we reached the top and descended into the doorway of the temple.

When our arrangements were complete we returned and brought the ladies up. The procession was picturesque. Two blazing torches led the way, and four more brought up the rear. Our English friends had arrived just after the *Phantom*, and joined us.

Never since the days of Remeses has his great temple shone so brilliantly. Every statue held bright lanterns, and for two hundred feet through the long rooms we placed them—rows of every color, shining on painted walls and lofty statues. The altar was in the shadow—for so we arranged it—hiding the lights behind it that they might shine on the faces of the gods, and not on the altar front. When all was ready we called in the ladies, and, as they entered, the sailors, who had busied themselves about the lamps, suddenly disappeared, and the temple was apparently empty. But at the moment of our re-entering, in place of the chorus of priests and attendants that was wont to arise in the hall, deep, sepulchral voices, from unknown recesses, uttered in loud and terrible unison the well-known cry, "Bucksheesh, Howajji!"

It was vain to resist such an appeal, and we answered it instantly; whereat the voices changed, and the men emerged from their hiding-places with shouts of thanks.

It was a gorgeous scene, worth visiting Egypt to look on that illumination; and we sat for hours in the hall, gazing with never-ceasing wonder and awe on the splendid statues and lofty walls. Then we wandered with torches through all the chambers, scaring the owls and bats from their hiding-places; and when it was nearly midnight we came out into the air, and there lay on the river and on the temple front such a moonlight as we dream of in other lands, but never see except just here. The hoary rocks looked like silver, and the gray statues gleamed in the mellow light, and seemed to know its beauty. We threw ourselves down in the sand, and drank in all the beautiful scene; and at last, when the ladies were gone down to the boat and were sleeping, I re-entered the temple, and sat down in the centre of the great hall alone, and watched the fading lights, and pondered on the old, old story of the decay of empire.

That altar seemed waiting the sacrifice, but who shall supply the victim or kindle the flame? The silent gods sat on their thrones and invited worship, but who will kneel to rock-hewn gods in Egypt now? There were times, said I to myself, when the tramp of armed men and the rustle of soft silks were heard in these halls; when priests and princes were here with maidens and matrons. There were times when men worshiped at that altar; when this stone was worn with the knees of devotees. Where are they all? One by one my failing candles answered the question. One by one they went out in gloom. A flicker, a spark, a little smoke, and all was over; and at length all were gone but three that stood behind the altar, and all was gloomy except in the holy room; and then, suddenly, as if a bat or an owl swept over them, they too vanished, and the blackness of darkness was around me.

One can hardly imagine a place on earth where a man could be more emphatically alone than I then was at midnight, two hundred feet from the air, in the deep caverns of Abou Simbal. Bats were flitting around me, and certain sounds were not pleasant to hear, sharp rattling noises that were much like scorpions. I had killed one in the temple that evening. But I have felt more alone in my own country many a dark night than I did here.

It was but a few paces in a direct line, and when I had taken them the hill of sand was before me, and up this, creeping on hands and knees through the doorway, I emerged into the pure atmosphere. My shoulder had by this time become exceedingly painful, and sleep was out of the question. So I managed to get myself up into the corner, under the ear of the great statue at the north, and here I sat and waited till fatigue well-nigh overpowered me, and then, hastening down to the boat, I lay in my bed all night, restless and in pain, and glad to welcome the dawn.

While we were at breakfast a confused sound of voices outside puzzled us not a little; and on going out we ascertained its cause in the presence of about seventy fine stalwart Nubians, sent over by the sheik of the village opposite to dig out the temple, in obedience to my instructions at Derr. We had countermanded the order when we found the interior accessible on our upward trip; but Abd-el-Atti had failed to transmit the direction, alleging as his reason a desire to impress the people with the importance of his masters. The next travelers whom our worthy dragoman takes up the Nile will find that it was his desire to magnify his own importance for future purposes.

The poor fellahs were most glad to be excused. A holy horror exists in their minds toward digging out this temple. They have been several times compelled to it at severe loss of life in hot weather; and they laid their hands on the tops of their heads with profound gratitude when I sent them back to their boats to re-cross the river.

The mountain, in which the great temple is hewn, slopes down to the river at an angle of perhaps forty-five degrees. It is solid rock. In the front of this mountain a niche is hewn out about one hundred and twenty five feet wide, and deep enough to allow of a perpendicular face of ninety feet. Across the top of this perpendicular face is carved a cornice. In the niche, when it was hewed out, were left four gigantic blocks of stones, which were cut into sitting statues of the monarch whose was this great work, the Remeses, known to fame as Sesostris.

Between the two middle statues is the great doorway, over the top of which, in a niche, is a colossal statue of one of the gods of Egypt, which seems less than life-size in contrast with the giants in front of it.

Some idea of the size of the colossi may be gathered from a few of the dimensisons of the face and head of one of them. The length of the nose is three feet five inches; height of the forehead, to the edge of the cap or crown, twenty-eight inches; width or length of the eye, twenty-nine inches; width of the mouth, four feet; distance from the nose to the bottom of the chin, three feet; length of the ear, three feet. The entire length of the head is about twelve feet, including an estimate of that part of it concealed by the cap or head-dress. A remarkable circumstance in connection with one of the colossi, the second from the north, is a fracture of the right arm, probably contemporary with the making of the statue, for the elbow is supported by a stone wall under it, on which are carved many hieroglyphics.

The smaller temple stands two hundred yards to the north of the large one, the ravine, down which the sand pours, being between them. Both temples are of the same period—that of the great Sesostris, whose name is carved on every pillar and portion of the walls. This great monarch appears to have devoted much of his wealth to beautifying this spot. Why he chose it for such expenditures tradition or story saith not. No mounds remain to mark the site of an ancient city, nor is there evidence of a palace or royal residence near it. Possibly some great event occurred on the Nile at this point, which led him to mark the bank in this manner; and future ages may succeed in reading the story on these tablets.

We passed the forenoon in measuring and examining the temple, of the interior of which I have already said sufficient. I would suggest to future explorers the examination of the wall on the left as you enter, that is on the south side of the great hall. I am convinced that there are undiscovered chambers within this wall, which may contain matters of great interest.

As we left Abou Simbal, shooting rapidly down stream, we passed a niche in the rock in which is a seated statue. Had I seen it before, I should have paused to examine it. None of the books mention it, but it is worth stopping to look at. It was late, however, and we were literally by it before I caught sight of it, and it was too late to return, and I was, withal, suffering too much from my wounded arm to climb up to it.

29.

Northward in Nubia.

We reached Derr again on the 28th, and Abdul Rahman was on the shore, with his suite, to receive us. The large boat could not approach the city for want of water, and we accordingly took the small boat, and the ladies sat in that, and dropped slowly down stream, while we walked with the governor and his attendants along the shore to his residence, under a large sycamore fig-tree, the largest, with the exception of one near it, that I have seen in Egypt. Here we had pipes and coffee, and here, to our surprise, Abdul Rahman produced various presents which he had been collecting for us since we went up the river. Foremost among them he literally trotted out two ostriches, for which he had sent off to the desert, and which stood up in the square as proudly as desert lords. It was something to own ostriches, but what to do with them? Either they or we must move off from the boat if we took them on board. We felt very much like the celebrated individual who became suddenly possessed of an elephant. A small and beautiful monkey was much more acceptable. He was just what we had been wishing for, and we received him with no little delight. The ostriches we retained in our possession during our stay at Derr, but when we left we were obliged to return them to the governor. He had also provided sheep, and fowls, and Nubian mats, and indeed loaded us with presents, for all of which we could make no return then, but which I had it in my power afterward in some measure to repay, by procuring for Abdul Rahman a transfer to a post which was much more to his taste.

We formed a procession to go to the temple of Derr, not very similar to ancient religious processions. Trumbull, Abdul Rahman, and myself followed the ladies, and a motley crowd of naked Nubians followed us. The entire city turned out to look at us.

The temple is in sadly ruinous condition, and of little interest except for its great antiquity. Amada, a few miles below Derr, on the opposite side, is of much more interest, as well as possessing much beauty of painting and sculpture. We passed some hours very pleasantly at Derr, and then returned to our small boat, with the governor in company, and pulled down to Amada, where the large boat was awaiting us.

Let no traveler miss this beautiful gem of antiquity, which lies on the sand a little way from the river. The paintings are beautifully preserved, and the period of the temple, not far from the date of the Exodus of the Israelites, makes it especially interesting.

Here we parted with Abdul Rahman and the doctor and resumed our downward passage. As we went swiftly down the river, nearly at Korusko, while seated at dinner table, there was suddenly a cry that came in at the window with startling effect.

"Ya Reis Hassanein ?"

It was from a boat upward bound, and the demand was interrogative, that he might know if this were the boat he wished to speak.

"Ya Reis Abdallah," went back.

"Stop, O Hassanein—we have writings for Braheem Effendi !"

Letters! Braheem Effendi and his friend were in the small boat before the reis had time to shout that the letters were on shore where the Howajji of that boat was shooting. We pulled to the land, and in a palm-grove met a gentleman in an English shooting-jacket and otherwise loosely appareled, for the weather was warm. We did not pause to exchange names. He handed me a package of letters and I thanked him heartily, sprang into the boat and pulled back as rapidly as possible to gladden those who had suffered more than we who were stouter, from this long delay in hearing home news.

I had an opportunity at Thebes of thanking Lord Paulet, for it was he who had found this package lying at Luxor on Mustapha's table. Knowing how welcome its contents would be he brought it up the river, directing his men to look out night and day for our boat and under no circumstances allow us to pass them.

Who shall describe the keen pleasure of letters from home in such unexpected places.

When they had been read and re-read, I went out and took my place on the cabin deck, where I usually sat facing the crew at their oars. Every eye was full of delight, for every man enjoyed our pleasure. There was never a Nile boat where the crew became so strongly attached to their employers. This was the effect of constant kind treatment and attention to their comfort.

"Have you heard from your people, O Braheem Effendi?" asked Hassan Hegazi, who pulled the stroke oar, standing up to it at every pull.

"Yes; this paper has come to me from my city."

Alas! that I knew not enough of Arabic to give them the idea that is in that English word of words, *home.*

"How many mahatta is it?"

Mohammed Ali established Khans along the Nile for his army or his caravans going to and from Upper Nubia, to rest in. They are at variable distances apart, but average about twelve miles, and that is the only measure of distance, except by hours, that they know of here.

"It is many mahatta—more than five hundred."

"Mashallah! Tell us the news from your city, Braheem Effendi."

"I will. Do you know that there is a country away north of this where it is always cold, and ice and snow?"

"We have seen snow."

"Yes; but there it is always snow. The water is all ice, and the land all white with snow; and, years ago, there was a brave Englishman sailed to that country in his ship, to find a way through the ice to countries beyond, and he never came back."

"Inshallah!"

"And before I left my city, there was an American, a young man of most excellent heart and exceeding brave spirit, who went out in a ship to find the Englishman, and bring him to his own city and his wife; but he was not heard of again, for he too did not come back from the country of cold."

"Bismillah!"

"And then the government in my city (*beled* is the only Arabic word to express city, country, or state, to the intelligence of the common classes) sent out another ship to find them; and when I came from America, they had gone to the land of cold!"

"Mashallah! another!"

"And these writings tell me that the last ship, sailing in the great ocean, saw another ship lying in a harbor, which had in it the very men they were seeking, who had traveled far over snow and ice, and found this ship, and were going to England, all safe and well."

"Allahu Akbar!" and they shouted all together over the safety of Kane and his companions.

It was nearly midnight when we reached Saboa—the Valley of Lions, so called from the lion sphinxes, an avenue of which was in front of the temple. The moon was up, and we determined to see the temple and go on. Coming to the land near the village, we climbed the bank, and found profound stillness among the huts. Not even a dog barked at us. There was a donkey tied near the houses, and Abd-el-Atti mounted him and performed some feats of riding for general amusement, but no one awoke. They sleep soundly, these poor dogs of Nubians. So we walked up to the temple and around it, and viewed its ruins, and returned to the boat and were away. These moonlight views are, after all, the pleasantest memories we shall have of Egypt. The temple at Saboa dates from the time of the great Remeses, and around it hang the memories of thirty centuries. It is as well to have seen such a spot in the silver light of the moon, and not by broad day, for one can thus better imagine it the abode of ancient stories. The men had other ideas of night and moonlight, and on our return to the boat we found each one of them loaded with fuel for their cooking, which they had stolen in and near the village.

Next morning I awoke with the boat rolling and pitching as if we were on the Atlantic in a small gale of wind. I hurried out on deck and found that we were in a narrow part of the river where the current was rapid, and the wind blowing against it strong from the north made a heavy sea, while, of course, we made no progress, but, on the contrary, rather drove up stream. The reis and crew were invisible. Every man of them was rolled up, head and heels, in his bournoose, and sound asleep. I turned in again and slept an hour, and went out again. We had gone a mile up stream, and they were all asleep as before. I shouted to the reis, woke him up and asked him why he didn't attend to his boat, and how long he intended to pitch us about in that way; and on the crew coming to their senses, we laid her in shore and made fast to the bank.

I passed the day among the hills and in the villages on the shore, learning what I could of the domestic life of the poor Nubians. Their houses and furniture were simple enough, and their dress even more so.

The purchase of milk had been a source of amusement as well as difficulty all along the river, and while waiting here we endeavored to secure a supply. Abd-el-Atti sent for his pail, and we sat on the rocks among the huts on the hillside, and told the women to bring their milk and pour into it. Singularly enough the great objection which they had to parting with it originated in their love of butter. Not for eating purposes. That would be a waste of precious material. It was for their heads only, to soak their black locks withal. Hence one brought but a pint, and another half as much, and another but a little more. Before they would pour the milk into the common receptacle they must have the money; and as for copper, they would not touch it. No, it must be silver. But we had no silver coin small enough to pay for such small amounts of milk, and after a long parley, Abd-el-Atti made a dash at the calabashes and poured them all into the pail together.

Then arose a cry, and while three or four of them shouted their indignation, one, a tall and beautiful girl, one of the most elegantly-formed women that I have seen, and displaying her beauty in unvailed freedom, seized the handkerchief which Abd-el-Atti had laid on a rock, and in which was a dollar or so of money, and sprang like a deer up the side of the rocks to a high point, where she turned and shook it at us with a shout of delight. Abd-el-Atti raised his gun and pointed it at her, but she knew well that it was only a threat, and she did not fear it.

The entire fearlessness of the women in this part of the world is remarkable, and appears to be an evidence that they are well treated. In all the blows that I have seen struck here I never saw a man strike a woman; and oftentimes when I have observed a man putting to flight a crowd who surrounded a doorway or who annoyed travelers, the women remained undisturbed, never apprehending violence. It was a long time before we could induce the girl to return with the money, but when she did, she approached without a moment's fear of personal violence.

A woman near this scene was grinding the castor-bean between two stones, and obtaining the oil for anointing purposes. Others were pounding corn into meal and making bread; and all were stout, fat, sleek women, looking as if fed on the fat of the fattest of lands, instead of the dry meal of Egypt. One man in America could not live a day on what will keep a Nubian family in good feed for a week.

While I was wandering over the hills in search of foxes the wind went down, and the reis, with a stupidity for which he had become somewhat remarkable, cast off the fasts and went on down the river without looking for his passengers. I saw this from a hill-top nearly a mile away from the river, and had the pleasant consciousness withal, that every one on the boat had probably gone to sleep, and I might follow them till night in vain. Abd-el-Atti was somewhere among the mountains also, and I determined instantly to look him up, and at that moment saw him a mile below the boat, hurrying to the bank of the river. He stopped them, and I came up an hour afterward, foot weary and glad to get on board again.

At nearly midnight that night we were at Dakkeh, and determined to see it, as we had seen Saboa, by the light of the moon, which in fact had not yet risen. The villagers were sound asleep, and did not hear us as we pulled the dry corn-stalks from the roofs of their houses, wherewith to build a fire in the desolate court of the temple.

By their light I copied a quaint picture of a man, or a devil, or a god, playing on a harp. It is on one of the pillars at the left of the door as you enter. This temple is well worth a visit, if only for the exquisite state of perfection in which many of the sculptures remain, especially those in the small sepulchral chamber on the east of the adytum, where, but for the smoke and blackness, one might almost imagine every thing fresh from the builders' hands.

Returning from the temple, we found some of the villagers awake, and pushed into their houses. There were the usual strange groups lying on the ground in profound slumber, forgetful for the time of the labors and the ills of life. An old man and an old woman, very old, lay by the embers of a fire, and when I entered rubbed their eyes at the strange vision that interrupted their slumber, and looked piteously at me, as if they thought I had come to disturb them in their few remaining days. I dropped money into their hands, and they looked like new beings. Some antiques were here, a few broken vases, a coin or two, and some trifles of that kind; and having bought all that were of any value, we left them to sleep again, and hastened back to the boat. It was a grand night again. The moon lay in the east with an air of majesty and calmness that I never saw surpassed, and I had blessed sleep that night and the dreams that most of all I longed for. Thank God again for dreams!

30.

Northward in Egypt.

In the morning after we left Dakkeh we were approaching *Gerf Hossayn.* We were welcomed at the shore by a crowd of hostile looking Nubians, and a demand of money for the privilege of landing. This is one of the spots in Nubia celebrated for outrages and rebellions. It is the Lyons of Egypt, where the government has more or less to do every year, in putting down insurrections and punishing not a few bold and daring offenders against its authority.

The temple at Gerf Hossayn is like that at Abou Simbal, cut out of the rock of the hill. The remains of a colonnade in front of it lead to the doorway, which admits the visitor to a large chamber, the roof of which is supported by six colossal statues, all of which have been brilliantly painted, of which paint much brilliancy yet remains. In the walls of the chamber behind the openings between the statues, are eight niches, four on each side, in each of which are three seated figures. The second chamber has the wall supported by four large square pillars, and beyond this is the adytum with its altar and four seated statues behind it, the gods that have waited for thousands of years the return of the devout of old times—who, alas, are wandering in shades of darkness, seeking vainly the abodes of their deities. There is a sublimity in the appearance of these stone gods sitting behind their cold altars, in the profound stillness of the mountain's very heart, which awes the careless stranger. I stand before them as before the very embodied thoughts of olden times. I look at them as I would look at the visible presence in the flesh of one of Homer's heroes. Nay, more than that—men's throbbing hearts have been hushed in awe before this stone. Woman's breast has been bared to seek a blessing from their cold, calm eyes. Red lips have trembled in convulsive prayer, have quivered in the agonies of hope deferred and failing faith, before the silent gods. The eyes of millions, generations after generations of the changing races of men, have been fixed with adoring gaze on their voiceless lips, and the faith of those generations had given sanctity to what might otherwise pass for stone and nothing more. If the voice of THE GOD should but speak into life those silent companions, and bid them utter their histories, what bones would shake in the vaults of old Egypt as the fearful stories of century after century came from those eloquent lips!

We did not leave Gerf Hossayn in peace. One native, blacker than any dream of darkness, grew specially insolent to me, and I was compelled to order the crowd outside of the front colonnade, and forbid their entrance, placing Mohammed Hassan on guard with a pistol to enforce obedience. This one rascal, however, threw stones at my sentinel, which was more than he could put up with. It was a miracle that he did not use the pistol. Instead of that he threw the pistol to Hassan Hegazi, another of the sailors who was with us, and sprang at his foe. The yell of the spectators brought me out of the temple in an instant, and I found the Nubian on his back under his powerful assailant. I cleared a ring, and commanded Mohammed to drag him into the colonnade, which done, I allowed him to administer such justice as left our Gerf Hossayn friends convinced of the impropriety of interfering with the pleasures of a Howajji. When we returned to our boat we found alongside of her a small boat which proved to belong to Abdul Rahman, and was then upward bound to Derr. I wrote him a note, suggesting one of the annual visitations to Gerf Hossayn which the government were accustomed to make, and, before I left Egypt had the pleasure of hearing that he had acted on my recommendation, caught the especial offender, whom he would have no difficulty in recognizing by his sore head, and administered a proper amount of justice in the regular way.

We passed Dendoor in the afternoon, going ashore only for an hour to examine the heap of ruins that mark the site of a temple, once beautiful and elevated on a fine terrace above the river, and that night we laid the boat up at Kalabshee.

The next morning was the last day of December and of the year.

The large temple of Kalabshee is interesting, as having been once very gorgeous, and still retaining remains of its golden chambers; but the small rock-hewn temple on the hill-side is more interesting, as built or hewn by Remeses (Sesostris), and as having in its front two columns or pillars, which are among the oldest in the world, since they must date between 1300 and 1400 B.C., and whose simple polygonal shafts are very like the Grecian Doric in appearance. The representations of the deeds of Remeses, which were on the sides of the court in front of this temple, are defaced, but enough still remains to enable us to trace much of interesting history from their ancient lines.

At noon we were again on the river, and as the old year died along the Nile and the new one came with curious eyes to gaze on the wonders of Egypt of the ancient days, we were falling quietly into the little bay under the shadow of the temple that overhangs the eastern bank of Philæ the beautiful.

All day long that New-year day we wandered among the stately ruins of Philæ. We had a sort of claim to possession of the island, for we had been its discoverers this winter, being the first travelers up from the lower country; but we found an English gentleman in actual possession, and in the course of the day an American party came up on donkeys from Es Souan to see the most beautiful of islands. Three ladies, dressed in black, and wearing the broad black English flats on their heads, looked down on us from the summit of the lofty tower of the propylon of the temple of Isis, and we, sitting among the ruins at the north end of the island, considered them as in some respects interlopers on our domains. Nevertheless it was pleasant to see females from civilized lands once more, and to know that we were returning into the company of fellow Christians.

We sent the *Phantom* down the river early in the morning. Of her fearful passage of the cataract we had great accounts in the evening at Es Souan, when we rejoined her. How she went bravely down the first great rapid, danced like a bird through the foam and wild dash of the long reach of the cataract; how thereupon Bag Boug sprang at Reis Hassanein and seized his turban, which is by custom the fee of the reis of the cataract on a successful descent; how old Reis Hassan seized the other end, and a fight ensued between the four cataract reises, during which the boat struck a rock and went over on her side, and a loud yell rose from fifty throats; how Abd-el-Atti threw Bag Boug into the river and knocked

Selim overboard after him, and made terrible work generally among them, till the *Phantom* swung off into deep water; all these things we heard in the evening from Reis Hassanein, who sat contented on the top of the kitchen watching the preparation of our New-year's dinner, and from Hassan, the bright-eyed cabin boy, whose heart had been in his mouth a dozen times between Philæ and the foot of the cataract.

As the sun was going westward, we hailed an old boat that lay under the bank of the main land, and a naked boy and a miserable old man with a ragged cloth around his loins paddled it across. It had an awning of coarse straw matting across the stern, and under this we lay down while they ferried us over to the main land, where we met donkeys which Abd-el-Atti sent up from Es Souan on his arrival there.

I have before spoken of the road to Es Souan. I had walked part of it with our missionary friends on a moonlight night some time before, and now by daylight the road was scarcely less picturesque and wild.

Our donkeys were none of the best. I had not used mine five minutes before it became evident that he had a weakness in his hinder parts, incapacitating him for carrying a hundred and seventy odd pounds of American flesh and blood, and I took to my own means of locomotion.

It was evening when we reached Es Souan, and here a gay scene awaited us.

There were seven boats here, besides our own, carrying American, English, French, and Prussian flags, and after dinner, when it was about noon at home, we followed the illustrious custom of the Knickerbocker city, and made calls, while the ladies on the *Phantom* received. When we returned, we found some twelve persons in the little cabin, and a merry evening that was for us, returning, as it were from exile, suddenly into all the refinements of civilization.

When our friends had left the boat, we amused ourselves and the natives with a few fire-works, and the various boats saluting, we made the rocks of Elephantina echo all night to the sound of fire-arms.

Next day, at eight, we left, with a chorus of the rowers, as they lay down to their oars.

It was a dark and threatening day, but we went swiftly down stream, pausing nowhere, and at nine in the evening passed under the hill on which stands *Koum Ombos.*

I was shooting along shore, next morning, for a head wind kept the *Phantom* back, when Mohammed Hassan, my constant attendant, shouted, "Yasmin! Yasmin!" and dashed at a bunch of green leaves, with a zeal that aroused, if it did not surprise me. Jessamine is a wood most highly prized by the Orientals for pipe-stems, and here was a quantity of it.

Reis Hassanein, seated on the cabin deck of the *Phantom*, a mile away, saw us and shouted aloud to know what we were doing. The distance at which these Arabs talk is incredible. Mohammed replied, and I saw the reis tumble down into the small boat in a great hurry. He hastened ashore to share the plunder. We secured as much as would have cost eight or ten dollars to purchase in Cairo, and this I sent on board, with bunches of the fragrant blossoms, for Amy and Miriam. I went on shooting along the bank of the river, getting sundry rabbits, pigeons, and partridges.

I arrived, at length, at the vast sand-stone quarries of Hagar Silsilis. Their extent is very great, and their chief feature of interest consists in deep, narrow, rock cuts, roads hewn from the river back into the hills, not more than twenty feet wide, and having sides often from fifty to a hundred feet high, perpendicular. I was lost in one of these, and found my way to the river just in time to hail the boat as it drifted by. They put me across to the other side, where we all landed to see the various rock-hewn tablets, and small temples, or praying places, which here abound. Many of these are of the deepest interest to the Egyptian scholar, and the attention of Egyptiologists is just now directed very carefully to the inscriptions at Hagar Silsilis.

Many of these open chapels are exceedingly beautiful, and on some the brilliant painting remains with very much freshness. Perhaps the most interesting is the most northern corridor, where we find repeated often the cartouche of Horus, the successor of the great Amunoph who is the original of the vocal Memnon. These chapels were probably used by the laborers. The quarries, which are of very ancient date, furnished the stone for most, if not all of the great temples along the river below this point. Thebes and Karnak were doubtless hewn out of these hills. I looked in vain for a cartouche of *Remai*, which Wilkinson saw on the rock somewhere near here, a king who was of a very early period, if he be, as that learned gentleman has thought possible, identical with *Mœris.*

The place derives its name from a large rock standing, column like, near the river, which is here very narrow. The word *hagar*, or *hajjar*, as it would be pronounced in Syrian Arabic, signifies a *rock*, and Silsilis *a chain*, there being a tradition that in some ancient time a chain was stretched across the river here as a barrier against southern invasion.

I walked on down the river until dark. An Arab had shot two crocodiles, and wanted to sell me their skins, but it was not in my line. Toward evening I hailed the boat, and the small boat came and put me across the river, where Abd-el-Atti was shooting along shore as I had been. While waiting for him, I observed that the shore was covered with cornelians and agates in large quantities. I filled my pockets, and threw nearly a half bushel into the boat, from which to let the ladies make selections, and then returned on board.

A loud cry, and a sudden thump on a sand-bank, interrupted our quiet, in the evening, and the next moment the reis nearly broke his neck as he fell off the front of the cabin to the main-deck. He had been dozing there, as usual, droning out a chorus for the men to row by, and when she struck, he toppled over forward, and came down in a heap in front of the door. Then ensued the usual demand for medicine and surgery, and so the night passed on.

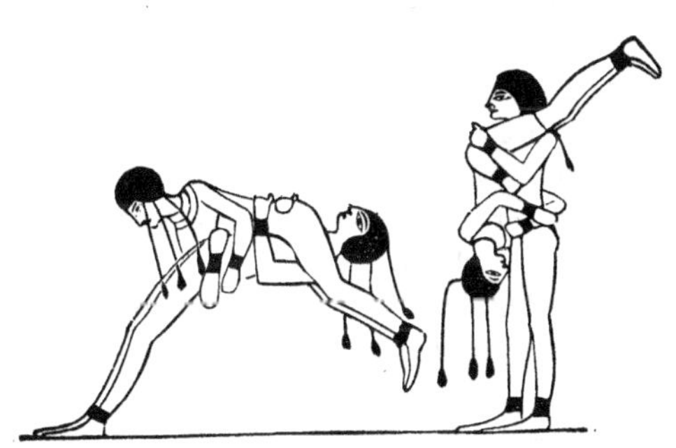

31.

Arrakee and Antiques.

Early next morning we were near Edfou; and as I had visited the temple alone on the upward passage we, of course, had a stop to make here.

The reis, being in a desperate hurry to get to land before another boat which was close behind us, plunged the *Phantom* on a sand-bar, where the pelicans and cranes laughed at us for three hours of a bright morning, and the *Breeze*, the other boat, following us blindly, fell on the same shoal, and stuck fast on the same bar. The men heaved, and pulled, and braced their backs under the boat, and strained their brawny limbs, and looked wistfully at their breakfast on deck, which the reis wouldn't let them have until they got the boat off; and so the sun went up high, and the chances were that we should lie there till the next flood of the Nile.

Trumbull, who had been sitting on deck, quietly smoking his chibouk, and had now finished it, called out to Hajji Hassan to make a rope fast to her stern, and take it off across the stream, where three of the men took hold, standing nearly up to their necks in water. A few easy pulls in that direction started the sand under the keel, and she swung gently off, while the poor wretches who had been working under the sides, swung themselves in with an exclamation, "Mashallah!" and took to their breakfast as if starving. Fifteen minutes more brought us to the land, at the same spot in which we lay on our way up the river; whence we started on foot, while the ladies rode donkeys, up to the village and the temples.

The travelers from the other boat were a party of four from Albany, three ladies and a gentleman, and they soon arrived, so that there were five American ladies and three gentlemen in the temple at Edfou together. I have spoken of this old and magnificent building on my way up the river, and I shall not pause here to describe it. It is one of those wonders of Egypt best described by saying that a large part of the modern village, a part containing several hundred inhabitants, is situated on the roof of the rear portion, the *adytum*, of the temple. The filth of centuries is accumulated within; and I record here the fact, that I did not enter the adytum, as this was the only hole, large or small, in Egypt, which there was any object in entering, that I shrunk from. It occurred on this wise. I was loitering around the entrance, looking at the vast towers of the gateway, while the ladies sat in a picturesque group in the grand court, under the shade of the western corridor.

"Antika, antika kebeer, antika tieb keteer minhenna!" said an Arab boy to me.

I had heard it from so many that I thought there must be something worth the seeing, and shouting to Miriam that I would return soon, I pushed on after the boy, who led me, with a motley train behind me, up to the village, which was on the roof of the adytum, and through two or three of its dirty alleys. The crowd of women and children began to increase around me, and at length my leader pushed open the board entrance of a mud hut, and told me to follow him. I followed him, and they followed me. They were of all grades and colors, and stages of nakedness and filth; some fifty Arab or Egyptian women and children, not a man among them; and I looked around me in the dim hut, thinking myself the centre of altogether the worst-looking group of humanity that ever radiated around my person. Up to this time I entertained the idea that I was to find an antique for sale, and I had some doubts whether it would turn out to be a mummy or a vase; for every valuable curiosity is most diligently concealed from the government officers. But the boy demanded now whether I had a candle, and on my replying yes, and producing my never-failing companion and some matches, he seized the candle, lit it, while I looked on patiently, and then dropping flat on his face on the floor, vanished out of sight.

It was magical. I was for an instant in astonished silence, till the group began shouting, "Antika tieb, tieb keteer!" and pointing downward, directed my attention to what I had not before observed, that the side wall of the hut was the upper part of the wall of the temple, and that the boy had crawled through a hole about a foot high, by two or two and a half wide, and was actually gone, by this "hole in the wall," into the holy of holies, which priests and princes of ancient days were accustomed to enter in lordly processions of solemn grandeur.

I stooped and looked in. The boy was calling me. I lay down and worked my way in, snake fashion, far enough to see that I was in a sculptured room, half filled with dust, and straw, and filth, and then seven fleas attacked my feet, seventeen my waist, and sevenscore my neck, and I returned to outer light, and the stifling presence of the women and children, who vociferously demanded if it was not a magnificent antique, and if my bucksheesh would not be proportionably grand. I scattered some coppers on the floor, whereupon there ensued the usual rough-and-tumble scene, a confused heap of heads, arms, legs, and bodies in the middle of the room; and I came out into the air. As I passed the front of the temple on my way back to the ladies, a hard-looking old case of an Arab whispered in my ear that if I wanted to see some good arrakee he was just the man who could gratify me. I thought he was, from his personal appearance. He was, in fact, the one-eyed scribe whose close attachment to the old governor I described in a former chapter; and I now had an additional explanation of the red face and blear eyes of that functionary, of whose diligent pursuit of my brandy I before wrote.

Willing to see all that was to be seen, I assented, and the old fellow led me to the spot. For the benefit of future travelers who may wish to drink at Edfou, I will inform them that it is in the street running from the front of the temple, third door on the left; knock once and say something low about bucksheesh, and an old woman—if she is not dead, as she seemed likely to be soon—a facsimile of the old man, will open the door, lead you through a court into a smaller court, and exhibit altogether the most primitive still that your eyes will ever rest on, wherein, by aid of dates and fire, there is manufactured wherewith to poison the poor devils who lie lazily around the temple to pick up travelers' coppers, and insure them a poor reception from the Prophet after they are dead. On the whole, however, it was good arrakee that the old man made, although the stuff is detestable. The taste is anise seed, the effect that of the lowest grade of whisky. I tasted and departed. As I came out of the hut into the street, where were now at least a hundred natives crowded around our party, who were purchasing antiques, I saw the old man slide up to Mr. R——, the Albany gentleman aforesaid, and whisper as he had to me, and a few minutes later Mr. R—— came out of the hut with a comical expression of countenance, and it was difficult to say whether it was owing to the oddity of the circumstance or the vileness of the tipple.

There was a little girl in the crowd, innocent of drapery, who came up to me repeatedly with four coins at a time in her hand, which I repeatedly purchased before I observed that it was the same child each time. I then saw that there must be a treasury of them somewhere. Obviously she could not carry them about her person, that was too manifest, and I made her take me to her home, a mud hut a little way off. It was inhabited by an old woman, who denied entirely that she had any more; but persuasion and promises produced the result at length, and she brought me out some hundreds of coins, chiefly of the eastern empire, but many more valuable. I selected and purchased all that I wished; but the stock will last her for years, and any one wishing for coins may find her there. Street and number I can't give.

It was a delicious afternoon. The memory of it haunts me. I can not say why, except that earth, air, and sky were in more perfect unison of beauty that day than ever before. We dined early, and after dinner I took my gun and strolled down the river, leaving the boat to follow when it would. The evening came on, and I found myself on the beach, where a long point of mud or sand, running two miles down the river, completely shut me off from communication with the boat if she should come along, but as yet I saw nothing of her. Retracing my steps with Mohammed Hassan, my constant companion in such walks, close behind me, I took to the point and followed it down, shooting an occasional wild fowl, for Edfou abounds in every species of duck, and the river is filled with geese and various other water fowl, which find excellent feeding-ground in the lake and flats back of the village.

A boat coming slowly up the river with full sail set, passed close to me, and I exchanged salutes with her owners. She carried English colors. The last rays of the sun lit them joyously as she swept on up the stream, and I was left alone with my Arab attendant on the sandy point, and the swift night was coming down on us, as it always comes in that land of clear air and deep skies. At length it became manifest that it was unsafe to walk further. The bar on which I was walking was of mud and sand mingled, and had now narrowed to less than two hundred feet, while it oozed and sank under my feet at each step that I made in advance. It was that peculiar mud, too, which reminds one of what, when boys, we called *leather-ice*, which was apparently tough and strong, and yet would yield under a steady pressure, so that we could run across it, but could not rest on it. I could strike the breach of my gun down heavily and firmly on it, and it would not give, but by tapping it gently I would change the consistency of it to mere loose mud, and then a small circle would sink and leave clear water in its place. Taking our position on the highest point of the ridge, a foot or two above the river level, and changing our feet constantly from place to place, we waited impatiently the coming of the boat. The *Breeze*, Mr. R——'s boat, shot by us, and sent me a halloo and a salute, to which I replied by waving my hat, and a few minutes later the *Phantom* was visible leaving the land. It was now a question whether they would see us or not, as it was growing so dark; but the voice is heard an incredible distance over these still waters. Our call was heard and answered more than a mile away, and the small boat came down rapidly for me. But it could not approach within thirty feet of the land, and I waded off to it, declining the proffered shoulders of the man, lest by contact I should take off what is as bad as disease, and much worse than dirt.

As I came on board the men lay down to their oars with a will, and it appeared that they had agreed on a race with the crew of the *Breeze*, which was now far ahead of us. In the evening, as we were seated quietly at our round table, we felt a sudden increase in the velocity of the boat, and, looking out, saw that we were alongside of the other boat, whose crew had waited for us. Then the swarthy Arabs sprang to their oars, and the reis, seated at the top of the ladder to the upper deck, led them in a song, to which they gave a stout and hearty chorus, while the other boat sang another refrain; and the two flew through the water at a speed far surpassing any thing I had supposed possible with such heavy objects. Now one boat was ahead, and now the other. Now the *Breeze* led us half a length, and now we came up with her and edged slowly by her. It was impossible to write at the table, so fast did we go, and so much did the boat spring to the strokes of the oars, and the race was not over till we both came to the land under the shade of the sont trees that line the bank at *El Kab*, the ancient Eileithyas, of which the reader will remember I spoke in a former article.

Here we had proposed to pass a day, and here we found one of the most interesting points in Egypt. The ruins of the ancient city are more extensive than of any other in Egypt, but these consist almost solely of crude brick remains, walls, and heaps which cover a great space, included within the circuit of a gigantic wall, whose height and thickness must have been cyclopean. It is not in these, however, that the interest of a stay at Eileithyas consists, but in the tombs of the Egyptians with which the hill back of the plain is perforated, some of which are among the most curious and instructive in Egypt.

One or two of these are among the most ancient known in the Nile valley, containing very curious chronological tables of kings' names which are, as yet, a puzzle to the scholar. The ruins are chiefly of Roman times.

I was awake, as usual, at day break. Trumbull was never behind me. We were always out with the first rays of light, and I commenced my day invariably with a plunge in the ancient river. The *Breeze* lay close by us, and all was profoundly still on board of her, as we went out with our guns for an hour's shooting among the ruins of the old city.

It was a scene of indescribable desolation. The only spot in all Egypt where there are remains of the houses of the ancient inhabitants. These, being built of crude brick, have elsewhere disappeared, but Eileithyas was inclosed in an immense wall of the same material, not less than twenty feet thick and forty or fifty high. The remains of this wall have acted as a preserver of the dusty walls of houses within its circuit, at least from winds, and they are, therefore, left, in ruins, but enough of them standing to show that here the people of ancient days had habitations. Here families lived, children played, mothers bore offspring; all the home passions, emotions, incidents, affections, and sorrows of life had succession here; and any one of these little inclosures has held a world of thought and hope two thousand years ago, all gone now—all utterly vanished—all as pure dreams now as is yonder blue sky, beautiful, glorious, distant, intangible, unapproachable.

In a hollow, where was once a sacred lake connected with one of the temples, we started a fox, and in the low water that filled the bottom of the hollow, we put up a dozen snipe and shot three or four of them.

As the sun came up pigeons began to fly, and we stationed ourselves on the highest point of the old wall and shot two or three dozen as they went over.

Meantime, on board the boat, Hajji Mohammed was busy at his breakfast arrangements, which were kept in abeyance till the ladies came out of their cabin, and then

Ferrajj was despatched to find and call us. Such was the morning routine always when the boat was not sailing.

Never were two ladies in brighter condition than Amy and Miriam, and never were donkeys more miserable brought for ladies to ride on than now awaited them on the bank above the boat. But these were the best that the country afforded, and they mounted, while Trumbull and myself declined the proffer of similar conveyances, and started on foot across the plain, which stretched away to the foot of the mountain, shooting as we went at whatever wild animals we found haunting the ruins of the ancient palaces of the Romans. Half an hour brought us to the foot of the hills, and lending our own assistance to the donkeys, we succeeded in carrying the ladies up the steep ascent to the platform in front of the first and chief row of sepulchres, when they dismounted, and we proceeded together to examine the empty chambers that were once fitted up for the long abode of mortality awaiting immortality.

I shall not pause to describe these tombs. We sat in one of them and welcomed the arrival of the party from the *Breeze*, who now came up, and we looked out on the flow of the river, and up toward Edfou, and down toward Thebes, and again we talked of the grandeur of the sepulchral spots which the men of old time selected, as if they designed to look out on the flow of their lordly river in the solemn nights, when ghosts of all ages have been permitted to walk abroad.

I believe that I mentioned, in my description of my voyage up the river, that I passed a morning at this place searching for antiques. We desired to do so again, and having given directions to our boat to drop down the river, we went on to the village, which lay a few miles down the plain, crossing the same broad plateau on which, a few weeks before, I had my fast run on an Arab horse. I was now on foot, and went along very quietly in the hot sunshine. At the village we were surrounded by the inhabitants in an instant, and, their curiosity having been first satisfied, they brought us what they had collected during our absence up the river.

The stranger to Egypt perhaps wonders what sort of antiques we can expect to find in such places. Certainly it must be something smaller than a statue or sphinx, for these are plenty, and whoever wishes to load a ship with one or a dozen may do so. But the tombs of Egypt inclose unknown treasures of antiquity. Of these, to the traveler, jewelry and articles of personal ornament are usually most curious and desirable, and the tombs often furnish these of great beauty and value.

It was in hopes that we might find something valuable that we made constant purchase of all the trifles that the people brought to us; and, after loading ourselves with earthern figures, images of various sorts, and coins in profusion, of various ages and conditions, we came down to the boat, which had dropped down the river to a point opposite the village. On the broad plain of El Kab that day we had a perfect mirage; so perfect, that with a full assurance of the impossibility of seeing the river, we disputed the possibility of a mirage on so small a plain, and refused to believe it was not water until we marked its boundary, and rode up to that boundary.

That afternoon we cast off from the shore, the *Breeze* being ahead of us, and Mr. R—— having come on board our boat. After dinner, while we were quietly sipping our wine, we were roused by the Arabs crying out that there was an American flag ahead, and rushing out on deck we saw a boat coming up with a fresh breeze, and behind it yet another, carrying also the stars and stripes. It was a sight worth seeing that, and not very common any where in the eastern world. Four American boats together on the Nile! Of course we all shouted—every body must shout under such circumstances. Trumbull, Mr. R——, and myself sprang into our small boat and boarded the other boats—the ladies having only waved their hands and helped the shouting a little. The *Phantom* and the *Breeze* went drifting down the river, and we went up with the new-comers, who could give us late news from home and from the civilized world, to which we had so long been comparative strangers; and at length, as evening approached, we suddenly remembered that the *Phantom* and the *Breeze* were gone.

We sprang ashore and hastened down the bank of the river. A mile below, we found our small boat waiting for us, and into this we hastened. The sun was setting—short twilight followed. The night came down, dark and cold. There were pipes in the boat, and tobacco plenty, that universal solace. Let me see the man that dares talk to me of the "deleterious effects of nicotine," when I am recalling its delicious consolations in such times as was that.

Eight—nine—ten o'clock, and still the men rowed, and still no signs of the *Phantom* or the *Breeze*.

"Now, men—lay on well—pull, pull—you shall have Tombak to-night;" and they sent her through the current, six of them pulling well, until my pistol was answered far down the river, and the red light flashed out at last. The boats were side by side, their bright cabin lights shining on each other.

Were you ever abroad on a cold night of autumn, and driving homeward over weary hills? and do you remember the delight of the warm room, the cheerful lamp, the hissing tea urn, and the welcome of pleasant lips? Such was ours in the cabin of the *Phantom*.

32.

Achmet the Resurrectionist.

At midnight we were at Esne, and in the morning I went again up to the temple.

The mummies lay as I had left them some weeks before, no traveler having ventured to disturb their repose. There were several boats at Esne, and while I sat in the portico of the temple, one, and another, and another stranger came in, and voices of various lands disturbed the quiet of Ptolemaic times.

The governor had no donkey that suited me or Abd-el-Atti, whom I represented. He came down to the boat with a drove of them, large and small, gray and black, male and female, but he said himself that he could not scare up one that he could recommend, and I left a general order to have one sent down by boat to Cairo, and so we departed.

I was dozing on the upper deck after an evening chibouk, discussing with Trumbull the shape of some hieroglyphic about which our memories differed, when the *Phantom* brought up with a plunge on a sand bank that sent the rowers over backward into each other's laps, and disturbed Reis Hassanein's stupidity to an alarming degree. He raved, stormed, swore, called on Allah, and vowed over and again that there was no Illah but Allah, but it was all of no use. Three hours she lay there, and two more on other banks before the morning, and then as we approached the Gebelein it was blowing a hurricane up the river and he couldn't get along an inch, and we lay-to from morning till nearly sunset. Two or three boats dashed up the river in glorious style, exchanging salutes with us as they passed. Seeing one with American colors coming up, we pulled out toward her, and as they saw our flags, for the *Breeze* was lying near us, they let their sheet fly and rounded to close by us, and made a call on the ladies. It proved to be the boat of two gentlemen from New Orleans, who had met some of the party on the *Breeze* some where in Europe months before. These pleasant *reunions* are among the most inspiriting incidents of foreign travel. They made a half-hour call, and then flew on before the breeze, of which we could not wish them a continuance, for we were by it kept back from Thebes, which lay half a day from us.

I strolled off over the fields with Abd-el-Atti and a milk-pail. Among my pleasantest recollections of Egypt are those adventures with Abd-el-Atti among the fellaheen. While he sought some one who would sell him milk, I sat down in a sunny place and chatted with the crowd of curious people who came around me. Once in a while I bought a valuable antique, and many rare coins I picked up in those places. There is but one memory of that day that is specially fixed on my mind.

On the bank of the river, near this village, I sat down and watched the women coming for water. One and another came, each helping the one before her to lift the enormous jar to the top of her head.

At length there appeared one of the noblest specimens of feminine beauty that I remember. A tall and splendidly formed girl came down close by me, the wind blowing back her single thin cotton garment so as to reveal the outlines of a perfect form, one that Praxiteles might have dreamed, one such as it is seldom permitted human eyes to see. Her tunic was open from neck to waist, and her bust, contrary to the common appearance of the Egyptian women, was full and of delicate outline. Her face was Greek, her lips classical in their severe beauty.

Imagine my astonishment as this vision swept by me, not three feet distant, and paused within a rod to dip water in a heavy jar. I gazed admiringly at her, as who would not? She returned my gaze with cold curiosity, and eyes devoid of interest, but dark, lustrous eyes withal, that had fire in them which might be made to flame.

She had on her neck a string of antiques, chiefly scarabæi. I had seen them thus before, and had purchased some curious antiques from the necks and wrists of the women. I walked up to her and took hold of them. She stood like a statue, motionless, with her black eyes fixed on mine, but was silent, and allowed my examination without fear or objection.

"How much shall I pay you for your necklace?"

She looked, but made no reply, and stooping down, lifted her jar; a friend helped her swing it to her head, and then, dropping her hands, she walked up the bank in stately style, nor looked back, nor seemed to have the slightest interest in the fate of Braheem Effendi. To be cut thus by an Egyptian! On reflection, I have thought that she was perhaps deaf and dumb—possibly idiotic, but I think not that, for she was too splendidly beautiful.

It was after midnight—a calm, still night—when we swept around the lower point of the island, and swinging into the branch which comes down from the eastward, laid our boat at the land close under the columns of the Temple of Luxor. The men were very still in all their movements, for the ladies were sleeping, and we had a crew that were remarkably intelligent for Arabs, and remarkably attentive to our wishes.

Trumbull and I sat on the cabin-deck, wrapped in our cloaks, for the night was cool, and watched the growing magnificence of the temple as we approached it. It seemed to rise in the air before us, and its stupendous proportions became gigantic, even supernatural, in that dim light which seems always to be the fitting shroud of Egyptian grandeur. The columns of the principal court—which are now the only portion fronting on the river, the rest being concealed by mud houses—appeared, in their lonesome greatness, like the memorials of a race of men that knew and talked with gods. In their shadowy presence we could well imagine the ghosts of the departed watching our arrival.

There were no boats at Luxor. The fresh wind of the previous day was too valuable to upward-bound travelers, and they had all gone on without pausing to look at Thebes. It was well for us that it was so, for it appeared more as if we were arriving at the desolate site of an ancient city, and less like a resort of modern sight-seers. A few days later, when there were four or five boats lying at the shore, and morning and evening saw ten or fifteen gayly-dressed ladies and gentlemen strolling across the open space which lies between the temple and the beach, the scene was very different, and almost modern. But now all was profoundly ancient. The very skies for once looked old, as they bent down over the site of a city of a hundred temple-gates, and the stars—

What a vigil theirs has been above the mighty Nile! The steady march of Time has been below; God never yet permitted him to tread the sapphire floors above. There, all is as it was when Eve was young in Eden, and human love and hope were as pure as the hopes and loves of angels. Below, all is changed; the mark of years is on every thing. But nowhere on the surface of the little globe that we call earth—nowhere, has the vigil been as sad as here.

It was in the morning of the new world—in the very dawn of human existence after the flood—that the foundations of this city were laid. He who led his followers here had heard the story of the deluge from Noah, perhaps had seen its subsiding waves. And after him nations and races swept over Egypt, and dynasties changed with the shifting desert sand, and the river rose and fell, and rose and fell, and the same solemn, calm watchers, looked down, night after night, on all.

I thought of one scene as I sat that night on deck. You may think it an imagination, pure fancy, or what you please. It is vain to forbid imaginations in such a place as that. Midnight, profound and calm; moonlight, holy as the memories that seemed verily to compose it; stars, watching with deep eyes the plains of their long vigil; ruins, that were gray centuries ago, and on whose mystical forms the men of early ages gazed with as much of awe and wonder as we do now—all this in a land where men had lived and toiled, had walked and talked, and eaten, and drunken, and slept, had lived and perished, in successive generations, since a period to which neither record nor tradition can assign a date—all this, I say, was certainly enough to rouse imagination, and quicken fancy to its freest play.

Once, as the boat was coming to the land, I looked across to the western hills, above the throne of Memnon, and for an instant saw a flashing light, that might have passed for a will-o'-the-wisp among the graves of the ancient Thebans. I knew it was no ghost light, and I knew as well that it was a veritable farthing-dip, and no doubt held in the hands of an Arab who was so intent on his work of robbing a newly-opened tomb, that he forgot his caution for a moment, and allowed his light to shine out on the plain. Perhaps no other person saw it, but it was enough to call before me the scene on the hillside, and in an instant all of its wild strangeness was present to my imagination.

This hillside, as the reader already knows, is full of the dead. It is very manifest that a broad street once crossed the plain, near the head of which Memnon and his silent companion sit now as then, and the passage between them led onward, by temple walls and stately erections, to the place of burial—the place where now, from day to day, we open tombs and disturb the rest of ancient Egyptians. That all is changed, no one need be told. The great plain of Thebes is a cultivated field, and Memnon and his nameless companion sit in solitary grandeur, looking with mournfully-fixed gaze half the year on the flood that spreads around their feet, and the other half over the desolate site of the great city. But Memnon would not sit so quietly on his rocky throne if the desecration that is carried on behind his back were perpetrated before his eyes. It would rouse an Egyptian god from his stony silence, and startle the very sleep of granite kings to see the hideous disentombment of their ancient followers, and the profane pollutions of the sanctuaries they built to sleep in till the return of Osiris.

It was up this broad street of temples, statues, and palaces that the funeral processions in former days were conducted, and the dead were carried with kingly pomp to tombs that are now invaded by the Arabs of Goornou, who work by night for fear of the government.

Achmet was abroad that night. I thought it was he, and he told me next day that I was correct. He had discovered the entrance to a new tomb, and when his light flashed on my eye, he and his companions, ten half-naked Arabs, had at length burst in the rocky wall, and the magnificent starlight of Thebes shone on the resting-place of an ancient prince.

Long ago, longer ago than with our feeble powers we can count, in the days when Joshua was judging the children of Jacob in the land of Canaan, that tomb was closed on the last of the group of sleepers that lay in its gloom. He was a prince and priest, and yonder, across the plain, stands the great temple within whose walls he had worshiped, and offered incense and sacrifice. One by one he had laid in this tomb the beloved dead of his household. Men had affections in ancient days as now. Men loved in old times as in modern. They looked on fair brows, lost themselves in the depths of blue eyes, clasped graceful forms to their breasts with all the passionate fondness of men in these days. And women were as lovely then as now. Who on earth could be more ravishingly beautiful than was the wife of Abraham, whom kings adored? Who more divinely fair than Rachel, whose young and delicate beauty won the heart of Jacob when it was growing cold in years that we think now almost too old for human passion?

Why, then, may I not imagine that she whom this great prince loved was young and very beautiful? That her brow had on it the stately light that I have seen before the sun arose on the cold, calm brow of Remeses, and that her eye had the liquid beauty and unfathomable glory of the sky that was above me that night, in whose serene, calm distances the eye of a lover could see worlds of beauty and starry radiance? Her form was of the mould of the olden time, not long removed from that of Eden. There were but a few generations (for generations were centuries long) between her and her mother Eve, and she had somewhat of the music of paradise in her voice. And she too was woman, and was human: woman, for she loved him; human, for she died. Woman, for that her heart poured out her overflowing love on him; and human, for that with that love went forth her strength, and he could not keep her back from the dark road on which she went away.

Yea, she died. There are pictures of such scenes on the monuments. With her slender arms wound tight around his neck, with her warm throbbing breasts pressed close to his, with her hot lips on his, and her breath thick with kisses, she went from him. He laid her young head, heavy with golden tresses, on the pillow, and before he left her, gazed one instant with unutterable longing on the face he should behold no more until those distant times when he and she would wake at the voice of Osiris. Other hands—for such was the custom—robed her for the grave, and wrapped her precious body in the spices and perfumes that should keep it safe from decay, and he followed her with feeble steps to the tomb, and closed it on the light of his life.

What vigils, outlasting the vigil of the stars, he kept! What long nights of his agony went heavily by as he sat and looked toward the hill in which she slept, who can tell? But there came an hour—the hour that comes to all men—when there was a darkening of the light, a gathering of gloom, and then the blackness of darkness, and he too was gone into the unknown abodes into which Egyptian philosophy had vainly sought to look. If, as they sometimes in their varying forms of belief had thought, the soul of the dead prince hovered around its late residence until it was laid by the beloved dead in the hill, then his spirit once more looked into the tomb and beheld the dead girl that had been so startlingly beautiful lying in the calm and profound repose that resists all the endearing epithets with which broken-hearted affection seeks to awaken the dust, and then his dust slept beside her.

The flashing torches that had accompanied his funereal pageant lit the recesses of his tomb once more, and the rays of Sirius and the faithful stars penetrated the inner gloom once more, and were once more shut out with his departing soul as it sought the distant and unknown residence of the Osirian shades. And then they fell on the sculptured stones before the door, and then on crumbling rocks and drifting sand, and when a thousand years had been three times told on the circles of heaven, the gray rocks of the western hills, in ragged desolation, lay piled deep over the silent company that there waited the return of the immortals.

And they came. Imagination may be pardoned thus far. When Achmet and his Arab companions tore down the last pile of rock, and broke through the wall with their rude picks and skeleton-like fingers; when the starlight sprang joyously into the gloom, among that group of gaunt men were shadowy forms flitting in the varying light, and looking with an interest more intense than any mere human being could feel in the presence of clay that had been living man three thousand years ago.

They, the Arabs, entered the silent place, and before them, in quiet that might have startled a man, but which was nothing to the inanimate souls of these poor dogs—the quiet of uncounted centuries—lay the dead prince and his dead wife, as they had wished to lie until the reunion of body to soul. With what emotion they beheld the breaking up of that long and calm companionship I dared not think. The light of Achmet flashed far out on hill and valley, and was extinguished, and then they carried them away. What fingers tore the coverings from her delicate arms! What rude hands were around her neck, that was once white and beautiful! What sacrilegious wretches wrested the jeweled amulet from its holy place between those breasts, once white and heaving full of love and life, and bared her limbs to the winds, and cast them out on the desert sand!

33.

Thebes the Magnificent.

Our stay at Thebes was to be limited only by our inclinations. Dr. Abbott had lent me a tent, which we pitched on the shore close by the boat, carried into it our deck sofa and the Nubian mats which Abdul Rahman had given us, spread our Persian carpets, and over it set the American flag by way of notice to all travelers that here was a temporary American home.

Many a pleasant evening we had in that tent, and I recall it with chiefest pleasure as the place of meeting with my friend Whitely, who subsequently wandered with me through Holy Land, along the coasts of Asia Minor, in Stamboul and up the Bosphorus to the "Cyanean Symplegades," in Athens and along the bay of Salamis, in Italy and through many sunny valleys of Europe, to be forever remembered.

In that tent many beautiful women of many lands sat in the starry evenings. In that tent I met frequently a young Englishman, an artist traveler, and talked with him of art and antiquity, and before I left Thebes I buried him in the dust of that ancient plain.

The memories of that tent on the shore of Luxor are varied and pleasant, and its evening histories alone would fill a volume.

Walking down Wall-street a few weeks ago I met just

in front of the Custom House a man whose grasp on my arm was as firm as if he had been the sheriff, and I had been—no matter who. I looked up in his face and recognized one of a party that praised Hajji Mohammed's coffee many a pleasant evening in the tent, when, tired with the long day's labor of sight-seeing or of study, we gathered around the bright eyes of Amy and Miriam and reminded ourselves of home-scenes in far off countries.

Mustapha Aga was down early in the morning to report progress in the excavations I had directed, and after breakfast we crossed the river, commencing our strolls among the ancient ruins of Thebes with Medeenet Habou. Understand, once for all, that the ruins of what is commonly called Thebes lie on both sides of the Nile, although we usually distinguish those on the west by this name as separate from Luxor and Karnak, which are on the east. The broad plain of Egypt, which is here more extensive than on any other portion of the banks of the Nile above the Delta, was once covered by the city, which has come down to us, in tradition and song, as one of the most magnificent of the Old World. But there remain of it now only a few isolated groups of ruins. Of these the greatest by far, and the most magnificent relic of ancient grandeur on the earth, is Karnak, situated on the east bank about a mile from the river. Luxor (*El Uksorein*—the Two Palaces) is also on the east bank.

On the west side of the river, at the southern extremity of the plain, lie Medeenet Habou and the group of ruins around the temple palace of Remeses. This is at the base of the western hills, and three miles from the river-bed, but the inundation reaches its very walls. To the north of this the two colossi sit on the plain, a little nearer to the river than the straight line which would connect Medeenet Habou and the Remeseion, or Memnonium. The latter is the next great ruin north of the colossi, and then nothing of importance is found until we reach the temple at Goornou, three miles further north. All these ruins are at the base of the hills and edge of the plain, being at the extreme limit of the inundation, and behind and around them all are the countless tombs of the dead of old times.

A crowd of donkey-boys and men were on the western bank awaiting our landing. It reminded one of a New York steamer landing. We selected a certain number of the small animals for constant use during our stay at Thebes, and, mounted on these, crossed the sandy shore and the dry bed of a branch of the river, ascended the true bank, which lies west of this branch, and were on the broad level plain over which the colossi, grand and majestic, gaze with steadfast eyes. Riding toward them a mile, and then diverging to the left, we reached Medeenet Habou, and entered its ruins with profound awe. Neither shall I pause here to describe the ruins of old Egypt. Human power of description is vain in the attempt to convey any idea of the grandeur of these colossal ruins, or of the startling effect produced on the visitor, who finds lofty corridors and columns exposed to the winds of centuries, yet gleaming with the brilliant colors which were laid on them thousands of years ago.

This temple, or these temples and the palace connected with them, are the work of the great Sesostris, as are most of the grand relics of ancient Egypt now standing in the upper country. In the front portions of the buildings were his private rooms, and these are especially interesting as affording us an occasional insight into the private life of the monarch. Here he was accustomed to retire from war, or from the council, and the walls are covered with sculptured designs, showing him engaged in games, and in the repose of home life.

It is interesting to remark him in one picture playing at a game of draughts, nor is this the only instance on the monuments where this game is represented.

Passing into the grand hall of the principal temple we sat down in silent admiration and reverence before the splendor of that scene. It was a sudden stepping from the present into the past, and although it was the dead and half-buried past in one respect, yet in others it was the living; the mighty days of old even before our eyes, and demanding our reverential awe.

The deeds of the great Remeses were recorded around us in sculptures that needed no interpreter. Here he pursued his flying enemies, and his shafts carried death into their disordered ranks; there he conquered lions that rushed on him from a thicket; here was a naval combat; there the fiercest fray that was ever known on Asiatic fields. Here his chariot went rushing over dead and dying; there he carried his captives in triumph home, and received from his accountants the tongues and hands of the slain as trophies, whose hideous number is carved on the wall.

There was the pedestal of a giant column standing in the court, from which the column had been hurled. The sun was not far westward, but the lofty architrave hid it from us, and in the cool shade we sat around the pedestal which Ferrajj had transformed into a table, loaded with eatables, where we made a most hearty luncheon. Two English gentlemen, strangers to us, who were rambling through the ruins, accepted our invitation to try our claret, and I have often wondered since who they were, and whether they remember that luncheon in the temple of Remeses the Great.

I am describing our first visit to this grand ruin only because that is first in my notes and my memory. No one will suppose that it was our last, or expect me to describe each and every pilgrimage that I made to these or other ancient shrines. It was not till the sun was setting behind the western hills that we turned our faces homeward.

The ladies mounted their donkeys and went off over the plain toward the colossi at a flying gallop, attended by the boys, and half a dozen Arabs who wished to sell antiques. The long shadows of the hills were stealing across the plain, and we all sat down in the dust before the cold face of Memnon and gazed on his gray figure—that figure that has been more celebrated in history and story than any other antiquity on the earth's surface—until the gathering twilight warned us to be away.

We dined on the boat, and had coffee sent up to us in the tent, where we were joined by half a dozen ladies and gentlemen from other boats just arrived, Mustapha Aga and Sheik Hassan, of Goornou, who came to talk about some new excavations to be made, and Mr. Tonge, the young English artist, of whom I have spoken, who was making sketches at and near Thebes. The scene within the tent was brilliant enough for home-land, and Amy and Miriam will neither of them be apt to entertain a gayer or more picturesque company than sat on their Persian carpets that evening on the shore at Luxor.

In my notes of visits to various places of interest about Thebes, I shall not attempt to confine myself to the order of the days or visits as I made them. I was constantly among the ruins, now superintending excavations, and now visiting places of famous name.

I do not recollect what day it was that we first visited the tombs of the *Assaseef*, which lie on the eastern side of the hill, and not very far distant from the ruins of the Remeseion. To reach them, it was necessary to go across the plain, passing the great statue of Memnon, and passing also the ruins of the Remeseion, in which we paused on our way.

We mounted our donkeys at the shore opposite to Luxor, and started off in fine spirits, I myself being on foot; for by this time I was able to walk miles without fatigue, and to pass an entire day on the tramp without having occasion to regret it in the evening. We paused a moment, as we always did, under the shadow of Memnon, and looked up at his colossal form, while one rushing wave of thought rolled over us, as it always must and will in presence of that mighty relic of antiquity, and then we passed on to the temple ruins and to the hills beyond. We did not go by the temple without the usual mob of antiquity-venders approaching us with their wares, consisting of every thing, from mummies' heads and feet to newly-manufactured scarabæi, wherewith to entrap the green Howajji. But by this time they had gotten to knowing us well, and they retired rapidly, except one old Copt, who had a curious and valuable antique that he wished us to buy, but which he valued at a price not much less than a quarter of what Dr. Abbott asks for his entire collection. Again we paused a moment.

Though we had visited the Remeseion again and again, there was a sublimity about its ruins, and, more than all, about the fallen statue of the great Sesostris, that mighty trunk that lies on the sand in solemn silence amidst the broken fragments of his ancient throne and the fallen walls of his once glorious temple—a sublimity that commanded our respect however often we passed before it, and we did homage once more to the presence and power of the great past. The high sun looked down with awe and subdued splendor on that scene, and there was a quiet sereneness with which his rays fell among those ruins that I thought very different from the glare on the outer desert, or the broad plain of modern Thebes.

A solitary vulture sat on the summit of the great propylon, and looked on me with sleepy eyes as I sat on the sand in silence and gazed on the fallen Osymandyas.

The beauty and gracefulness of the grand hall of the Memnonium or Remeseion perhaps surpasses any other ruin in Egypt, and one might linger here for weeks, lost in admiration and astonishment. But this morning we had a day's work before us, and it was necessary to press on. So, remounting their donkeys, the ladies rode on, and we walked out among the ruins, made more ruinous in appearance by recent excavations, and passing through the courts, emerged on the hillside behind, and struck across the mounds of sand and rock to the great tomb which we designed visiting.

The hills which bound the plain on the west, as I have already had occasion to remark, are a honeycomb of tombs. From the very edge of the water-level of the plain to a point more than a thousand feet high, every inch of the rock is occupied by the dead of ancient Egypt, or has been occupied until the modern resurrectionists of England, France, Germany, or Goornou, broke the slumber that was to have been eternal. Many of these tombs have been opened. Myriads remain undisturbed. Untold treasures lie buried here, and from day to day portions of them are brought to light by the Arabs, who dig in secret, and conceal what they discover until a traveler presents himself ready to make purchases. But it must not be supposed that it is an easy matter to open tombs in this hillside. The falling stone of a thousand years, and the drifting sands of the desert, have changed the form and surface of the ground so much that it may require weeks of excavation to reach a burial-place, and the searcher may then find that he has but opened a tomb that was rifled ten, twenty, or a thousand years before. Still a plan pursued by the French and Prussian expeditions has been found very successful—namely, to run a trench in a straight line for a considerable distance. In this way they have opened many curious tombs. For a mile the earth is a succession of mounds heaped up by excavators, and hollows left by them. Up hill and down, therefore, the path is tiresome and difficult, to approach the tombs of the Assaseef; but at length winding down a hillside into a basin that was dug out by one of the great expeditions, we found ourselves in a half-acre hollow, upon the side of which opened a great tomb, one of the most wonderful in Egypt. The hollow, as I have called it, was, in fact, the court in front of the tomb, and at the western side of this the great entrance was visible, in the stately style of old Egypt. Through this we could see the distant end of the first corridor, beyond which all was blackness. The front was carved in the usual style, with representations of gods and men, and the immediate entrance or doorway was covered with small hieroglyphics, beautifully cut in the white stone of the hill, which was left for the portico.

We had provided torches for entering, for although I desired as far as possible to avoid adding to the smoke which already blackens many of the walls of the formerly white or elegantly painted tombs of Thebes, yet I knew that this, the greatest of the private tombs, was already far beyond injury of that sort. No one knows at what period its silence was invaded, or by whose order the mighty priest and prince who rested here was disturbed in his repose. In the course of years, and even of centuries, the walls have become blackened throughout its extent by torches, and by bats which inhabit it in myriads. We could sometimes scarcely advance, so thick were the clouds of these animals that dashed in our faces and clung to us.

This vast tomb has been described by so many travelers that I shall not pause here to relate our progress through its labyrinthine halls. The blackness of darkness was reigning every where throughout its extent, as it had reigned for thousands of years, except when broken, as now, for a few moments by the torches of travelers penetrating with doubtful footsteps the abodes of death. That he was a great man who dug this tomb for his bones there is abundance of evidence, since his name is found on one of the gates of the temple at Medeenet Habou, as its erector. But of more than this—his name—we know nothing. He was a man, and he built a gateway to a temple, and he needed a tomb. He was a mortal, and he believed in immortality. After all we know considerable of him in knowing that much. It is not every man that leaves behind him enough for us to know that much, even when he has a blazoned epitaph over his dust.

But why he built these vast halls, why these crossing and recrossing corridors and galleries, which cover an excavated space of more than twenty-three thousand surface feet, it is left for us to guess.

We walked on in wondering awe, even after we had seen the glory of Abou Simbal. There is one part of this tomb which illustrates well the manner of concealment adopted in many sepulchres, but which the ingenuity of man has readily made vain.

After passing under ground to the right and left, and left and right, through various galleries, descending a long flight of steps, and again passing through long dark corridors, the traveler, pausing for a moment to glance down a deep pit that falls into a grave hewn in the rock forty-five feet deep, shrinks back in horror from the fatal edge, and turns to the distant entrance, glad to escape the dark and foul residence of birds of night and death. If he had brought with him a coil of rope, and directed his attendants to let him down into that pit, he would have descended to the bottom of it, and found it a simple tomb, and nothing more. Nevertheless, half way down its depth, if he has kept his eyes open as he descended, he will have seen a doorway, and swinging himself back so that he may on the return catch his foot on the edge, he will enter another passage, and then follow on through stately chambers and corridors, carved with all the images of ancient times and the dark language of the years that followed the flood; and he will ascend by stairs hewn through the rock, to a point above the chambers he first examined, and so pass on from room to room, till he grows weary with the vast extent of this subterranean palace for the dead dust of an ancient priest.

I don't know how long we remained in these halls.

When we emerged, the open air appeared beyond description beautiful, and we threw ourselves down on the sand to enjoy its richness and purity. At length the servants, who had spread luncheon in the open doorway of a smaller tomb, announced that it was ready, and we sat down to our chicken and claret with a zest that no one knows any thing about who has not spent two hours under ground among bats and mummies.

While we were eating, Mr. R—— asked Trumbull and myself if we would go with him to a place not far distant and examine a mummy which was in possession of an Arab, and which he proposed to purchase. The ladies were safe with our servants around them, and we readily consented.

On learning the name of the Arab I was satisfied that we should lose nothing by going, for it was my old friend Achmet, whom I have several times mentioned, and who is an accomplished resurrectionist and a great scoundrel. He led us in a very circuitous manner, to a point not far distant from the tomb of the Assaseef, which we might have reached by a path one half shorter.

This I saw and remarked to him, but he muttered something about an excavation to get round, and I reflected on the well-known and very proper anxiety of the discoverers of treasures to conceal them from the government, but told him that he would do better to trust us frankly, and not make a fool of himself by attempting to deceive us. At length he came to a cavernous opening in the hill fronting the north-west, it being around a spur of the mountain, hidden from the plain of Thebes. Entering this, and passing in a hundred feet or so, we came to a sudden break in the floor, and were obliged to descend by a jump of about eight feet. Here I observed that the cavern branched, and the other branch led to the right, while we took that to the left, and commenced a difficult passage on our hands and knees, holding our own candles, and at length came into a comparatively open space, where lay, in solemn silence, the mummy of an ancient Egyptian. The case was of a very ordinary kind, painted highly, but not so as to indicate great wealth in the deceased, or great value to the mummy. We asked Achmet where he found it, and he replied, "Here."

"In this cavern?"

"Yes."

"You lying dog!"

On the honor of an Arab it was just here, he protested over and over again.

"But," said R——, "this is not the mummy I was to buy?"

"O yes, it is!"

"O no, it isn't!"

"But it certainly is!"

"Then I won't buy it, and there is an end of it, Achmet. You showed me a better mummy than that the other day, and if you want me to buy it, show it up again."

While they were talking, Trumbull and I had exchanged a few words, and were quietly working our way a little further along into the cavern. Achmet caught sight of us, and began shouting that we were at the end; there was nothing there; but if we would come with him the other way he would show us the real mummy, the Simon Pure. But the more he shouted the more we were satisfied there was something to be seen beyond, and having climbed a heap of fallen stone, and squeezed through an opening between it and the roof of the cavern, we found ourselves in another chamber, and in the presence of three more of the departed Egyptians of Pharaonic times. Here was a discovery!

"O you fool of an Achmet! So you never examined the cave any further. These are my mummies, old fellow! I have found them. You didn't know they were here? Eh, Achmet?"

Achmet looked sheepish, and still more so when we turned around, and raking down a heap of stone, showed the sunlight streaming across the valley of Thebes, and pushing through the hole in the wall, emerged in the scamp's own hut, built on the hillside. He had led us this long roundabout way to conceal from us the natural and easy access to the cavern, which was, in fact, the cellar of his house. In case of the presence of suspicious characters, either in front or rear, he could readily convey his treasures to spots as inaccessible as those in which they had lain for ages.

There was something hideous, and yet quaint and strange, in the assembly of the old dead that this Arab scamp had gathered. They lay side by side, their coffins staring on us with those startling and fixed smiles that are always found on the unmeaning faces which the Egyptians painted and carved over the countenances of their dead, and one was lying partly on his side, with a cant toward the other two, that seemed to intimate a knowledge of their presence, and a satisfaction at finding himself once more in company.

But we had not yet seen the mummy that R—— was to purchase, and now coming out of the cavern, and going around the end of the hill to the same place at which we had before entered it, we followed Achmet again to the jumping-off place; but instead of going down this, he turned into the other passage, and leading us by a narrow ledge around the descent, entered a long gallery, which brought us, after much winding and creeping, to a small chamber, in which were two other mummies, one an elegant one of Ptolemaic times, and the other one of those plain, dark mummies of remote ages, that looked verily as if it might have been a companion of the sons of Jacob.

"Now," saith my reader, "what under heaven did the gentleman want a mummy for?"

Very proper question. But will you step into Dr. Abbott's museum in New York some day, and look over some curious jewelry there. Witness a necklace of gold and precious stones, and then let your delighted eye rest on a gem of gold and lapis lazuli, representing the flight of the soul to the land of Osiris, or some similar idea, and then examine the rings and various charms, and trinkets, and stones carved into scarabæi, and other quaint shapes; and now imagine a case wherein lies a dead man of old time, or a lady of the court of Shishak, or the times of Thothmes III., and that upon unrolling the coverings you found such a necklace on her neck, such a gem on the breast, such rings on the hands, and such charms here and there about the person. In the brief phrase of modern times, "Would it pay?"

I have seen many ladies wearing the jewelry of thirty centuries ago. Indeed there is at present a great passion among the ladies resident or traveling in the East to become possessed of such treasures, and hence the price at which the Arabs sell them is enormous.

Still, aside from all this, there is a great interest in examining the mummy of an ancient Egyptian, independent of his ornaments, and it is no waste of time or money to open a case and unroll the sleeper.

We came out as we had gone in, and returned to the Assaseef, where the ladies were seated in the porch of the great tomb, waiting patiently for us.

We had yet a long day's tramp before us ; for we designed visiting a number of the private tombs which have been opened in the side of the mountain, hundreds of which are of the utmost interest.

This is, in fact, the grand source of our knowledge of the manners and customs of the ancient Egyptians. In burying their dead they were not only accustomed to place in the tombs many of the utensils of ordinary life, the work-basket of the lady as well as the sword of the soldier, but they took care to paint on the walls of the tomb all the prominent events in the life of the deceased, and oftentimes all the paraphernalia of his daily living.

On another day we made an examination of one of these tombs, that which is now known as No. 35, which I may describe as an example. This is one of the most interesting of any of the tombs, and were it possible for me here to give a reduced copy of the paintings on its walls, I should be able, without a word of explanation, to describe to the reader a vast portion of the public and private manners and customs of the ancient Egyptians.

The shape of the tombs is almost invariable. The outer door opens into a sort of cross hall or chamber running to the right and left, while a deep passage or chamber penetrates the hill itself. Of course all is darkness within, and the visitor is compelled to make his examinations by candle light. If he uses torches it is at the risk of blackening the wall, and defacing these very curious memorials. But this is already almost accomplished. The most of the tombs which are interesting have been seized on by the natives as cellars, and their mud huts are built in front of them, so that it is sometimes difficult to obtain admittance. No. 35 is of this class, and we found it piled half full of doura (cornstalks), and inhabited by colonies of fleas. Nevertheless we devoted ourselves to its examination carefully.

One of the most interesting painted groups in Egypt occurs on the wall of this tomb, an extract from which the reader will remember that I gave in a former chapter when writing on the subject of brick-making, and the illustration there given will show the style of representation in this and other tombs. Conjecture, of course, has not been slow to suppose that these men, who are represented as making brick under the lash of masters, are the children of Jacob. I before remarked on the reasons for denying this supposition. But the date of the tomb is not far from the period of the captivity, being in the reign of Thothmes III., whom we suppose to be the Pharaoh of the Exodus.

In the first chamber, the transept, is found a procession of princes of foreign nations bringing tribute to the king. Some are black, some red, some white; some have long, and others short hair. The dresses vary, as does the nature of their presents. One party bring leopard skins and monkeys, ivory, ostrich eggs, gold rings, a giraffe, and various other Ethiopian products. A second group have an elephant, a bear, a chariot, and long gloves, which indicate a more northern residence. Still a third and a fourth line of men and women appear with ostrich eggs and feathers, gold and silver cups, ebony and ivory, bags of jewels, vases of precious metals and porcelain, and a hundred other objects which have long afforded subjects of study to the scholar and antiquarian.

The inner chamber, which is the long hall I have spoken of, contains various subjects illustrating the private life of the proprietor of the tomb, who, from the subjects in the outer room, we may conjecture was a person high in authority under the king.

Here are represented the daily occurrences of life, and all the artisans that he had occasion to employ are here pictured in their various labors. Carpenters at work, rope-makers twisting their cords, sculptors busy on a sphinx which they are finishing, as well as two colossal statues of the king.

The minuteness with which scenes in daily life—in the house, in the garden, and in the chase—are here represented, enables us to see the life of the Egyptians as if it were furnished for the express purpose of illustrating volumes on the subject, and indeed the illustrations are ample in themselves without the aid of description. The same is true of the tombs near this, and of hundreds which lie open every where among these hills.

34.

The Palaces of the Dead.

STRANGERS to Egyptian antiquities are surprised at the freedom with which scholars speak of the manners and customs of the men of three thousand years ago. But a visit to Egypt removes all surprise. Old Egypt is still here. The tombs opened are a resurrection of the ancient times. The paintings are sufficiently minute to exhibit life in all its aspects, and the articles discovered in the tombs are themselves precisely the articles that did duty in the long-gone centuries.

That some of these antiques are manufactured, is well known; but no one familiar with them can be imposed on.

I was seated at my table in the cabin of the *Phantom*, one evening, Trumbull and Amy having gone by moonlight to Karnak, and Miriam being on one of the other boats making a call. Having a considerable amount of writing to do, I had not gone out into the tent as we usually did, and the ordinary evening assembly that we had there was not gathered. In the afternoon a steamer had arrived from Cairo, but instead of landing at Luxor, it had stopped two miles below, on the western side of the river, and we had no idea who was on board of her. I had dispatched Abd-el-Atti, in the evening, to ascertain what she was, and was hoping for news from civilization, when two gentlemen were announced by Ferrajj, and entered the cabin.

"We saw an American flag on your boat, this afternoon, and judging that we should find fellow-countrymen here, have taken the liberty of calling."

"I am delighted to see you. My name is Prime, and I am from New York."

"Is it possible? and mine is Righter, from Constantinople."

It was no less a surprise to me. He was the oriental traveling companion of my brother two years before, and had returned to Constantinople, where he now resides; but had come to Egypt, and finding a party made up for a swift trip up the Nile on a steamer, he had joined it. He knew that I was in the East, but had no idea of finding me here. His companion was a reverend gentleman from Illinois, and the two were as welcome visitors as one might hope to receive of a winter night in Egypt.

Ibrahim, the old Copt, whom I have before spoken of as the chief manufacturer and vendor of *modern antiques*, had repeatedly urged us to visit his laboratory. He had long ago become sufficiently well acquainted with me to know that I was past hoaxing, and he then became confidential, and frankly let me into the secrets of his trade. I took this opportunity to accept his invitation, and all our party having returned, we made a sally in the moonlight to the village and the house of Ibrahim. Passing through the narrow and silent streets, we entered a dark passage into the mud walls, and going to the rear of his house, mounted a crazy flight of steps and entered his sanctum.

It was a queer hole, not unlike the rooms of antiquarians that I have seen in America. Masses of stuff, broken coffin-boards, and mummy-cloths, lay piled in heaps around, while on shelves, and tables, and chairs, were the relics of ancient Egypt. The old fellow frankly confessed that nine-tenths of all that we saw was modern Arab manufacture, and the ingenuity of the laborers is deserving of all praise. The astonishment of my friends was increased fourfold when they recognized numbers of articles which, they said, had been offered for sale at the steamer that same afternoon, and *fac-similes* of which had been purchased at enormous prices by travelers in their company. One article, in particular, attracted the attention of one of the gentlemen. He had been bargaining with an Arab for one precisely like it, and an Englishman had bought it before his eyes at the native's price, whereat my friend had been decidedly and justly offended. He now saw its counterpart lying here, and asked Ibrahim if that were modern? The fellow took out a box and showed him a dozen precisely like it. "It's a favorite, and sells well," said he. It was a beautiful thing; and when I asked for the original from which the copy was made, he produced it from a secret place, and asked me ten pounds for it. It was but a piece of stone, four inches by five, with a figure in relief on one side.

By far the most remarkable discovery of the past year in this neighborhood has been a sort of undertaker's shop. Some Arabs, digging as usual in the night, opened what appeared to be a tomb, but on entering it, the contents were as astonishing to them as they have since been to antiquarians, being neither more nor less than cases containing some two thousand mummy shawls. The reader is, of course, aware that the mummy of an ancient Egyptian was rolled in long pieces of cloth, of which we find from twenty to thirty yards on one mummy, and often much more. These strips were cut and torn to suit the shape of the body, and were laid on with a skill of bandaging which modern surgeons are accustomed to envy. When this was complete, the mummy was wrapped in shawls of more or less expensive character, the cloth being fine linen, sometimes ornamented with beads, while a very common form was a shawl made entirely of earthen beads strung on thread, and worked in graceful figures. Such shawls I found on two mummies which I unrolled at different times.

These shawls were all of linen, varying in fineness, and this was evidently a dépôt or shop for the sale of them, being situated near the great burial-place, and doubtless near the mummying establishments; for the Egyptians did not mummy their own dead, but sent them to the undertaker's, where they were kept for from twenty to fifty days, and then returned in the shape of a roll of cloth, with head and feet alike enveloped and unrecognizable. This custom accounts for the fact that we not infrequently find the mummies of males in coffins elaborately ornamented with the hieroglyphical descriptions of females, and, *vice versa*, females in the cases which should contain males. It would be very curious if, in the great establishments, where hundreds of dead were brought weekly for embalming, there were not such mistakes constantly occurring; and hence the error of Mr. Gliddon, which caused so much amusement in Boston a few years since, was not owing to his having mistaken the legends on the coffin, nor should it at all detract from his deserved reputation as an Egyptian scholar.

I procured some twenty of these shawls. The one which lies before me as I now write is, like the rest, about three yards in length by one in width, made of the finest linen, with a fringe surrounding it; and the most curious circumstance in connection with it is that each shawl has a price-mark on the corner. Incredulous persons, given to denying that the objects which we find can possibly be antiquities, and asserting the incredibility of the idea that these shawls have been lying two thousand years under ground, say, on seeing them, "You have been sold; these are modern, and made for the Egyptian antiquarian market." The same thing I have heard such persons assert a hundred times in the collection in New York, on looking at its wonderful specimens. The only and the complete answer to such persons is this: "I bought the twenty shawls for three piastres each, being about three dollars for the whole." A friend of mine, who is a large dealer in, and a manufacturer of Irish linens, has examined what I have left of the twenty, and informs me that no factory in the world could make the articles for less than one dollar and seventy-five cents each, first cost from the factory, for each shawl, or thirty-five dollars for the lot, which cost me three. The Arab, therefore, who attempted to sell us made a poor speculation of it. But the character and quality of the articles determines their antiquity; and having unrolled some dozens of mummies, and become familiar with their clothing, I do not think I could be deceived in purchasing mummy cloth by even a Yankee speculator.

The western hills, to which I have so often referred, the reader need not be informed are the eastern boundary of the great desert of Sahara. They are themselves totally destitute of vegetation. Not a blade of grass, not a weed, or wild-flower, finds root on their rugged sides or summits. They are barren rock, whose crumbling debris lies heaped in the hollows, at the foot of their precipitous sides, and are the fitting barrier between civilization and the wastes of the Libyan plains.

Irregular in shape, and broken into numerous hills, whose height varies from one to three thousand feet, they have among them numerous ravines and deep gorges, whose desolation surpasses the conception of man, and far exceeds the power of the pencil.

One of these enters the hills, at a point not far north of Goornou, and penetrates several miles, scarcely ascending from the level of the plain of Thebes. The hills on each side of this narrow gorge hang in frowning crags above the adventurer who enters its gloomy recesses. The sunshine has a sombre, solemn appearance as it falls quietly into the silent depths. Here and there a solitary vulture sits like a resident demon eyeing the approaching stranger; and he is not surprised when he reaches the ends—for it branches into several ravines—to find that the kings of old Egypt selected this gloomy retreat for their burial-places, where, in stately halls, dug deep into the heart of the mountain, they should sleep in kingly slumber.

I say in kingly slumber; for, though the dead dust of a king was in no respect different from the dust of his meanest subject, and though his sleep was no more or less deep and profound, yet it was something to be laid in a granite sarcophagus in the centre of a vast hall, and to lie surrounded by household servants, guards, and retainers, all ready to spring to life when one should call whose voice should be loud enough to penetrate these deep caverns. The queens lie elsewhere, in a valley by themselves; or rather there they did lie, and there are now their vacant tombs.

The tombs of the kings, of which seventeen are now known and open to visitors, have long been celebrated as among the chief wonders of the ancient world. Many of them were open, and had been robbed of their dead two thousand years ago; and the writers of that period have given us descriptions that indicate which ones they knew and had visited. Others have been discovered in later periods, and some quite recently.

We made an early start in the morning for our first visit, and having crossed the river, mounted donkeys at the shore, and rode to the temple at Goornou, which we examined, and then went on up the valley of the tombs. It had been my desire to make an excavation here over a point which I had fixed on in my mind (having never yet seen the place), where I was confident of discovering an unopened tomb. Sheik Hassan of Goornou accompanied me for the purpose of taking my orders on this subject; but the day proved too short for even the cursory examination I desired to make, and I was obliged to put off my excavations to another time.

Without wearying the reader with tiresome description, I may be pardoned if I devote a brief space to the great tomb, No. 17, commonly called BELZONI'S, because discovered by him, and No. 11, or BRUCE'S.

The descent into this tomb is more rapid and sudden than into the others. A long, gradual slope of some hundred feet usually leads the visitor slowly downward. But here he descends twenty-four feet by a very abrupt staircase, and finds himself in a passage or gallery, eighteen feet in width, down which he proceeds between walls gorgeously painted and sculptured, until he reaches a second staircase, and again descends twenty feet, or thereabouts, and continuing onward through two doorways and intermediate halls, enters a chamber in which Belzoni found a deep pit, and the apparent end of the tomb. This pit was designed to deceive invaders. Belzoni filled it up and tried the wall beyond it. With a palm-tree battering-ram he burst his way through into a hall of almost fabulous splendor, and pursued his way to a second and almost precisely similar room, down yet another staircase, through two passages and a smaller chamber into the grand hall, a room about twenty-seven feet square, supported by six pillars, in the centre of which he found an alabastar sarcophagus. This appeared to stand on a solid rock floor, but experiment showed that the floor behind the sarcophagus was hollow, and when this was broken up, the sarcophagus was standing on the summit of an inclined plane, which descended more than a hundred and fifty feet further into the mountain, with a staircase on each side of it. The crumbling rock filled up its extremity, and how much further it led, or what lay beyond, is left to imagination.

From commencement to end, this great cavern is ornamented with sculpture and painting, and the remark is literally true, which has been so often repeated, that the colors have the freshness of yesterday. They appear like newly finished and *varnished* paintings. Of the subjects of many of these paintings I have already repeatedly spoken in connection with private tombs, while the largest and most numerous class have reference to the supposed future history of the soul of the deceased monarch. The entire length of this tomb is four hundred and five feet, and the descent from the entrance to the lowest point is ninety feet.

The tomb No. 11 is known generally as Bruce's tomb, and not quite so frequently as the Harper's tomb.

The first name it received from the fact that the lamented Bruce, on his return from Egyptian travel, published an account of this tomb, and described the splendid paintings he had seen in it, and was laughed at as an egregious liar by the entire literary and scientific world.

The other name is derived from the painting of the harpers on one of the chambers which Bruce described.

This tomb is supposed to be that of the third Remeses, but other royal names occur in its sculptures. Its length is the same as Belzoni's, but the descent is only thirty-one feet. The entrance passage is remarkable for a series of small chambers opening out on each side of it, which seem to have been designed as sepulchres of the royal caterers and servants. In the first on the left we find the royal kitchen represented on the walls, where men are killing, preparing, and cooking meats, kneading bread and going through the countless employments of an ancient kitchen.

Many of the scenes are very curious. In the room directly opposite to this are boats with various shaped cabins and sails. The next chamber is covered with representations of arms and armor, and the succeeding room has elegant chairs, painted and gilded in royal style.

These are among the most beautiful existing evidences of the style and splendor of royal furniture in days so long gone. Beyond these rooms are others on both sides, and in the last on the left are the two harpers, one of whom at least was blind.

This tomb has afforded us great information on the subject of the manners and customs of the ancient Egyptians, as the reader may gather from the subjects delineated in these chambers.

The shades of evening were gathering in the outer world while we were still treading these dark passages in the mountain; and we were now warned that if we did not hasten, darkness would overtake us long before we had extricated ourselves from the gloomy ravine. We had several miles to go before reaching the river, and having directed our small boat to meet us at Goornou, we had still four miles of sailing on the Nile to reach our own boat.

Although we made swift progress toward the shore, it was profoundly dark when we reached it; and here we found the boat. It was blowing a fierce gale of wind from the northward; and having packed ourselves into the boat, and wrapped shawls closely around the ladies, we were ready to be away. I was unwilling to trust the best Arab boatman with the precious freight we had on board. I took the sheets into my own hands, and she sprang away before the desert wind like a bird.

I never saw a boat fly more swiftly. The little lateen sail swayed forward at first, and then held a steady, strong full, and she went over the water as if she knew in what haste we were to be at home.

But it was no common gale. The wind was out in his wrath, and the desert storm came down on the river. My eyes were blinded with the sharp, swift sand, and I could with difficulty see the lights at Luxor, toward which we were flying. The current in the river was stronger as we approached, and, being against the wind, caused a heavy swell, into which the boat plunged with a will; but though the foam flew high, we held on toward the lights, and as we passed the first boat lying at the beach, we were greeted with loud shouts, that passed along the line of boats as we rounded the point and ran up alongside of the *Phantom*. Every one had been alarmed on our account, and a bright look-out was kept for our appearanee.

After we had dined we held a levee in the tent. Hajji Mohammed made capital coffee; and no boat was in our neighborhood for a day without finding it out. Every evening the tent was full, and coffee and chibouks circulated till midnight. That evening I well remember with especial satisfaction. There were some cards on the table when we reached the boat, names, none of which we recognized, but which, being American, were received most gladly. In the evening, when the tent began to be filled with visitors, the canvas was thrown up, and three gentlemen came in, one of whom the reader will hear much of if he follow me into Holy Land.

He was a tall, well-formed man, young, broad-shouldered and exceeding stout in his build, who looked like just the man to select for a companion in a tussle with Arabs or any other evil meaners. I little thought then how many miles we should ride together over hill and plain, how many nights we should sleep together on the starry plains of Holy Land.

35.

He Sleeps Well.

We had been at Luxor for a week or ten days, and again we were without company. All the boats which had been with us had gone on up the river, and no others had arrived; so that we were lying alone, with the exception of a freight-boat which had met with some accident, and discharged her cargo on the shore while she was repairing.

The day had been one of hard labor, but I can not now say what that labor was. I only remember that Trumbull lay at full length on the diwan on the one side of the boat, and Amy on the other end of the same, while Miriam and myself occupied the other side; for the diwans were thirteen feet in length, so that there was just room for four of us. *Derry*, the monkey that Abdul Rahman had given us at Derr, whence his name, was sitting on his cage with one eye shut, dreaming of new mischief; and I was smoking my chibouk in perfect kief; while in the cloud of smoke I saw those visions of beloved forms that follow the wanderer forever; and I was hearing those musical voices that he hears over mountains and plains, over sands and seas, those voices that earth is not broad enough to prevent his hearing, heaven not so far away from the poorest sinner of us all but that they reach him from its radiant homes.

It was ten o'clock—had there been a clock there to

mark it—and all was profoundly silent on river and plain, except the melancholy, but sharp quick bark of the jackals, seeking their food between Karnak and Luxor. The appearance of that cabin is vividly before me now. Entering it from the deck, there was a diwan on each side and a round table in the centre, while opposite to the front door was the curtained doorway that led to the sleeping-rooms. On each side of this last doorway was a mirror, and a shelf containing a drawer. Over the diwans were the windows, five on each side, and at the right and left of the front door were glass-covered shelves containing the table silver and furniture. Over the windows and on the various shelves were placed our arms and ammunition—four fowling-pieces, three revolvers, and one repeater, ready to be seized and used in an instant, were there any occasion for it. The diwans were covered with soft cushions, the windows curtained with crimson, and similar curtains hung over the front and rear doorways, so that in the evening our room had the appearance of perfect comfort and retirement. A more delightful arrangement could not be made; and when within such a room you place four persons so closely attached to each other as we four were, and as familiar with the antiquities we were searching out as Trumbull and I had endeavored to make ourselves, you can not doubt that we had reason to be satisfied with traveling on the Nile, and a fair prospect of enjoying our life so long as the voyage should continue.

But there was a sad interlude to this perfect luxury, which for awhile forbade our enjoyment of it. Other travelers were not so comfortable as we, and close at hand was one who was even then fast passing, in pain and agony, into the silent land beyond the deep river.

Ferrajj's black countenance was visible as he put his head in by the door curtain—

"Mustapha Aga has sent down to say that the English gentleman in his house is very sick, and he wishes you would come up and see him."

Mustapha is a nobleman—not by any writ or grant, for aga is the lowest title known to oriental society, meaning about as much as esquire does in our country—but he deserves rank among the highest, and his position as English and American consular agent at Luxor enables him to take it—and he is a nobleman of the heart, and a good fellow in every sense of the phrase.

I have before mentioned the visit at our tent of Mr. Tonge, the young English artist who was passing the winter at Luxor. He was about thirty years of age, and one of the finest looking men that I have known. His face was one of high intellectual appearance, his eye black and keen, and quick as starlight. He wore a dark beard and mustache curling over a well-shaped mouth, while his thin hair was brushed back from a high broad white forehead. He was ill when last in the tent, and he had talked somewhat despondingly of his condition; but none of us imagined that he was very ill, nor do I think he did so himself. The next day I saw him sketching near the great temple of Luxor, or rather he was giving some final touches to a water-color drawing of that temple, within the ruins of which Mustapha's house was situated.

Mustapha has the grandest front to his house of any man, private or public, in the world. It is not much of a house; something of a pile of mud, but clean and whitewashed within, consisting of five or six rooms, all on one floor, around an open court in which he has some few trees and shrubs. But he has selected for the location of his house the interior of the grand court of the temple, and the doorway is between two of the large columns, while the huge architrave towers above it. The contrast is somewhat severe on a near approach, but from a little distance in front you may see, any fine morning or evening, Mustapha quietly smoking his chibouk on his front steps, surrounded usually by a half dozen of his neighbors and friends, and the profound silence, the magnificent columns, the curling smoke, and the strange oriental dresses make a picture that an artist would love to sketch, but which, once painted, a person unused to such scenes would pronounce a fanciful mixture, not like any reality in the world.

Mustapha is a Mussulman, but although he drinks no wine himself he is amply supplied with abundance, and he can give you a bottle of nominal Johannisberg, or sparkling St. Peray, that will go to your heart in old Egypt, nor is it impossible that he may furnish you with mountain dew that will make you able to see Pharaohs without number on the plain of Luxor that slopes down from his grand portico to the water's edge; for every traveler who touches at Luxor experiences his kindness, and he is invaluable in his capacity of American and English agent. Some time since he was removed from office by the English consul, and his rivals and enemies sent him down to Cairo in chains to answer sundry charges, which he did successfully. Our excellent consul, Mr. De Leon (whom may government long preserve in Egypt for travelers' sakes), placed him in the same position as American agent, and the English consul then restored him. The only repayment that can be made for his attention must be some small present, since he receives no salary from our government, and of course no money from travelers. Many a dozen of capital wine finds its way into the cool temple of Luxor, and Mustapha, having no use for it himself, opens it for every guest, and of course never succeeds in diminishing his stock or its variety.

Mr. Tonge had arrived at Luxor some weeks previously, bringing with him, as is the custom with travelers in the

East, his bedstead, bedding, and ordinary camp furniture. Mustapha gave him a room in his house large and comfortable in all respects, at least as much so as could be expected in a rough, mud-brick structure, for it was clean and whitewashed, and had one window ten feet from the floor with glass in it, and here, surrounded by his painting materials, the artist was accustomed to live, and here he was to die. It was a dismal-looking room at best in the night time, and when Trumbull and I entered, it was almost impossible to see across it, so dense was the smoke of tobacco from the chibouks of his Arab attendants, of whom three sat on the floor puffing most resolutely, and with the utmost stolidity waiting God's will in the case of their master.

He was in so much agony that I do not believe he had once thought of their presence. Certainly he had not appreciated the closeness of the air and density of the smoke. First of all, therefore, we cleared them out and threw open the room to the air of night, that soft, rich air of Egypt, that glorious air of Thebes the ancient, laden with memories as with the odor of flowers, and which now stole in across the forehead of the dying artist.

He was dying. It was vain to look for help on earth; and he, too, as millions before him on that plain, was going into the presence of older times than those when the temple wherein he lay was built—into the presence of the Ancient of Days himself. The wanderer was nearer home than he had supposed, and it was a sudden but a forcible thought which his position brought to our minds, that after all we might not be so far away from home as but an hour before we had been dreaming.

It was a strange place for a Christian to die. I had read of such scenes, I had written of them when I wrote imaginations, but I never thought I should see the life-light grow dim in the eye of a fellow-Christian in a distant land, among the columns of an ancient temple, on the very spot where thousands of thousands had worshiped the gods of Egypt in the long gone years of Egyptian glory. The dread past and the awful future seemed standing before me there.

It was but little that we could do for him. He did not think he was dying. He was a man of peculiar sensitiveness, and I have often smiled sadly as I remembered his interrupting himself in a fit of severe pain, by suddenly apologizing to us for the impossibility of giving us a better reception. So little did he think his case desperate that he lit a cigar and insisted on smoking it, hoping to obtain some relief to the pain from its sedative effect.

The night wore on slowly. It was already midnight when we were called, and toward morning we left him for a little while and returned to the boat. The ladies were sleeping, and I threw myself on one couch while Trumbull took the other, and we slept profoundly.

But a messenger called us long before the sun was up, and springing to our feet we hastened to the house. The cold sky of a winter night at home is not more clear than was that sky above the ruins of old Thebes, and the stars looked through it with perfect beauty. Passing rapidly through the corridor of noble columns, and up the steps of Mustapha's house, we entered the room where the sick man lay.

Already there was a terrible change, and it had been very swift. But a few moments previously he had said to Mustapha, "I am free from pain," and then said, "I am dying," and that was the last sound he uttered on earth. As I entered he lay on his back, his face calm, white, placid, and a smile of content, as if the satisfaction of relief from pain, was on his features. He was breathing calmly, but did not know us, and I sat down at his head while Trumbull stood at his side, and we waited in silence the coming of the great change that comes alike in Egypt or in England, or our home, that no man can escape, flee he never so far to distant lands.

And the great sun came up once more on the land of the Pharaohs, and as his first rays fell across the valley and touched the lips of Memnon on his ancient throne, our friend heard a voice, but it was not the fabled voice of Memnon, a voice out of the deep that overhangs the land of Memnon and old England alike, and he departed in obedience to the call.

No convulsion marked the mighty change which had come over him, the Eternal receiving the child of time. A sigh, one long deep respiration, the smile that had flitted over his countenance rested on it in perfect quiet, and he was dead. I leaned over him and laid my hand on his forehead. It was warm but pulseless. I pressed it on his heart, but it had done with the heavy labor of beating the swift hours of existence. I took his hand in mine, but the skillful fingers that had grasped the pencil but yesterday returned no answering grasp, and so I knew that all was over, and he was in the dread assembly of the departed.

So all was over. The promises of childhood and the hopes of maturer years, all love, all ambition, all labor, anxiety, strife, and care, all wandering travel, all restlessness, every thing that was earthly of him was ended here, in this ancient temple, and we alone beheld the end, and were left to record it.

If the studio of a dead artist be a mournful place after he is gone, what think you was the aspect of that room as we rose from his bed-side and looked in one another's faces, and then around us? His easel stood where he had left it two days previous, and upon it a finished painting of the ruin in which he died. His pencils lay where his fingers had dropped them, never to be resumed; his clothes where he had thrown them in his hasty undressing. His Arab servants sat at the door with knees lifted to their chins, and Ali was weeping bitterly near the feet of his dead master.

I looked back at the now changing face of the artist, and bowed my head in silent, solemn assent to the power that had overcome that mighty thing that we call man.

Then I crossed his arms over his breast in token of the hope that alone remains when dust is dust; and walking slowly out into the soft sunshine, lay down under the great columns and looked toward the western hills and the tombs of the ancient Pharaohs.

There was a gloom in the sunshine of the next morning that I can not well describe. It was the same sunshine, and it shone as quietly and warmly on the valley of the Nile as ever before, but for all that it seemed to me sombre and mournful.

We had marked out this day for a visit to Karnak, our first visit there. It was, perhaps, more a subject of my thoughts and desires than any other ruin in Egypt. From boyhood I had been accustomed to think and dream of these ruins as the chief and most wonderful in Egypt or the world. I had read of them a thousand times; had passed hours in gazing on pictures of them; had written descriptions of them to read over to myself, and had compared every wonder that I saw or heard of with them.

One of my most distinct recollections of college life was that which recalled professor Dod, long since dead, as he sat before us reading his eloquent lectures on architecture, and the enthusiasm with which he described the stately grandeur of Karnak, and contrasted it with the puny works of Greeks and Romans. Aside, therefore, from desires for study, my great hope in visiting Egypt was to see these stupendous remains, and, in going up the river, we had agreed that we did not wish to make a hurried visit to them, but would reserve them for a first calm, quiet, long day's view.

Miriam and Amy went off early on donkeys with Trumbull and the Arab attendants. I remained to finish a letter, and then walked up to Mustapha's house, and entered the room in which poor Tonge was lying.

Mustapha had agreed to take charge of the arrangements for the burial. Indeed, he volunteered every service imaginable, and behaved as if his brother lay dead in his house instead of a roving traveler, unknown to him a few days previously.

The room was little changed. We had closed and sealed his trunks and packages, and every thing looked as if he were ready to leave on a journey, and was but lying on the bed a little while to rest hinself, and would start up and be away when the time should come. Alas for him, the desert stretched far away to the east and to the west, and the strong river flowed swiftly downward to the sea; but he would not cross the desert, nor set sail on the river. He was already gone on the long journey beyond the desert, beyond the dim light of the desert sun, beyond the sea to the land where there is no sea.

I stood alone within the ruins of the great Temple of Luxor by the body of the young artist, and—nay, I will not conceal it, know it who will—there were tears wept for him that morning, though his mother was far away, and he was buried in the sand long months before her ears rang to the terrible story of his death.

I covered up his face and left him there, stepping quietly out into the shadow of the great columns of the temple, and thence walked swiftly through the streets of the village toward Karnak.

Outside the village, to the eastward of the great avenue of sphinxes that once extended from Luxor to

Karnak, is a mound elevated a little above the plain, and so far raised that the overflow of the Nile can never reach it. I am not able to say what that mound covers. Whether it be the ruin of a temple, or of an ancient house, or of some other structure of olden time, must be left to conjecture. It is a desolate spot. No grass grows on it; but the dust of the desert and the plain are mingled with broken pottery and stone. No rain falls on it, nor water of the Nile reaches it. It stands up a little above the surrounding land, so as to be visible from Karnak and Luxor alike. Upon this mound there is a grave. The Arabs said it was the grave of an Englishman. Perhaps—probably—it was. Here we had directed them to dig a grave for our friend; and before I went to Karnak I walked around by this spot to see that the work was properly executed.

Two fellaheen, naked, gaunt, and bony, sat on the mound by their completed work, and demanded bucksheesh for it when I approached. It was an Arab grave, five feet long and three deep; no more. They were astonished at my dissatisfaction; and when I gave them a stalk of doura seven feet long, and told them to dig it as long and as deep as that, their astonishment was unbounded. But they went to work with their pick and fingers, and I left them diligently engaged, and walked on over the desolate plain, covered with halfeh grass, along which formerly extended the most magnificent avenue of sculptured stone that the world has ever seen.

I passed the day at Karnak, and returned as the sun was going down. Mustapha had completed his arrangements strictly in accordance with good taste. He had provided a coffin—a rough affair indeed—but he had concealed the roughness by tacking over it the blue cotton cloth of the country, the only cloth to be procured in the village; and, with a feeling that astonished me in a

Mohammedan, he had trimmed the coffin on the edges with white tape, and nailed two strips on the lid so as to form the sign whereby we are accustomed to signify our faith in the Saviour.

Once more I looked in his face. Mine were the last eyes that should look on those features until the far-off morning, and I alone of all the earth was to preserve the memory of that marble countenance, so that if in my future wanderings there should by chance be any one—mother or brother, sister, or better loved than all, who should demand of me how he looked when the light was forever shut away from his white brow, I could answer. At that moment there went a swift thought homeward. I thought if I were he; if that pale forehead were mine; if that dark mustache and heavy beard were mine; if that closed eyelid were this one, and that hushed lip this lip, what sad lament would there be in my far home, what grief to my old father, what heart-breaking agony to my beloved mother, when some one should come in on them, in their home among the trees, and tell them "He is dead!"

I looked wistfully—how wistfully!—into that face and asked yet again and again, "Is that all?" Strange inconsistency, it seemed, that yesterday I thought nothing of that man, and now death has been here and his dust demands reverence as never living dust demands it, even though it be the crowned brow of an emperor. Yesterday I might have forgotten him—now he is an immortal, and I shall remember him forever.

He was a man of like passions with myself. He lived, labored, sinned, and suffered as do I. But this is not he. There is no sin here. This is a pure, sinless body. What was his faith I do not know, nor whether he believed in God or Saviour; but this much I know, that he is gone, and this that lies before me is the image in which God made man, and death has sanctified it by his holy touch, and somewhere, on this sorrowful earth, there are those who would give years of life to stand where I stand now and look once, but one instant, on those calm features and that holy clay. And is this all?

Yes, that was all! A brief day—a brilliant morning, and a sudden darkness. That was all? He had lived his life through swiftly and passed to the presence of the mighty dead. A voice out of the deep—I know not whether it was the voice of one loved on earth and gone onward long ago, or but the deep voice that all men hear—a voice had called him, and he had heard it and was gone.

The old Coptic bishop stood a little way off as I covered up his face, and caught my gaze as I lifted my dim eyes from that last sad look. He was a venerable looking man, large and commanding in appearance, the representative perhaps of as pure a line of apostolical succession as the world can furnish. But he was not a worthy successor of Mark. He came, not for respect to the dead, but for bucksheesh from the living; and I think his Christian sympathies were not strongly excited toward the American branch of the church by the manner in which we treated his demand.

Four American gentlemen, travelers upward bound, stopping at Luxor for a day, arrived at this moment, and we proceeded to carry him out for burial. It was a simple procession. Six Arabs lifted the coffin, and seven Christians followed them. The unsatisfied Coptic functionary fell in behind us, and a straggling crowd of two or three hundred Arabs came on, respectfully and in silence. We passed through the village streets and out by the market-place, and down the hollow, and up to the ready grave. It was not very much like home, O gentle reader of these lines, who prayest every night that God will let you die and be buried with the beloved of old times. It was not like that quiet church-yard in the up country—that holy spot where, with feeble footsteps and quick floods of tears, we laid her darling head in all its young beauty below the myrtle and the violets. As I walked that sad distance, I bethought me of all that. The coffin on the table under the pulpit; the old clergyman leaning over it, and weeping bitterly for her he too loved beyond words to tell; the broken words of faith and hope that fell from his lips at length, and the deep sob that would not be restrained from her—the gentle friend of the dead girl—who sat in the choir and strove once more to sing, but could not, though the song was one of triumph; the lifting of the coffin and the heavy tread as they carried it down the aisle, and out to the corner under the elm-tree, and the soft sunshine falling through the branches into the grave as if to hallow it for her whose life had been one long sunshine on our lives, gone out indeed in black and sudden night; the reverential pause, the deep and solemn silence as the dust was let down slowly to its kindred, and the low wail of agony that God heard on his great white throne and answered with the words of everlasting life—all these were before me now.

The sun was on the horizon's edge as we approached the grave and for a moment set down our burden on the surface of the ground. Karnak, in majestic glory, was before us. Luxor looked down on the scene, while, far off across the ruin and the plain, Memnon of the stony eyes gazed on the group as he had gazed in thousands of years on burial-scenes from the pageant that followed Amunoph himself to this.

The natives crowded around. Children, naked and filthy, crawled on hands and feet between the legs of the older spectators and surrounded the edge of the grave, gazing curiously into its depths, while one naked young

Arab, bolder than the rest, forced his head between my ankles and lay flat on the ground, content with the view that he thus obtained of this mysterious rite.

We read certain passages from the burial service, lifted our hats reverently from our heads, and then laid him in the grave; and with our own hands and feet, for shovels are unknown in Egypt, we threw in the earth, and so buried him in the dust of that old land where God will find him when he calls the Pharaohs and their followers to meet him in the awakening.

Nearly a year after the occurrence of these events, it was my melancholy pleasure to meet in England the friends of the unfortunate Mr. Tonge, whose fate I have described, and to communicate to them the particulars of his death and burial. A rude brick monument, which we caused to be erected over his grave, will preserve its locality till this generation and all who knew and loved him are themselves epitaphed.

36.

The Glory of Karnak.

THERE are some places on the face of this old earth where antiquity sits throned and crowned, compelling homage to its old but radiant splendor. Such a spot is the Parthenon, where the ancient is beautiful and glorious, and the modern traveler bows in delighted adoration to the splendor of that beauty and glory.

There are other places where antiquity is crowned with roses, and claims in the hearts of men a kindred spirit of joy and joviality; where we seize the old by the hand, clasp it in our arms, treat it as of the same blood and passion with ourselves, and draw down the regal dignity of age to the level of our own humanity. Such a place is the house of the tragic poet at Pompeii, such the vast halls of Caracalla's baths in a sunny day at Rome.

There are places where the ancient wears a brow of serene dignity, and is crowned with gray and reverend locks. Such places are awe-full. Such is the summit of Cheops, such the shrine at Abou Simbal, such preeminently the grand hall at Karnak.

Beyond a question this ruin is the most stupendous relic of antiquity, the most grand achievement of human art, ancient or modern, that the world has seen.

Karnak is a greater wonder than the pyramids. The heaping of stone together in such a mass was, indeed, a kingly idea of Cheops; but here was the same royal thought, the same masses of rock, hewn into graceful forms and shapes, that indicated taste and design, and grouped in a temple, or in temples, that surpassed the pyramids in extent. I have no doubt there is more stone in the ruins of Karnak than in the pyramid of Cheops. The size of many of the stones is greater than of any in the pyramids, and the work of elevating them to the tops of lofty columns, and arranging them in the form of the architraves of this temple, was certainly much more difficult and laborious than any of the labor in erecting the tombs of Cheops and Cephrenes.

The reader can with difficulty obtain an idea of the extent of these temples, which, connecting one with another, form the ruins which we call Karnak; nor shall I pause here to weary him with statistical information about them. Enough, however, to say that the immediately connected ruins extend for a space of three fourths of a mile, by half a mile, on which lie heaps of stone, fallen columns, obelisks, and towers; while here and there portions of the ancient buildings stand high up in their original grandeur and perfection, defying the power of time. The buildings which we may call the chief temple are about 1200 feet in length, by 330 in breadth.

It was not storm nor decay that overthrew the temples of Egypt. Time had no more power over them than he had over the stars above them. The last mark of the chisel which the sculptor left on the stone remains as it was left, and the pencil-lines drawn to direct his future work are uneffaced, and literally as fresh as the moment after they were drawn.

This is a fact which every person who has examined Koum Ombos can verify, where, on the portico of the temple, exposed to every wind that blows over the lofty hill on whose summit the temple stands, remain the outline sketches, in red and brown, made by the sculptor to direct his chisel, and the last touches of the chisel among them, as if he had but yesterday laid down his mallet and would to-morrow resume it. And this among fallen columns and the scattered ruins of the temple.

What, then, worked the ruin? It was not earthquake; for those parts which earthquakes could never have shaken are scattered over the plain. What shattered the colossal statue of Osymandyas and broke his granite throne?

The answer is with God. Conjecture vainly seeks to account for the ruin. Probably the conquering armies of invading nations wasted their energies in the vain attempt to efface the memory of the conquered.

I am more than ever impressed with the conviction that the ancient Egyptians built temples for immortality. That they expected in their own proper persons to return to these plains, to worship at these altars, possibly with the visible presence of their gods.

For this they sought tombs in the solid mountains, whence they could walk out in later days and view the redemption of the land of Misraim; for this they embalmed their dead, that in the resurrection they might know each other, and souls might not wander in deep darkness seeking in vain a clay tenement. From this arose the fable of the ghosts wandering on the banks of the river Styx, and it is worthy of remark that to this day, under Mohammedan teaching, the Egyptian hurries his dead into the grave, believing that the angels who are to question them for admission to heaven will not approach them till the grave is closed over them. For this resurrection they piled these grand temples. An artist friend of mine one day proposed to fill the background of a picture with a broken column of Egyptian style.

"My friend, it will not do—there is no such thing in Egypt as a broken column."

"No columns in Egypt?"

"Yes, there are hundreds, but I never saw one broken —they are either erect or prostrate, never broken. They are too grand to be broken. No earthquake could break one though it might hurl it from its pedestal."

This remark applies, of course, only to monolithic columns. Those which are built of separate layers are often scattered in fragments.

Approaching the great front from the river (not as we came from Luxor, which is south of Karnak, but entering from the west), we have before us the two propylon towers, whose vast size and height surpass all others in Egypt. Long before reaching the gateway between them, we are passing through an avenue of sphinxes, or crio-sphinxes, as Wilkinson calls them, but in fact rams of colossal size, facing the worshiper on each side as he approaches the temple. Passing through the pylon or gateway, we enter a court two hundred and seventy-five by three hundred and thirty feet, with a corridor on each side of it, and the remains of a double row of columns through the centre, one only of which is standing. On the opposite side of this court stand two other lofty and grand propylon towers, passing through which, we enter the great hall of columns. This hall is three hundred and twenty-nine feet in breadth by a hundred and seventy in length. When complete, it consisted of a central aisle, which was higher than the naves or the remainder of the room, being supported by two rows of columns, six in each row; one hundred and twenty-two other columns supported the rest of this vast hall, of which I counted one hundred and two now standing, and the others lay prostrate. The twelve central columns are standing.

These central columns are each sixty-six feet in height, without counting the base and capital. Including these, they are ninety feet high. The diameter of each is twelve feet. I beg the reader to mark out these figures on the ground, describing a circle of twelve feet diameter, and endeavor thereby to get some idea of the size of these columns.

The other hundred and two columns are each forty-one feet nine inches in height (pedestal and capital not included), and nine feet one inch in diameter. No other spot on earth realizes so perfectly the idea of a forest of columns.

Without pausing now to express our wonder and awe in this vast hall, we pass out of it between two lofty towers, as before, into another court, now a heap of stone, in which stands an obelisk of granite, its mate lying broken to pieces near it. Again we pass between two towers, not so large as the others, and now lying in ruins, and enter another court, in which stands the great obelisk, ninety-two feet high and eight feet square at its base, while its companion lies in broken masses by its side.

Already, I am aware, that I shall lose my reader for a companion if I attempt to lead him any further through these vast buildings, and yet we have not approached the sanctuary in which the gods sat of old to receive homage and sacrifice.

Other towers, another court, another court, a granite gateway, and another broad area lead to the holy place, and beyond it the buildings stretch to the eastward even further than to the west, whence we have come. All these vast courts and areas, obelisks, towers, and halls, are or were surrounded with columns, sphinxes, and statues, and every column and stone is covered with carving, and brilliantly painted. Not only was the temple colossal in its proportions, but it was gorgeous beyond all description in its furniture and adornments.

Of its age I hesitate to speak, since it is a subject on which Egyptiologists have differed widely; but there can be no doubt that the more ancient parts, those eastward of the sanctuary, were built prior to the arrival of Jacob and his family in Egypt, while the grand hall was erected at a later time. Some portions of this vast temple, doubtless, stood in the days of Abraham, and it is not impossible that the traditions of the Arabs may be correct, and that Noah himself may have stood within its walls. Certainly it was but a brief time after the deluge that the foundations were laid. Of the monarchs who erected the different parts it is not difficult to speak, since their names are blazoned on every stone laid by their orders. But of the period in the world's history when these monarchs lived and reigned it is more difficult, indeed next to impossible, to affirm.

There is, however, one portion of the temple which possesses a more profound interest to the Christian traveler.

On the outside of the south wall of the grand hall is a representation of a god, leading many captives to a king, who is seated to receive them.

The cartouche gives the name of the king—Sheshonk, or Shishak, who is mentioned in 1st Kings, chap. 14, 25; and 2d Chronicles, chap. 12.

This cartouche is well known. It appears on a very interesting piece of scale armor in the New York collection, of which a fac simile is given at the end of this chapter.

The name of Shishak would be of great interest in

itself, but in this instance is of a thousandfold more intense interest from the names of the captives that are before him, each of whom is represented, as in the vignette at the head of this chapter, which is the most remarkable of them all. The characters in this peculiar figure, the battlemented outline of which represents a fortified city, are AIUDAH MELK KAH, and the whole sign translated, signifies "The fortified country of the king of the Jews."

The discovery of this record of Scripture history on Egyptian stone is one of the most interesting in Egyptiology.

Fears had been entertained and expressed that there would not be sufficient confirmation of Scripture found in Egyptian sculpture, and those who but half believed their Bibles were afraid of the monuments—a strange fear that is found in the history of every progressive science. He whose faith in revelation is firm, always springs with delight to the investigation of new fields, *knowing* (not hoping) that he will find full confirmation and new assistance to his faith and understanding. Before Champollion visited Egypt this sculptured group had been often looked at with curious eyes, but no one had for a moment imagined its significance, or value in a historical view. The king's name was, indeed, known as Sheshonk, Shishak, as our translation of the Old Testament has it; but although a hundred scholars had seen the rows of captives, no one of them had read here any thing by which to connect this with the Scripture history. Champollion landed at Karnak on his way to Upper Egypt, and remained an hour or two in the vast halls that are the wonder of modern wanderers. But his keen eye was not idle, and as he passed this group, reading name by name in it silently, he started, astonished at the blindness of his friends who were before him, and read aloud to them the name MELEK

AIUDAH, or the King of Judah. The oval in which it was inclosed represents a fortified place, and the sign at the bottom of those within the oval represents a country. It was like a voice out of the ancient ages, that sound among the ruins of Karnak, as the great scholar read the story of the son of Solomon on the wall of his conqueror's temple. It was the greatest, as it was almost the first of the new discoveries, and a tribute to the truth of God's revelation that at once consecrated and sealed the truth of the scholar's investigations and their results. That wall at Karnak is the most interesting spot among the fallen temples of the land of the Pharaohs. While other records have been effaced, that one seems to have been kept expressly that the world might discover it, and, this done, it is crumbling.

I observed that the corner of the stone is badly broken, and the next name, which was perfect in Champollion's time, is now completely effaced. This will soon follow. But hundreds of travelers have seen it, and copies of it are placed on record forever, so that future ages can not doubt that, in the nineteenth century after Christ, Champollion read on the walls of Karnak, among the captured countries of Shishak, the name of the kingdom of Solomon, and the name that was hallowed to all eternity afterward when Pilate nailed it to the cross of the last and greatest KING OF THE JEWS.

There are several temples near the great temple, and many magnificent structures, gateways, lofty towers, and the most stately obelisks in Egypt scattered here and there in this vast burial-place of temples, for I know of no other title so fitting as this. The huge mounds are like monster graves, and there are old shrines under them. There are hundreds, I believe I may say thousands of sphinxes, colossal rams, dog-headed gods, and statues large and small, scattered over a square mile of ground.

There are two sacred ponds, one of which has been the scene of Mohammed Ali's sacrilege. He broke up a vast amount of the stone and threw it into the lake, that the water might dissolve the nitre with which the stone was impregnated, and afterward he evaporated the water and gathered the nitre for his gunpowder works near by. Thus much old sculpture was destroyed.

I visited Karnak at all hours of the day and all days. One Sunday I passed the entire day sitting in the grand hall and endeavoring to people it with its long dead worshipers. Mohammed Hassan, my faithful sailor, was with me and sat for hours as silent as I. I believe that the awfulness of the place had impressed him as well, for he would sometimes turn his large eyes toward me with a look that I could interpret as nothing else but an imploring anxiety to be told who were the builders of this gigantic edifice. I told him as well as I was able, but he could not appreciate that it was of thousands of years ago. To him a century was greater than his mind could grasp—what then the years of this house, or the eternity of which its builders dreamed?

I was often there by moonlight. Certainly there is no spot of earth that the moon so magnifies. I had been one day shooting over the plain till sunset, and went around by Karnak in the twilight, climbed the great tower of the western gateway of the grand hall, and sat down on its top to await the coming of moonlight. The weird quaint startling lights and shadows of the twilight deepening into the silver shine of a moon almost full, were exceedingly beautiful. I lingered with eyes fixed on the tall obelisks that pointed their taper fingers to the inaccessible God beyond the sky of Egypt far up above its massive structures, and wondered how many myriad eyes had gone upward like mine from that granite pedestal, up, up to the everlasting stars.

Though it was a false worship, it was nevertheless a spot like that where Jacob slept, for above that shaft directing eyes to heaven, in ancient days had been the ladder that angels trod; for thoughts are angels, messengers of men if not of God, and right there away more thoughts had traveled to the unknown abode of the Almighty perhaps than at any other point in mid air between earth and heaven.

As I walked home that night I turned out of my way to visit the grave of my poor friend. Two jackals sat on it. I would have shot them, but I could not so disturb the holy night that rested on that heap of earth—the last resting-place of the dead artist. How but last week he would have loved that silver light of Egypt that now blessed his grave! I sat down one moment on the mound.

O friend of mine! there is a grave-yard in which the moonlight falls to-night with white radiance on mounds of snow. In a summer evening such as that, I have been accustomed to go to that quiet spot with those well-beloved, and sitting down on the broad tablet that honors the memory of a man of God who now stands before his throne, talk of the village dead that lie around him in peaceful sleep, calm as the moonlight that falls through the branches of the willow on the grave of his daughter, the fairest child of the valley village. There, could I but uncover their faces as they were when laid in their resting-places, I have loved to think of the smiling countenances, the peaceful lips, the closed eyes, of man and maiden, father and daughter, I should see, who, a goodly company of happy people, will wait, in dust of which they are content to be a part, the voice of Him of Bethany.

Not so the moonlight grave-yard scene that night. The gray walls of Karnak and of Luxor stood up against the sky. A grove of palms close by the mound, cast a deep shade almost up to it. No grass, no shrub, no flowers grew there, but the moonlight was as pure on the dust of the Nile valley as among the violets of home highlands, and the dead slept as deeply, as profoundly.

When I remember that mound outside the walls of Luxor, in the dark nights while I sit here in America, no longer near it to watch over him I laid there, when I think of the loneseme nights of summer when the hot sun has been there all day long and the jackals wail there all night, no travelers for months to look at the mound, and he lying there—to-night—alone, I shudder and pray God I may die among my kindred.

37.

Memnon and his Daughter.

When we were at Esne, Suleiman Pasha, the governor of the section from Es Souan to Luxor, had proposed to us to amuse ourselves during one day of our stay at Luxor by an exhibition of the performances of horses. In fact, to get up what the natives call a Jereed play, in which the Arabs should display their horsemanship for our especial edification. He accordingly wrote letters to the nazir, Islamin Bey, whose dominion is inferior to his, and whose usual residence is at Luxor, as also to old Houssein Kasheef, the local governor at Luxor, directing them, on our demand, to summon all the Arabs in their dominions who were possessed of horses worth showing in such a performance.

We had little desire to see the exhibition, but Abd-el-Atti was anxious to have it done, and we allowed him, in our names, to present the letters, and fix a day for the Jereed. The day came, and seventeen horses and horsemen appeared. This was a failure. We wanted seventy at the least. Nor was it pleasant, for we had given up a day to it, and other travelers had done the same, on our suggestion.

Abd-el-Atti was in a rage. The nazir was at Goos, some thirty miles distant, but the letter had been sent to him, and he had paid no attention to it. He was, in fact, the only surly specimen of a Turk that we met with in Egypt, and he will not be apt to forget us, having leisure now to think of us. Houssein Kasheef was absent at Esne, and in no way to blame for the failure, but the nazir had the entire responsibility of it on his shoulders.

Abd-el-Atti proceeded, in the fashion of the East, to take the testimony in the case, and I observed him for three days sitting all day long, or always when I was at home, near the tent, with a crowd around him, taking the evidence that the nazir had refused to obey the letter, and had neglected to honor the firman of his highness, the viceroy, of which I had the honor to be the bearer. All this produced a sensation in the neighborhood, and on the arrival of Houssein Kasheef he sent for Sheik Abdallah, the sheik of Karnak, and between them they arranged the affair, and sent down to us to beg us to fix another day. Accordingly we named another day, and on the morning thereof we saw a very different looking place when we returned from an early canter to Karnak. The broad space which lies between the temple and the river's edge, and which contains some ten acres, more or less, of dry dusty soil, was covered by Arab horsemen in gay dresses, and the scene was altogether one of the most lively and inspiriting that could well be imagined. Houssein Kasheef and Sheik Abdallah had done their utmost, and every village and camp within twenty miles had turned out its finest horsemen and best horses.

The Jereed play has been an ancient amusement in eastern countries, having some resemblance to the tournament of the middle ages. The horsemen who formerly rode with tilting lances, and sometimes fought with them even to the death, adopted a less dangerous weapon, and were accustomed in these tournays to use the long, slender, and graceful branch or leaf-stem of the date palm-tree. But this was not a harmless toy thrown from the hands of a strong and skillful man; so that the government, finding that private malice not infrequently took advantage of the public games to inflict terrible wounds, forbade the Jereed, as it was called, and the riders were left to use such light and harmless weapons as they could procure, if they desired to continue their sport. An excellent substitute was found in the long and light stalks of the Indian corn, which grow to a very great height in Egypt, and which furnish a lance, or the imitation of a lance, ten feet in length. Each horseman carries half a dozen, as the Arab horsemen were at one time accustomed to carry lances or darts.

Over a hundred horses were gathered on the plain of Luxor. How they rode, how one would dash out from the ranks, and fly like the wind across the plain, throw his steed on his haunches, while he shook his lance in the air, then leap forward with a shout, and return to the ranks with his burnoose streaming in the wind; how a dozen, with flying garments and wild cries, would follow, and a dozen more give chase, and advance, retreat, fly and pursue, mimic the battle-scene, the attack, the fierce thrust, the parry, the steady backward retreat when hard pressed, leap by leap, the gallant horse and rider facing steadily the three-fold force of the enemy; how they divided their ranks, and placing half on each side of the plain, under old leaders, advanced at a fierce gallop, and met in the centre before us, with hundreds of lances flying through the dusty air, and shouts as if the conquered of the Battle of the Pyramids were all there; how they wheeled and advanced, retreated and plunged forward, until the fray became a confused mass and the dust covered them, and then out of the cloud

> "Fast, fast, with wild heels spurning,
> The dark gray charger fled,"

and Sheik Hassan, of Goornou, lay rolling on the plain; how when the fray became thickest, and the shouts most furious, and we heard some sounds which seemed to indicate that there was a growing seriousness in the fun that might result unpleasantly, and Houssein Kasheef rushed down the slope on foot and vanished in the melée; how at this instant there came a storm of wind, a whirling blast from its desert home, tempted, doubtless, by the combat on the plain, and gathering up the dust, now beaten to powder by the horses' hoofs, swept over all in the grandeur of a sand-storm, and drove horsemen, and horses, and Howajji ingloriously from the field; all this, alas, there was no troubadour to sing, and posterity must remain ignorant of.

In the evening after the Jeered performance, several of the *Ghawazee* came down to the boat hoping to induce us to engage their services for an exhibition, which we had hitherto refused to do, and still continued to refuse.

The Ghawazee have been celebrated by Egyptian travelers in numberless chapters; and there is scarcely a book on Egypt which does not contain more or less poetry on their beauty and gracefulness. Most writers follow a tradition, founded on a decree of Mohammed Ali, and locate the Ghawazee at Esne; but this, like their beauty and their grace, is very much in the imagination of the traveler; for though banished to Esne when they became too plenty in Cairo, they were allowed to consider Esne as reaching from Cairo to the first cataract, and they are to be found every where between the two places, and chiefly at Luxor. Some of them retain traces of the traditional beauty of their race; but by far the most of them are miserable drabs, and hopelessly degraded.

The two girls who came down to the boat were fair specimens of the class; one of them held a species of banjo or guitar in her lap, on which she beat a sort of tune, while the other danced slowly, and with some degree of skill, to the measure. Their taste in dress was far above the ordinary run of women in Egypt; for the natives of the lower classes, as I have already stated, wear but a single long, loose garment, while these girls were loaded with the usual full dress of the lady of the hareem.

But receiving neither bucksheesh nor prospect of engagement for a dance on deck, or in the room of the old house where they had performed the evening previous for a European nobleman and lady, they retired in disgust, and, I am sorry to say, left us with very similar impressions regarding them. They were like a hundred others that I saw in Egypt; and, out of Cairo, I think none better are to be seen.

The last day of my stay at Thebes arrived. Before breakfast I crossed to the island and shot a dozen pigeons, and knocked over a fox that looked impudently at me out of the edge of a corn-field, as if he did not believe in lead and charcoal.

Pigeon shooting in Egypt no traveler will pursue except for the purpose of supplying his table. There is no sport in knocking over these tame birds, born and bred in the village pigeon houses.

Away across the river, on the broad plain, Memnon sat silent and majestic on his throne, lord of all the upper country; and it behooved me to take leave of him with due solemnity before I should go northward.

I sent up to Houssein Kasheef for a ladder. A firman can bring out of a governor in Egypt any thing that is in him. He had never heard of a ladder, didn't know what it was. But his highness had given Braheem Effendi a firman, and Braheem Effendi wanted a ladder by virtue of the firman, and a ladder he must have. No one in Egypt ever thought of climbing any thing but a palm-tree. But an explanation that a ladder meant something to help a man up the side of a house, induced some one in the train to recollect that a French explorer, who had been some time resident here in former years, had used a curious combination of pieces of wood for such purposes, and it was forthwith hunted up. They found it in the subterranean chambers of the Luxor temple, where it had been used in copying inscriptions. It was about ten feet long, and likely to be of little use to me; but I had it brought down to the boat. Miriam and myself went off together. We, hoisting our little sail, dashed swiftly across the Nile, to the west bank, where our donkeys were standing, and then across the plain to the feet of him of the stony eyes.

Have I or have I not mentioned what every one ought to know, that Memnon is one of two statues that sit side by side, between whose thrones doubtless an avenue once passed, leading to the great burial-place, which is a thousand yards behind them. It certainly can not be necessary for me to inform any intelligent reader that the statue is that of Amunoph III. At what period it was selected as vocal and superior to its companion, we know not.

With the aid of my ladder we mounted easily to the pedestal of the old statue, and sat down between his feet. The rock of which he is made is full of beautiful agates; travelers cut these out for ornaments and memorials.

I wanted to climb into the lap of the statue, and examine for myself the sonorous stone, which, being struck, gives out the sound of a bell. This is by some supposed to be the fabled music of Memnon. An Arab boy went up like a cat and disappeared from our view. A moment later he struck the stones, first one, and then the other. One sounded somewhat like a bell—very little like it indeed—but the other was dull, heavy, and like striking a blow on any rock.

Mohammed Hassan held me on his shoulders where, standing up, I could reach with the ladder high enough to hang the upper round of it on a projecting point of the rock and lift myself up to the lower round. It was not a very safe climb at the best. As I approached the top I found that the round, on which the ladder and I hung, was nearly cut in two, and the chances were that in thirty seconds more I should fall thirty feet, as dead as Memnon. I sprang to a projecting corner of the broken rock, and wedged myself in the huge rift that was made by an earthquake in ancient days, when half the statue was thrown down. Here I found that my chin was just above the edge of his leg. I could look into the chasm in his lap. It was a hole deep and broad enough to hold three or four men, but if priests lay concealed there, as has been by some intimated, the question is, how they got there and got away again without being seen. For it is a clear case that no one could effect such a lodgment and escape without a ladder, and a longer one than I had.

I saw the Arab strike the stones, but I could not get into the lap of the old man of the plain. Perhaps I could have got into it, but how to get out of it again was the problem, and not choosing to attempt a practical solution of this I stepped back to the ladder, slipped down it, as if it were greased, to the shining shoulder of Mohammed, and so to the ground.

Whether it was an earthquake, or the destroying army of Darius that hurled down the upper portion of the statue does not now appear. Probably it was the Persian, for Memnon's companion sits monolithic in his ancient seat, undisturbed, while of Memnon all the body, shoulders, and head, are rebuilt of massive hewn stone. The other and less noted statue is much the more stately and perfect in appearance. But no tradition has hallowed him. He is but a carved stone, a rough rock, while his old friend and companion of stony silence for so many centuries has name and fame in history and story, and is known to the very children of remote and late born nations.

One half hour to stroll among the stately ruins of the Remeseion; one glance over the white hills under which lay the millions of Egyptian dead, and then, waving our hands to the old watcher for the sunrise, we left him to his throne and kingdom.

In starry nights of this western land in which I now write, I sometimes bow before a solemn, grand thought. He who has not seen Memnon can hardly appreciate what I mean. It is the thought of that stately old giant, sitting calmly on his rocky seat now as for thousands of years, while dew and dawn alternate on his cold brow.

Old Houssein Kasheef had behaved remarkably well in the matter of the Jereed play, and every day after that was accustomed to come down early in the morning, sit on the sand on the sunny side of the tent, and move his seat around with the sun till evening, when he joined the group within it, and smoked his chibouk in solemn quiet, wondering at the furious talk of the assembled Franks.

I liked him from the first, perhaps because he was so very quiet. He never disturbed me. If I were on the lee side of the canvas he came and sat down quietly with an Arabic good morning, and smoked the pipe of peace in silence. Hajji Mohammed never needed an order to send up coffee, but so soon as the old man made his appearance it would begin to come, and it never stopped coming till he left at night. He transacted all his business there, received and answered letters, examined prisoners, and, in point of fact, lived there altogether. The quantities of coffee that he consumed in a day's sitting were enormous.

I have called him an old man. He was about seventy; a small, calm-faced old Turk, with a mild, and rather pleasant countenance, very kind disposition, and, as I soon learned, very poor. The house which he occupied was a miserable mud affair, the largest in Luxor indeed, but the winds howled through it fiercely and furiously, and it was destitute of furniture, except only his bedstead and bedding, on which he reposed his weary and lonesome old limbs at night. I shuddered as I thought of it one day in his dreary room, for I had begun to like the old man, and I feared that some dismal morning they would find him cold and stiff on the split reed bedstead.

"Why do you live alone, Houssein Kasheef?" I asked him one day between two pipes. He heard me, and when Ferrajj had brought back my chibouk, fragrant and fiery, he replied,

"Because I can not afford to live otherwise."

"But you are married."

"Allah be thanked, I have one wife and ten children, at Goos."

"Why not here?"

"By the mercy of Allah, and the grace of his highness Mohammed Ali and his exalted sons, I have been governor at Goos for nearly twenty years. I have lived there since I was a man; my wife has always lived there, and her friends are all there. A year ago the government adopted a principle of changing officers from place to place. A good system; but it tore me from my family. I could not bring my wife and children here to this miserable hole. I left them at Goos. It is only ten hours from here; but my labors are, as you know, very arduous. I have seen my wife and children but once. When you arrived, O Braheem Effendi, I was at Goos. I found them all living and well, and have come back. I am too poor to give up my office. I must go where I am ordered, and I expect to die here. Perhaps I shall never see my wife again: Allah be merciful to us."

He was nearly a half hour in telling me this. It came out briefly, in smoky ejaculations. I listened, and pitied him from my soul.

The evening of our departure from Thebes was one of indescribable beauty. The moon lay on the water in silver glory. The air was a dream of splendor. The tent was struck at sunset, and the deserted shore appeared more lonely than ever. The *Phantom* was the only boat at Luxor. Every thing else had gone.

Abd-el-Atti had been making a purchase of an antique, on his own account, from an Arab of Goornou. He had learned that a mummy of the most ancient, rare, and valuable kind, had been found, and he had negotiated for and bought it. It belonged to a company of more than thirty of the Goornou resurrectionists, and they would not consent to bring it over to Luxor to the boat, lest they should be caught with it by some government officer, and lose mummy and some of their own skin besides, a not unusual occurrence. Therefore the dragoman was puzzled on the subject, not liking to lose the opportunity for speculation, and not knowing how to avoid it. At length he was relieved by this plan. He directed the Arabs to bring down the daughter of Pharaoh to the shore of the Nile, three miles below on the west bank, near a tree which we all knew, at midnight on the night of our starting. He went down early with the small boat and four men to receive the freight. On our appearance with the *Phantom* he was to board us.

Mustapha and Houssein Kasheef came down in the evening, and sat and talked till nearly midnight. Mustapha had a small cannon, presented him by some traveler who had carried it for saluting purposes, to which he zealously applies it, and he had loaded it to the muzzle for a grand discharge on our departure. But I determined to send him off quietly to bed with the idea that we would not go till morning, and let him save his gunpowder.

As the evening wore on, and we still sipped our coffee and smoked, while the candles burned dimly on the table, a messenger came in and whispered to Mustapha. He went out, and was gone half an hour. When he came back, he had something on his mind, and at length it came out.

"Would Braheem Effendi consent to be reconciled with Islamin Bey, the nazir, before leaving Luxor?"

Of course he would. If the nazir would for once be decent, and come down to the boat, he should have pipes and coffee, and a gentleman's reception.

Mustapha vanished. He came back soon afterward with downcast countenance, and told us the nazir was quite sick and couldn't come.

I told Abd-el-Atti, privately, to ascertain if it was true, and at length I learned the fact that the surly dog had told Mustapha briefly, in reply to his invitation, that we, our illustrious selves—two American pashas, of brilliant rank, worthy unbounded honors and admiration, to say nothing of our wives—might go to the devil; that was the long and the short of it.

Houssein Kasheef shrugged his old shoulders, and gathered his robes about him to be gone.

"I hope when I come back to Luxor I shall see you here yet my old friend."

"Ah, if you wish me any thing, wish that I may be at Goos, or dead; don't wish me long life at Luxor."

"If I could ask Abd-el-Kader to remove you to Goos—"

"I would take you up on my head, and carry you to see every ruin in Egypt, could you but get me leave to die at Goos."

So we parted. The old man looked sorrowfully back at the cabin, as he left it for his own miserable quarters; and I thought then that he would remember us with some pleasure. It was a gratification afterward to give him cause to remember us when he dies among his kindred.

Midnight was at hand. The moonlight lay like a dream of beauty on the river and on the ruins. Through the vast corridor of the temple a broad pathway of silver light came down, that made Mustapha's house seem like another Bethel at the foot of a heavenward way.

I sat alone in the cabin of the *Phantom*. The others were sound asleep, dreaming, I doubt not, of home.

When I came out on deck, the crew were lying here and there like so many piles of cloth, giving signs of animation only in the long regular heaving of each mass.

I stirred them up gently, making as little noise as possible, and ordered them to be as quiet. I did not wish to wake Mustapha's cannon. They moved about like ghosts on the moonlit shore, casting off the fasts. I took my place on the upper deck as usual, and gave my orders in pantomime, for the lowest utterance of the human voice echoed from the magnificent corridor in which Mustapha was sleeping.

The *Phantom* drifted slowly out into the current of the river. As she went out of the bight or bay in which we had been lying, the current took her and she shot downward.

All was still. Moonlight lay on the temple and on the shore. The tall group of palms, nearest to the mound on which we had buried poor Tonge, lifted their branches calmly into the glory of the moonlight. There my eye was fixed longer than elsewhere, and looking there I forgot to look at the temple, and so before I knew it we were away from Thebes, and all danger of rousing the echoes of the palace with Egyptian gunpowder were gone.

"Shil!"

They were ready, every man at his oar, and at the word the fourteen oars struck the plashing water together, and the *Phantom* flew down the river.

We coasted the western shore. Near the large tree that was the old landing place on that bank, they lay on their oars, and I looked ahead on the moonlit shore for some indication of Abd-el-Atti with his companion of Pharaonic days. There was a small grove of trees not far below us which was the appointed place of meeting, and here I saw something which looked like the small boat. The shore was three hundred feet broad, and the moonlight lay across it, making it appear as white as snow, while on the bank above there was a grove of trees. From this, as we approached, a group of fifteen men suddenly emerged into the moonlight, bearing something heavy, with which they hastened across the open beach to the boat. Then, retiring a few paces, they stood in a row, while the boat pushed off and joined us as we drifted by.

"Now—all together, men. Lift carefully and slowly. So she comes!" and the princess or priestess was hoisted to the cabin deck and laid on one of our vacant sofas, covered with canvas and blankets to hide her from curious eyes, and the men again lay down to their oars.

We swept close in shore by the row of silent Arabs; the Goornou resurrectionists' guttural "Salaam Aleikoum," came to us as we went along, and they retired into the grove.

So the daughter of the Pharaoh (who dares say she was not the daughter of Amunoph himself?) commenced her voyage from her ancient resting place and the graves of her fathers. Three thousand years of repose—then, the Nile-boat of a wandering Howajji—then, a curiosity-room in Cairo—and then the sea, the Pillars of Hercules, the Fortunate Islands, and a new world! There is verily no rest even in an Egyptian grave. This royal lady slept quietly on our cabin deck during the voyage down the river, and Abd-el-Atti transferred her to Dr. Abbott at Cairo, who, I suppose, will ship her to enrich the collection in New York.

38.

A Turkish Nobleman.

I SLEPT profoundly. It was hard to sleep on such nights. I often lay all night on deck dozing and dreaming till morning.

The next afternoon, at sunset, we reached the landing place of Gheneh. I had promised Abd-el-Kader Bey that I would not go down the river without seeing him. The temple of Dendera, on the opposite shore of the river, was by no means to bo omitted.

The same moonlight fell on the river and land again. At eight or nine o'clock the barking of foxes on shore tempted me out with my gun. The boat lay on the west side of what is at high Nile an island, but was now connected with Gheneh by the broad sandy bed of a dry branch of the river. In the upper part of this bed lay a lake of water extending down nearly abreast of our landing-place in a narrow canal-like strip. Between us and this was the high land of the island, and on this I heard the cry of the jackals.

Starting quietly along through the corn I came out in an open place where I could look five hundred feet between two rows of standing doura. I saw at the lower end of the row three foxes amusing themselves very pleasantly in the moonshine. It was a pity to spoil their sport, but I wanted specimens, for as yet I had not found out whether there was any difference between the fox and the jackal.

I knocked over two of them—one with each barrel. As the echo died away I heard a twittering and rushing of wings in the lake and the canal below me, which showed that there was game there and in quantity.

I reloaded and slipped down the bank to the edge of the water. All was still. Sundry dark spots seemed like the ducks I was after, but I was uncertain whether they were not low grass hummocks. As I approached the edge of the water, creeping on hands and knees, I heard a step crushing the corn on the hill above me, and the next instant two barrels of a heavy ducking gun sent down a load of lead into the water, directly in front of me.

Abd-el-Atti, hearing my shots at the foxes, had come out to my aid, and not finding me had poured down these loads on the water among the feathered animals.

The cloud of birds that rose from the water was arctic in its vastness and thickness. Thousands of the duck kind filled the air. My two barrels sent some hundreds of shot into the cloud and brought down nearly a dozen splashing in the bright water.

Abd-el-Atti was surprised. He had no idea that I was near him. The game circled awhile with loud cries in the air; then, as we lay motionless, and they could not see us, they settled again on the water, and we loaded and fired again. One barrel raised them, and the other three made terrible havoc in them as they spread their wings. I never saw such duck shooting, and I have had much of that sport from the Chesapeake to Montauk. It was absolute murder. After we had fairly scattered the flocks and driven them over into the Nile, we laid down our guns and clothes and went in after our game. They lay on the water in all directions, and it was with much difficulty we gathered them. But it was a glorious bath in the cool soft water, with such a sky and such a night over us.

I owe much to Abd-el-Kader. I would not have gone by without seeing him, had I not promised him to stop, for he was the most accomplished Egyptian that I had met.

He heard that I had arrived, and early in the morning his chief of the household was down with horses and an invitation to the governor's residence. I rode up. He was in his cool small reception-room, with the same four ebony boys that waited on him when I went up the river.

We had sherbet and pipes and coffee, while he finished his morning's business, heard a few petitioners, and received reports of his soldiers. Then we retired to a small and somewhat more cozy cabinet, where, lying on soft cushions, we smoked and talked as the morning slipped away.

"What think you, O Abd-el-Kader, is the first duty of a man in his worldly affairs?" said I.

"The Koran saith the first duty of a man is to his family."

"Yea, truly; and if the government so order that a man may not do his duty to his family?"

"The government doth wrong."

"My old friend, Houssein Kasheef, of Luxor, has a family at Goos, but Latif Pasha and Abd-el-Kader Bey have separated him from his family and sent him to Luxor to be old and cold and die. Send him back to his family."

My friend waved his hand to a scribe or secretary, who stood just outside the open door, and spoke a few words to him before he replied to me.

"The government have thought a rotation in office the better plan. When a governor resides long in one place he becomes acquainted with the people, and is too apt to favor certain persons, perhaps to accept bribes from them. It is better to change once in a while. Houssein Kasheef has been very long at Goos."

"Yes, but he is old; he ought not to be separated from his wife and children. He is faithful to the government, is he not?"

"Always. But he will learn new things at Luxor, and soon like it;" and so he continued for a few minutes to combat my wishes, very gently indeed, until the secretary reappeared with a written order, to which the governor affixed his seal, and then puffed his chibouk quietly, and enjoyed my surprise and pleasure, his own flashing out of his fine eyes, as his scribe handed the paper to me.

It was an order appointing old Houssein to Goos as I had requested. He gave it to me that I might have the pleasure of forwarding it to the old man myself. This I did without delay, and at Cairo I received a reply from him, full of gratitude, promising to remember Americans thenceforth forever.

I passed the day with my kind host, enjoying the luxury of fruits and coffee, delicious Latakea, and pleasant talk. I told him stories of home, of hunting in American forests, of the chase on the Delaware, and the buffalo on the prairie. He in return told me of Mohammed Ali, for whom he had a son's affection. He, when a boy, was a slave of that prince, had been by him educated in arts and arms, and he remembered him with a devotion that was admirable. Many stories of what he thought the greatest glory of Egypt he told me that I would gladly relate here if I had space.

Toward evening I left him. He despatched a servant for a branch of an orange tree, bearing two splendid oranges, which he sent with his compliments to the ladies.

In the twilight I strolled through the bazaars at Gheneh, crowded with Ababdee Arabs, carrying huge heads of matted hair, some curled in masses of pipe-stem curls, and some hideously filthy. At the corners were many dark-eyed Ghawazee, with white complexions and lithe forms carefully exposed to view. One, a fair-faced girl with flashing black eyes, who hung close to me as I bought some perfume at a drug shop, and held out her tattooed hand to be touched with the fragrant oil, had been of rare beauty, but was now sadly faded. There was a peculiarity about her face that attracted my attention. It was so very American. In home-costume I should have taken her for a heart-broken New England girl. Her complexion was whiter than the ordinary complexion of a New York lady's face, even than a blonde, and I started when I first saw her, and wondered what girl could have been left by a traveler's boat to shame and misery in this far city.

Next day, I walked from the river to the temple at Dendera, shooting over the plain. Pigeons were plenty, and I killed a fox. The temple is of modern times. We call things old, not from actual age, but in comparison. Old for a man is young for a tree, but old for a tree is young for a temple. This temple that was built in the days of Cleopatra, and has a portrait of her on its walls, is of little interest in comparison with those that were built in the days of Jacob or Moses. It is in very perfect preservation, and we wandered from room to room for hours. The great zodiac on the ceiling of the corridor remains there still, but a smaller one from one of the smaller rooms has been removed to Paris. I shall not weary my reader, who is already sufficiently be-templed, with any sketch of the group at Dendera. The capitals of the columns of the great corridor, which are in fact four-faced heads of goddesses, have been often described and engraved, as also the grotesque figures on the smaller temple. We should have remained here all day, but for an engagement to review Abd-el-Kader's troops at Gheneh, and we returned to the river, crossed, and went up to the palace.

The troops were altogether the best disciplined body of men that I saw in the East, and Abd-el-Kader prided himself much on them. They went through the evolutions with precision, uttering at each order or motion a guttural *hugh*, like a North American Indian's expression of surprise, which enabled them to keep perfect time.

We had coffee and pipes again in the cool reception room, and Miriam honored his magnificent amber and diamond mouth-piece with the touch of her lips. He presented her with a bowl, made from the horn of a rhinoceros, a rare and costly present, and one most highly prized among the Orientals. This bowl (a rhinoceros furnishes but one as large as this) it is said has a power of detecting poison, so that none can be administered or taken in it. It will fly to pieces on the touch of poison, if its fabled virtue is true.

When we returned to the boat, he had sent down a quantity of presents in the usual style, among which the most curious were a large variety of fowls, known only at Dendera.

39.

The Crocodile Pits.

I PAUSED a day at Es Siout and then went on to *Maabdeh*, on the east bank of the river, about five miles above Manfaloot. Here we found ourselves, one morning, on awaking.

Maabdeh is not the site of an ancient city. But it is the nearest point on the river to one of the most remarkable of the ancient catacombs of Egypt. Seven miles from the shore, beyond the eastern mountains, are the celebrated crocodile pits, which many travelers have attempted to explore. None, I think, have succeeded as thoroughly as myself.

These pits have their chief celebrity, in modern times, from the difficulty which travelers have experienced in entering them, and the fatality that attended Mr. Legh's attempt. As his account has hitherto been most relied on for description of the pits, I give an extract from it, that it may be compared with my own.

He proceeds as follows:* (I condense the statement somewhat.)

"We formed a party of six; each was to be preceded by a guide. Our torches were lighted; one of the Arabs

* Narrative by Thomas Legh, Esq., M. P. Philadelphia Edition, 1817. Page 148, etc.

led the way, and I followed him. We crept for seven or eight yards through an opening at the bottom of the pit, which was partly choked up with the drifted sand of the desert, and found ourselves in a large chamber about fifteen feet high. Here we observed fragments of the mummies of crocodiles; we saw also great numbers of bats flying about, and hanging from the roof. We now entered a low gallery, in which we continued for more than an hour, stooping or creeping as was necessary, and following its windings, till at last it opened into a large chamber, which, after some time, we recognized as the one we had first entered. Our guides at last confessed they had missed their way, but if we would make another attempt, they would undertake to conduct us to the mummies. We had been wandering for more than an hour, in low subterranean passages, and felt considerably fatigued by the irksomeness of the posture in which we had been obliged to move, and the heat of our torches in the narrow and low galleries; but the Arabs spoke so confidently of succeeding in this second trial, that we were induced once more to attend them. We found the opening of the chamber which we now approached, guarded by a trench of unknown depth, and wide enough to require a good leap. The first Arab jumped the ditch, and we all followed him. The passage we entered was extremely small, and so low in some places as to oblige us to crawl flat on the ground, and almost always on our hands and knees. The intricacies of its windings resembled a labryinth, and it terminated at length in a chamber much smaller than that which we had left, but like it containing nothing to satisfy our curiosity. Our search hitherto had been fruitless, but the mummies might not be far distant; another effort and we might still be successful.

"The Arab whom I followed, and who led the way, now entered another gallery, and we all continued to move in the same manner as before, each preceded by a guide. We had not gone far before the heat became excessive; I found my breathing extremely difficult; my head began to ache most violently, and I had a most distressing sensation of fullness about the heart. We felt we had gone too far, and yet were almost deprived of the power to return. At this moment the torch of the first Arab went out; I was close to him and saw him fall on his side; he uttered a groan; his legs were strongly convulsed, and I heard a rattling noise in his throat—he was dead. The Arab behind me, seeing the torch of his companion extinguished, and conceiving he had stumbled, passed me, advanced to his assistance and stooped. I observed him appear faint, totter, and fall in a moment: he also was dead. The third Arab came forward, and made an effort to approach the bodies, but stopped short. We looked at each other in silent horror. The danger increased every instant; our torches burned faintly; our knees tottered under us, and we felt our strength nearly gone. There was no time to be lost.

"The American cried to us to take courage, and we began to move back as fast as we could. We heard the remaining Arab shouting after us, calling us Kaffirs, imploring our assistance, and upbraiding us with deserting him. But we were obliged to leave him to his fate, expecting every moment to share it with him. The windings of the passage through which we had come increased the difficulty of our escape. We might take a wrong turn, and never reach the great chamber we had first entered. Even supposing we took the shortest road, it was but too probable our strength would fail us before we arrived. We had each of us separately, and unknown to one another, observed attentively the different shapes of the stones which projected into the galleries we had passed, so that each had an imperfect clue to the labyrinth we had now to retrace. We compared notes, and only on one occasion had a dispute—the American differing from my friend and myself. In this dilemma we were determined by the majority, and fortunately were right. Exhausted with fatigue and terror we reached the edge of the deep trench, which remained to be crossed before we got into the great chamber. Mustering all my strength I leaped, and was followed by the American. Smelt stood on the brink ready to drop with fatigue. He called to us, for God's sake, to help him over the fosse, or at least to stop, if only for five minutes, to allow him time to recover his strength. It was impossible—to stay was death—and we could not resist the desire to push on and reach the open air. We encouraged him to summon all his force, and he cleared the trench. When we reached the open air it was one o'clock, and the heat in the sun about 160°. Our sailors, who were waiting for us, had luckily a bardak full of water, which they sprinkled upon us, but, though a little refreshed, it was not possible to climb the sides of the pit. They then unfolded their turbans, and slinging them round our bodies, drew us to the top. Our appearance alone, without our guides, naturally astonished the Arab who had remained at the entrance of the cavern, and he anxiously inquired for his hahabebas or friends. To have confessed they were dead would have excited suspicion of our having murdered them. We replied they were coming, and were employed in bringing out the mummies we had found. We lost no time in mounting our asses, re-crossed the desert, and passed hastily by the village to regain the ferry of Manfalout. Our kandjia was moored close to the town, and we got safe on board by five o'clock."

Many travelers since Mr. Legh's time have, with great justice, condemned him for deserting his men under such circumstances. My own experience in these pits convinces me that he was decidedly wrong. The account of his failure and that of subsequent explorers did not deter me from the attempt I now proposed.

Early in the morning I began to make arrangements for guides among the villagers, but I found great difficulty in persuading any to go with me. The reason was not that given by Mr. Legh, fear of the pits, but they said that we must pass through a village near the mountains, where the inhabitants would assuredly beat them off and take us into their merciful protection, whereby they, the shore guides, would lose their pay beside getting a thrashing. It was only on assurance of pay, beating or no beating, that I could persuade two of them to go with me. Abd-el-Atti and Abdallah, one of my boat's crew, the two guides and myself, formed the party who started for the mountains, crossing the largest grain field that I have seen in Egypt. It was almost prairie-like in appearance, being three miles or so in breadth, and stretching up and down the river as far as I could see—one long waving field of green wheat flashing in the sunshine.

Crossing this we arrived at a narrow branch of the Nile, now dry, but apparently quite recently filled, and near this a village, the one of which our guides had expressed their fear. The custom which they stood in dread of is said to be prevalent in this neighborhood, but to our and their surprise no molestation was offered us at this crossing, the men of the village being absent on some prowling expedition, or possibly engaged in the fields. Climbing the side of the mountain, which is here not more than six hundred feet high, consisting of beetling cliffs of white rock that overhung our path, and which had, in some ancient times, been quarried for the purposes of a city now wholly gone, we arrived on the elevated table-land of the Arabian desert.

Such appears to be the character of the land on both sides of the Nile, resembling in that respect portions of the upper Mississippi. The valley is a deep depression or rift in a vast table of high land.

We had still some miles to go. I am entirely unable to estimate the distance, but can safely say that it was not less than five miles from the landing place, in all. Our path was over a sandy soil, with broken rocks jutting out here and there, but no sign of vegetation whatever visible. The peculiarity of it was a crystal of what I suppose to be gypsum over which we walked all the way. My feet crushed in it like walking on dry moss. Enormous quantities of it, thousands of bushels, were on the surface of the ground, to be gathered up by any one. I know not what commercial value it has, but it seemed to me a desirable matter to be examined by some one interested in Egyptian agriculture if in nothing else.

In crossing the plain I had been overtaken by a party consisting of two English gentlemen, their dragoman and a sailor from their boat with a guide, who learning of our guarantee had consented to bring them along and take the risk of passing the village safely. Their boat had arrived just as I was coming away from mine.

We had joined forces and come on together, presenting a formidable array which it required some courage in any party of Arabs to attack. At length we found ourselves in a water shed toward the east, and this narrowed to what was apparently the bed of a torrent, finding its way downward to the south-east, the hills on each side sloping toward it.

The ground was still covered with yellow sand but further along the torrent bed was bare gray rock, and now the guides stopped.

I saw no hole or entrance till I was close to them.

They paused on the edge of a hole in the sand, about six feet long by four wide at the widest end, narrowing to a point at the other. It descended perpendicularly about ten feet to a floor of sand. Originally it was much deeper, but the sand flowing into it in every wind, has filled it much. It is only marvelous that it was not long ago quite filled. There was nothing outside to indicate its existence. No ruin, nor stone; persons might pass a hundred times within twenty feet of it and not see it. The sand was unbroken to its very edge.

After resting a few moments I prepared for the entrance to the pit.

As it was by no means certain that the villagers from the foot of the mountain would permit us to finish our examination unmolested, and as Abd-el-Atti now strenuously objected to entering the hole himself, I left him sitting on the ground at the entrance with the sailor from the other boat, and the donkey-boys, taking Abdallah with me; he seeming very willing to go in, and not at all influenced by the tales of horror with which the guides had amused us along the way. I took off all the clothes that I had worn and put on an old shirt and a pair of brown linen pantaloons of the coarsest sort. This was my total equipment.

Having no coat and no breast-pocket, and mindful of the disasters which had occurred to various travelers solely from want of stimulants in this cavern, I put my small pocket brandy-flask, a glass flask covered with wicker, into my pantaloons pocket, each of us having in the first place fortified himself with a single swallow of the liquor.

The descent into the cavern was by sitting on the edge, swinging off with one hand on each side of the hole, and dropping into the depths below, where a soft bed of sand received us, in a chamber just large enough to hold the eight persons of whom the party consisted, all standing in a stooping posture while we lighted our candles and arranged for our progress. I tossed my tarbouche and takea up to Abd-el-Atti, and left my head bare. Then, following the principal guide, I lay down flat on my face, holding my candle before me, and began to advance with as close a resemblance to a snake's motion as human vertebræ will admit of. My other guide and Abdallah followed me; the English gentlemen next, and their dragoman and guide bringing up the rear. I progressed slowly, and with great difficulty, constantly bruising my back on the sharp points of the rock above me, some five or six yards. Legh calls it eight, but I think it not so much. We were now able to stand up again, in a stooping posture, the ceiling being a little over four feet high, and thus advanced eight or ten yards further, until we reached the chamber of which Mr. Legh speaks.

I am of opinion that we had now arrived just under the bed of the torrent I have spoken of, and that the entire cavern, which I afterward explored, is a natural fissure in the rock running under this point of meeting of two hills, and following the line of the valley between them. This is, of course, but a conjecture, as I did not take a compass with me to determine the course.

This chamber was a small, irregular, cavernous room, the floor of which was covered with shapeless masses of stone that had fallen from the roof. Over these we stepped with great difficulty. I need not remark that the darkness was profound, and the air already became so close that our candles burned but dimly, so that each man was obliged to hold his own at his feet to determine where to set them. Crossing the room, we stepped over a chasm between a mass of rock and the wall of the chamber, to a point in the wall, which presented a ragged edge, and from this into a narrow doorway, about four feet high. I call it a doorway, for it resembled one, though I could find no signs of artificial origin about it. It was almost square, and opened into a sort of gallery, the floor of which was covered with broken rock, and interrupted by huge deep fissures. A ledge at the side afforded tolerable walking for some distance, in a stooping posture; and then we again lay down on our faces and crawled through a passage twenty feet in length, entering the largest chamber in the pit. It was a vast irregular cavern, perhaps seventy or a hundred feet in diameter. Entrance to it was almost forbidden by clouds of bats that met me in the narrow passage through which I was crawling, dashing into my face, wounding my forehead and cheeks, clinging by scores to my hair and beard, like so many thousand devils disputing the entrance to hell. I can give no adequate idea of this chamber of horrors in which I now found myself. Profoundly silent, we had crawled along, each man having a fast-beating heart, and listening to its throbs; and now, as I emerged into this room, the loud whirr of the myriads of bats was like the sounds of another world into which I had penetrated. I staggered forward to a rock and sat down, when a piercing yell started me to my feet. It rang through the cavern as if the arch-fiend himself were there tormenting some poor soul. But it was only one of my poor friends who were making their first entrance to an Egyptian catacomb, and had never before encountered the bats, with whom I was thoroughly familiar. The one who was in advance was overwhelmed by the army that met him as he approached the room.

"What is it?" I shouted.

"These bats: they are devouring me."

"Push on; they'll not harm you."

"My light is gone, and I can see nothing."

"Here is my light; come toward it." I had re-lit my candle, which had been put out as his was, and was now seated in the centre of the cavern, on a black rock, holding it up before my face. As he emerged into the room and caught sight of me, he uttered a howl of mingled astonishment and terror.

"Pluto or Sathanas, by all the gods," said his friend, coming up behind him, and looking at me. My appearance must have been picturesque in my primitive costume, now begrimmed with dirt, and seven bats (they counted them) hanging on my beard, with a perfect net-work and Medusa-coil of them in my hair. I was very little disturbed by the harmless little fellows, although, before coming to Egypt, I scarcely knew of an animal in the world so disgusting to my mind.

But the atmosphere, if it may be so called, of this chamber was beyond all description horrible. It was not an air to faint in; there was too much ammonia for that. It was foul, vile, terrible. I confess, that, as I found myself panting for breath, and drawing long, deep inspirations, to very choking, without "reaching the right place" in my lungs (I think every one understands that), I trembled for an instant at the idea of going further. It was but an instant, however, and the desire to see the great repository of the sacred animals overpowered the momentary terror.

"Abdallah."

"Ya, Howajji."

"If any thing happens; if I fall down, give out, or faint, don't you run. Tell the guides that I have ordered Abd-el-Atti to shoot them man by man as they come out, if one of them appears without me. Do you pour this down my throat, and drag me out to the entrance. You understand?"

"Aiowah, Ya Howajji. Fear not; I will do it."

"Recollect that if I die, you all die. That is arranged, for, as surely as you, one of you, attempt the entrance without me, Abd-el-Atti is ready for you."

The guides had listened attentively, and, having seen me hand my pistols to my trusty dragoman before coming down, they believed every word of it, though it had never occurred to me till this instant.

The guides were all at fault here, precisely as they were in Mr. Legh's time, and that of every traveler since. This chamber has been the end of most attempts to explore the pits. The intense darkness is some excuse for this, since our eight candles wholly failed to show a wall any where around or above us. The men proposed that we should sit still while they tried various passages opening out of the room. To this I objected, much preferring to trust myself at a juncture like this. In that intense blackness it was not easy to find even the way we had come in at, for, of course, there was no guide to north or south, except my recollection of the shape of the rock on which I was seated, and its bearings as I approached it. The reader will bear in mind that the whole floor of this room was covered with immense masses of rock, among which we moved about in search of outlets, leaving always one person on that rock to mark its locality.

After trying three passages that led nowhere, I hit on that one which the guides pronounced correct, and the party advanced. For the benefit of future explorers, if any such there be, I may explain that it is the first passage which goes out of the chamber to the right as you enter it. That is to say, keeping the right-hand wall will bring you to it, leaping a chasm at its entrance. This is the chasm of which Legh speaks. I found it to be only about six feet deep.

The passage which we now entered ran so low that I found it necessary to creep on my hands and knees, and sometimes to crawl, snake fashion, full length. It continued for a distance that I hesitate to estimate. It is wholly impossible to guess at the progress one is making in such postures. Henniker, I think, makes it four hundred yards. I should think a thousand feet a very large estimate, but it may be as much. The air was now worse, lacking the ammonia. It seemed to be almost pure nitrogen. The lungs operated freely, but took no benefit or refreshment from it, while the heat was awful, and perspiration rolled down our faces and bodies, soaking our clothes and making mud on our features and hands, with the fine dust that filled the atmosphere. At length the passage became so narrow, that my progress was blocked entirely. My broad shoulders would not go through, and I paused to consider the matter. The hole was about eighteen inches wide, and a little more than two feet high. Evidently Mr. Legh did not pass beyond this. I was obliged to lie over on my right side, presenting my body to it narrow way up and down, and pushing with all the strength of my feet as well as pulling with my hands on the floor and rocky projections, I forced myself along about eight feet. In this struggle my brandy flask, which was in my trowsers pocket, being under me, was broken to pieces, and my sole hope, in the event of a giving out of my faculties, was gone. At the time, I thought little of it, laughing at the occurrence as I called out to those who followed me; but afterward I remembered the incident with a shudder. The only argument that had allowed me to persuade myself to attempt this exploration was a promise to myself that I would take brandy with me, which no one else had done, and, if necessary, secure artificial strength thereby. It was gone now, and I was more than a thousand feet from light and air, in a passage that did not average four feet by two its entire length.

A vigorous push sent me out into a more open passage

and a sort of doorway opened into a gallery on a level two feet lower. Jumping down this step I was, for the first time in nearly a half hour, where I could stand upright. My English friend shouted for help behind me. His light was gone out, and he was literally stuck in the hole. I returned, touched my candle to his and gave him a hand to drag him through, and in a few moments we were all standing together. We now advanced some hundred feet, perhaps three, perhaps five hundred, in a stooping posture mostly, but occasionally crawling as before, and, at length, as we crept, the rough and very low parts of the gallery and the roof began to lift, and I found that I was actually crawling over mummies. There was just here a sort of blind passage at the side of the chief passage, in which the French expedition had carved their names. The walls were covered with a jet black substance, like the purest lamp black, which the point of a knife would scratch off, exposing the white rock. Numerous stalactites hung from the ceiling, all jet black, and some grotesque stalagmites at the sides of the passage startled me at first with the idea that they were sculptures. This black sooty matter I can not account for unless it be the exhalations in ancient times from the crocodiles which were laid here, for we were at last in the depository.

The floor was covered with crocodile bones and mummy cloths. A spark of fire falling into them would have made this a veritable hell. As this idea was suggested, my English friends, whose experience in the narrow hole had been sufficiently alarming, vanished out of sight. They fairly ran. Having seen the mummies, and seized a few small ones in their hands, they hastened out, and left me with Abdallah and my two guides. Advancing over the mummies and up the hill which they formed, I found that I was in one of a number of large chambers, of the depth of which it was of course impossible to get any idea, as they were piled full of mummied crocodiles to the very ceiling. There was no means of estimating the number of them. When I say there were thousands on thousands of them, I shall not be thought to exaggerate after I describe the manner in which they were packed and laid in.

Climbing to the top of the hill, and extinguishing all lights but one, which I made Abdallah hold very carefully, I began to throw down the top of the pile to ascertain of what it was composed, and at length I made an opening between the mummies and the ceiling, through which I could go on further, descending a sort of hill of these dead animals, such as I had come up. In this way I progressed some distance, in a gallery or chamber that was not less than twenty feet wide and probably twenty or thirty feet deep.

The crocodiles were laid in regular layers, head to tail and tail to head. First on the floor was a layer of large crocodiles, side by side, each one carefully mummied and wrapped up in cloths. Then smaller ones were laid between the tails and filling up the hollows between these. Then, and most curious of all, the remaining interstices were packed full of young crocodiles, measuring with remarkable uniformity about thirteen inches in length, each one stretched out between two slips of palm-leaf stem, which were bound to its sides like splints, and then wrapped from head to foot in a strip of cloth, wound around, commencing at the tail and fastened at the head. These small ones were made up in bundles, usually of eight, and packed in closely wherever they could be stowed. I brought out more than a hundred of them, of which my friends in Egypt seized on the most as curiosities, but I succeeded in getting some twenty or thirty of them to America with me.

This layer completed, a layer of palm branches was carefully laid over it, spread thick and smooth, and then a second and precisely similar layer of crocodiles was made, and another of palm branches, and thus continued to the ceiling. These palm branches, stems, and mummies lie here in precisely the state they were in two thousand years ago. No leaf of the palm had decayed. There could have been no moisture from the mummies whatever —or if any it had no effect on the palm branches.

Among these crocodiles I found the mummies of many men.

Sitting down on the hill, by the dim candle light, I overhauled gods and men with sacrilegious hand. It was a strange, wild, and awful scene. Among all the pictures that my memory has treasured of wandering life, I have none so fearful and thrilling as this. It was hell—a still, silent, cold hell. All these bodies lay in rows, in close packages, like so many souls damned to eternal silence and sorrow in this prison. Five bodies of men that I drew out of the mass lay before me, and cursed me with their hideous stillness and inaction. I dared them to tell me in words the reproaches of which their silent forms were so liberal; reproaches for penetrating their abode and disturbing the repose of twenty or forty centuries.

These were of the poorest and most common sort, destitute of any box, wound in coarse cloth and laid in the grave with the beasts that were sacred to their god. One I found afterward in a thin plain box, but it contained no indication of its period, and bore no mark of its owner's name or position, much to my disappointment.

"Let us go further," I said to the guides, at length.

"There is no further."

I was satisfied that the entrance we had effected was not by the passage known to the ancients, and that some other outlet lay beyond these chambers. I pushed my way over the piles of mummies to a point where another low passage went on, but it was too difficult of exploration to tempt me into it. It may lead to an outlet in the desert hitherto unknown, or that outlet may be long ago covered over by the shifting sands.

What was the object of all this preservation of the Nile monsters it is not within the scope of this volume to discuss. It is at least a mystery, for we know so little of the Egyptian theory of a hereafter that we can not understand what part the birds and beasts were to take in the resurrection.

Time flew fast, and I began to think that if I remained much longer I should be in a fair way to await the resurrection of the crocodiles before I should emerge to light.

I much desired to bring out with me a gigantic fellow, nearly twenty feet long, but the impossibility of it made it more manifest that he never came in by the way I had entered. He was one of the ante or immediately post-diluvian sort, a crocodile of the days when there were giants. Perhaps he had survived the flood, who knows? He may have laid that huge jaw on the edge of the ark in stormy times and fixed those hollow eyes on the strange ship of Noah. He may have fed on dainty limbs that were swept down to him from the wrecks of palaces. I wonder how long a crocodile lives. What rags these are that fill this cavern. Rags of grave-clothes. The last thin covering of the dead, torn to tatters! These young fellows have paddled in sacred fountains and been fed in costly vases in temples? These silent men were guardians, keepers, feeders of the sacred animals, and were buried with their charges—or possibly, they were crocodile embalmers, privileged expressly to rot—no—to preservation with their hideous companions.

O friend, there is pleasant thought, in our land, of

graves in shadowy church-yard corners, but think of life in such employment and burial here! If I thought that I were to be laid in that horrible company—I would—I would—if they did lay me there I would rise up and walk from very horror and find another grave for myself.

I crawled out as I had crawled in. Before I came away from the chamber of horror (Madame Tussaud's is nothing like it) I laid the wreck of my brandy-flask on a projecting shelf of rock where the next explorer will find it. The chances are that it will turn up in the British or Prussian Museum, as evidence of the bad habits of the ancient Egyptians thus proved to be strong in death.

I never saw a light so clear and beautiful as was the daylight that fell in the entrance of the cavern. As I approached it its tints appeared deep violet only—exceedingly rich.

"What is that?" I exclaimed, not recognizing the divine sunshine from which I had been for some hours separated.

My appearance must have been hideous as I sprang out on the sand, and fell down exhausted at the very side of the pit. The desert air seemed piercing cold, and the brandy being all gone, I could but wrap myself in a boornoose, and seek to get warmth in the sunshine.

My arrival was opportune. It was about three in the afternoon. The bellicose villagers had been collected after our coming on to the mountain, and were just now making their appearance in a body of about twenty. They paused at a hundred yards' distance, and sent one, a huge fellow with an uncommonly bold air, to be spokesman in their demands. His brave and impudent way of demanding by what right we were on the mountain was deserving of a better fate than awaited him.

"Is the mountain yours?"

"Yes, it is ours; no one has a right to be here without paying us. Who is to pay me, now?"

"I will," said Abd-el-Atti, springing at him, koorbash in hand, which he laid on furiously over his head and shoulders. The astounded Arab endeavored to assert his rights again, but the whip fell fast, and at length, completely routed, he fled toward his allies, and they joined him in the flight, while the indefatigable dragoman pursued the entire party, brandishing his weapon in the air, to their immense horror and our infinite amusement.

As he paused, they stood and shouted a defiance that was ludicrous under the circumstances, and preëminently so their threat to go down to Manfaloot and inform the governor that a traveler, with an Egyptian dragoman, had committed this wrong on their prescriptive rights. From Mr. Legh's account, it seems probable that in his day the Manfaloot governor was, to a certain extent, under the influence of these men, but we laughed at them as we turned to our claret and luncheon, which I devoured with a voracious appetite. I am compelled to admit that it tasted of mummy. I can not deny that every thing that I ate for a week had the same flavor. Countless washings would not clear my mouth and throat of the fine, impalpable dust that covered its interior, and my moustache was mummyish for a month, spite of Lubin and Piver.

Stopping on the way back to visit a small Coptic church near the village at the foot of the mountain, we reached the boat at three o'clock in the afternoon, and my first movement was to plunge over the other side into the river. Until this was accomplished, it was useless to hope to be recognized in the cabin of the *Phantom*. My complexion was dead crocodile, my odor was dead crocodile, my clothes were dead crocodile—for I had not changed them on coming out of the pit—I was but little removed from being a dead crocodile myself.

While we dined, the boat drifted down the river four miles, to Manfaloot on the west bank.

Reis Hassanein's request to be allowed to go by without stopping could not be granted, and indeed he had begun to think better of it. He disappeared on our arrival at the city, and reappeared in an hour with smiles on his face.

I went, so soon as we had finished dinner, to the Coptic convent, which is one of the most interesting in Egypt, but that is not saying much.

The Coptic church is most sadly degenerated. Ignorance and stupidity seem to characterize the priests, and I found none of the laity who seemed to have even an ordinary idea of the fundamental truths of the Christian religion.

The church was a low, arched room, the ceiling supported on arches which rested on brick pillars. The altar was behind a latticed door, and at the opposite end of the church was a latticed place for the females. All was cold, damp, and dreary. There were some very curious old pictures on the walls, which were, indeed, my object in coming here, but the bishop was absent, and I did not talk with any one about them. They took us into the convent court, and we sat down a while with a half dozen monks to discuss chibouks and coffee, and some dry wheaten cakes—blessed cakes from the altar, if I mistake not, though we could not get the explanation of their peculiarity—and then I strolled up into the city.

In the bazaar I met the governor on his way down to see me, and I turned him back to go to his own house.

Taking a seat with him in the gloomy court, we lit pipes and had sipped coffee a few minutes, when our interview was interrupted by the entrance of a fellah, who demanded loudly for an audience from the governor, and presenting himself at his feet in the shadowy corner of the court, poured out a furious tale of wrongs that he had suffered on the opposite side of the river from a traveler and his dragoman.

The foolish dog had not once raised his eyes to see that the companion of the governor's diwan was none other than his enemy. Had he looked, he would scarcely have recognized in the tolerably respectable visage and clothing of Braheem Effendi, the dirty brown, half-naked object just emerged from the crocodile pits.

Terrible was his narration, and a governor of ordinary intellect must have been moved to indignation at some one, the lying narrator or the accused, by his admirable tale. But Ali Rashwan Bey was not the man to be affected by trifles, and his sagacious mind took in the whole.

When the accuser had finished, the governor was silent for a moment, while clouds of smoke—dire portent!—filled the air above the head of the devoted fellah.

"Hast thou heard him, O Braheem Effendi?"

"Yea, word for word, O high and mighty governor."

"How much is false, and how much is true, O Howajji Braheem?"

"All is false—save only this—that he, with nineteen other men of his village, did set on me in the mountain pass and would verily have robbed me, as they have robbed travelers oftentimes heretofore, but that we put them to flight. There are many bad stories of his village written in the books, and it would be well to punish them once for all, that the traveler may not hereafter be prevented from visiting the crocodile pits at Maabdeh."

"Lay the unrighteous dog on the ground." They have a knack at it in Egypt. I have never seen it done as well in other Turkish countries. Before he had time to howl he was lying on his face, a man sitting on his shoulders, and another on his legs.

"Name the nineteen companions who were with you on the mountain."

No answer.

A nod to the ready slave, and the blow fell. The victim howled, but it was evident that he howled as a matter of course. Eastern flogging, except when the bastinado is used on the feet, is a farce. The blows of a large stick on loose clothes do no harm until they have been often repeated. This is the explanation of the vast number of blows sometimes administered. Five hundred in Egypt is not equal to five dozen in the navy of England, scarcely indeed to one dozen. By the tenth blow there is a perceptible aching, but the hundredth may not be painful at all. After a few blows the character of the performance was changed, and the soles of his feet were turned up. This is a stinging infliction. At the fifteenth blow he shouted the name of a companion, and out came the whole row. Before I left Manfaloot next morning, every one of the nineteen were in prison there, awaiting sentence.

I returned to the Coptic church in the evening. The old bishop was there, and with a dim candle he and I entered the church. I showed him what picture I wished, and he pushed the bishop's chair under it for me to stand in and look at it, holding up the dip to its surface. But he would not sell it to me.

He insisted on giving it to me, if I would promise not to make him any present in return. He was old, very old, and they would say the old bishop had sold church property, and that would never do. I would not accept it on such terms, and then he lamented that he had offended me, and I, to convince him he had not, took him along down to the boat, where he comforted his old bones with such wine as he had never tasted before. Ali Rashwan came down directly, and sat on the opposite diwan. He was Moslem and could not drink wine. But he took coffee, cup for glass with the bishop, and one emptied the coffee-pot and the other the decanter by bed time. Bed time came early, for I was very weary, having accomplished the hardest day's work that I did in Egypt.

40.

"Desolate Places."

It was a pleasant afternoon when we approached Beni Hassan, but a dark cloud lay in the west, and the air was cold. A head wind kept the boat back, and we took the small boat, with sundry shawls, cloaks, luncheon and its accompaniments, and pulled down the river to the nearest point from which we could reach these celebrated tombs. We thus gained an hour or two on the large boat, and had time to examine the most interesting paintings.

The broad plain was to be crossed, here nearly or quite a mile wide, and the land being newly plowed, made the walking excessively fatiguing. But the hillside was more so, and to add to our trouble, a sharp pelting shower of rain came up as we were climbing the sandy slope, and we laughed at each other for being caught out in a storm in Egypt without an umbrella.

It lasted but a few minutes, and then the sun shone gloriously into the open tombs, which, being on the east side of the river, open to the west.

Beni Hassan was for a long time regarded with great interest, because of a painting on the wall of one of the chief tombs, which was supposed to represent the arrival in Egypt of the brethren of Joseph. There are several points tending remarkably to show that this is so, but others which perhaps forbid the idea. The tomb is of the time of Osirtasen, whom Wilkinson supposes to be cotemporary with Joseph. The picture represents the presentation of strangers to a person—not royal. The strangers are two men bringing a goat and a gazelle as presents, then four men leading a donkey, on which are baskets containing two children, a boy and four women following, another donkey loaded, and two men bringing up the rear. The number *thirty-seven* is placed above them, to indicate that these are but the representatives of that number. The name of the person into whose presence they are led is not Joseph, nor Zaphnath Paaneah, but Nehoth or Nefhotph; and names of his father and mother are also given.

It is, however, by no means certain that this is not a representation of that memorable scene. It may be that in this tomb the bones of Joseph awaited the exodus, or those of one of his mighty brothers lay till barbarian hands broke their repose.

But the tombs of Beni Hassan are interesting on other accounts than these. We find among them almost as many representations of scenes in the private lives of ancient Egyptians as at Thebes. The tombs of greatest interest open in a row, side by side, on a terrace some hundred feet above the level of the plain on the hillside. One of these contains admirable colored pictures of nearly all the animals, birds, beasts, and fish known to ancient Egypt.

Another is particularly interesting as containing representations of games and gymnastics, many of which are very familiar to moderns.

They play at ball, games of chance, and of skill. We passed the entire afternoon in going from one to another, sketching outlines of the drawings on the walls, studying the curious lists of animals, and looking out from the doors at the magnificent view over the Nile.

As the darkness approached we came down the hill and

crossed the plowed land to our small boat. The *Phantom* had gone on down the Nile, and we had hard work before us to overtake her. We were delayed longer by stopping to shoot a duck, and then the men lay down to their oars, and the boat flew through the water. A dark cloud again gathered and began to pour a shower on us. We sat close together in the stern of the boat and drew my boornoose over the whole party. It was a home-like shower. Suddenly Miriam, whose eyes were out of a hole watching the shore, shouted, "Timsa, Timsa," and the next instant a magnificent crocodile, who had fallen asleep on a sand bank and not woke up to see that it was getting dark, roused by our oars close to his nose, lifted himself high up on his legs, and as I sent a load of shot into his hide sprang into the air and fell with a tremendous splash in the water and vanished. He was the last of the gods of Egypt that I saw.

Ten minutes later we were startled by a very long low black boat, apparently crammed with men putting out from the shore, evidently to intercept us. The neighborhood of Beni Hassan is celebrated for robberies, and the prospect looked bad. But we held on, and as we neared her Trumbull shouted to them to put down their helm and sheer off, while we all three rose with guns raised, commanding them completely and ready to pour in a volley of six barrels. The next instant the loud voice of Ferrajj shouting his own name and imploring us not to fire, changed the seriousness of the scene to the ludicrous. The faithful fellow knew that we were without umbrellas, and had hired a shore boat to come up and bring them to us. The shower was now nearly over, but we were wet and cold, and it was much the most uncomfortable night we had experienced on the river. The cabin was welcome, and Hajji Mohammed's dinner as usual restored our equanimity.

In the intervals of a furious gale of wind that blew all night that night we drifted down to Minieh, where Latif Pasha was laid up with an attack of Bedouin fever. He called it rheumatism. But as he had recently hung a number of Bedouins, and their friends had sworn to have his blood, and as no steamer was at hand to tow his boat up to Es Siout, it was manifest that he did not dare to sail up the river on his dahabieh, and was laid up accordingly.

I found him in a quilted room. The walls were covered with quilted silk. No breath of air could blow through it. I sat a couple of hours with him, smoking a chibouk, of which the mouth-piece was amber with seven grand pearls around it, each one round, creamy, and worth a duchy.

He is, as I before remarked, one of the finest looking men I have ever seen. But he has a terrible reputation. He has hung more than a hundred and fifty men within twenty-four months, without law or form of trial, contrary to the statutes in such cases made, but confident of Said Pasha's approval. At Es Siout he never sleeps in the palace on shore. He dare not trust himself there; but always sleeps in his boat, lying outside a steamer, over which any attack from the land must be made, while he has ample force to beat off any pirates on the water.

He has much of the Ibrahim Pasha style about him; and nothing more delights him than the order to destroy a village. I inquired what was the meaning of the great collection of soldiers in the streets that day, and he replied, smiling quietly, that he was sending up to burn the villages at Beni Hassan. The people had gotten such a bad character that nothing short of extermination would answer.

I was often reminded by his conversation of the stories of Mohammed Defterdar, who cut a slave's head off as coolly as he would carve a chicken. Such occurrences are not unknown in Egypt even in this day. While I was in Cairo, Said Pasha gave Mohammed Bey, chief of police, seven days in which to catch a murderer; and when the eighth day came, and he was not caught, Mohammed Bey missed his head.

We left Minieh at noon, and made a tremendous run to Sakkara, where we arrived at evening of the next day. The pyramids of Sakkara are of little interest; but it was our desire to visit the tomb of Apis, recently opened by M. Mariot, and we paused for this.

The sun came up over the eastern hills, now known as Mokattam (*hewn*) range, because of the vast quarries which are among them, whence the pyramids were dug out. We awoke early, and found that a steamer had arrived in the night, and been laid up close by us.

The usual morning row on shore was greater than was common; and I hastened out to find Abd-el-Atti in a furious combat with an Italian gentleman, one of the party on the steamer. It appeared that the former, knowing the difficulty of obtaining donkeys at or near Sakkara, had dropped a man on shore five miles above, and directed him to find the necessary animals, and have them at the boat by daylight. The Italian gentleman had captured one of these useful vehicles, which, of course, was our especial property; and Abd-el-Atti had captured him in the very act of beating the donkey-boy, who insisted on being allowed to go to his rightful owner. Thereupon the dragoman, who recognized no superior in the world, except his employer and the government, "pitched into" the Roman with astonishing bravery; and the latter, overwhelmed by the suddenness of the onset, shouted for help. The steamer's crew hastened to the rescue, and the crew of the *Phantom* flew to the aid of their commander. Then ensued a combat that Homer's ghost regretted the impossibility of describing to mortal ears; and in the midst of it I rushed in on the battle and shouted a parley.

Seated on the bank above the steamer, in the simplest of costumes, a shirt open at the neck and a pair of brown linen trowsers, I held one of my extemporaneous courts. The southern European demanded justice on the Egyptian who had dared attack him. The Egyptian was silent, not precisely knowing what course his master would take in the premises. I have already remarked on the state of law in Egypt which entirely prevents the punishment of an offending foreigner, and which makes it very dangerous for a native to insult or injure a howajji. The Italian gentleman was furious in his denunciation, but fortunately Abd-el-Atti could understand him, and when he was somewhat out of breath I demanded an explanation of his side of the case. He gave it with suppressed rage, but with remarkable outward coolness, while the Italian interrupted him often with abusive language, and demanded that I should have him bastinadoed, bowstringed, or hung, then and there, for laying hands on him. When I learned the donkey story I began to understand the case, and as this was my quarrel I demanded if he had attempted to steal one of my donkeys in that manner. He replied that he had as much right to the donkey as I. I retorted that I was glad he was thrashed, and only regretted he had not received more of it, and then he sprang forward.

Before I could move, Abd-el-Atti had him by the roll of his vest, and for a moment they clinched in excellent style; then he backed him slowly toward the boat, and when the distance was correct, sent him flying over the toe of his slipper into the shallow mud and water at the edge of the Nile, a result that was received with loud shouts by four or five English or American gentleman who had been watching the entire fray from the deck of the steamer, and an emphatic *tieb! tieb!* from me. This desirable accomplishment effected, I went on board and dressed for breakfast.

The route to the Pyramids of Sakkara was through fields of corn, and grain, and glorious palm groves that grow on the site of ancient Memphis. At the village of Mitrahenny we paused among excavations made by various exploring expeditions, and looked at the statue of Remeses lying prostrate in the water, with his face downward, half-buried in the soil. This is one of the colossal statues, like those at Abou Simbal and on the plain of Thebes, bearing the names of kings and recording their kingly thoughts. This bears the name of Remeses.

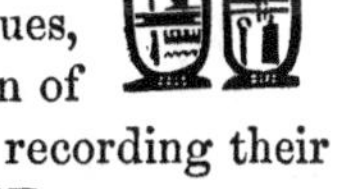

These colossal statues are something more than masses of stone. I remember once meeting with an eminent artist in Rome who laughed at the idea of admiring an Egyptian statue, devoid of form or comeliness, a huge, rough hewn mass of stone. But I am not altogether certain that the idea of hewing a mountain into a statue of Alexander was not a greater thought than the conception of the Venus de Medici, or the Apollo of the Apollos.

Our route was necessarily circuitous, on account of the Nile canals that intercept the plain in all directions. We met the large majority of the steamer party returning as we approached the pyramids, and, enquiring what treatment they received at the tomb of Apis, found that they had been subjected to a heavy tax by way of entrance fee. Pausing awhile to look at the pyramid, which is small as compared with Cheops, but large enough to be a wonder of the world, we pressed on over the sand hills, among hundreds of open tombs, to the great object of our visit.

We had been told that this tomb was in possession of

a tribe of the worst Arabs in the neighborhood of the pyramids, and that was saying much, for they are by far the hardest wretches hereabout that are to be found in Arabia or Egypt. Knowing that the tomb was regarded as specially interesting, more so than almost any thing near Cairo, they had taken possession of it, and demanded two dollars from every visitor as a fee for entering. Travelers usually go to this place soon after their arrival in Egypt, and before familiarity with the natives has bred that contempt which it soon does. We were by this time tolerably familiar with the debased Arabs of the Egyptian frontier, who are neither noble as the desert Bedouins, nor fearful of insulting travelers as are the fellaheen of the Nile valley.

When we reached the entrance to the tomb, in a hollow of the desert sand hills, west of the pyramids, we found it walled up with stone, although it was not thirty minutes since gentlemen had come out. Some fifty Arabs stood near, and a loud shout for bucksheesh was the immediate demand. I paid no attention to them, but advanced directly to the entrance and commenced throwing down the stone wall. To loud shouts ot "Stop, stop!" from fifty throats, I paid no attention, and meanwhile the ladies were dismounting close by me. We were four, Trumbull and myself, Abd-el-Atti and Mohammed Hassan, in this crowd of screaming devils—human they did not appear. I was continuing my work with my back to the noisy crowd, while Trumbull and Abd-el-Atti were keeping them off, when the sheik suddenly sprang at me and seized me by the shoulder over-rudely. He had not time to say one "Allah!" before my fingers were twisted in the neck-band of his shirt, my knuckles buried in his wind-pipe, and an ugly-looking volcanic pistol at the side of his head.

I backed him ten paces, and his retainers fell away behind him. Then I shook him off, and talked a little to him. The substance of my remarks was a warning against touching with unholy hands the shoulder of one who could throw him over the Nile into the Red Sea. Physical strength, of which I had sufficient for my purposes, intimidates the effeminate fellows, and the muzzle of a pistol is a dry hint that they are quick to take. I drew a line on the sand, twenty feet from the mouth of the cave, and told them that any man who came over that line should be shot on the spot. Giving Mohammed Hassan my fowling-piece, I seated him at one end of the line, where he commanded it, with orders to obey my instructions to the letter.

This done, we entered the cave. In its vast halls we found, what the successful Frenchman had found before, twenty-three great sarcophagi of polished basalt, in each of which had been a bull, such as Americans may see in Dr. Abbott's museum in New York. The dead apis was buried here in solemn state in those days when the Egyptians made him their God. The gloom of the long halls, the splendid coffins standing each in its arched niche, robbed indeed of all their distinctive marks—for M. Mariot has carefully concealed all his hieroglyphical discoveries in this tomb—the silence and awful solemnity of the place made it one of the most profoundly interesting that I had visited in Egypt.

When we came out, after an hour in the vast halls of this great tomb, we found Mohammed Hassan seated in the spot where I had left him, and the front row of Arabs on their haunches in the sand on the safe side of the line, while a hundred more stood, growling and furious, but cowards all, behind. We mounted and rode away, leaving them to fleece the next traveler who may be foolish enough to submit to their imposition.

Let the reader understand that these were not desert

Bedouins. I confess freely that I am too much of a coward to touch with my own hands a free, uncontaminated Bedouin of the desert, surrounded by his tribe.

We had directed the boat to drop down the river a few miles, and we returned from Sakkara by another route, stopping only a little while to examine the Ibis mummy pits. There are several of these open, containing many thousand of the sacred birds. Each bird is wrapped carefully in cloths, and enclosed in an earthen jar, which is closed and sealed tight. The jars are piled on each other in cords, filling the chambers to the roof. We pulled out hundreds of them, all alike in shape and contents.

There was a wild cry ringing through the palm groves as we came down on the level land. The soldiers of Said Pasha were abroad, impressing boys for the army, and had caught not a few among the villages on the plain. Their mothers and sisters were rending the air with wails of sorrow, for the parting was, as they well knew, likely to be final.

We approached the boat, and found her surrounded by two thousand soldiers, looking curiously into the windows, or down on her from the banks, but kept from intruding by Ferrajj who stood manfully at the plank, forbidding entrance to one and all, officer and private. It was sunset, and at the short twilight we dropped down to Ghizeh. Cairo, especially the lofty citadel and the mosk of Mohammed Ali, was before us, gleaming in the last rays of the western sun. On both sides of the river the banks were covered with soldiers, the viceroy having some fifteen thousand under arms in the neighborhood.

Ghizeh, as the reader already knows, is opposite to old Cairo, which is two miles from the walls of modern Cairo the grand. The pyramids are some six miles from the river, as are those at Sakkara. We laid the boat up at the shore of the village of Ghizeh, whence we designed making our excursions to the pyramids, preferring our floating home to the hotel at Cairo, which would have made a longer ride necessary every day both morning and evening, beside ending our pleasant life in the *Phantom.*

The pyramids and sphinx are old acquaintances to all readers of books of travel, history, philosophy, and religion. They have done service by way of illustration so many thousand years, that they seem old friends even to those who have not seen them face to rock.

It has been often said that they are not mentioned in the sacred Scriptures. It is indeed somewhat surprising that they are so seldom alluded to, but I can not think they are entirely omitted.

Moses, we suppose, wrote the book of Job. The great lawgiver was born and educated under the shadow of Cheops, and I have no doubt had those vast tombs in his mind when he placed in the mouth of Job, wishing for death, that expression—"Then had I been at rest, with kings and counsellors of the earth who built *desolate places for themselves.*"

I shall not devote any space in this volume to a description of the pyramids, already familiar to every intelligent reader.

At the first moment of reaching them we were surrounded, as travelers usually are, by scores of Arabs, demanding large pay to be employed as guides and assistants. But we were old hands at thrashing off the fellaheen Arabs, and our koorbashes, whistling over their shoulders, made open space around and largely diminished their expectations, as well as reduced their nominal prices.

How we, Miriam and myself, ascended Cheops and

looked back, up the lordly river, and up the river of time as well, for there is no spot on earth from which man can see so far into the past as from that same summit of Cheops, how we descended and entered the heart of the stone pile, with a crowd of vociferating Arabs, and how, when they had us in the king's chamber by the sarcophagus, they sought to frighten us as they had other howajjis, but woke up the wrong passengers, if I may use an Americanism, and how the whistling koorbashes made the atmosphere more clear and the darkness less noisy, how we sat down under the shadow of the sphinx and gazed at his stony countenance, whose calm, almost ineffable smile, seems, among the shifting sands and rifled tombs, now too sneering for a smile, and now too soft, and sad, and mournful for a sneer, how we looked into a hundred vacant resting-places of the old dead, and pondered much on the power of time and the oblivion with which age wraps nations, as with a grave-cloth and a grave, out of which their voices come in sepulchral tones; how, at length we climbed Cheops once more and swept our eyes over the plain, and up the Nile, and far away over the Libyan desert to the dim horizon that seemed as distant as the days of Moses—all this he who would know more of, must seek in the books of other travelers, since we did but as they.

It was the last night on the *Phantom*. We pushed out into the river in the evening, and went drifting down by the island of Rhoda, and at length reached the bank at Boulak, where we had set sail in November previous. The moon was not now on the river, but the night was starry and calm, and divinely beautiful. No sounds announced our approach to a great city. All was still, quiet, profoundly silent. The lapse of the river among the boats along the shore was but audible silence, so softly musical was it, and every thing conspired to sadden us on this last evening of our Nile life. I have never felt more regret at leaving a temporary home. We clung to it with the utmost affection. To-morrow we would be no longer in our own house. Hereafter, wanderers once more, at the mercy of hotels and unknown servants, we could not be willing to go.

Hajji Mohammed won my heart, finally and forever, that night, by a dinner that Apicius might have died over. Every thing was perfect—magnificent. We sat long over the wine, and then, on deck, in the soft air, and then—slept.

Dire was the confusion that awoke us in the morning. A livelier port than Boulak the world can not show. Thousands of voices, in a dozen languages, rent the air, and when the sound at length overpowered my sleepy faculties, I sprang up, astonished at finding myself once more in the world of active, business men.

A carriage was waiting for the ladies, but Mohammed Olan, and Barikat, and Achmet were on board with their donkeys, and a thousand stories of what had happened since we left Cairo, and we mounted the old animals, as one bestrides his own favorite horse at home, and cantered up the avenues of sont and lebbek, to the Ezbekieh gate and Williams's hotel, where our rooms were awaiting us.

41.

Visions and Realities.

They were a fortnight of keen delight those last two weeks in Cairo. There was much that was home-like in coming back to a city in which we had passed a month of the previous autumn, and the heavy discounts of the bankers were not enough to spoil the pleasure with which you talked with them and allowed yourself to be shaved in true western, Wall-street style. Drafts on England cost only five per cent., and it was worth that to sign your name in respectable chirography, instead of dirtying your fingers with your seal-ring and India ink as I had been doing for some months, whenever a paper required my hand.

It was pleasant to meet the same faces in the mouski shops and in the Turkish bazaars, to ride along the shaddowy streets and be greeted by some old Turk who had cheated you outrageously last fall, with a jovial—as jovial as the guttural would permit—"Good-morning, Braheem Effendi."

It was even gratifying to see the same beggars, and when I sat under the shadow of the lebbek-trees in the Ezbekieh and smoked calmly while Abd-el-Atti and Hajji Mohammed were putting up and taking down tents for my examination, preparatory to our Syrian journey, to be interrupted by the same blind boy and old woman that I administered copper to some months ago, with the same "Bucksheesh Ya Howajji."

It is useless to resist the impression that this demand for bucksheesh is instinctive in the Arab character. It is the first word which children utter. That I am convinced of. It is the last on the lips of the dying man, if the vision of a foreigner crosses his failing sight. Dr. Abbott vouches for the fact that he attended an Arab in a long and severe fit of illness and cured him. When the man was well he called on the doctor, as the worthy physician supposed for the purpose of expressing his gratitude for visits that had been regular twice a day for a month. That he had nothing but gratitude to give, the doctor well knew.

"I am well," said the man.

"Yes—I am glad to see it—you are well."

"I am well," repeated the Arab.

"Yes, so I see. Thank God for it," said the doctor.

"Yes—but—isn't there any thing more? You see I am well."

"Certainly I see you are well, and you have had a hard time of it. Go to work now and keep well."

"But isn't there any thing more?"

"More—more—what more?"

"*Bucksheesh?*"

"For what?"

"For the experience you have had in curing me!"

"I had cured him for nothing and paid for his medicines, and the dog came to me for *bucksheesh!*" said the doctor.

Nor was this a solitary instance in his practice.

There are some places in and around Cairo which, you will not need to be told, I revisited with new delight. There are places in which it seems to me now I would be content to doze away a life-time.

First of all I sought out my old friend Suleiman in the bazaars within the chains. He welcomed me with a "salaam aleikoum," an honor forbidden to be wasted on a Christian and so much the more to be prized. Seated on his shop-front with the same chibouk, the same tiny cups of coffee, the same calm old eyes looking into mine, I could not believe that even a week had elapsed since I was last there and that I had meantime been far beyond the barriers of Syene.

The blue smoke curled up in the lofty aisle of the bazaars, and the soft sunshine stole in on it and lit it up in graceful forms that floated before me as I sat and dreamed. There were outlines of fair and gentle persons in the solemn air, delicate outlines of rare beauty. There were blue eyes gazing out of indescribable distances on me (how well I knew those eyes of blue!) There were a hundred shapes and shades in the air above and around me. I could have rested there a century in that delicious kief, that no man may know in any other spot on earth.

I know what it is to lie down on the desert sand in the sunshine when the air is cool and lifegiving, and the sunshine warm and heavenly. I know what it is to swing in my hammock on a long sea, with the breeze well off on the quarter and home right in on the lee bow. I have smoked Tombak in silver narghilehs in the kiosks of Damascus, and Stamboul tobacco by the sunny side of the tomb of Sultan Mahmoud in Constantinople. I have drank lager-bier with the stoutest of Prussians in Prussia, have sipped golden Ivourne and flavored it with the pleasantest of Swiss tobacco in the Alpine valleys; I have —I have smoked tobacco everywhere that my wanderings in many years have led me, many kinds and flavors thereof I know, and I have loafed, and lounged, and dreamed, and slept in very many lands. But there is no spot on all the world's surface to which I look back with a memory of such perfect calm delight, such undisturbed repose of mind and body as the shop-front of Suleiman Effendi in the bazaar within the chains in Cairo the Victorious.

Seated there one afternoon, I saw old Selim Pasha stalk by followed by his retainers, and by diligent questioning I got from Suleiman enough to confirm a story I had before heard, on what I supposed good authority. It is very difficult to persuade a Mussulman to repeat a story of his neighbor's wives. Scarcely ever, indeed, is a female name mentioned by their lips. In fact, not in one instance in a hundred does a man know the names of his most intimate friend's wives, or any of them. The hareem is a forbidden subject of conversation under all circumstances, and to ask a Moslem if his wife is well would be insulting and unpardonable.

The romance of the hareem is well-nigh ended forever. But once in a while a true history comes out with startling effect, as its incidents become known, and we begin to fancy the days of the Arabian Nights not wholly gone. Such is this story of Selim Pasha, governor of Upper Egypt under Mohammed Ali.

He was a Circassian slave, in high favor under that great prince. Young, noble, ardent, and brave, he won the affection of his master and lord, and was always near his heart. Well he might be. No hand was so cunning with the sword, so firm on the rein, so steadfast in the battle. No foot was so strong in the stirrup, so swift to do his master's will, so constant at the palace door. Step by step he rose, as slaves often rise in the East, from his low estate to honor, wealth, and fame. Still he was young, and still unmarried. Whether in the restless dream of his ambition, for he was ambitious, there were ever mingled memories of his mountain home and the beloved ones of his infant years, whether in the battle under the pyramids he heard the voice of his mother as he had heard it in far-off Circassia, calling him back to a peaceful home, whether in the desert fray, when the sun was hot on his head, and the faint blood lay heavy in his heart, he remembered the cool breezes that used to steal down from the snow-capped mountains, and the delicious streams that murmured at his feet in long gone years, none may tell now. I have sometimes thought that even now, when he is old and gray and passes feebly along the streets of Cairo, surrounded by his hordes of attendants, those memories must haunt him with fearful power.

He had never loved. The old viceroy was of a gentle turn of mind occasionally, and he bethought him to make Selim's home a happier one. He knew a young and strangely beautiful woman, who would be worth his loving. True, she had lain in his own arms, and was his slave; but his embraces were forced. She did not love him, and oriental custom permitted and sanctioned the giving her to his slave Selim as his wife. Her fame had already reached his ears, and he had sometimes wished to see her. She had seen him. Had watched from the lattices when he came and went, had waved unknown, uncounted kisses to the splendid soldier, the young and noble slave. It was a moment of untold joy to her when she learned that she was free from the hated embraces of the old pasha, and was to be the wife of Selim. He was her first and only love.

Love is not here what men call love in cold western climates. This is the land where love climbs turrets, scales fortresses, swims rivers, destroys cities. This is the land of Helen and Cleopatra.

Great was the rejoicing in Cairo the Beautiful, when the wedding was announced, and great the preparation for its celebration. Selim was most glad of all. From a hundred directions came tales of the beauty and loveliness of his promised bride, for although no men's eyes ever saw her face, it was not difficult through other men's wives to hear every line of her features described, and, though all this was fifty years ago, there are many whom I have seen who remember the splendor of that beauty as described by those who had seen it. She was of the rare mould of the eastern Venus, a worthy representative of Helen the beautiful. She was not tall, but exquisitely formed, her limbs the very soul of grace, her eyes wells of love and glory, her lips the ruby portals of maddening kisses. Alas, how a half century has changed the beauty of Hafiza the beloved!

He could not see her face till she was his own. Such is the eastern custom. The man knows nothing of the features of his bride until she is shut up in his house and left to his care and love. That is a fearful moment for the wife when her features are for the first time exposed to his gaze.

Great were the feasts and magnificent the presents which did honor to the nuptials. Mohammed Ali loaded them with his bounty, and Cairo rang with music, laughter, and song, from the citadel to the gate of the Ezbekieh, as the procession marched in state from the royal residence to the palace of Selim, where he waited her coming.

They were alone together, and he knelt before her and with trembling hands threw back the vail that hid her from his eager gaze.

He had not dreamed of it, it was so gloriously beautiful. Her forehead was white as the forehead he saw when he did dream of his mother, and her eyes were bluer and deeper than the sky of Araby the Blessed. The brown hair rolled back like a river of jewels from her splendid head, and her lips were—he thought not of her lips an instant after they had whispered "Selim, my beloved," and she lay close against his breast and wept the life of her joy out on his heart.

What strange thrill was that that shot through his brain when she spoke, and made him clasp her closer to his breast? It was a voice he had heard in all his dreams. It was a voice he had loved in all his wanderings. Doubtless it was the prophet's goodness that had permitted him to hear her speak who was to be his wife, though he did not know it then.

But what was there in that blue eye that so bewildered him. Had he seen her in dreams as well as heard her voice?

They spoke of all the past and tried to open up the vistas of their early years, each to the other's gaze.

She was from Circassia.

And he!

She remembered her home. It was in a valley of the fairest part of that land and a stream of water flowed down by the door and dashed over rocks a hundred yards below.

How like his boyhood's home!

Never had the names of familiar places seemed to him so musical as they now sounded from her lips.

But when she named her father he sprang to his feet, and at her mother's name he called on Allah!

Like a flood swept over him the terrible discovery. He seized her in his arms, tore from her bosom the covering that concealed a mark he remembered in childhood, and thrust her from him with a cry of anguish.

She was his sister!

Selim Pasha sought service in a distant field and lived to be an old man, and withal to become a tyrant. His sister married another man, and is still resident in Cairo, where Selim Pasha also resides since he ceased to be governor of Upper Egypt.

The story is fully credited in Cairo, and there is no reason to doubt its correctness. I give it on the faith of the shop-front of Suleiman Effendi in the bazaars within the chains.

There was another spot, outside the walls of Cairo, to which I was accustomed to resort with Miriam in the afternoons, to watch the sunset beyond the pyramids. There, on the last evening of our stay in Cairo, we rode with Whitely, who had now joined us.

It is a high hill of pottery, on the north side of the city, commanding the desert eastward, as well as the Nile valley.

Forever, in this miserable land, you are interrupted in your holiest thoughts by something that drives sentiment to the winds. If you see a fine marble, a splendid column, lying in the dust, a stone covered with hieroglyphics, or any thing on which your eye rests with interest, it is certain that before your thoughts are fairly in the train you wish, some Arab woman will be sitting on it, with a girl kneeling before her, while she investigates the contents of her bushy hair with her fingers. In the most splendid mosks you see the most filthy persons; and even in the gorgeous mosk of Mohammed Ali, where silver itself seems out of place, half-naked and vilely dirty Arabs lounge in and out with curious eyes, making the air foul with their presence. The miserable, abject, wretched appearance of nine tenths of the population of Egypt beggars description. Clothing they have almost none, and such as they have but adds to the misery of their looks.

I saw a man bathing near the base of the hill. When he came from the water and took up his solitary garment to put it on it was ludicrous to see his perplexity. Somewhere in it there was, or had been, a hole, intended to admit of the passage of his head, but he could not find it among the others. He tried it once, and it went through the wrong place. He tried it again with no better success. I left him trying it. I doubt whether he ever succeeded.

The brief twilight hastened along. The camel-train from Suez came more rapidly, but its end stretched far away toward the desert. On the western horizon the majestic outlines of the pyramids broke the line; Cephrenes, as always, looking over Cheops.

I had devoted much time that day to a task set for myself in Cairo—seeking some memorial of the burial-place of John Ledyard, the American traveler. I knew only that he died in a convent; and in my former visit I had inquired at all the convents, but utterly in vain. No records, no books, notes, minutes—nothing remained of him. I found an old man, one about old enough to have been there when he died, and I talked with him; but his wits were wandering, and he was of no use to me.

It was only left to me to stand, as on this hill, and sweep my eyes around the city walls, and know that of this dust his dust formed part. That somewhere beneath the changing mounds that stout heart was loosed of all its bands. He was a man of noble hope, never-to-be-satisfied ambition. Lo! here the end of it all—death among strangers, and burial among dogs!

I did not heed that evening stole over us, as we sat on the mound of broken pottery. Two skulls lay white and ghastly in the moonlight, and sundry powerless bones of human limbs scattered here and there around us, as if dogs had dragged them from graves.

Probably no soil on the earth's surface has been so often made over in the image of God as this same soil of Egypt; and that has sanctified it. It is this that makes hallowed ground. It is not because Abraham was here; not because old Israel was here; not because the Pharaohs shook off this clay from their sandals; not because Solon, Plato, Aristotle, Herodotus, or a hundred other philosophers and historians have walked along these banks; not even because Mary and her holy Child sat under the shade of the trees of the valley. Not for any one, nor all these things that I honor and love it.

"Why then?" said Miriam; and for the first time I knew that I had been thinking aloud.

"Listen, my child, and I will tell you. More than three thousand years ago there was a scene just here that you have often read of, but perhaps have never before fully appreciated. You see that rocky hill, and the desert road around its base. You see the camels treading it with slow steps. It is now forty centuries since the grandson of Noah broke that path in the sand, and left the first human footprints on it. It was then, as now, bright sand. The foot of Misraim sank deep in it. That rock was then as brown and red as now, and the shadow fell in the morning on the shore of the great river as it fell to-day. Then the pathway was worn; and year by year, and century by century, the sand grew hard under frequent footsteps, and men by millions had trodden it down.

"At length there came over that road a caravan, in which there were men of stately presence and women of rare and glorious beauty. They knew not, the Egyptians knew not, the world knew not, that in that procession was more of royalty, more of magnificence, more of splendor, than all the courts of all the Pharaohs could boast, though it was but the train of an old and worn man, with his sons and their descendants, seeking the face of a lost son and brother who had risen to power and position in the land of Egypt. They paused yonder at the foot of the hill, and waited for messengers from the palace to direct their footsteps to a resting-place. Examine them more closely. The old man, the father of the three-score and ten who surround him, is of kingly presence and bearing, his eye looking as it learned to look when he once saw heaven open and the angels of God entering its brilliant portals. His sons were giant men; every man fit to be father of a race of kings. It is of those sons I would speak. There was stalwart Judah, the lion of his family; there was the mighty Reuben, and the cruel Simeon; there was the beloved Benjamin; and, while they wait, the first lord of Egypt, attended by a royal train, comes to meet them, and throws his arms around the old man's neck, and kneels before him for his blessing. Yes, the air that is so still around us now, that lies so calmly on this desert plain, has heard the voice of Joseph, and has trembled on the lips of Israel.

"There is no point in all the history of the race of man that possesses to me a more profound interest than this. A century before, the altar of Abraham among the oaks of Mamre was the only altar on earth erected to the true God. And now, while those two embraced, and the group gathered closely around them, yonder, on the sand of the desert, within the sound of the feeble voice of Jacob, stood every man that was living on the face of the earth who acknowledged and worshiped the God that made it.

"But it is not this that sanctifies the land to me. Years fled apace in those old days, and men lived, loved, and died, much as they now do. A century passed away after this scene of which I have spoken. The bones of Joseph lay waiting the exodus. But, somewhere in this dust of the valley of Egypt, somewhere along this narrow strip of land, lay the dead dust of Judah, of Levi, of Simeon, of Manasseh, and Ephraim, and of the beloved Benjamin. Think of it. This that I hold in my hand, this grain of dust, may have been part and parcel of the clay that throbbed against the heart of Joseph; may have grasped the sword of Judah; may have felt the pressure of the hands of blind old Jacob. Yes; this very dust may have heard syllabled those sublime prophecies that told of the glories of the twelve tribes, and the coming of their Lord at last. We will follow some day the dust that is not here, and seek it among the flowers of Canaan. But, now, I think this delicate mimosa, this tree of rare and beautiful foliage, must have sprung first from the dust of Benjamin, and that stately lebbek may have found root over the grave of Simeon. None but a palm could grow of dust that formed the lion-heart of Judah. It is this that makes Egypt sacred to me. They are somewhere here, all those eleven giant sons of Jacob; all here in the valley, within sound of the cannon from yonder citadel.

"Nay, more than this. Not alone the fathers of that mighty race lie in this soil, but their mothers as well. There were fair and beautiful women that lay in the arms of those stout men, whose lips were accustomed to their caresses, whose arms often enfolded them, on whose fair breasts they laid their flowing locks. Somewhere under this ground, lies the queenly wife of Joseph; and somewhere here the dark-eyed wife of Ephraim. Perhaps they are not dust. Perhaps—does it not startle you to think of it—perhaps, ten feet below this very spot where we sit, stern, solemn, calm, as in his life, four thousand years ago, lies the tall form and massive arm of Judah; his features set in that last long gaze with which he looked into the loving eyes of Joseph bending over him. What would you give to see that look of love and penitence?"

"Let us dig," exclaimed Miriam.

"Perhaps beneath us lies the fragile form of the young maiden that loved Manasseh. I have sometimes thought of her, and wondered that no one else had named or thought of the mother of Machir. She was—she was—let us imagine it—the daughter of Benjamin, a girl of fair and splendid beauty. In the long moonlight nights of Egypt, the light of yonder moon, that rests now on the Mokattam hills, Joseph and his brother walked together and looked at the crags of that same hill, and the elder told the younger of the beauty and majesty of their queenly mother, whom Benjamin never knew, and of her gentleness; and how, in her young girlhood, a shepherdess on the plains of the East, she won their father's heart; and how old Jacob, in his age, was yet willing to serve her father seven years of his life for the love he bare her, that made the years seem but as days; and how, in her glad beauty, she was like—so very like—to Rachel, his own beloved daughter, that was in the grove behind them; and then, to see his mother once again, to look into her dear eyes again, to think himself not now the lord of Egypt, but the boy of Canaan, he called to him the daughter of his brother, and she came, closely followed by Manasseh, and he looked into her black fathomless eyes, and took her hands in his, and as he sat by the fountain, looked up at her tall, slender form and speaking face, and fancied that he saw the dawn that always shone on the brow of his dead mother. When she looked thus, he knew that it was love of him that shone on her forehead from her radiant eyes; but whom could this child love?

"'Thou hast never loved yet, Rachel?'

"'I love Manasseh.'

"No simpler story could be told; none more full of meaning. The brothers smiled each in the other's eyes, and so it was all settled, and they left the young lovers in the grove, and the moon went onward from the Mokattam hills to the pyramids.

"It was a royal wedding. Never was such before or since in Egypt, as that when Joseph's son married the daughter of Benjamin. Doubtless, as now, they made processions in the streets, and there was much of pomp and ceremony, and the pyramids and the eastern hills were lit with the blaze of beacons, that told all Egypt, from Elephantine to the sea, that their lord and benefactor rejoiced in his palace. Perhaps she slumbers here! Who knows how near us are the beloved features that wear in death the look that Rachel wore when she closed her dark eyes at Bethlehem.

"Laugh who will, but this is no land for laughing at even these imaginations. Your veriest skeptic in antiquity stands respectully before the doors of modern tombs that are opened here, and admits the reckoning of forty centuries, while the stoutest arguments of infidelity are directed, not at the supposed antiquity of the remains we have found here, but at their *want* of antiquity. No man disputes that they are at least four thousand years old. The only other claim is that they are nearer forty thousand. It is well known that mummies have been taken from the tombs of the valley that must ante-date the Exodus. There is one standing in the collection of Dr. Abbott, in New York, that is of the period of Moses and Aaron—a woman who, from her princely titles, may well have been one who had seen the great lawgiver, and had stood by the bones of Joseph. Why then doubt that in some great tomb under this ground, in some mighty room built by the servants of Joseph, some cavernous sepulchre whose arches are on granite columns set in the solid rock, stand, side by side, eleven grand sarcophagi, carved with the names that the high priest of the temple wore on his ephod, and in them, man by man, waiting in solemn silence the voice of Joseph and the angel, lie Judah and his brethren!

I am aware that some persons, reasoning from a passage in the seventh chapter of Acts, hold that the twelve sons of Jacob were brought up into Canaan by the Israelites when they brought up the bones of Joseph.

It is certainly very improbable that Moses would omit such an important item in his history of the pilgrimage, when he carefully speaks of the body of Joseph and its fate. In Exodus xiii. 19, the reason for removing Joseph is given as the oath he had himself required, and certainly had his brethren been removed their translation would here be alluded to.

The passage in Acts is not historical, nor intended to be so, for it is manifestly incorrect in other respects.

"So Jacob went down into Egypt and died, he and our fathers, and were carried over into Sychem, and laid in the sepulchre that Abraham bought for a sum of money of the sons of Emmor, the father of Sychem."

Jacob was not carried over into Sychem, nor did Abraham buy the sepulchre. There is probably an interpolation here, or some error in the early copies of Luke's manuscript. No tradition now exists at or near Sychem that the patriarchs were buried there. A learned Jewish Rabbi, to whom I have lately mentioned the subject, tells me that he has no idea that the patriarchs, other than Joseph, were ever removed from Egypt.

I have already wandered on beyond what I said in my preachment to Miriam and Whitely, and the curious gaping donkey-boys, who seemed to be overpowered by the unexpected eloquence of Howajji Braheem.

From the far past to the far future, the change of thought is necessarily instantaneous. The mind rests with intense interest on a point in that future, which is the only one that human foresight can with any certainty fix—I mean the day when God shall summon up the dead of this valley to stand among the living of the resurrection. What an awakening will that be! I know no spot on all the surface of the earth where the scene will be like this. The followers of the prophet, the swarthy Bedouins, the black Nubians, the bearded Turks, and the pale Circassians—millions on millions will rise from this dust which contains their generations for a thousand years, and start in horror to find the places from which, in their proud self-religion, they drove all other creeds as false and infidel, already occupied, crowded, and overflowing with the men of Memphis and ancient On! The men of the Pharaohs will see among their dark-browed host a few tall forms and calm faces uplifted to the heavens, and will be awed to silence at the majestic appearance of the men they trampled on and despised. The very sand of the desert will spring to life. If it could but now do so! If the lips that are dust here now under my feet would but syllable words!

At length my arrangements were complete. The tents were pronounced perfect. The same servants enlisted for a Syrian journey, and I sent them with the heavy luggage to Alexandria, where I overtook them the next day. A week after that, our camp shone in the white moonlight on the shore outside the walls of Joppa, and I began my TENT LIFE IN THE HOLY LAND.

APPENDIX.

A.

A SKETCH OF THE HISTORY, RELIGION, AND WRITTEN LANGUAGE OF ANCIENT EGYPT.

B.

ADVICE TO TRAVELERS VISITING EGYPT.

A.

SKETCH OF THE HISTORY, RELIGION, AND WRITTEN LANGUAGE OF ANCIENT EGYPT.

I.—HISTORY.

He who would maintain that any one of the oriental nations is older than all others, must be prepared to combat the theories of various scholars, supported with an amount of learning, ingenuity, and earnestness, sufficient to appall any one but a thorough student in eastern languages, literature, and history. That the Sanscrit is the root of all languages, may seem plausible until a Hindoo scholar demolishes our theory, with what is probably very intelligible to him, but is all Hindoo to us. That Nineveh was built close by, and close after the tower of Babel, is certainly a very probable idea, until some learned Brahmin or Chinaman shows you up a city that must antedate the creation itself, if Bishop Usher's chronology be correct, and proves his creed thereabouts by a mass of strange characters and inscriptions, pages of black letter work and oriental roots, sooner than attempt any argument against which you, unless much set in your opinions, rather yield at once, and admit that it must be true, and all that must prove something.

It is unsafe, therefore to whisper, even privately, to your friend that Egypt is the oldest nation in the world. I tried it once, on the quarter-deck of a steamer, in the moonlight of an evening at sea, running down the banks. A learned pundit overheard me and knocked me down, in the saloon, an hour afterward, when I went below for coffee and a bone, with such an array of Sinaitic and Semitic, Cuneiform and no form inscriptions, all which he drew on the mahogany with weak black-tea—no sugar in it—and the point of a silver fork, and having got me down, there was no let up till I admitted that Egypt was the youngest of the old nations, beyond a doubt, and so got rid of him.

But Egypt is the father of nations, for all that, and from Egypt Greek and European civilization traces its genealogy, nor is it possible to show that Egyptian mythology, philosophy, or life, had its origin in any other nation known to history, or to that geology of history, if I may be pardoned the expression, which digs among the bones of nations, the accumulated strata of the early years, for relics of Megatherian nations, or shapes and moulds of extinct and unrecorded dynasties and races.

Chronology is at fault in the years that immediately succeed the deluge, and there can be little doubt that we have erred in our commonly-received chronological tables in the space of time which followed that event and preceded the descent of Jacob into Egypt.

Herodotus relates, that the name of the first king of Egypt was MENES, and Diodorus also states, that he succeeded the gods and heroes who had previously reigned. Herodotus adds, that in his reign the whole of Egypt, except the province of Thebes, was a marsh, or in other words, that what we call the Delta, was then in process of formation. This places the time of that monarch at a period long anterior to Abraham. Of course the authority of Herodotus was but the tradition of Egypt, when he was there, about B.C. 450, but that was a time when the monumental records were read with ease by all the learned men of Egypt, and the story of Menes is therefore entitled to more attention than the vague traditions of the heroes and the gods who preceded him.

It has been by some supposed, that Menes was identical with Misraim, the grandson of Noah and the son of Ham, to whom Egypt fell as an inheritance, and whence it derived a name well known in Scripture, and preserved to this day in the Arabic name of Cairo, which is MUSR. Others have supposed, that *Menes*, which signifies *eternal*, was a figurative name, designed originally to convey the idea that the race was without beginning, or possibly that it had its beginning from THE ETERNAL.

Of the time between Misraim and the arrival of Abraham in Egypt, we are almost destitute of any cotemporary record, either in Scripture or on stone.

Colonel Howard Vyse, an energetic Englishman, who, by his

excavations in 1847, discovered more of value to history in the pyramids of Egypt than had been found for two thousand years before, in forcing his way through the heart of the great pyramid above the king's chamber, and opening room after room, which had been left above that chamber to relieve it of the superincumbent weight that would otherwise have rested on its top, found the cartouche of Suphis or Cheops scrawled on the rocks, which no eye but his had seen since the day they were laid there.

This scrawl of an idle workman, with red chalk or earth, on a stone that he sat on while he ate his onion and bread at noon, is a solitary memorial of the grandeur of Cheops, the builder of the pyramid.

In Dr. Abbott's collection there is a heavy golden signet ring, found in a tomb near the pyramid, which bears the same cartouche, and is one of the most interesting relics of antiquity extant, as possibly having been worn on the royal finger of the same Cheops.

These, and one or two opened tombs near the pyramid, are the only monumental confirmations of ancient history wich give the name of Cheops as the founder of the great pyramid of Ghizeh.

Colonel Vyse opened also the third pyramid. Herodotus ascribes it to Mycerinus. Colonel Vyse found in it a broken mummy case and some bones of a mummy. Fortunately the upper board of the case was preserved, and on it in plain characters—hieroglyphic, of course—was the name of this monarch, in connection with the usual title given to the Egyptian monarch on the monuments. The coffin-board and the bones of this monarch lie now on a shelf in the British Museum.

The second pyramid of Ghizeh, next in size to that of Cheops, and somewhat higher in fact, from standing on higher ground, was built by a monarch variously styled in ancient history Cephren, Chemmes, Sensaophis, and Cephrenes. He was a brother of Cheops. Mycerinus was the son of Cheops. In the tombs immediately around the three chief pyramids of Ghizeh the name of Cheops and the names of other unknown kings (as yet undeciphered or untranslated) have been discovered; while that of Mycerinus is found in one of the smaller pyramids not far distant. The other pyramids scattered along the west bank of the Nile are either unmarked, or, if containing names, are of unknown date.

These, then, are the only monuments of the period before Abraham that we are possessed of, and from these slender materials we are left to construct a history of the nation for an indefinite space of time.

Manetho and other ancient historians of Egypt afford us no aid, since they give no authority for their stories, and are too often contradicted by the existing monuments.

Of the date, period, and departure from Egypt of the dynasty called the Shepherd Kings, we have no other information than this, that if such a dynasty did exist, it was in the period we are now writing of.

During the period of from four to eight hundred years, Egyptian power and wealth attained an unexampled height. No nation in the world so advanced in the arts and sciences, nor is there any known relic of that period, or of any period approaching it, which compares with the monuments in the land of Menes. Whatever, therefore, may be asserted of Phœnician or other origin to Egyptian arts and learning, it is very evident that at a point of time two thousand years before Christ no nation in the world rivaled the sons of Misraim.

There is no reason to suppose that at this time the religion or general condition of the people was materially other than in the days of Herodotus, who describes them so minutely. We know that they already built temples and worshiped the bull Apis, and numerous other gods. But who were the kings of Egypt, save only those three whose names we have mentioned, is a secret in the unrolled scrolls of history.

Manetho says that after Menes sixteen kings reigned at This or Abydos, and when This fell Thebes arose and seventeen kings reigned there.

It is impossible to tell which part of Egypt was first populously settled. Herodotus's account of the marshy condition of the Delta is not without foundation in reason, for we find the obelisk of Heliopolis now deeply imbedded in the ground which has accumulated around it by the annual deposits of the Nile, and it is not unlikely that the remoter and dryer regions of Thebes would be selected as the capital of the country and the residence of the kings.

It is probable that there were at least three different governments in Egypt at the same time. One at Memphis or Heliopolis, one at Thebes, and a third at Elephantine, the first cataract. There were also minor communities, which were independent, having their own sovereigns, as at Heracleopolis.

Thus much of the dark ages before Abraham.

The next endeavor of history is to fix his date. But this can be done only by working back from a known point. The monuments of Egypt are carved with kings' names, and we are able to form a tolerably correct list from the time of Osirtasen I. to the days of the Cæsars. But to find the date of Osirtasen we must take that of Shishak, which is already fixed, and go backward. Egyptian scholars differ vastly on this chronology, nor is it possible to affirm who is correct. Sir Gardner Wilkinson, whose reputation is certainly not inferior to any, while his critical skill and impartial mind render him a cooler examiner and more trustworthy guide than Lepsius, fixes Osirtasen I. at B.C. 1740, the arrival of Abraham in Egypt being at 1920, while Dr. Sharpe and others suppose that this obelisk of Heliopolis erected by Osirtasen may have been seen by the Father of the Faithful.

This monarch erected the oldest portion of the temple of Karnak at Thebes, and from the solitary obelisk which remains at Heliopolis it appears probable that he adorned and beautified that city, which Abraham, and Jacob, and Joseph visited. Some of the tombs at Beni Hassan are certainly as old as his time. From this reign we date the oldest existing monuments which are sculptured, both in the upper and lower country, and it is evident that he included all of Egypt in his dominions. It is possible that he was the first monarch who united Upper and Lower Egypt, which continued at all times afterward to be spoken of as two countries. One of the common titles of a Pharaoh was, "Lord of the Upper and Lower Country."

There are various tablets in Egypt which record the names of successive monarchs. On that at Abydos, we find that Osirtasen I. was succeeded by Amunmeit-Thor II. (the first of that name probably preceded Osirtasen), and by Osirtasen II. and Osirtasen

III. Wilkinson supposes one of these four monarchs, probably Osirtasen I., to be the king whom Jacob saw, and who elevated Joseph. The present prevailing opinion among scholars is, that the Exodus took place in the reign of Thothmes III., an intermediate king, Amosis, being the king "who knew not Joseph."

It is not the design of this sketch to discuss these chronological questions. Already before the Israelites arrived in Egypt the arts and sciences had progressed to a great extent, as we have abundant evidence in the paintings and sculptures of the early tombs. Colonel Vyse found an iron instrument in the pyramid of Cheops. The granite obelisk of Osirtasen was beautifully cut. The polygonal columns which remain, of his portions of Karnak, are elegant in design, and evidently suggested the Grecian Doric. The civilization of families must have been equal to the best days of Rome. Articles of luxury, gold and silver ornaments, fine colors and embroideries, all abounded, and it appears evident that the splendor of life among the wealthy in Egypt, at the time of the captivity, was never surpassed, even in the days of Cleopatra. The government was priestly. The king was the high priest.

Among the kings who reigned during the century immediately succeeding the bondage, Amunoph III. is among the most distinguished. He built the great temple at Luxor, and erected on the plain of Thebes the two colossal statues, one of which became vocal in tradition as Memnon. About 1400 B.C., Remeses the Great ascended the throne. He was the great monarch of Egypt, the Sesostris of ancient history. The reader of this volume has already observed the number and splendor of his works in the Nile valley. He carried the sword into other countries. His temples at Thebes and elsewhere are covered with the accounts of his victories, the number of his captives, and the valuation of his conquests, while his name is recorded in distant countries through which he marched as a victor.

The period of Remeses Sesostris has well been styled the Augustan era of Egypt. The Nile valley was a continuous row of prosperous cities, magnificent temples, and royal palaces. The arms of the country were every where triumphant; the arts were cultivated and adorned the cities, houses, and most of all the tombs; nor is there at this remote age an article of household luxury, a fauteuil or a cooking utensil, a harp or a set of toys, that does not seem to have its counterpart in the splendid tomb of this monarch, now lying open at Thebes.

After him Egyptian history continues through a long line of kings, among whom are Shishak, whose cartouche I have spoken of at Karnak, and So, Psammatichus, and Neco, who are mentioned in the sacred writings.

We now approach a period of more definite dates.

The Greeks, who had long been in the habit of trading with the Egyptians, had established colonies in the Delta, where Naucratis, their chief city, grew to be an important colony.

Thales of Miletus visited Egypt about B.C. 548, and Solon came to Naucratis with olive oil, to exchange it for Egyptian corn. Plato gives a full account of what the great lawgiver learned in the old country, whose priests professed to possess records of nine thousand years. Pythagoras, too, about this time resided in Egypt for twenty years, and until the Persian invasion.

The reign of Amasis was to Egyptian history what the reign of the fourth George was to England, a period of high art, polished literature, learning, luxury, and power—when all the world flocked to her temples and palaces to learn arts and arms, philosophy, theology, and all that appertains to life, earthly or eternal.

It was about 529 B.C. that Cyrus died, and in the fourth year of his son Cambyses, the Persians invaded the Nile valley. Amasis was dead, his son succeeding him. Crossing the desert by way of Petra, Cambyses entered the Delta, and routed Psammatichus, in a pitched battle, under the walls of Pelusium. Thence he followed up his victory to Memphis, and the throne fell into his power. He made the conquered monarch's daughter and the children of the nobility of Egypt carry water for him, and wear the dress of slaves, to show their complete subjugation, while he adjudged two thousand of the young men to death.

This was the end of the glory of ancient Egypt. The Persians passed up the narrow valley of the Nile, sweeping away the splendid structures whose age even then was fabulous, and whose duration was intended to be eternal. Osymandyas fell from his throne before the invader, and his granite fragments were scattered on the sands of the Theban plain. Memnon, that had greeted the morning suns for a thousand years, was hurled to the ground. The obelisks of Karnak, that pointed their taper fingers heavenward, were scattered; one only standing, calm and serene as the face of an old friend among the chaotic fragments of a delirious dream.

The successor of Cambyses, Darius Hystaspès, permitted the Egyptians to be ruled by Egyptians, and Memnon was repaired, and the temples were then in some measure restored. But the age of giants was passed, and there were neither men nor souls to rebuild Karnak, or replace the granite statue of Sesostris at the Remeseion. It was during the Persian dynasty, about 460 B.C., that Herodotus visited Egypt, and wrote his curious notes on the history, manners, and customs, religion, and laws of the people, from which we derive much of our information about them.

Alexander the Great conquered Egypt, and Ptolemy was made governor, B.C. 322, in the name of Philip and Alexander.

The history of the division of the kingdoms among the followers of Alexander on his death, is already too well known to need repetition. The Ptolemaic dynasty continued until the Roman power in the East. During the period of this dynasty arts flourished, and many splendid temples were erected in the upper country, which are distinguished for their florid architecture and elaborate adornments. It is remarkable, that of the architectural antiquities of Egypt now remaining, nine tenths are Ptolemaic or of the days of Sesostris.

Alexandria sprang into power in those days. It had been an insignificant Egyptian city, but became for a time the capital of the East, and when Cleopatra won Antony to her arms it was the centre of all the luxurious refinements of the world.

The scattered Jews had settled in large numbers in Egypt, and especially in and near Alexandria. It was here that the tradition of the church brings the Apostle Mark about the years A.D. 50–65. He remained in Alexandria twelve years, preaching boldly with great success, and founding a church, of which Annianus was the first bishop. Eusebius gives a complete list of his successors, and there is no reason to doubt the regularity of the succession from that time to this.

The Christians of Egypt shared the variable joys and trials of Christians all over the world. They were persecuted with sword and flame, they were offered up as sacrifices to heathen gods, and burned for torches in the public highways. Thousands of souls went to God in triumphal chariots from martyrdom on the Nile plain, and among the hosts in white that surround and sit on the thrones of heaven, there will be none with brighter crowns than some of those who came from this land of all manner of idolatries.

II.

RELIGION.

The brief sketch of the ancient history of Egypt will suffice to convey some idea of the various influences which had importance from time to time in the formation of Egyptian mythology and theology.

At what period of the world men began to worship false gods we can not at present know. The roar of the deluge had not ceased in the ears of the sons of Noah when they had forgotten the God of the storm. A few centuries had passed, and among the oak-trees of Mamre there was an altar to the living God, but no other smoke of sacrifice—so far as we now know—went up to him from all the earth that he had created.

The origin of idolatry was not every where the same. In Assyria it was doubtless in hero worship, and the canonizing of the great dead. But in Egypt this was not done. Herodotus is correct in his statement that they gave no divine honor to heroes. No trace of such worship exists in their theology.

Doubtless the religion of Egypt became idolatrous from an attempt to define the several attributes of the Deity. This is a very natural and easy method of falling into, precisely what the Egyptians did fall into, pantheism. For the religion of the Egyptians was pure pantheism until it became debased in the later centuries.

They, like all children of Noah, worshiped the God of the deluge. But in process of time his character, which was originally understood as a Unity, became unintelligible to them. Then they deified his attributes. The living God, the eternal, unchangeable, the Father of lights, the Creator, the Preserver, each was a different deity.

But that they at first united all these in one God, and had some notion of them as being various manifestations of the same Deity, appears to me sufficiently evident.

There was in all that they did an idea forever prominent of the one mighty Lord. To him the converging lines of the obelisk pointed. To him the open courts of all the temples permitted the voices of worshipers to ascend. To him they built their most magnificent temples, erected their most expensive shrines. Nor did the presence in the temples of other and lesser deities at any time fully remove the vague idea that they were in some sense emanations from the Supreme One.

Such, then, was the origin of Pthah, Amun, Khem Maut, and other deities, representing the Creator, the Powerful, the Father, the Mother, and other great attributes of God. At what period in Egyptian history they were introduced to the Pantheon it is impossible to say, but it must have been in that indefinite period before the date of Osirtasen I., since at the time of that monarch portions of the temple of Karnak were built and dedicated to these deities.

But it is necessary to account for far more than this simple pantheism if we would attempt to explain Egyptian theology.

The most profound mystery in the subject hangs around the chief object of Egyptian fear and adoration, the God Osiris.

But that his worship antedates even the days of Abraham, we should be disposed to believe that there was some dim conception of the theory of the Messiah, in his character, which is the grandest fact of the great system of Egyptian worship.

He was a God who long before the days of Menes reigned in Egypt. He had come to the earth as the "teacher of good and of truth:" such is his title. He was put to death by his son Typhon, the Satan of Egyptian mythology, and then being dead was made the judge of all the dead, who in turn must appear before him.

In regard to the time, the manner, and the causes of all this, doctors differed as theological doctors now differ. Some held to his burial and resurrection, others that he was cut into pieces and the pieces scattered through Egypt, and that Isis went on a mournful search after them and gathered them together. All agreed that the island of Philæ had a peculiar sanctity as his burial-place. To all he was the God of the judgment, and whatever particular deity was specially honored in one or another city, Osiris was every where respected as the final judge.

From worshiping the manifestations of the Deity in his great attributes, it was an easy transition to worshiping his great works, in which there seemed to be an active principle of life. The sun and moon were to all nations first in the catalogue, and the earth perhaps next. The sun was peculiarly near in its relations to divinity from its life-giving power. It seemed the source of animal and vegetable life, and thus to be almost an essential part of the creating power of the Deity. Nature, acting with the influence of the sun, brought forth plants and various forms of life. She was of course deified.

Later in succession, a species of transcendentalism seems to have entered into the religious philosophy of Egypt, and it is not uncommon to find on the monuments representations of kings, the external and visible man, offering votive presents to his own inner self standing before him as a god.

Few animals were actually deified. There has not been sufficient distinction made in this respect between deification and a making sacred, which perhaps might be called canonizing.

The crocodile was a sacred animal. The origin of his canonization was probably in villages situated back from the Nile on broad parts of the valley, the fertility of whose lands depended on keeping open the canals of the Nile. Building a temple with a sacred pond and therein preserving, feeding, and taking care of these animals, the people were instructed that the fertility of their lands depended on attending to the wants of the crocodile, chief among which was the necessity of free access to the Nile. Therefore the people kept the canals open. A similar reason may be given for the respect paid to the Ibis, while the attention which was given to cats and other animals, living or dead, originated in the idea that each of these animals was in some respect typical of the attribute worshiped as one or another deity.

It is my object in this brief article only to sketch the rise and progress of Egyptian theology in its earlier existence. It afterward became a hideous mass of idolatry, without form or order—a madness without method.

Temples to gods were erected at a very early period. The older parts of Karnak antedate the arrival of Abraham in Egypt. One almost invariable plan was adopted in building these temples during two thousand years. Two great towers stood on the sides of the grand gateway which opened into a court, surrounded by a colonnade, and this opened into a chamber which was the holy of holies. More or less chambers surrounded this, for priestly uses. Images of gods and goddesses were common. At Abou Simbal, and at Gerf Hossayn, the stone gods sit even to this day behind their altars, waiting the return of worshipers.

That the Egyptians believed in the immortality of soul and body, there can be no doubt. This led to the custom of mummying the dead, and I presume that this led to the excavation of costly sepulchres. It appears evident that they expected to return to their original bodies at some future time, and desired to find them not only perfect, but in such habitations as they might not be ashamed of. I believe I have already remarked, that it seems to me probable that they built their temples with reference to this return, as if they intended them to outlast the changes of time, and be ready to receive them in the second life. That they expected to resume these bodies, and inhabit the Nile valley, can not, I think, be questioned.

The state of the dead between this life and their return, was a subject of constant thought and study among Egyptian philosophers and priests. The tombs abound in representations of that state. The dead were always led to Osiris for judgment, and by him consigned to one or another fate as their balance of evil against good was smaller or greater. For I am not aware than any tomb has been found among the hundreds containing this judgment scene where the evil did not outweigh the good. If they did not believe in original sin, they undoubtedly believed in the total depravity of the human race, and while the doctrine of an atonement was unknown to them, they taught and believed that sin must have its punishment after death, whether the sinner were king or clown.

III.

WRITTEN LANGUAGE.

Whether Moses, educated in the house of Pharaoh, wrote the books of the Pentateuch in Egyptian characters, or whether he had learned another and more simple alphabet, or had invented one for himself, is a question that will forever remain unsettled.

Although very great advances have been made within the present century in deciphering the hieroglyphics of Egypt, we are still very much in the dark when attempting to read monumental inscriptions or records on papyrus. Enough is known to establish the general character of the alphabet, but not enough to follow the various signs through their different names and sounds which they probably possessed in different locations and connections.

The history of the discovery of the method of reading the hieroglyphic writings of Egypt is among the most important parts of the history of this century. It is a striking feature of the age in which we live, that the monuments which have lain for nearly two thousand years, showing their broad legends to the sun and the eyes of the learned and curious, are now for the first time legible and intelligible to men.

In this brief paper I can do no more than outline this history, but I am not without confidence that even a cursory statement may prove interesting.

He who has read this, or any other volume on Egypt, is of course well aware that the sacred sculptures (*Hiero-glyphs*) are found on almost every ruin of old times in the valley of the Nile. Temples are covered without and within with these figures and forms. Columns, from pedestal to capital, are blazoned with them. Even in the streets of Cairo your donkey treads on carved stones, bearing the names of old kings. Walls of tombs are minutely adorned with stories of the dead, and prophecies of their future fate. Tablets here and there in palace temples record lives of kings and queens. All these are in the hieroglyphic character.

Besides these we have articles discovered in tombs, household utensils, furniture and toys, which are marked with these or another style of character. And we have also immense quantities of papyrus, found chiefly in tombs, which contain histories, poems, essays, and other writings, in the Hieroglyphic and two other styles of character, which we call the Hieratic, or priestly, and the Demotic, or popular. The Hieratic bore to the hieroglyphic much the same relation that our written characters in common handwriting bear to an elegant printed page. It was the same character, but shaped for common, rapid, epistolary use.

The Demotic, or people's style, was probably a corruption of the hieratic. It is found on papyrus as well as on household articles.

Illustrations of these three styles of writing will better enable the reader to appreciate their distinction than any amount of description.

Hieroglyphic.

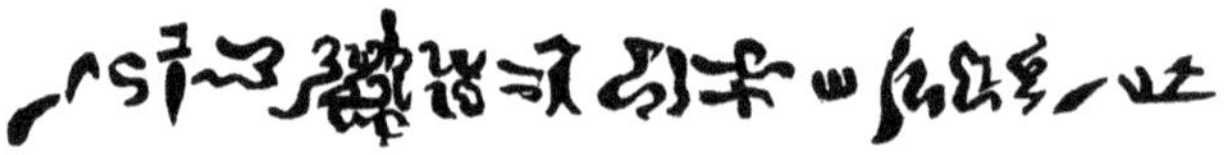

Hieratic.

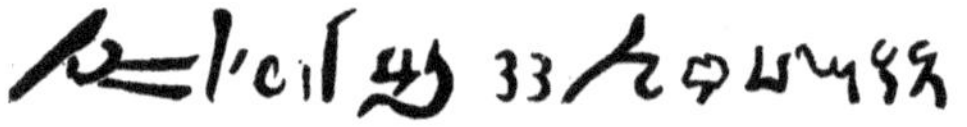

Demotic.

In one or the other of these characters the learning of Egypt was preserved from generation to generation, and age to age. Immense treasures of that learning have been forever lost.

The literature of Egypt was doubtless very extensive, vastly more so than we are accustomed to believe. In the great Alexandrian library, there must have been many thousand volumes of Egyptian history, law, metaphysics, theology, and general literature.

The forty-two books of Hermes, known to the Greeks, were hierographic. We are fortunate in possessing considerable portions of them in the papyri most commonly found in the tombs, and especially in the papyrus of the Turin Museum, which contains one hundred and sixty-five chapters. This, usually called "The Ritual of the Dead," is often found in whole or in part as the companion of a mummy. In later days the form was much shortened. It consists of prayers to be recited by priests at the funeral services, formulæ which the deceased must be acquainted with, for his guidance in the unseen world—prayers to the gods for the dead—services and orders, by means of which the deceased will oppose evil spirits and fiends of all kinds—will recover his head, his heart, and his body—will pass through the mystical regions of hereafter—and, in general, instructions of the dead for their guidance in the future world.

Besides these, however, the books of Hermes consisted of works on astronomy, music, law, theology, and medicine.

We learn from ancient writers that there were also works of King Cheops, builder of the first pyramid, on theology; of Menes, who was a physician, and of Necho, an astrologer, as well as numerous books of priests and learned men.

Diodorus and Herodotus allude to works on law, medicine, and astronomy. The laws of the country were known in eight volumes.

We have abundant evidence that hieroglyphic writing was used for ordinary literary purposes. Even songs were written in it. An example, familiar to Egyptian scholars, is taken from a tomb at Eileithyas, where it appears written over oxen treading out grain. (*Vide post*, page 490.)

The language of ancient Egypt was a derivative from the old stock, branching at Babel. This was preserved with much purity in the priestly writings and legends, but corrupted by the people in its common use, receiving words and ideas from every nation conquered by, or conquering the Egyptian, even to Greek and Roman times. The Coptic of the centuries after Christ bore a very distant resemblance to its original Semitic root, and was finally lost, except only in the formulas and services of the Coptic church, where it is still used, neither clerk or priest pretending in four cases out of five to understand a word that he reads. I questioned them in many Coptic churches, and found their ignorance of the language frequently and usually total.

The problem, therefore, to be solved, was this: Given an unknown language, written in an unknown character; required to translate it into English.

It would be impossible in these pages to recount one in ten of the attempts which have from time to time been made to solve this problem.

As early as 1529, Valeriani published a folio attempt.* Kircher, in 1653, fathered most amusing and extravagant notions in a larger publication,† and was followed by a host of authors in octavo and folio for more than a century, no one of all whom made the slightest progress in the work. The waste of time, paper, and press-work on these essays, was enormous. Perhaps no subject has exhausted so many brains to so little effect. Zoega,‡ in 1797, suggested the first valuable idea on the subject, to wit, that the hieroglyphical figures which we commonly call a cartouche, contained the name of a royal personage, and that the ordinary characters might be alphabetical. This suggestion was never acted on, however, until the days of Dr. Young and Champollion.

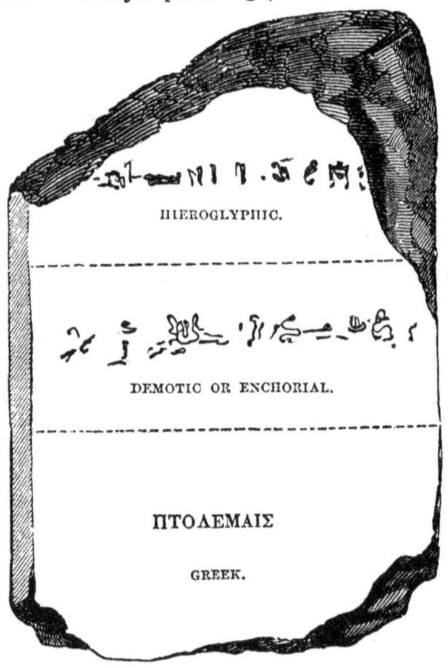

ROSETTA STONE.

In 1799, a stone was discovered in the Delta, near Rosetta, of the shape of which the drawing will give an accurate idea. It bore an inscription of great length, in three characters. The first was the Hieroglyphic; the second, the Demotic or popular; and the third, Greek. This is the famous Rosetta stone which proved the key to the hidden Egyptian characters.

* Hieroglyphica. Lugdun. Batav. 1529. † Œdipus Ægyptiacus. Romæ; 1652-4.
‡ De origine obeliscorum, Romæ; 1797.

In 1818, Dr. Young published an article on the subject, and actually gave the names of some royal persons from the monuments, with the phonetic value of certain of the letters composing them. He did, in fact, discover the value of five characters, but he went no further. Champollion le Jeune had published his Egypt under the Pharaohs, in 1814.* He was an ardent young Frenchman, and devoted himself with skill and spirit to the solution of the problem.

Mr. Banks had discovered at Philæ a Greek inscription on the base of a small obelisk, which he and others had believed to be the translation of the hieroglyphic inscription above it. The latter contained a cartouche answering to the name of Cleopatra in the group.

Champollion took this cartouche and compared it with one on the Rosetta stone, which occurred as often as the name ΠΤΟΛΕΜΑΙΟΣ (PTOLEMAIOS) occurred in the Greek, and which Dr. Young had identified as that name.

The reasoning of Champollion was very simple. His theory was that each hieroglyphic was a letter possessed of phonetic value.

If true, then the first letter, K, in KLEOPATRA, would not be found in PTOLEMAIOS. It was not. The second letter, L, should be fourth in Ptolemaios. He found it so. The third letter, E, should be fifth in Ptolemaios, and was there, as also the seventh and eighth. The fourth letter, O, should be third in Ptolemaios. It was there.

The P was in its proper place in both names. The A of Cleopatra was not in Ptolemaios, but occurred twice in the cartouche of Cleopatra. The T was not alike in the two names. It was the first failure of the theory. The R was not in Ptolemaios.

It was soon evident to Champollion that the difficulty in the T originated in the use of different signs to express the same sound, and this was another great step in learning the lesson he had before him.

It is hardly necessary to explain how rapidly after this Cham-

* L'Egypte sous les Pharaons. Paris, 1814.

pollion advanced his system. Taking up a cartouche which contained the A and L, and R, which he already possessed, he said, this is Alexander, and by comparison with others, verified his supposition. Every oval or cartouche thus furnished new letters to his alphabet, and at length he was able to read sentences outside of the royal ovals.

The rapidity with which Champollion pressed to a result is astonishing. In a brief space of time he published a grammar and dictionary of hieroglyphics, of great extent, in which later investigators have been able to detect so few errors, that there is no other assistant in Egyptian studies yet competent to supply their places.

The result arrived at was this. The hieroglyphic writing of Egypt is in substance alphabetical. The alphabet consists of a very large number of characters, the total being even yet unknown. Each picture has the phonetic value of the first sound uttered in pronouncing its name. Thus a reed, *Akke*, would be pronounced A (the two reeds represent the diphthong AIO, or AI, in Ptolemaios, of which the sound may be not unlike a double *aa*), a lion, *labu*, would be L, a hand, Tut, would be T; or to take an English illustration, a picture of a lion would be L, of a hand H, of a reed R.

I can not leave Champollion's name without recalling to the reader's mind that remarkable occurrence in his visit to Egypt, which I have before described,* which at once stamped the truth of his system and dedicated it to the uses of Christian theology.

On his arrival at Karnak his eye was attracted by that remarkable group of captives before the monarch Shishak, and ran over

the hieroglyphs with astonishing result. In one of the compartments he found these characters, and read them aloud to his sur-

* Page 392.

prised attendants and the savans who had been at work on them before his arrival, Judah Melk, *the King of the Jews.*

This example may suffice by way of illustrating some further explanatory remarks.

The last character is indicated as Kah. The word is translated *country.* The figure itself represents rolling land. Its value is not phonetic.

This is one of a class of characters forming an important feature in the hieroglyphic system, commonly called *determinatives.* In this instance it indicates that the previous words refer to a country.

A name with a picture of a god after it, would be understood as the name of a god. If a man follows it, it would be the name of a man. In this instance there are two determinatives. The entire name (see cut on page 386) is enclosed in a figure representing a fortified place, and the translation of the whole idea is, "The fortified country of the King of the Jews."

Another class of determinatives was soon discovered, consisting of pictures introduced to explain the precise sound of a syllable or value of a letter—as if in English after the letter A in the word STAND, a picture of a man were placed to indicate that the letter was to be pronounced as in pronouncing *man.*

Abbreviations were found to be common. The head of an animal was enough for the idea of the whole animal; a dot, with a ring round it, was the representation of an eye.

It must not be supposed that the hieroglyphs were always phonetic. On the contrary they were sometimes symbolical, even when occurring in alphabetical sentences; and oftentimes whole inscriptions, and extended legends were in symbolic characters. Thus certain characters acquired symbolical value. A jackal was the emblem of knowledge—a flail, of power—a feather, of truth; and these and other characters which possessed phonetic value also would be selected in writing names and words, on account of their symbolic value agreeing with the idea of the word written. The fact that the same hieroglyph possesses at one time phonetic and at another time symbolic value, is, as must be evident to the reader, one of the great difficulties in the way of reading the Egyptian records, especially as this double use may occur in the same sentence or inscription.

Before concluding these remarks, I venture to give the illustration which I have before alluded to, of a song found in one of the tombs at El Kab, or Eileithyas, by way of showing briefly a few of the characteristics of hieroglyphic writing. The ordinary rule is, that the lines are to be read from the direction toward which the animals are looking. This song will therefore be read from right to left.

The first line, Mr. Birch writes,

hi ten en ten

The character at the end of this line is a direction, *twice* or *repeat.* The same direction occurs at the end of the third line. The song is thus translated:

"Thrash ye for yourselves,
Thrash ye for yourselves,
Thrash ye for yourselves, O oxen;
Thrash ye for yourselves,
Thrash ye for yourselves,
Measures of grain for yourselves,
Measures of grain for your masters."

A comparison of the English with the original will afford an interesting occupation for the reader who may have leisure for it. Such obvious characteristics as the symbolic representation of the words thrash, oxen, measures of grain, the plural being indicated by the three marks under them, I need only mention to show the thoughtful reader the prominent characteristics of this ancient style of writing.

This song is among the oldest pieces of written poetry extant.

Scarcely so old as the words of Lamech, but perhaps quite as ancient as the triumph of Miriam.

Thus much must suffice, in this brief paper, on a subject which volumes would be required to make a complete history of. The reader will find ample assistance in the English and French publications, should he desire to pursue the subject further than this outline may instruct him. At the present time, learned men in almost every nation except our own, are devoting their labor to the development of the system. Some, indeed, remain unconvinced of its value, but nearly all scholars have yielded to the clearness and conclusive force of the reasoning, as well as the results, of the Champollion system. Dr. Seyfarth, in Germany, holds to one of the old theories, and has published elaborate and voluminous works since 1844 in its support. This theory requires all the pages of Dr. Seyfarth's works to explain, and then in a most unintelligible manner. He supposes the hieroglyphics to have certain relations to astrology, and to possess variable value according to the zodiacal position they may occupy, or in which they have been used. His system has one advantage, that it enables him to translate any passage or inscription to which his attention is directed, it being competent to suppose the hieroglyphics were used in any astrological connection necessary to give the translation desired, and no one can establish the falsehood of the version so produced.

The steadfast progress of the method of Champollion has sufficiently settled its truth and value.

The system is far from complete, and as yet the results have been meagre in historic value, as compared with the reasonable expectations of its discoverer and his followers. This arises from the peculiar character of the Egyptian sculptures. The monuments abound in addresses to the gods, repetitions of prayers and sacred formulas, but historical sculpture, or papyri, are rare indeed. The habits, manners, and customs, and religion of the ancient Egyptians, are before us in a thousand pictures and in these sculptures. But the succession of kings, and the relation of events in Egypt to events in other parts of the world, can be but roughly guessed at from such tablets as those at Philæ, Abydos, El Kab, and elsewhere, on which occur names and successions of royal personages, but no dates, periods of reign, life, or cotemporary history.

When, as in the case of the subjugation of Rehoboam by Shishak, we find allusions to cotemporary history, we have starting-points fixed, but intermediate monarchs, their succession and the length of their several reigns, can not be accurately and conclusively determined, until we find some more complete historical papyrus or tablet than is as yet known.

If there were extant a history of Egypt in hieroglyphics, our present knowledge is ample to translate it with correctness. Hence the importance of additional searches in Egypt, and government excavations. Each new sculpture, or papyrus, discovered, may be the most valuable yet known.

I can not forego the hope that our own government may in time lend its aid to these investigations, in which there is a field for American talent and enterprise, discoveries in which will add to the glory of the country, while they may tend to the confirmation of the Christian religion, and will increase the great sum of human knowledge.

B.

TO TRAVELERS VISITING EGYPT.

For lovers of all that is luxurious in travel, of all that is glorious in memory, of the grand, the beautiful, the picturesque, and the strange, Egyptian travel is the perfection of life. For invalids it surpasses any country in the world, and the voyage on the Nile is perfect *dolce far niente.* I do most seriously recommend a winter in Egypt to invalids, especially to such as have pulmonary affections. The climate is even, calm, and delicious. In the shade it is not hot, and the evenings and nights are profoundly still, clear, and beautiful. Day and night the atmosphere is the same. There are no changes from heat to cold, or the reverse. There is no labor in visiting ruins. All of Egypt is on the Nile. Your boat is a home that becomes, like your own in America, inexpressibly dear to you, and it floats along from temple to palace, from pyramid to tomb, from old glory to old glory. The day, the week, the voyage, is one long dream of delight, and the memory of it an inheritance of pleasure. Medical attendance in Cairo, of the highest order, is always to be obtained, and advice for the voyage, should the invalid be in condition to need it.

As for the comfort of the voyage, I have only to repeat that there is no hotel in Europe, from Morley's or the Hôtel du Louvre down to the vile inn at Capua, in which the traveler will live so well in all respects as on his Nile boat. The larder is always full of game, and the shore abounds in chickens, eggs, turkeys, and mutton.

The insects, of which so much has been said in oriental travel, are but a small annoyance. For every one that I found in Egypt there are ten in Rome. Italy is in this respect much worse than

Egypt. Fleas abound, but a Cairene invention of flea-powder is a perfect safeguard against them. Lice are sometimes found by the traveler on his person, after being carried on the shoulders of a native. We had no mosquitoes above Cairo. No vermin need be found on the boat if the traveler take proper care of its cleanliness before hiring it.

I know by experience the necessity of the few pages which I here add by way of advice to my roving countrymen.

Americans leaving home to go to Egypt need make no preparations in this country. The direct route is from New York or Boston to Liverpool or Havre, thence to Marseilles, and from Marseilles by steamer to Alexandria.

The Peninsular and Oriental Company's steamers from Southampton touching at Gibraltar would, under ordinary circumstances, offer the most pleasant conveyance, but they are invariably taken up by the India passengers. Gentlemen traveling alone will do well enough on them, but ladies going only to Egypt will fail to find cabin room.

The French steamers leave Marseilles every two weeks, touching at Malta, where they lie over night. They are miserable, second-class vessels, as are nearly all the French Messagerie Imperiale steamers on the Mediterranean.

Were I going again at this time, I should without hesitation go from Paris to Vienna and Trieste, taking thence the Austrian Lloyd's steamer to Alexandria, which is a better steamer than the French, and better manned. The Mediterranean trip is much shorter by this route, an important consideration on a sea so notoriously disagreeable. This route, however, has this disadvantage, that it affords no such opportunity for making purchases on the route, preparatory to a winter on the Nile, as the voyager will find at Malta.

Ladies of the most delicate constitutions need have no apprehensions in passing a winter in Egypt. The climate is delicious, the Nile boat is as comfortable as a hotel, and every luxury is provided by a careful dragoman that the most fastidious could desire. There is no such thing as "roughing it" in Egypt.

The purchases of which I have spoken are not many, but a few are important.

A first-rate fowling-piece is indispensable to a gentleman on the Nile. Water fowl of all kinds abound, and the shores are lined with flocks of pigeons, a variety precisely like our common blue barn pigeon.

Arms are useful only for show in Egypt. It is well to have a good pistol, and in Syria it is necessary. I found the *volcanic pistol*, as it is called, much preferable to Colt's. The latter was constantly getting out of order, and from the falling of the cap between the cylinder and the hammer, was useless twice out of three times after the first shot. I carried the fixed ammunition of the volcanic pistol with me in all climates, and found it infallible. It is compact and safe. I recommend it to the eastern traveler.

Take plenty of gunpowder and shot from Malta. They are very scarce and very expensive in Egypt.

A first rate opera-glass is preferable to a telescope for Nile uses. Purchase this in Paris, or better still, if you pass through Germany, in Munich, where very small glasses of great power can be procured.

What wines you wish, buy in France or in Malta. If you go from Marseilles by French steamer, purchase your supply there, for your entire eastern tour. You will have no trouble in the Alexandrian custom-house.

Buy no Spanish wines in Marseilles; leave them till you reach Malta. Drive directly to Woodhouse's on your arrival in Malta, and let him send on board your steamer what supply of Marsala wine you wish. This is probably the best wine you can take to Egypt. It is as a matter of health, preferable to claret, and the latter will not stand a winter on the Nile. I found a quarter cask of Marsala more than sufficient for our party of four, seeing, as we did, much company.

Books are an essential to the pleasure of the voyage. Wilkinson's works, and Murray's edition of Wilkinson (Murray's Guide-Book for Egypt), Lane's Modern Egyptians, and any books of travel by way of hand-book will be sufficient for the ordinary pleasure traveler. Others will increase this stock, and general reading books are not out of the way on a Nile boat.

Make no arrangements with a dragoman in Malta. Under no

circumstances be induced to take one till you reach Cairo. English is spoken by every one at Alexandria with whom you will be likely to meet.

On arriving at Alexandria, go on shore without a commissionaire or guide. You will find donkeys, and donkey-boys who speak English. Probably the regular commissionaire from one of the hotels will be on board. If so, let him take care of you and your luggage. If not, leave your luggage on board, and send from the hotel for it.

At Alexandria, go to the Hotel d'Europe or the Peninsular and Oriental, on the grand square. The Victoria, not on the square, is kept by an Englishman, and I believe is comfortable.

Employ a dragoman as a guide for the few days you remain in Alexandria, but no longer. The regular price all the world over is five francs a day. You go to Cairo by rail.

At Cairo, go to Williams's India Family Hotel. It is more home-like than the others, which are large barns. I have heard that Shepherd has sold out. If so, the hotel that was his may be tolerable, which it was not last winter.

In selecting a boat for the Nile voyage, leave nothing to your dragoman, but go and examine every boat yourself. Insist on it being newly painted and varnished. Be particular about the varnish, for the paint never dries without it.

There are two sizes of boats. There are a dozen for that matter, but the traveler need only inquire for this distinction, whether the boat is too large to ascend the first cataract. If his voyage is only to the first cataract he may take a large boat; if beyond, it must be somewhat smaller.

All the provisions and furniture for the voyage may be obtained at Cairo. If the traveler make such a contract as I made, he need give himself no concern about this whatever. If he prefer to pay a dragoman by the day, he must hunt up his own food and fixtures in the shops, as well as along the river.

In selecting a dragoman it is impossible to advise. The best of the class are great scamps. I have no doubt that Mohammed Abd-el-Atti is one of the best dragomans in Egypt. I saw no one that I considered his equal in intelligence and ability. He proved a faithful servant to me during more than seven months of life among the Arabs, from Abou Seir to Damascus, and I learned his faults as well as his virtues. He has a furious temper and an ardent love of money. These are his sins. Let who can find one of his class without them. Treat him as a gentleman should treat an educated and respectable interpreter and courier, and he will serve you most faithfully.

My contract was made for a longer period than most persons will wish to pass on the Nile, and the rate payable per diem, after the exhaustion of the pay days allowed by the contract, was three pounds, which for four persons was about three and three quarter dollars each per day. I paid much more than was necessary, and if going up the Nile again, should have no difficulty in making the trip in the same style for four dollars per day for each person, and three dollars for extra days of stoppage.

The expense of a winter in Egypt is less than in almost any other part of the East. A reference to the contract which I give in full on page 122, will show precisely the expense which a party of four persons are at for the most comfortable and luxurious arrangements that are ever made on the Nile. Gentlemen traveling without ladies, should under no circumstances pay more than four dollars per day for the Nile voyage, unless they travel singly, which they will find too lonesome by far. Any one paying over a pound a day alone, or four dollars if with another person, may regard himself as cheated.

If you desire to become acquainted with the people, and their manners and customs, select an Egyptian dragoman.

If you take a Maltese, look up Francis Abrams, an honest fellow for a Maltese, who served me faithfully for some weeks.

You will need in Egypt ordinary clothing, such as would be worn in New York in May or the latter part of September, with overcoats for cold changes. No special provision in this respect need be made.

Medical advice is not wanting in Cairo, where Dr. Abbott will be found, a skillful and learned physician, long resident, familiar with all the necessities of the climate, and himself an agreeable and delightful companion. His name is already well known in America.

With these few hints in his mind, the traveler who desires to go to Egypt for the winter, may pack up his baggage and go, heedless of the thousand doubts and apprehensions which a journey to a remote and almost barbarian country almost necessarily suggests. With this advice before him, he may go to Egypt as confidently as to England or France.

THE END.

Vagabond Life in Mexico.

By Gabriel Ferry, for Seven Years Resident in that Country. 12mo, Muslin, 87½ cents.

Madeira, Portugal, &c.

Sketches and Adventures in Madeira, Portugal, and the Andalusias of Spain. By the Author of "Daniel Webster and his Contempories." With Illustrations. 12mo, Muslin, $1 25.

Life and Travels of Herodotus.

The Life and Travels of Herodotus in the Fifth Century before Christ: an imaginary Biography founded on Fact, illustrative of the History, Manners, Religion, Literature, Arts, and Social Condition of the Greeks, Egyptians, Persians, Babylonians, Hebrews, Scythians, and other Ancient Nations, in the Days of Pericles and Nehemiah. By J. Talboys Wheeler, F.R.G.S. Map. 2 vols. 12mo, Muslin, $2 00.

Ewbank's Brazil.

Life in Brazil; or, a Journal of a Visit to the Land of the Cocoa and the Palm. With an Appendix, containing Illustrations of Ancient South American Arts, in recently discovered Implements and Products of Domestic Industry, and Works in Stone, Pottery, Gold, Silver, Bronze, &c. By Thomas Ewbank. With over 100 Illustrations. 8vo, Muslin, $2 00.

Squier's Central America.

Notes on Central America; particularly the States of Honduras, and San Salvador: their Geography, Topography, Climate, Population, Resources, Productions, &c., &c., and the proposed Interoceanic Railway. By E. G. Squier, formerly Chargé d'Affaires of the United States to the Republics of Central America. With original Maps and Illustrations. 8vo, Muslin, $2 00.

Ross Browne's Yusef.

Yusef; or, the Journey of the Frangi. A Crusade in the East. A new Edition. By J. Ross Browne. With numerous Illustrations. 12mo, Muslin, $1 25.

Waikna;

Or, Adventures on the Mosquito Shore. By Samuel A. Bard. With a Map of the Mosquito Shore, and upward of 60 original Illustrations. 12mo, Muslin, $1 25.

Kendall's Santa Fé Expedition.

Narrative of the Texan Santa Fé Expedition: comprising a Description of a Tour through Texas, and across the great Southwestern Prairies, the Camanche and Caygüa Hunting-grounds, &c. A new Edition. By G. W. Kendall. With a Map and Illustrations. 2 vols. 12mo, Muslin, $2 50.

www.ingramcontent.com/pod-product-compliance
Lightning Source LLC
LaVergne TN
LVHW021320110826
845150LV00003B/623

* 9 7 8 1 4 2 5 5 5 6 6 5 5 *